Revolt of the Ministers

By the same author:

Seeds of Trouble: Government Policy and Land Rights in Nyasaland, 1946–1964
Development Governor: A Biography of Sir Geoffrey Colby
State of Emergency: Crisis in Central Africa, Nyasaland 1959–1960
Retreat from Empire: Sir Robert Armitage in Africa and Cyprus
Sir Glyn Jones: A Proconsul in Africa
Johnston's Administration: A History of the British Central Africa Administration, 1891–1897
Education and Research in Public Administration in Africa (with A. Adedeji)
The Evolution of Local Government in Malawi
Ife Essays in Public Administration (with M. J. Balogun)

Revolt of the Ministers
The Malawi Cabinet Crisis 1964–1965

COLIN BAKER

BLOOMSBURY ACADEMIC
LONDON • NEW YORK • OXFORD • NEW DELHI • SYDNEY

BLOOMSBURY ACADEMIC
Bloomsbury Publishing Plc
50 Bedford Square, London, WC1B 3DP, UK
1385 Broadway, New York, NY 10018, USA
29 Earlsfort Terrace, Dublin 2, Ireland

BLOOMSBURY, BLOOMSBURY ACADEMIC and the Diana logo
are trademarks of Bloomsbury Publishing Plc

First published in Great Britain by I.B. Tauris 2001
Paperback edition published by Bloomsbury Academic 2021

Copyright © Colin Baker, 2001

Colin Baker has asserted his right under the Copyright,
Designs and Patents Act, 1988, to be identified as Author of this work.

All rights reserved. No part of this publication may be reproduced or
transmitted in any form or by any means, electronic or mechanical,
including photocopying, recording, or any information storage or retrieval
system, without prior permission in writing from the publishers.

Bloomsbury Publishing Plc does not have any control over, or responsibility for,
any third-party websites referred to or in this book. All internet addresses given
in this book were correct at the time of going to press. The author and publisher
regret any inconvenience caused if addresses have changed or sites have
ceased to exist, but can accept no responsibility for any such changes.

A catalogue record for this book is available from the British Library.

A catalog record for this book is available from the Library of Congress.

ISBN: HB: 978-1-8606-4642-3
PB: 978-1-3501-8025-3
ePDF: 978-0-8577-1642-2

Typeset by Ewan Smith, London

To find out more about our authors and books visit
www.bloomsbury.com and sign up for our newsletters.

Contents

List of Illustrations	vi
Abbreviations	vii
Glossary	viii
Note on Terminology	ix
Preface	x
Maps	xii

1	Introduction	1
2	Banda and His Lieutenants: Early Relationships	4
3	Banda Consolidates His Power: August 1960 to September 1961	17
4	In Government: September 1961 to February 1963	42
5	Self-government: February 1963 to July 1964	69
6	The Revolt: July–August 1964	88
7	Banda's Retaliation: September 1964 to January 1965	140
8	Chipembere's Attempted *Coup d'État*: February 1965	204
9	Chipembere's Evacuation: April 1965	237
10	The Fate of the Ministers	274
11	The Ministers' Revolt and Its Legacy	299
	Notes	325
	Biographical Notes	355
	Sources	359
	Index	363

Illustrations

1. Dr Kamuzu Banda, Chikela Airport, 6 July 1958.
2. Dunduzu Chisiza, 1958.
3. Henry Chipembere and Dunduzu Chisiza, Gwelo Prison, 1959.
4. Orton Chirwa, Dr Kamuzu Banda and Dunduzu Chisiza, Federal Review Conference, London, December 1960.
5. The Governor, elected ministers and parliamentary secretaries, September 1961.
6. Executive Council, September 1961.
7. Legislative Council, September 1961.
8. Kanyama Chiume, 1962.
9. Kanyama Chiume, Dr Kamuzu Banda and Henry Chipembere, 1963.
10. The Governor, Sir Glyn Jones, and the Prime Minister, Dr Kamuzu Banda, 1963.
11. Kanyama Chiume and Henry Chipembere, on tour, 1963.
12. Dr Banda, 1963.
13. Legislative Council, 1963.
14. Henry Chipembere, in hiding in the bush, January 1965.
15. Henry Chipembere's house at Malindi, destroyed by security forces, February 1965.
16. The Fort Johnston Ferry, February 1965.

Abbreviations

BHC	British High Commission
BSAP	British South Africa Police
CCAP	Church of Central Africa Presbyterian
CDP	Christian Democratic Party
CIA	Central Intelligence Agency
CID	Criminal Investigation Department
CRO	Commonwealth Relations Office
DC	District Commissioner
DPP	Director of Public Prosecutions
FCO	Foreign and Commonwealth Office
HMG	Her Majesty's Government
KAR	King's African Rifles
LMY	League of Malawi Youth
MCP	Malawi Congress Party
MLA	Member of Legislative Assembly
MLC	Member of Legislative Council
MP	Member of Parliament
NAC	Nyasaland African Congress
OAU	Organization of African Unity
OHMS	On Her Majesty's Service
P&DA	Provincial and District Administration
PC	Provincial Commissioner
PDP	People's Democratic Party of Malawi
PMF	Police Mobile Force
UFP	United Federal Party
WNLA	Witwatersrand Native Labour Association
ZAPU	Zimbabwe African People's Union

Glossary

Askari	African soldier
Atate	Father
Bambo	Father
Boma	District headquarters
Bwana	Sir, Mister
Chimkango	Big lion
Chisilu	Traitor
Coloured	Person of mixed race
Kamuzu	Dr Banda's forename, literally 'little root'
Katundu	Luggage
Malawi police	Dr Banda's private bodyguard
Mankhwala	Medicine
Mbadwa	A political party in opposition to the MCP
Mchona	A person who left his home long ago
Ngwazi	Title given to Dr Banda, literally 'warrior'
Singanga	Native doctor

Note on Terminology

The names of countries and places are spelled as they were at the relevant time, and not in their present-day form where this is different. For example, Nyasaland, Tanganyika and Northern Rhodesia, pre-independence, are so called and Malawi, Tanzania and Zambia, post-independence. Similarly, places such as Port Herald and Fort Johnston are so called instead of Nsanje and Mangochi as they subsequently became.

Preface

Exactly six years after he returned to the country of his birth in 1958, following forty-three years' absence, vowing to secure Nyasaland's withdrawal from the Central Africa Federation and its independence from Britain, Dr Hastings Kamuzu Banda, having secured the Federation's abolition six months earlier, became prime minister of the independent state of Malawi.

The course to sovereign status had not been smooth. Following mounting violence, civil disruption and fears of a plot to murder senior government officers and Africans loyal to the government, a state of emergency had been declared nine months after Banda's return, and more than 1,300 members of Congress had been detained. Banda himself had spent over a year in Gwelo prison in Southern Rhodesia. He had been released in April 1960, though his principal lieutenants had not been freed for a further six months. With an alarming amount of politically inspired violence, including brutal murders, the country had moved swiftly towards a de facto one-party state: at the last elections before independence none of the seats for the legislature had been contested. Despite these and many other worries, the general impression was that the country was firmly united behind its powerful, if somewhat unusual, prime minister and that he headed a unified, solidly loyal and progressively dynamic cabinet, devoted to the country's progress. The government was adopting a realistic approach to the fragile state of its finances and economy, and the country's political stability, under Banda's strong, pro-Western leadership seemed beyond question.

Yet, well within three months of Malawi becoming independent, all save one of his cabinet ministers resigned or were dismissed. All but one of the former ministers fled the country. A number of actively pro-Congress Europeans, including a former cabinet minister, fearing for their lives, followed them. Severe fighting, including killings and arson, occurred between the followers of the former ministers and Banda's supporters. The cabinet, composed almost exclusively of university graduates, each with significant experience of government, was replaced by a largely non-graduate cabinet in which only the prime minister and one colleague had ministerial experience. Many African civil servants openly opposed Banda, and the business of government was, for a while, disrupted and left exclusively in expatriate hands, without political guidance. Friendly countries were alarmed by what was happening, and much distress was experienced by those who had placed great confidence in Malawi's future as a member of the community of nations. For a while, the former colonial master, the British government, which had staunchly backed Banda and which was keeping the country afloat financially, hedged its bets as to which side to support.

It is the purpose of this book to examine how this apparently sudden and potentially catastrophic state of affairs came about, how it was handled by the major participants and what the aftermath was. The bulk of the book is devoted to the cabinet crisis itself, but it is preceded by a study of the elements that accumulated over the years and ultimately led to the crisis. It is followed by an examination of the longer-term fate of the principal individuals involved and of the country itself as a result of the ministers' revolt.

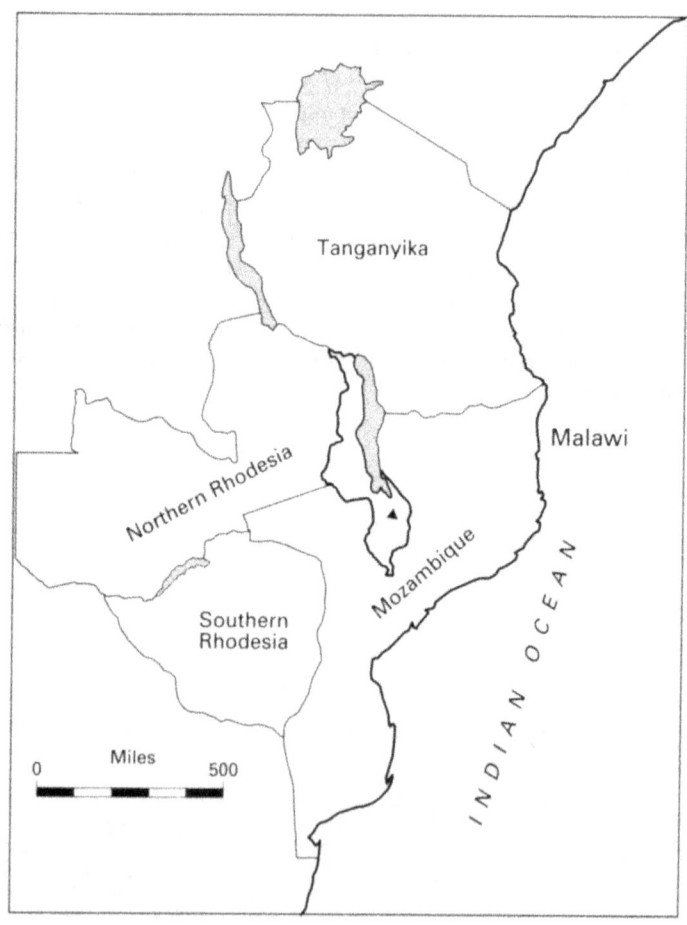

Map 1 Malawi in Central and East Africa

Map 2 Malawi: Location of places mentioned in the text

Map 3 Malawi: the Southern Region

CHAPTER I

Introduction

THE British government declared a protectorate over the Shire Highlands on 21 September 1889, primarily to prevent the Portuguese moving into the area. The declaration was in response to strong representations made by the Church of Scotland, which had established mission stations in the area from 1875 onwards. The Church took a keen – and often proprietorial – interest in the government of the country ever thereafter. On 14 May 1891 the protectorate was enlarged to cover present-day Malawi, and a Commissioner and Consul-General appointed. In 1907 the protectorate's name was changed from British Central Africa to Nyasaland, the Commissioner was restyled Governor and executive and legislative councils were created. Various piecemeal changes resulted, by the early 1950s, in an entirely European executive of three ex officio and two nominated official members, together with two non-officials; and a legislature of ten European officials sitting with ten non-officials – six European, three African and one Asian – all nominated by the Governor. With the Governor as president of the legislative council, there was still an official majority, and the Africans – first appointed in 1949 – were in a marked minority on the non-official side of the house.

Further constitutional development was complicated and retarded by the imposition in 1953 of the Federation of Rhodesia and Nyasaland against the long, consistent and strongly expressed opposition of the African population. It was accompanied at its inauguration by riots in which eleven Africans were killed and a large number injured, and it was followed by a period in which the Nyasaland African Congress, founded ten years earlier, went into decline.

Although the introduction of the Federation complicated and retarded constitutional advance in Nyasaland, it did not stop it. At the end of 1953 two additional non-officials were appointed to the legislature, one European and one African. In 1956 a new constitution provided for a legislature of eleven officials and eleven non-officials – six Europeans and five Africans. The Africans were still in a double minority in the legislature: with the Governor in the chair, the non-officials formed a minority and within that minority the Africans were still outnumbered by Europeans. The executive council was unaltered: five officials and two non-officials – all European. It had taken six and a half decades for Britain to advance the Africans to this stage of preparation for governing themselves. The successful Africans were H. B. M. Chipembere, M. W. K. Chiume, N. D. Kwenje, J. R. N. Chinyama – all four Congress candidates – and D.Chijozi, a Congress sympathizer.

> Their success did much to restore Congress's self-respect, and it took on a more militant mien. In the Legislative Council, Chipembere and Chiume ... required answers to awkward questions, demanded an end to discrimination, vilified Federation, and generally made life difficult for the Government. Among educated Africans, Hansard quickly became a best-seller; no one before in Nyasaland had dared to question so openly the motives and methods of colonial autocracy.[1]

Chipembere, born in 1930, had been at university in South Africa and returned to Nyasaland in 1955. He acknowledged his militancy and admitted to holding violent views: 'I certainly had very extreme views, very violent views ... and I certainly did advocate at the time extreme methods.'[2] He joined the civil service as an administrative assistant and then resigned to stand for selection to the legislature. Chiume, born in 1929, had been to school in Tanganyika and to college in Uganda. He taught for a while in Tanganyika before returning to Nyasaland at the very end of 1954. He started a coffee farm at Chikwina in the northern province and then campaigned for selection to the legislature.

Chipembere and Chiume realized that, despite their success and militancy, they needed a person older than themselves to lead Congress: 'a man of about fifty or sixty, an intellectual, with a character combining nationalism with honesty, self-denial and a spirit of cooperativeness'. They knew the man for the job. Dr Banda, already almost sixty years of age, had left Nyasaland in 1915, worked in South Africa and went to high school and university in the USA, where he qualified as a doctor. He lived in Britain from 1939, became a successful and respected medical practitioner there, campaigned against the introduction of the Federation and in 1953 moved to Ghana, where he continued to practise medicine. While Chipembere and Chiume could have managed without Banda, they recognized that it would take them very much longer than it would him to turn Congress into a mass movement and persuade Britain to hand over the reins of power. They, particularly Chipembere, set about persuading him to return to Nyasaland. Of all the letters written to persuade him, Chipembere's were 'by far the most urgent'. He was dissatisfied with the current leadership of Congress, primarily because on the last day of 1956 it had overwhelmingly rejected his and Chiume's strong urging that the Nyasaland members of the federal assembly should immediately resign. That Chipembere and Chiume pressed this point, against Banda's clear advice that the members should remain in office for another two years, indicates that they were concerned more with his potential leadership than with actually accepting his views and acting on them. Chipembere could see that 'although it [was] wrong to be led by a single man placed in such a powerful position, still human nature is such that it needs a kind of hero to be hero-worshipped if a political struggle is to succeed'.[3]

> [He] said quite frankly that Dr. Banda's reputation would have to be built up. He told him that he was known as a name, as an African highly educated doctor in London of Nyasa birth, that ... little was known about him among the masses. He must not be frightened if he was heralded as the political messiah. Publicity of this sort could be used with advantage; it would cause great excitement and should precipitate almost a revolution in political thought.[4]

Eventually, the doctor agreed to return to Nyasaland, but only on the adamant condition that he should be made president of Congress and given an unfettered hand to run it as he wished.

Earlier, Lennox-Boyd, Colonial Secretary, had urged Welensky to prohibit Banda entering the Federation, but the federal prime minister had not done so.[5] Banda arrived back in the country of his birth on Sunday 6 July 1958 and received the tumultuous welcome of three thousand Africans gathered at Chileka airport to greet him. In introducing him to the crowd, Chiume said that the doctor came not only to lead but to carry out the wishes of the people, and he, like anyone else who did not follow their wishes, would have to go. He repeated this point later in the day at a public gathering at Soche: 'Dr Banda should be our leader so long as he toes the party line.' That evening Chiume, Chipembere, Dunduzu Chisiza and other Congress leaders met secretly and agreed that Banda would remain their leader as long as he accepted their policy, but no longer. From the outset, the lieutenants' views on Banda's role were clear.[6]

Although present when the first two of these statements were made, Banda may not have fully grasped what was being said, for although he very soon became competent in Cicewa – much more so than he let on – it may be that, after so many years' absence, his ear was not immediately attuned to the language. In any case, since it had been agreed that he was to be president of Congress, with complete freedom to run things his way, he may not have much minded what Chiume was saying.

CHAPTER 2

Banda and His Lieutenants: Early Relationships

BANDA had been away from Nyasaland for over forty years. Whatever the political, economic and social changes that had taken place during his absence, they have to be set against the infinitely greater changes he had personally experienced. His experience of the First World War was in Southern Rhodesia and South Africa; that of the inter-war years, including the Depression, was in the USA; that of the Second World War was in Britain; and his post-war experience was in Britain and Ghana. He left Nyasaland as an impoverished teenaged schoolboy and returned as a well-educated and highly qualified professional man, widely travelled and much respected in the West. In many ways he was more European than African. Chipembere wrote of Banda's lack of understanding of African life, and his general treatment of Africans, in contrast to Europeans:

> At his party residence in Blantyre he had a living room in which he received only Europeans, including officials working under us. Africans were invariably received in the inferior living room, except for selected visiting dignitaries. When an African visitor had a call of nature, he was shown the toilets at the servants' quarters; a European was shown the bathroom inside the residence. At one time he told one of us: 'I trust Englishmen; they never lie.' [This demonstrated] Dr. Banda's lack of understanding of African life caused by his prolonged absence from Malawi, and ... the aloof and aristocratic life he led. [His] leadership philosophy is that: 'familiarity breeds contempt. A leader must live above the people. He must be different from them. They are proud of him when they know that he is someone different and exceptional.' [1]

Although, particularly during his later years abroad, he stayed in touch with his home country, his expectations of what he would find on his return were not fulfilled. His recent personal experience of Africa was in Ghana, from 1953 to 1958, and this did little to prepare him for Nyasaland, which was much less advanced politically, educationally and economically. He was disappointed with the level of development in these spheres in Nyasaland. Within a few weeks of his return, he told a district commissioner that he was appalled by the low level of Nyasaland's advancement, and exclaimed, 'What am I to do?'[2] It was to be expected, therefore, that he would welcome and pin his hopes on any indications of promise in individuals whom he encountered.

Before he returned to Nyasaland, Banda had met relatively few people from the country. Governor Armitage had made a special point of inviting the doctor to visit him in London in June 1958 when he was on leave, and a few other members of the administration had called on him. Over the years, too, a number of Nyasalanders had visited him but few of the currently significant Nyasaland African political leaders had met him. Chipembere had, but not Chiume, who recalled:

> A few weeks before he came [back to Nyasaland] some disquieting murmurs still circulated the country, centred round the criticism that Banda was a *mchona* [one who left the country long ago, had not returned and was out of touch]. It was therefore decided to send a delegation to Banda in May to brief him on the situation in Nyasaland and the sort of difficulties he might encounter. The delegation [consisted of] Mr Chipembere and Chief Kuntaja.[3]

Chiume soon set about consolidating any gains he had made through being one of the small group who had pleaded with Banda to return to Nyasaland and lead Congress, and making up any loss he may have suffered through not having previously met him. It was he who made the introductory speech at Chileka on 6 July. Three weeks later Congress held its annual conference at Nkata Bay, and Banda stayed with the Chiumes at their home. He was struck by what he saw there and wrote that Chiume was 'one of the few sensible young men who realised that Nyasaland is an agricultural country'. They had a fifteen-acre coffee farm and the doctor took a stroll each morning, noticing the coffee berries ripening, and he enjoyed drinking the coffee that was 'grown, roasted and ground by hand on the farm'. In a rather Western way, he found it 'most delicious, far more tasty than the stuff one buys from shops'. Mrs Chiume, who showed him round the farm and provided refreshments each day, was 'a charming and very industrious young lady'. He wished there were more couples like them in the country. Chiume had been inspired by a plea made at the 1955 annual Congress meeting that 'all present should go out and help bring economic betterment to Nyasaland' and he had immediately begun working with the local chief in the Chikwina area to encourage the villagers to grow coffee.[4] Banda was clearly most impressed with the Chiumes.

Banda was elected president-general of Congress at the conference and given sole power to appoint other officers and the members of the central executive. He appointed Chipembere treasurer, Chiume publicity secretary and Dunduza Chisiza secretary-general. He appointed the four other members of the executive committee and in general 'ignored the older, more experienced and more moderate leaders and took on the younger, more volatile and extreme people'. The Devlin Commission, which inquired into the 1959 state of emergency, had 'no doubt that the real power on the executive committee was concentrated in the hands of Mr Chipembere, Mr Chiume and Mr Chisiza'. On the other hand, Chipembere told Devlin that Banda did not always accept the advice he and Chiume gave him. Also, from the very time of his arrival back in Nyasaland there were signs that Banda was intent on being the boss and demonstrating this to his colleagues. When, soon after his arrival, he called on Armitage, Chipembere was with him and pulled up a chair, clearly expecting to stay, but Banda immediately told him to leave, much to Chipembere's obvious surprise and displeasure. Later, when Banda visited Portugal, Chiume, who accompanied him, was made to wait outside 'like an office boy' while Banda talked to the minister of foreign affairs and shortly to Salazar.[5]

A change in Banda's attitudes to social contacts with Europeans can be seen between the short period before the conference and thereafter. Within a few days of his arrival in the country he made courtesy calls on the Governor and other senior officials.[6] On his way north to the conference he went to his home district, Kasungu, and while there he accepted an invitation from the district commissioner and his wife – a fellow doctor – to dine with them:

> He came and visited his home, Kasungu, and we asked him to dinner and he came. He was very interesting. He was then talking of setting up his dispensary in Blantyre, and my wife, being a medical officer, he asked her many questions about drugs, and local illnesses and so on, and she agreed that she would make out a price list of drugs for him. He was then going up to the Nkata Bay conference, so we asked him to stay with us on his return. He was very friendly and charming. Then he came down and I heard that he had arrived. We waited for him and he did not come. We heard that he was staying nearby, so I sent over a letter asking if he was coming over to us, but we got no reply. Then I wrote the next day and said that we still had not heard: 'Do come and stay with us if you like.' We still had no reply. The third day I sent a messenger again and said 'Give this letter actually to Dr. Banda himself.' The messenger said that he [Banda] opened the letter and he was sitting next to Mr. Chiume and he handed the letter across to Chiume and said, 'Right,

there you are.' Then he tore the letter up, threw it on the floor and said, 'Right, as you say, no further relations with Europeans,' and told the messenger to go back and say there was no reply. [He returned the letter torn in half.] But the first time, as I say, he was very interesting, very charming.[7]

At this time, too, Banda failed to turn up, without sending an excuse, at a cocktail party arranged by the provincial commissioner at Blantyre to meet members of the judiciary and a number of fellow medical practitioners. Jones, the Acting Governor, intended to have a quiet word with him about this breach of civility, but in the event did not do so.[8]

Two or three months previously, Chiume had spoken of his attitude towards social relations between the races to a visiting American, who recalled:

> I asked if he had noted any improvement in the inter-racial situation, and Chiume said he could think of no successful inter-racial activities now. How about the colour bar in hotels, I asked; isn't it in fact possible for Chiume now to go into Ryall's Hotel in Blantyre? Chiume said he wouldn't go into Ryall's Hotel (and implied that he would despise any African who did). 'I'm not interested in the small advances; I want the things that really matter.'[9]

In December 1958 Banda and Chiume attended the All African Peoples Conference in Accra, Ghana, and the doctor subsequently made a number of interesting remarks about their attendance:

> The flight from Johannesburg to Accra was uneventful ... but at Leopoldville the plane on which I travelled picked up a number of delegates ... And to my surprise Kanyama Chiume among them. It was more of a surprise to Kanyama to see me than it was for me to see him. He did not know I was attending the conference ... I had already sent him away when I decided to go to Accra ... [During the conference I] deliberately kept in the background and allowed Mr Chiume to do all the work on each committee on each of the items on the agenda. Since I took over the supreme responsibility of directing the affairs of the NAC, it has always been my policy to give my lieutenants and subordinates as much work and responsibilities as possible. I believe in teaching others who must succeed me one day, by allowing them to do things and share responsibilities with me now, as much as possible ... In the case of Mr Chiume I knew he would be equal to the task imposed on him. He is a very able and energetic young man, who thrives on hard work, as a committee man and as a negotiator. Few in NAC are his equal and none is his superior ... As it turned out, I had never been more right in any decision in my life than I was in allowing Mr Chiume to do the majority

[of the work] for Nyasaland at the Accra conference – who acquitted himself with credit to himself and Nyasaland, and made an excellent impression on all those with whom he worked or came in contact, and they were many.[10]

Banda was clearly still much impressed with Chiume, despite the general view that the doctor himself had given a poor performance at Accra and might well have been overshadowed by Chiume. Chiume had been away from Nyasaland, and out of Banda's critical view, during much of the time since the doctor's return to Nyasaland, so he was continuing to enjoy the good opinion which Banda first formed of him. Indeed, he did not return to Nyasaland for another eighteen months: he was outside the country when the state of emergency was declared in March 1959 and did not return until May 1960, when the emergency was about to be lifted. He was not present at the emergency meeting of Congress in January 1959, though he allowed Congress to use his private box-body truck extensively during his absence, among other things for transporting members at the emergency meeting.[11] At this meeting, it was alleged, a murder plot was hatched to assassinate the Governor, senior government officers, and other Europeans and Africans loyal to the colonial government. Chiume thus neither suffered the hardships of detention nor benefited from the political kudos which it conferred. He spent most of the interim period in Britain, working and lobbying on Banda's behalf – and in the process enhancing his international reputation – while Chipembere and Dunduzu Chisiza and part of the time his brother, Yatuta, were detained in Gwelo prison with Banda.

Being impressed with Chiume did not prevent the doctor being critical of him when occasion demanded. As Chipembere recalled:

> There was a time when Nasser donated £10,000 to our freedom struggle and it was Chiume who received it just before Dr. Banda was released, and he banked it in the name of the Malawi Congress Party in London ... When he reported it ... Dr. Banda was angry with him and said, 'You should have opened it in my name.' There were no explanations. It is possible that he felt that money was safer when the money was controlled directly by him.[12]

Like Chiume, Chipembere was one of the small group responsible for persuading Banda to return to Nyasaland, and he played a large part in building up the doctor's reputation as a messiah: 'I became one of [Dr Banda's] right-hand people and ... in the first years he was very much grateful to me and one or two of my colleagues who took the initiative to call him from abroad to lead the independence struggle.'[13] He was a leading figure and speaker at the January 1959 emergency meeting of

Congress. He was arrested on 3 March 1959 and detained in Gwelo prison. When they were together in prison, Banda and Chipembere got to know each other better. This had both benefits and disadvantages for Chipembere that Chiume did not share. The doctor later referred to those who were in Gwelo with him as his 'immediate top lieutenants'.[14] Banda seems to have entrusted even some domestic and personal affairs to Chipembere, who many years later recalled:

> As a result of this very close relationship I was able to know the man very thoroughly and can explain some of his deeds in terms of what I was able to observe in him at close quarters especially during the time that he and I and two friends – the Chisiza brothers – were locked up together in [Gwelo]. For fourteen months we were together, apart from the first three weeks in which we were not allowed to communicate, in which we were all in solitary confinement. We spent the rest of the time together most of the day, a little reading in the morning and the rest of the afternoon discussion and so on. We got to know the man very thoroughly during that time – the changes of mood, philosophy of life. It is impossible to conceal your feelings from somebody you see every day for fourteen months, talking together.
>
> We were in Gwelo and planning what he was going to do. His former nurse had got married. [She was] a relation of his – and he was just thinking who was going to take her place. He asked me to find a good girl who might take the place of that other one. I wrote to [Cecilia Kadzamira]. She was about to get married but such was the patriotism in those days that she said, 'O.K. I am willing to delay my marriage so as to work for the old doc.' She thought that after working for a few months or years she would be able to get married. The Doctor told me to tell her that she would be sent abroad for training – I don't think he intended that and he has never done that. It created an additional attraction for her to take up the job.[15]

Banda had begun to know Chipembere quite well before they were detained, and there were aspects of his make-up which disturbed him, particularly his occasional losses of temper and the immoderate behaviour that accompanied them. For example, at a public meeting in Zomba in mid-January 1959, Chipembere was so upset at the arrest of a number of women supporters that he delivered a speech that was violent in tone and in which he made obscene remarks about the royal family. Banda was sufficiently disturbed by this as to tap him on the back and tell him to quieten down. Later that day he delivered a reprimand to Chipembere for his unseemly behaviour.[16] Banda was aware, too, that Chipembere lost his temper from time to time in Gwelo prison and, for example in December 1959, 'he had, in a moment of irritation, thrown some doubt over the ancestry of the prison superintendent [who] had thereupon removed all privileges for two weeks, including seeing visitors'. While in detention he spent so much time reading that his warder – who thought him 'the most likeable' of the detainees – chided him and thought he would 'crack' if he did not do something else. Thereafter he relaxed by making fishing nets, which he enjoyed: 'I naturally find net-making a reviving change from long hours of pacing round my cell or our yard or sitting down for hours reading all the conflicting things that the great brains of this world have to say about ideal constitutions and systems!'[17]

The early change in Banda's attitude towards social contact with Europeans may have been the result not only of Chiume's but also of Chipembere's influence. Devlin was given a good deal of evidence that Chipembere was anti-European and 'rabidly racist', including that of two district commissioners with whom he worked before standing for selection to the legislature. The first found:

> He was an extreme fanatic, especially over his relationships with Europeans, and I have always said that he is mentally most unstable. He would get into the most dreadful rages and harangue against Europeans, and on many occasions I said, 'If you think like this, why on earth are you working for the Government?' He told me that when he was at school he was once caned by a European, and he said that from that date to this, so far as he was concerned, Europeans were dogs ... Apparently one day I passed his wife in the street and he asked me, 'Why did you not take your hat off to my wife?' I said I was very sorry, but I had not seen her. He harangued for a long time. He would never come to my house, never ... and on several occasions I asked him to dinner. He never replied. When I taxed him with it he said, 'No. In my position I cannot be seen mixing with Europeans.' As I say, I have always thought that he is mentally most unstable. One day he will go off his head. He gets into these dreadful rages, almost like a fit, but he is undoubtedly a very intelligent man.[18]

Devlin found this evidence 'most valuable and helpful'. When asked about Chipembere's attitude towards Europeans, the second district commissioner told the commission: 'When I knew him I would say that he accepted them as a rather unpleasant form of life ... he just had nothing to do with us towards the end.' Youens, later secretary to the prime minister and cabinet, attributed Chipembere's attitude to his having been boxed over the ears by a European schoolmaster for some misdemeanour. He was reputed to have had the floor of his office painted white so that he could walk on it daily. Chipembere routinely rejected invitations from Europeans to attend social functions, as did Chiume. Chiume felt, for example, that when Armitage was entertaining African members of the legislative council he was trying to 'mellow [them] from the twin objectives of secession and independence [but he] was left in no doubt that he could not succeed in his policies ... by traditional methods of being nice to the Africans'. Later Chiume said, 'We did not intend to be softened so easily and ... refused to attend [his] luncheons.'[19]

Chipembere was not released from detention until September 1960, with the other members of the elite group of 'camp finalists'. Again, his long confinement and late release had physical disadvantages and political benefits, which Chiume did not share.

The other lieutenant detained in Gwelo with Banda was Dunduzu Chisiza. Born in 1930, he went to school at Uliwa and Livingstonia in the northern province of Nyasaland. In 1949 he went to Tanganyika and worked briefly in the police as a records clerk. He then went to college in Uganda and spent two years touring the Congo. He returned to Uganda and then went to Southern Rhodesia, where he worked as a clerk in the Indian high commission. He was deported to Nyasaland in July 1956 for political activities. He was appointed Congress's organizing secretary in 1957 before going off to Britain to study economics. He was recalled to Nyasaland in 1958 and made secretary-general by Banda. It was Chisiza who was primarily responsible for initiating and organizing the January 1959 emergency meeting of Congress. He was arrested and detained on 3 March 1959, but a little later in the day because he was not at his usual house when the police arrived to arrest him. During the morning he telephoned the officer in charge of police and asked him – unsuccessfully – to provide a vehicle and to come personally to take him into detention. He also contrived to have his arrest witnessed by journalists and photographers of the international press. In Gwelo he spent a good deal of time studying economic development and pondering Nysaland's economic future. In addition to reading several economics texts he also particularly asked for a copy of Dale Carnegie's *How to Stop Worrying and Start Living*. He remained with Chipembere in detention when Banda left Gwelo and was not released until the camp finalists were freed on 27 September 1960.[20]

Yatuta Chisiza, Dunduzu's elder brother, had served in the Tanganyika police force, where he reached the rank of assistant inspector. During that period, he was asked by the Tanganyika government

> to infiltrate and report on the activities of the Tanganyika African Union (TANU). This he did but when TANU suspected these activities, he was posted from Iringa to Tukuyu. From there he left the police force and returned to Nyasaland in 1957. He pretended to do so in the nationalist cause of Nyasaland but in reality, Chiume believed, he was fleeing from TANU.[21]

12 · Revolt of the Ministers

In January 1959, at the emergency meeting of Congress, Yatuta was appointed to be Banda's private secretary, paid for by Congress, and to do 'some personal work for [him] at his house', paid for by the doctor.[22] In effect, he became Banda's personal bodyguard and was with him when he was arrested. Although he was not incarcerated in Gwelo all the time, he did spend a portion of his detention there with Banda, Chipembere and Dunduzu. The Devlin Commission found him to be lying when he denied all the violent passages in the transcript of a speech he made in February 1959. Devlin then played the tape recording of the speech – which indeed contained many violent statements – to Chisiza, who still declined to reconsider his evidence. Devlin concluded that there was no point in continuing the questioning.[23] Yatuta was a prison graduate and a camp finalist.

In the three or four years leading up to the creation of the Federation in 1953, one of Banda's most frequent correspondents was Orton Chirwa – born in 1919 – who strongly opposed federation. 'In the villages and townships mass meetings were held at which Orton Chirwa, wearing academic robes, stirred up a ferment of anti-federal feeling the like of which Nyasaland had never seen before.' He then added a barrister qualification in London to his arts degree from South Africa. Armitage recorded that Chirwa 'was known to have been in close association with Dr. Banda while in the UK and since [his] return [late in 1958]'. He acted as legal counsel for Congress but did not become a member of the executive committee, possibly, it was thought, because 'he was afraid that Banda's entourage would take decisions which he, as a lawyer, could not condone'. In March 1959 he was detained, but only for a short period. He was not accommodated with Banda, Chipembere and the Chisiza brothers at Gwelo. He was not arrested on 3 March as were the other lieutenants, but a few days later with other members of what the government saw as the second eleven: John Msonthi – who was authorized by Chisiza to take over the secretary-generalship of Congress in the event of members of the executive being arrested – Dr Harry Bwanausi, Willie Chokani, David Rubadiri, Moir Chisuze and Vincent Gondwe. Indeed, Chirwa was disappointed at not being arrested on 3 March, and, at his request, was allowed to accompany Chipembere and others to Chileka airport – but no further – prior to their being flown to Southern Rhodesia. The arrest of this second eleven – all graduates – and especially Chirwa, caused much concern in Britain, where a number of parliamentary questions were asked about it.[24]

Shortly after his release Chirwa founded the Malawi Congress Party with Aleke Banda. Aleke, then aged only twenty, had been born in Northern Rhodesia and educated in Southern Rhodesia, and had recently been deported to Nyasaland, as a political agitator. His parents' country of origin was Nyasaland, but they had left there twenty-five years earlier. The Chief Native Commissioner considered his security file 'so shockingly subversive' that he 'just could not take a chance on keeping him in Rhodesia'. Chirwa and Aleke in effect re-created the proscribed Nyasaland African Congress under a different name, openly saying they were creating, expanding and keeping it going ready for Banda to take it over when released. In this respect Banda owed a good deal to them. Unlike Chipembere, Chiume and the Chisiza brothers, they were moderates. Chiume tried to prevent Chirwa creating the MCP, fearing that he was entering into a deal with the government in which he, Chirwa, would become Nyasaland's first prime minister. It was alleged 'that he had been visited by a Nyasaland Government official when he was detained in Zomba prison, and offered his freedom' if he would form a new party. This is most unlikely to have been the case. Chipembere confided to an American visitor to Gwelo gaol in September 1959 that 'Orton Chirwa's idea of forming a new party is not approved by us', and when he was asked if this included Banda, he said, 'Yes.'[25]

While Banda and his leading colleagues were still in gaol, Chirwa became the principal representative of Congress. During the last two months of 1959, in particular, he enjoyed a public role he had not experienced before. He had meetings with the Governor and accepted an invitation to visit the Colonial Office in the middle of November. There were two meetings, both with Iain Macleod, secretary of state. Chirwa was very self-confident, speaking, as it were, on behalf of the Nyasaland Africans. Although he had prepared a memorandum, he preferred 'an informal meeting in which he could develop freely the various points he had to make'. He told them that through his professional and personal relationship with Banda he was able to influence him and, having provided an instrument for non-violent political activity – the MCP – he felt he could keep Banda on a constitutional path. Despite Chirwa's confidence – bordering on arrogance – Macleod, Armitage and Colonial Office oficials saw him as 'certainly not a political leader', not that this mattered because Chirwa was 'perfectly ready to admit that the party had been specially created as a vehicle for Banda'.[26]

Banda was released from detention on 1 April 1960. This was done without the knowledge of those detained with him in the same prison; they did not accompany him to freedom. He was taken to Government House to meet the Governor and the Colonial Secretary. A little later in the morning Chirwa and Aleke Banda were brought to Zomba to meet him. They were the first Africans to know of his release and he was in effect entrusted to their care when later that morning they took him to Blantyre.[27]

A week later Banda went to Britain and the USA and was away for several weeks. He did not take any of his colleagues with him. Shortly after his return, the state of emergency was brought to an end, but not before legislation was passed to ensure that about a score of the hard core were kept in detention, including Chipembere, the Chisizas, McKinley Chibambo – who had been in restriction in Port Herald from 1953 until his detention in 1959 – and Gwanda Chakuamba, one of Banda's 'staunchest young supporters'.[28]

Chiume returned to Nyasaland on 8 May, and with Chirwa and Aleke Banda accompanied Banda to the Lancaster House constitutional conference in July and early August. The doctor had vowed not to go to the conference unless the remaining detainees were released, but Armitage talked him out of this, apparently with no great difficulty. The agreements reached at that conference were arrived at without Chipembere's and the Chisizas' participation and fell well short of what they strongly wished to secure, despite Chiume's presence.

In the period up to September 1960, the old guard – men like the other members of legislative council, Chinyama, Chijozi and Kwenje, and former office-holders in Congress, Thamar Dillon Thomas Banda and James Frederick Sangala – passed into virtual oblivion and were rarely heard of again. The membership of the new guard, Banda's principal lieutenants, became clear: Chiume, Chipembere, Dunduzu Chisiza and Chirwa. The individual parts played by the leading members of Congress varied a great deal.

Chiume got off to a good start in his relations with Banda. On the positive side he was one of the small group instrumental in bringing the doctor back to Nyasaland; he and his wife created a highly favourable impression on Banda at a time when he was disappointed in the general level of advancement that he found on his return to Nyasaland; his performance at Accra impressed the doctor on an occasion when he wished personally to keep out of the limelight but did not want Nyasaland to be so treated; he kept the flame of Congress alight in Britain and internationally when the NAC was proscribed; and he accompanied Banda to the Lancaster House constitutional conference. On the negative, but none the less beneficial side from his point of view, he was away from the country for long periods when any defects were less likely to come to Banda's notice. He seems to have been sufficiently influential on Banda as to induce him to change his attitude towards social contact with Europeans. Indeed, one of the non-official members of executive council told the Governor that Chiume was intercepting Banda's mail and insulating him from moderate European opinion.[29] On the other hand, although he offered to return to Africa and join his colleagues in detention – an offer Banda declined[30] – not being detained with them, and especially not being among the elite last group to be released, deprived Chiume of the politically important titles of prison graduate and camp finalist. It deprived him, too, of membership of the small group in Gwelo which planned Nyasaland's future. While Chiume was unable to learn more about Banda through close association in Gwelo, Banda was not able to learn more about Chiume – which, on balance, was probably to Chiume's advantage.

Chipembere also got off to a good start by being one of those inviting Banda to return to Nyasaland, and he was especially influential in persuading him to do so. It was he who agreed to Banda having sole power to control Congress as the price for his agreeing to return to Nyasaland. He was primarily responsible for ensuring that the doctor was built up as the saviour and messiah – though the actual building up was done mainly by Chiume. When the state of emergency was declared, he was flown in the same plane as Banda, with no other detainees, to Southern Rhodesia – indeed the plane's departure was delayed until he arrived at the airport – and he was incarcerated with Banda for the next thirteen months. During this period he was able to learn a good deal about the doctor – who also learned a good deal about him – and, with Dunduzu Chisiza, frequently discussed and planned with him Nyasaland's future. For the first six months in Gwelo he joined Banda in financially helping the Chisiza brothers, who had no money with them. When his legislative council salary was discontinued, however, he was no longer able to help in this way.[31] He was the longest imprisoned of all those detained, being among the first to be arrested and the last to be released: he was both a prison graduate and a camp finalist.

Dunduzu Chisiza's start was also good. Before going to Britain for further studies, he had joined Chipembere and Chiume in a delegation in September 1957 to press the Governor for constitutional advance. He was specially chosen by Banda to be the secretary-general of Congress and had to abandon his studies to take up the post. He accompanied Banda, Chipembere and Chief Kuntaja to make representations to the Colonial Secretary in London in June 1958. He was arrested on 3 March, and was able to learn a good deal about Banda – and he to learn about him – while spending thirteen months in Gwelo with him. He spent long hours discussing and planning Nyasaland's future economic development with the doctor there. He continued the study of economics, which he had abandoned when he was called back from Britain, and, in effect, he became Congress's economist. He, too, was a long-serving prison graduate and enjoyed the prestige of being a camp finalist.

Yatuta Chisiza's position as Banda's personal bodyguard placed him in close contact with the doctor, who must have reposed considerable confidence in him, at least physically. He did not, however, share the sort of confidence enjoyed by Chipembere and Dunduzu and he did not join in their discussions planning Nyasaland's future, possibly because he was somewhat less well educated than they were. When they discussed with Banda in Gwelo gaol the cabinet to be formed on self-government, they excluded Yatuta, 'to his intense annoyance'.[32] Though a prison graduate and a camp finalist, he was not one of Banda's principal lieutenants.

Orton Chirwa had been active in supporting Banda's strong opposition to federation and he kept in contact with him while the doctor was in Ghana. His not having been long detained, and especially not being a camp finalist, was compensated by his co-founding the Malawi Congress Party and building it up ready for Banda to take over. Consequently, when Banda was released he had a ready-made party organization to use in continuing the fight for secession and independence. Chirwa's studies in Britain made him, in efffect, the Congress lawyer, and in this capacity he accompanied Banda to the Lancaster House conference.

Although Chiume and Chirwa were free when Banda was released from detention, it was not until September 1960, when Chipembere and Dunduzu Chisiza were freed, that the principal lieutenancy became complete.

CHAPTER 3

Banda Consolidates His Power: August 1960 to September 1961

BY early August 1960, Banda's power was already considerable. Its initial source was the British government which, without reference to any electoral test, accepted him as the Nyasaland Africans' leader. As early as February 1959 Macmillan had foreseen that the British and Nyasaland governments would have to deal with him.[1] By September that year many outside government were convinced that the stalemate produced by the emergency could be broken only by recognizing him as the Nyasaland leader and including him in the processes of government. Macleod reached this conclusion within a few weeks of becoming secretary of state. But there were other strong sources of Banda's power. He had been asked back to Nyasaland specifically to lead Congress. He had been given sole power to run the party and had selected his own principal and other lieutenants. He had a well-organized and fast-growing party ready and waiting for him on his release from detention. He had the sympathy of many influential people and organizations throughout the world, who felt that his long incarceration without trial was harsh and unjustified. He had been built up as a messiah. Devlin had been far more critical of the Nyasaland government and of his principal lieutenants than he had of him. As the Africans saw it, he, and not the government, had been right: he was at least the match of any white man. He had devoted his period in Gwelo prison to planning the future and to influencing – and assessing – two of the principal lieutenants, Chipembere and Chisiza. Within a few months of his release he had secured for Nyasaland a new constitution that gave Africans a dominant position in the legislature and a significant presence in the executive. His standing as leader of the Nyasalanders was very high indeed. He spent the next twelve months consolidating and furthering his personal power over his party and his lieutenants, and to extending it to encompass the head of government himself, the Governor.

Armitage went on leave early in August 1960, and Jones, the chief secretary, was appointed Acting Governor. Macleod's tactic was so to handle Banda that he would become involved in the work of government by joining executive council. In this way he hoped the doctor would learn that federation had distinct benefits for Nyasaland. To achieve this the government had to strive to create an environment in which he could gradually move towards the centre – politically in the sense of a non-violent, more moderate, more democratic approach and leadership, and constitutionally in the sense of a more balanced approach to continuing association with the Rhodesias, in particular being prepared to consider the Monckton Report and attend the federal review conference scheduled for December 1960. Whatever attitude Banda might take to these ideas, it was clear they would be utterly unacceptable to his lieutenants.[2]

Banda raised the question of his membership of executive council with Youens, the deputy chief secretary, two days after Armitage left. He was 'willing, indeed anxious' to accept nomination, but neither he nor any of his colleagues could possibly accept appointment or 'sit in the same room' with the current 'nominated stooges' – the four nominated African legislative councillors and the two executive councillors. Furthermore, if they 'were not dispensed with',

> he certainly would not take a seat on either council, nor could Government hope to get the cooperation from him which he was willing to accord ... If the Government would not act reasonably in this way, then ... the former pattern of events would be repeated. The Government would be 'pig-headed' and he would be 'pig-headed'. Tension would increase and stability would not be achieved.[3]

Four days later, the doctor discussed the matter with Jones. He was adamant that the existing nominated African members would have to be removed before he would take a seat. Jones, knowing Macleod considered it unthinkable that he should accede to this demand, simply asked Banda to think about it carefully and discuss it with him again. Banda agreed, but held out no hope that he would change his mind. There the matter rested, mainly because a related and more pressing matter overtook it.[4]

In his conversations with Youens, Banda had hinted that in his view 'the time had now come for the Government to declare a general amnesty in respect of all those presently detained, to restore Chipembere and Chiume to their rightful places in Legislative Council'. On the day he himself had been released from detention Macleod and Armitage had assured him that if peace and order were maintained 'they would consider not only the question of the release of the rest of the detainees, but also lifting the whole state of emergency'. It is likely that he thought the former would be easier than, and would precede, the latter, and he was puzzled that this did not turn out to be the case, although the remaining detainees had been moved from Southern Rhodesia to Kanjedza in Nyasaland. It was this assurance that persuaded him that day to agree to broadcast a message calling for peace and calm.[5]

A few days before Armitage went on leave he had discussed with Jones and Youens how to handle a query from Macleod about how to deal with those still in detention. As Armitage recorded: 'We want to play the game as slowly as possible ... We don't yet know what Banda really wants.'[6] The doctor, however, was quick to make clear precisely what he really wanted and he certainly did not want the game played slowly.

On 5 September Banda had separate meetings with Youens and Jones and again raised the question of releasing the remaining detainees. On the one hand, it had been made more difficult for the government by recent physical attacks on Banda's political opponents and their intimidation and vilification by MCP members. On the other hand, Banda was under considerable pressure from Chiume. The MCP annual convention was shortly to take place at Kota Kota and Chiume warned him that:

> already there were open murmurings against his having agreed to be released ... without the knowledge of his colleagues and leaving them behind. His standing at the Convention certainly would [be] lowered if they [were] not ... released before or at the Convention [and I] put before him forcefully, the dissatisfaction of the people and the Party in the continued detention of the [remaining detainees].[7]

The first meeting was with Youens, who found it 'an uncomfortable interview'.[8] Twice the doctor 'evinced an intention of abandoning it but though he got near the door, in the event he never actually went through it'. Banda was 'utterly dismayed' at the government's 'entirely unreasonable' attitude, which showed a complete lack of appreciation of the difficulties he had to overcome and the compromises he had to make with his own conscience in going to the Lancaster House conference and accepting the agreement there. It was clear to him that all the government's talk about making a new start and creating the circumstances in which all could work together was so much 'hypocritical eyewash'. Did the government seriously think he could come on to executive council and cooperate while they kept his followers 'rotting indefinitely in gaol without trial'? Such a situation made the Lancaster House agreement quite worthless. He would prefer to join his followers in prison. If the government failed to see sense he would have to abandon any plans for cooperating with them. Instead, he would concentrate on organizing the MCP with a view to putting the differences between him and the government to a 'final test'. 'It will be back to March 3rd 1959 all over again.' Banda was pushing this question hard and was using the most powerful of threats: a return to emergency conditions and the reimposition of an impasse – eventualities he knew Macleod and Jones would do almost anything to avoid.

Youens told the doctor that it was in his own power to improve the situation to an extent that would be conducive to further releases. He could, for example, make it publicly and consistently clear that he condemned and abhorred all acts of violence and intimidation. He could also require his followers to respect the freedom of belief and expression of all people, and he could give instructions to his party explicitly prohibiting acts of violence, molestation and intimidation against political opponents. 'This theme', Youens told Jones, 'was played to the accompaniment of numerous expostulations by the Doctor and a sally towards the door.' Banda continued to dig his toes in, they got no further and at 4 p.m. Banda left for Government House to see Jones.

Banda was still steamed up after his meeting with Youens, and although a great deal of flak had been drawn from his attack, there was still a good deal left. He gave the Acting Governor a rough ride. Jones recalled:

> Banda went into the attack immediately ... against the Government and against me personally for continuing to detain people in Kanjedza. He said that he was disappointed to see that I was becoming infected with the Zomba virus; he had hoped to see a new policy initiated by me with a total release of people detained for political reasons without trial but he was sorry to see that I was the same as all other civil servants in Zomba ... He displayed considerable emotion at this stage.[9]

Jones had arranged that Banda should take tea with him, his wife and his daughter after the discussion, but the doctor – following Chiume's warnings about the dangers of 'the traditional methods of being nice to the Africans' – said he could not drink tea with them when he was so distressed about Jones's refusal to see his point of view, and about his complacency in thinking there could ever be peace in Nyasaland while any of his followers remained in detention. Jones tried to soothe him by saying they were releasing detainees as the situation warranted and he had no intention of keeping them all in detention indefinitely. Banda retorted that he could not accept gradualism: they must all be released at once. While any remained in detention his people felt so upset that it was impossible for them to avoid creating incidents and impossible for him to impress upon them a respect for law and order. The only way to achieve tranquillity was to release all the detainees. 'Their continued detention made a mockery of the Lancaster House agreements and he would not participate in the new constitution if they were not released.' This last remark was designed to put additional pressure on Macleod, whose reputation for having pulled off a masterstroke in securing the agreements would be in tatters if Banda decided not to let it work. Similarly, his comments about Jones being infected with the Zomba virus and being like all other civil servants in Zomba were designed to put additional pressure on the Acting Governor whose personal position in Nyasaland depended on his being seen to be different from more reactionary colleagues. He, as Banda well knew, would have been particularly concerned about these personal jibes.

Jones eventually concluded that prolonging the discussion would lead to their parting with hard feelings and might prejudice their future relationship. With great difficulty he enticed Banda into the drawing room, where he had tea 'and went off the boil'. This was the first time Banda used angry, threatening and indeed rude language in his contacts with Jones. On no occasion did he act in a similar way with Armitage, and though he became angry and used threats in his subsequent dealings with Jones, he was never rude. He was, however, keenly aware of the efficacy of 'shouting at and denouncing' those who did not accede to his demands.[10]

Two days later Banda asked to see Youens urgently. This time he was in 'an entirely different mood'.[11] He acted reasonably and quietly, there were no explosions or emotional outbursts and they departed, after taking tea and toast together, amiably. Banda said his position with his followers was becoming daily more impossible. When he told his colleagues he had made no progress over releasing the detainees, they responded violently and vowed to organize a large crowd to release them by force. Only after a heated discussion in which he said their proposed action would lead to bloodshed and could not possibly have the ultimate effect they desired, was he able to dissuade them. Clearly, at this time, Banda's lieutenants – led by Chiume – were not averse to telling him what they thought and to pressing a course of action upon him. Banda now asked that Youens and Jones should try to see things from his perspective. He was keen to cooperate but they had to realize it was impossibe for him effectively to advocate cooperation without showing something tangible for it. Banda begged that Jones should see sense, and if he did not, then he must accept that the situation would inevitably degenerate to emergency conditions similar to those of the previous year. There would be nothing he could do to prevent it. If they were released, he was confident he could ensure their good behaviour.

After long discussion with his official advisers, following this meeting, Jones concluded that he should consider the early release of the remaining detainees and lifting all the remaining control orders. He would make it clear to Banda that, if he did this, he would expect him to cooperate with the government and control his followers. He hoped that this would produce an atmosphere in which Banda would consider some form of continued federal association.[12]

Macleod had not expected Banda to raise the detainees question to crisis point, but now that he had, he agreed on balance with Jones's proposed way of tackling it, so long as there was any prospect of inducing the doctor to adopt a reasonable attitude towards federation. He expected, however, that with the release of the final detainees, especially Chipembere and the Chisiza brothers, there would be increased pressure on Banda to raise his demands as high as possible about implementing the new constitutional arrangements before the federal review conference and about accepting a seat on executive council.[13]

When Banda saw Jones on 15 September, he was hostile, but once he was persuaded that his representations were being taken seriously he quietened down.[14] He was grateful to Jones for consulting Macleod on this vital matter because it was making it 'impossible for peaceful conditions to emerge'. He repeated that he would publicly call for peace and denounce violence once he received an unequivocal assurance that all detentions and restrictions would be lifted. He guaranteed that the 'three Cs' – Chipembere and the Chisiza brothers – would be amenable to his influence and would cause no trouble. Jones, privately, was not convinced: 'One would have to accept that for what it was worth.'[15]

A week later they met again.[16] Jones started by saying that, if the discussion proceeded satisfactorily, he had great hopes the doctor would be satisfied the government was doing all it could to ease his situation and to remove all bitterness remaining in MCP minds. In the course of the next two hours' discussion he explained his difficulties, including the great anxiety that if Chipembere and the Chisizas were released, they would revert to their known bitter and violent tendencies.

> I then said that if I was to revoke the detention and control orders, I must be given a very solemn assurance that this would not lead either in the immediate future or later on to disturbances ... What I was proposing to do was an act of faith in Banda and I relied on him to be insistent that all his followers throughout the territory should keep the peace. He gave me his solemn assurance on this point.

When Jones raised the question of his cooperating by joining executive council before the elections, Banda said it was not an important issue for him. His tactic of linking the releases with membership of council had suceeded: he had secured the former and now dismissed the latter.

Jones then told him he would revoke the remaining detention and control orders. Banda thought they should be released early on 27 September and taken secretly to Kota Kota where the annual MCP conference was to be held. They could then be delivered to him and he could give them 'strong advice' as to their future behaviour as soon as possible: this would remove the danger of demonstrations in Blantyre-Limbe as a result of their release. It would also ensure that Banda could claim all the credit for the releases, and his colleagues none.

The exercise to release the detainees was codenamed 'Operation Stunt'. Three hundred and fifty control orders were lifted at the same time.[17] Banda kept the secret entirely to himself and there was no leaking of information about the operation. During 26 September, Youens visited Kanjedza and interviewed the detainees there because, Banda felt, the government was not fully satisfied with his assurance that he would control the detainees if they were released. He particularly spoke with Chipembere. As Banda shortly said:

> In the eyes of the Government ... Chipembere, the two Chisizas, especially Yatuta Chisiza, and [Kapombe] Nyasulu [Banda's factotum who spent part of his detention in Gwelo] were the most dangerous or still are the most dangerous. In all my negotiations, it was Chipembere that I was always asked first if, when he were free, he would keep the peace. In fact ... they did not want to release these men ... and they maintained that Chipembere, even more than the other three, would not keep the peace, once they were out. I told the Acting Governor and others ... they had the wrong impressions of ... Chipembere, the Chisiza brothers and Nyasulu.[18]

In the early hours of 27 September the remaining detainees in Kanjedza were placed in the camp bus and told they were being taken to Kota Kota, where they would be formally released.[19] They were encouraged to keep their heads down as they travelled through Blantrye at the beginning of the journey so that no one would recognize them. They entered into the spirit of the secret and made no noise as they left the camp, still in the dark. They kept quiet throughout the whole of the journey. As the bus travelled through Lilongwe, one of the camp officials travelling with them suggested they duck down so as not to be seen. This they did and successfully passed through Lilongwe with no one knowing about them. A few miles south of Visanza, Banda passed the bus in his car, without the occupants of either vehicle making the slightest sign of recognition. Five miles short of Kota Kota, they stopped at the house where Banda was staying and were then handed over to him. Even then, no one in Kota Kota knew what was happening. They had been in detention just short of nineteen months.

Back in Blantyre-Limbe, no news of the releases became known until about 4.30 p.m., when Chirwa was told by someone in the MCP office. Expressing great surprise and pleasure, he immediately rushed to Kanjedza so that he personally could take them to Kota Kota. He was astonished – and no doubt somewhat deflated – to learn that they had left fifteen hours earlier. Soon after they arrived in Kota Kota, Banda presented them to the assembled MCP conference.[20] This was a major political coup and further strengthened his standing as leader of the party. Chiume, who had been reinstated as publicity secretary of the MCP and officially number two in the party hierarchy, was virtually in charge of the convention and was already at Kota Kota. He recalled: 'The detainees, as well as the convention, were overwhelmed by [the releases]; no wonder Dunduzu Chisiza ... was so emotionally carried away that he [took the step] of declaring Banda, before the crowd of over 100,000 people, Life President of the MCP, without prior consultation with the others.'[21]

The camp finalists were dressed in red prison graduate gowns, an idea proposed by the Zomba branch of the MCP Women's League. These gowns were, to Banda, 'the outward, visible and tangible expression of the honour and esteem' in which the detainees were held in the country. He wore a black gown, given to him by the Zomba women three weeks earlier to indicate that he was 'Prison Graduate Number One'. He was not, it seems, going to let the finalists steal his thunder and he was at pains to tell his audience how strongly he had emphasized his desire himself to be the last detainee to be released, when the chief secretary had visited him in Gwelo. In the course of his speech Banda referred to Youens's visit to Kanjedza on the eve of the detainees' release, and asked Chipembere to repeat before the huge audience the assurance of good behaviour he had given Youens three days earlier. He did so.[22] He was then reinstated in his former post of treasurer-general, Dunduzu Chisiza was reinstated as general secretary and Yatuta Chisiza became administrative secretary of the party. All the lieutenants were now free.

Banda went off to Nigeria on 21 November and then to the federal review conference in London. In Nyasaland the security situation deteriorated almost as soon as he left. The review conference started on 5 December and Banda was joined by Dunduzu Chisiza and Chirwa. No doubt miffed at being left behind in Nyasaland, Chipembere and Chiume were extremely worried that Banda would agree to the country remaining in the Federation. Chiume recalled:

> There were three of us, Chip[embere], Augustine Bwanausi and myself. We toured the whole country by car, train, boat and air to mobilise the people against a heavily rumoured possible sell-out by Banda at the conference. There were strong speculations ... that Banda would have agreed to Nyasaland being part of a modified Central African Federation ... In the circumstances we felt it our duty to forestall this criminal deal and thus the campaign to expose it before the people and prepare them for an inevitable showdown should Banda, in the teeth of African opposition,

have decided to accept the imposed and detested federation however modified.²³

There was a general feeling that Banda did indeed succumb to Macmillan's charm during the conference – which was adjourned and never reconvened. As Short put it: 'the principal delegates were invited to spend the weekend at the British Prime Minister's country house, Chequers. Alone with Macmillan, Banda set out to be at his most engaging. The two men got on well, sharing a love of history and a peculiarly English sense of snobbery.'²⁴ On Banda's return to Nyasaland Armitage remarked on the way in which Macmillan, and no longer Macleod, was the doctor's hero. The Governor, too, thought this was snobbery. Later, Banda was to say both that going to London allowed him to 'meet a great Prime Minister' and also that he did not want to be subjected again to 'the Chequers treatment'.²⁵ Chiume had given early warning of the dangers of the 'traditional methods of being nice to the Africans'.

The first dangerous incident after Banda left for Nigeria was at Port Herald on 1 December. The LMY attacked a police van, stones were thrown, tear gas was used and riot squad reinforcements were called in. Chipembere and Chiume were 'making a lot of rabid speeches condemning ... government and stooges' and threatening to deal with them severely once Congress got into power. Soon Finney, head of Special Branch, was reporting on how active the LMY was being and how they were causing trouble also in Nkata Bay and Karonga, where they were 'very anti-police, anti-government and anti-European'. He believed Chipembere's and Chiume's tactics were to 'keep up the task of frightening the government', confident that Macleod would not allow force to be used against them again.²⁶

Following a particularly vigorous speech by Chipembere in Blantyre, the police were stoned and two constables injured. After the crowd was dispersed by tear gas, a mob of about eighty stormed the house of Chester Katsonga, founder and leader of the recently formed, Catholic Church-backed, Christian Democratic Party. They burned his house to the ground, and he, his wife, father and three children were only just able to escape from it. Chipembere later, in attempting to defend his actions, told Banda the 'it was the UFP, the Special Branch and [the Congress Liberation Party] who burnt it in order to discredit Malawi'.²⁷ Armitage, returning from leave in November, wondered why Chipembere and Chiume were behaving in this fashion and concluded, correctly, that they feared Banda might compromise in London and cooperate with the Europeans. He also thought they were angry at not having been taken to London and were trying to undermine Banda and show him where the real power lay.²⁸

Finney thought prosecuting Chipembere 'would ignite a powder train' and consequently he should be warned in the hope that he would then behave himself. He and Armitage considered arresting him and letting him out on bail, but feared he would then continue his tour of the country, even if restrictions were placed on his movements and on his making speeches. Remanding him in custody 'might set the country alight'. They concluded that Chiume had done nothing to merit prosecution. In any case he came from the north, where his position was strong and the LMY predominant; reaction to proceeding against him would consequently be acute. For this reason the Colonial Office thought a control order against him would be a more serious matter than a prosecution against Chipembere. Armitage was sufficiently concerned about the escalating violence to call for a review of the security forces available and where he might obtain others, for example from Britain.[29]

Armitage told Macleod he was contemplating prosecuting Chipembere for a speech in which he said 'Give me the living body of Blackwood [Nyasaland leader of the UFP] to tear it to pieces. I'll do the job in two minutes.'[30] He also considered prosecuting Chiume for speeches in Zomba and Blantyre. He thought that whatever Banda might do to calm the situation, the damage done could not be undone. He made it clear that if there were to be no prosecutions it would be because he, the Governor – and not Macleod – had decided it was not in the public interest. He did in fact prosecute the Karonga MCP chairman, Flax Msopole, a hard-core camp finalist, four members of the executive committee of the LMY in Blantyre, and others. Macleod asked him to stay his hand in respect of Chipembere until he had spoken with Banda.

Just before the doctor left London after the conference, Macleod told him he hoped he would keep the peace and eschew intimidation. He also told him that Armitage was going to prosecute Chipembere. Banda was in a good mood and gave Macleod the assurances he was seeking about keeping the peace and rejecting intimidation. As for prosecuting Chipembere, he said the law should take its course. Just before he landed at Chileka the Nyasaland police issued a summons against Chipembere on charges of making seditious speeches and proposing violence. When the summons was served, Chipembere accused the police of being afraid of actually arresting him.[31] The matter was not without humour, for when the detective superintendent served the summons at MCP headquarters, as he recalled: 'It was rather embarrassing. Chipembere mistook me for a member of a BBC team who had come to interview him, and greeted me with a handshake and a beaming smile. This entente rapidly disappeared when I slapped him with the summons.'[32] Banda advised Chipembere to 'bury [him]self in some office and refrain from crowds' until his trial, and this he did.[33]

On Christmas Eve Finney had his usual Saturday-morning meeting with the Governor. He had already told Armitage of the confusion in Congress stemming from Banda's attendance at Chequers and his association with Welensky during the conference. Now he said there had been criticism of the doctor in Karonga district for some time and there was a more widespread feeling that, since Banda had not achieved secession, a more militant leader should be sought. Presumably they thought this leader should be a northerner, possibly from Karonga, and, if this was so, it meant one of the Chisiza brothers, probably Dunduzu. Finney also reported a growing split between Chirwa and Aleke Banda, and between Banda on the one hand and Chipembere and Chiume on the other, 'with Chisiza as yet uncommitted'. Banda's relative moderation and lack of success in breaking up the Federation was 'not appreciated by many' and Armitage thought 'Banda will need good health and [to] keep a jump ahead of these extremists if he is to hold them': 'We shall be in a jam if he can't last the pace.'[34]

Early in the new year Banda summoned MCP delegates to a 'peace and calm' conference in Blantyre. He was worried by the effect Chipembere's and Chiume's speeches and the ensuing violence might have on the forthcoming elections – on which so much depended. If Britain were to continue to recognize the MCP as the major party in Nyasaland and Banda as its leader, their positions needed to be legitimized by elections. Polling might be postponed if violence continued, and he told the delegates that it must stop, no matter what the provocation: 'Remember this: there is too much at stake. We must have the elections.'[35] Although the conference itself ended violently – there was a riot in which a man was killed – the violence did shortly die down.

In January 1961 Chipembere was tried, convicted and sentenced to three years' imprisonment.[36] Banda had done nothing to intervene, was almost certainly relieved that his most militant lieutenant was now out of the way, and may have thought this would encourage others to behave themselves. Given this success, Armitage reconsidered prosecuting Chiume and concluded that he should not proceed. Although he had a good case against him, he now considered Chiume of 'not much account' and not popular, principally because he was not a prison graduate.[37] Chiume and Bwanausi had both been expecting to be prosecuted, and were now expecting to be called as witnesses in Chipembere's trial. They were suspicious of Chirwa, who defended him – and not nearly as forcefully as they had expected – and thought he might have been asked by Banda not to call them, in order to drive a wedge between them and their supporters.[38]

While in prison Chipembere wrote to Banda a number of letters. Though some were authorized, more were unofficially smuggled out.

The first of these smuggled letters – which opened 'My Dear Atate [Father]', and ended 'Your loving son, Masauko' – was written a few days after his conviction.[39] He was concerned with reports of plans to kill him by poisoning his food. He was reassured when the convicts who cooked his food told him they woud never allow themselves to be used to harm 'a fellow son of Kamuzu'. He thought the reports might conceivably be a 'UFP scare story' designed to 'make the prisoners react violently and get shot or create a disturbance that might embarrass [Banda] and delay the release of political prisoners which is strongly rumoured to be imminent'. He reported the matter to the prison authorities and was then confident that 'this "murder plot", if it is at all genuine [cannot] be carried out now, since the officers know that it has been leaked out not only to me but also to other prisoners and, since there are discharges of prisoners every day, to the public as well'. He had harsh things to say about the European prison officers: 'diehard Welensky men ... in touch with the worst white supremacists in Zomba clubs and bars'. They victimized the MCP prisoners, imposing severe punishments on them: solitary confinement, reduced rations and loss of remission. So far, he continued, 'I personally have not been molested in any way. I continue in my rigid isolation, but I face no other hardships. In fact, I don't intend to give them any chance or excuse for molesting me.'

The Chipembere affair – his release from detention and his early reincarceration – contained a number of important elements. First, under pressure from Chiume, Banda fought hard – first blustering and then pleading – to secure his release and that of his hard-core colleagues. He energetically – and at times rudely – argued with Jones and threatened to go back to Gwelo. This success was a private triumph for Chiume and a public triumph for Banda. Also it was the first time the doctor played the 'Gwelo card', and he must have been gratified with its effectiveness when used against Jones. Second, Chipembere, Chiume and Bwanausi distrusted Banda and felt he might compromise over federation. Consequently, to prepare the people for it and be ready to react with a 'showdown', they set out on a speech-making tour in which Chipembere and Chiume addressed audiences in violent and seditious terms. This was the first time – and it passed vitually unnoticed – that Bwanausi's name was so closely linked with the other two. Third, Banda, in respect of Chipembere, said the law must take its course and as a consequence Chipembere was gaoled. The effect of this – deliberately or otherwise – was that Chipembere was out of Banda's way for a couple of years and was of little or no direct influence either on MCP supporters at large or on Banda himself, though he remained in touch through Chiume, Bwanausi and others and by means of smuggled letters.[40] Fourth, the government recognized the strength of Chipembere's following in the country and avoided having him arrested. He was probably right when he told the police they were afraid to arrest him – not personally in fear, but acutely apprehensive of the inevitable widespread consequences. Fifth, Armitage changed his mind over the danger of prosecuting Chiume, believing him to be of insufficient consequence and influence for him to do so. This change may be interpreted as the Governor believing that Chiume, in conjunction with Chipembere, commanded wide and dangerous support, but without him commanded little. Sixth, Chiume believed that Chirwa failed to do his best when representing Chipembere and that this was under Banda's direction or influence. Seventh, the attack on the leader of CDP is an early example of what was later to become distressingly common: the victimization and intimidation of members of opposition parties or simply people who refused to become members of the MCP. It was an early case, too, of a church running foul of the MCP: the Roman Catholic Church supported the CDP. Eighth, it is probable that had Jones, rather than Armitage, been in the gubernatorial seat at this particular time, Chipembere would not have been prosecuted.[41] Finally, in prison, Chipembere looked upon himself as a political prisoner and he quickly became the centre of attention of other prisoners – especially the 150 convicted MCP members, as opposed to what he called 'non-political prisoners' – who communicated with him, reassured him over the safety of his food, helped to smuggle out letters and looked upon him as a hero and their leader. He was determined to take no risks that might give the warders the excuse to punish him and delay his release.

Shortly after Chipembere was sent to prison, the MCP party headquarters issued an instruction that in future party songs should praise only Banda and no other party leader.[42] With this prohibition and Chipembere's absence from the political scene, Banda's undisputed leadership was still further ensured, though it was not yet completely secure. He was pushed hard by Chiume to secure the release of the final detainees, and without this pressure might have acted differently – he did not seem to mind Chipembere shortly being sent back to prison. He felt it neccessary, when the camp finalists were released, to emphasize that he was one of them and indeed was 'Prison Graduate Number One'. Chipembere, Chiume and Bwanausi were in effect questioning his leadership in their speech-making tour. There was criticism, too, in Karonga and a wider feeling that a more militant leader should be sought. Early in 1961, Banda sent Chiume off to West Africa and England, and Chisiza off to India, possibly to avoid them engineering any backlash to Chipembere's conviction.[43]

The registration of electors under the Lancaster House constitution started on 13 February and passed off peacefully and efficiently. Banda devoted a great deal of time and energy to touring the country, encouraging as full a registration as possible and appealing for peace and calm.[44] He personally chose the MCP candidates for the election. In exercising this significant extension to his personal power, in general he chose moderates, people such as headmasters and prominent businessmen. Perhaps he felt he already had enough extremists and professional politicians to handle. Under pressure to nominate Chipembere, who was in prison, he instead, 'by something of a master stroke',[45] chose his father, Archdeacon Chipembere, thereby – genuinely or otherwise – giving the impression that he regretted the imprisonment of the archdeacon's son.

Although the registration period was peaceful and orderly – and it was in Banda's interests that it should be, in order to maximize the number of people able to vote for him – in the lead-up to the elections themselves there was a deeply disturbing outbreak of intimidation and violence against opposition party members. This came to a head in the Visanza sub-district of Kota Kota district in late July and early August. During the night of 26–27 July six houses of prominent Africans were destroyed by fire. They were all within a radius of two miles and four of them belonged to leading members of the UFP, including their local candidate. The following night a further house, two cattle kraals and two food stores belonging to the same people were destroyed. Jones, who had succeeded Armitage as Governor in April, suspected 'political arson by LMY thugs' in all these cases, and he immediately sent a Police Mobile Force platoon and a CID team to the area. Banda said he 'deeply regretted' all such incidents and publicly appealed for peace and calm.[46] Dunduzu Chisiza quickly decided to visit the area. On Saturday, 29 July, he set off from Limbe to drive to the central province 'with the avowed intention of trying to assist the police', because the local population were not cooperating. Near Ncheu on his way north he was involved in a motor accident and was seriously injured with a suspected fracture of the skull. He was in hospital for some days before being released.[47]

Reporting on the troubles generally in Visanza, Jones told the secretary of state:

> I am satisfied that, whilst burnings were result of planned hooliganism with a political bias by a group of as yet unidentified persons (probably local adherents of the LMY) after a beer drink, they were not acts of political intimidation inspired by Malawi [Congress Party] hierarchy against UFP. [The] constituency is Malawi stronghold and intimidation of opponents would be pointless. There is also some evidence that incidents have been touched off as a result of provocation by local UFP representative in the area who is a known trouble maker.[48]

Although intimidation in this particular area might not be necessary for the MCP to win the seat, it need not be pointless, because it could be designed to induce those in other, less secure, areas to vote for the MCP candidate.

Jones was disappointed that John Msonthi, the MCP candidate in the area, failed to condemn the burnings, and he told the provincial commissioner to see Msonthi, express his serious view of these events and warn him that the obvious disquiet in the area was prejudicing free elections and they might have to be postponed in his constituency.[49] It is unclear how much the trouble, and particularly Msonthi's failure to do anything to reduce it, disturbed Banda. The last thing he wanted was the election to be postponed, since this would be a major setback to all that had been gained at Lancaster House. On the other hand, he knew the British government would be extremely unlikely to agree to a postponement, whatever Jones's warnings. That would return the country to the stalemate out of which they had so desperately wished to extricate themselves by releasing Banda, holding elections and thereby proving themselves correct about having selected him as Nyasaland's leader. Effective intimidation of his opponents, whether or not he disagreed with it, was, of course, to his electoral advantage. In the event, intimidation declined sufficiently for Jones not to order a postponement.

Roberts, later secretary to the president and cabinet, was to look back on the build-up to the general election of 1961, when the MCP candidates made 'extravagant promises ... to the newly enfranchised electorate'. They almost unanimously led the people to assume, once federation was brought to an end, independence had been achieved and the MCP was firmly placed in a position of supreme authority, that poverty and economic oppression would come to an end, Africans would rapidly take over all important positions and their salaries would increase to the European levels, 'there would soon be an abundance of food and other material benefits and taxation would be reduced'. Banda was probably the only Nyasaland African who 'had the honesty to disassociate himself from these wild election promises', repeatedly warning his audiences that after the election they would have to work harder than ever.[50] It was the case that Chiume also realized it would be with independence that their real difficulties started.[51]

At the election held on 15 August 1961, in a huge poll, the MCP won all the lower roll seats with more than 99 per cent of the votes cast, and their supporters won three of the eight upper roll seats, the remaining five going to the UFP. It was a massive victory for Banda and the MCP and a humiliation for Blackwood and the UFP.

From prison Chipembere smuggled another letter to Banda, congratulating him on the 'resounding electoral victory [in] one of the most historic elections in Africa'.[52] He reminded Banda that when they parted in January the doctor 'intimated that [he] would, some time after the

Election, ask the Governor to exercise his power of Executive Clemency' in favour of the political prisoners. All the MCP prisoners firmly believed they would now be released, but he had warned them that 'the release of political prisoners will have to take its proper place among the priorities' that Banda had set for the benefit of the whole nation. It was the effect on the prisoners' relatives that worried him, because they might not understand the delay, and he was keen that the position should be explained to them quickly 'lest some hot chaps begin an irresponsible fuss and agitation about it'. He advised that the negotiations for release should be conducted secretly by Banda alone: 'I fear that Sir Glyn [Jones] might, if the matter is made public, be compelled to give a "No" from which it will be embarrassing for him to retreat soon after.' He knew that Jones and Macleod were bound to refer to him, Chipembere, as a security risk when the doctor negotiated their release, and he wished to emphasise that he was 'as always, completely loyal' to Banda and would '*not* resort to any methods not authorized' by him. He hoped Jones would 'find it easy and wise' to accept Banda's request that the prisoners be released, for 'Nyasas being what they are, our prolonged stay here could inflame feeling'. He explained his alleged violent speeches the previous December as being the 'result of temporary defeat by my own passions'. If Banda ordered him 'to take action' he would, of course, be at Banda's service, otherwise he would keep out of the public eye. If Banda wished, he would even leave the country for an overseas study tour, 'just to be away during the critical months, lest I'm tempted to incite'. It sounds as if Chipembere found his violent outbursts and incitement beyond his control. He hoped the British government would give Banda 'the one higher roll portfolio' that he deserved, and would convert the two nominated seats on executive council to elected seats immediately rather than later, so as secure six seats for the MCP. Finally, he went into some detail as to how the releases might be effected and on what conditions. The tone and content of his letter indicate that he was entirely confident all the MCP prisoners would soon be released, in conformity with what he claimed Banda had intimated when he was convicted.

At the first meeting of the new legislature, at the end of November, Dunduzu Chisiza made an impassioned, but unsuccessful, plea for the release of Chipembere and others:

> This is a matter on which we harbour very strong feelings ... If His Excellency the Governor, if the Leader of the Majority Party, if this Government is to look the parents and relatives of these people in the face ... if we are to forget the past and look to the future it seems vitally imperative that those men who are in prison should be set free. There should be a general amnesty somehow.[53]

Now the elections were over, the way was clear for a new government to be formed. There were two important aspects of this: the questions of which parties were entitled to how many executive council seats, and the questions of how many and which ministries should be created and who should fill them. The first of these was the more difficult to resolve: to how many of the five non-official seats on executive council the UFP and the MCP, respectively, were entitled. It required the Governor to negotiate between Banda and Blackwood and, having done so, to reach decisions.

It had been expected that the upper roll election would result in a virtually complete victory for the UFP, and the lower roll in a similar victory for the MCP. Such an outcome would have produced an executive council of five official ministers, three MCP ministers and two UFP ministers, leaving control largely in official hands, since the UFP ministers would on most issues vote with the officials. The MCP, however, unexpectedly won three of the eight upper roll seats.

The constitution obliged the Governor, in appointing non-official ministers, to have regard to the composition of the parties in legislative council. On 19 August, four days after the elections, he saw first Banda and then Blackwood.[54] Banda 'strongly represented that his overall majority entitled him to all Executive Council unofficial seats, though he would welcome Cameron', despite his being an independent. He would not retreat from this position, saying he could not sit in executive council with members of the UFP. Rather, he declared, he would go into opposition. The Governor's discussion with Blackwood was easier because the requests the UFP leader made were simpler: two seats on executive council, and a parliamentary secretaryship which he was prepared to forgo.

A day or so later Banda again saw Jones. In the meantime he had received Chipembere's letter indicating that he thought the MCP was entitled to one higher roll seat, though additionally he wanted the two nominated officials replaced by elected members. Banda discussed with Jones the distribution of seats and eventually agreed to serve with one, but not more than one, UFP member, preferably without portfolio – which would 'suit him down to the ground'. He hoped Blackwood would reject an offer of only one seat, as indeed he did.[55] Banda was pleased, and said it gave him the opportunity to demonstrate his ability to govern in cooperation with officials and Cameron.

This outcome was important. The election had been fought on party lines and only a government of the majority party combining with officials could work in practice. In view of their opposed views, especially on federation, it was unrealistic to believe that a coalition of MCP and UFP members would cooperate for long. Given his overwhelming majority in the legislature, Banda knew that, to the government, his being allowed to boycott executive council was unthinkable. In opposition he could immediately defeat every measure the government brought forward in the legislature. It would, as he well knew, be a constitutional nightmare and one that could not possibly endure for long. The outcome also secured for him parity in council. If two seats had gone to the UFP he would have been in a minority because the UFP members would normally have voted with the officials on contentious issues. Now, however, he controlled five seats against the officials' five. Chipembere had hoped for six but by securing one upper roll and two converted nominated official seats. The constitution provided for this conversion, at the Governor's discretion 'at any time he thought fit, in the light of the working of the new constitution'.[56] It was not therefore open to Jones to make the change until the constitution had been in operation for a while. The outcome, however, greatly increased Banda's personal power to influence both the number and contents of all non-official portfolios, rather than only some of them, and also the selection of individuals responsible for them. It was these aspects of forming a government that he now proceeded to discuss with Jones. He was in a very strong position.

In the early stages, Banda's views were 'somewhat divergent' from Jones's, especially over the provincial and district administration, the chiefs, native authorities, African courts and district councils. Banda believed these should be in the hands of an African minister, and it was clear that he wished to have them himself. 'He took a fairly strong line that the people would not stand for it if these matters remained under the Chief Secretary.' Jones told Banda he would find it difficult to allow an elected minister to control the provincial and district administration, because at this stage of constitutional development it was normal for this responsibility to remain with the chief secretary. Eventually, the doctor, realizing he was unlikely to win the argument at this point, agreed to put it on one side.

Banda wanted a minister of justice as well as an attorney-general, but Jones felt this idea 'woolly' and that he could probably be dissuaded from it. Under the new constitution the attorney-general was ex officio a member of executive council, and this in effect precluded a separate minister of justice. After a while Banda agreed to drop the idea, provided the current attorney-general remained in post and had a parliamentary secretary attached to him. Under these circumstances he agreed, too, that the African courts should rest within that ministry. Somewhat surprisingly, he made no bid to control the police, law and order, being content to leave them to the chief secretary. He wished the current financial secretary to become the minister of finance – an unneccessary request, since the financial secretary was ex officio a member of executive council.[57] He also wanted the financial secretary to have a parliamentary secretary attached to him, and wished Chisiza to fill this post. Jones readily agreed to both these requests.

The doctor spoke of wanting land and mines included with natural resources under an African minister. Again it was clear he wanted the responsibility for himself, though Jones was hopeful of being able to divert him from insisting on this combination of subjects. They argued for some time and eventually Banda agreed, 'somewhat reluctantly', to land and mines being separate from natural resources and being allocated to Kettlewell. He was well aware that land and mines without natural resources were minor responsibilities and that Kettlewell's was a nominated seat replaceable by an elected member under the new constitution, so the question of his getting his own way was simply postponed.

Banda also wanted a separate ministry of development, but there was little discussion about it and it was not pursued. It is probable that he would have taken this ministry himself. It may be that he was simply exploring ideas and putting down a marker for the future. He did, however, want a ministry of labour and social development straight away.

Up to this point, the only non-officials Banda directly mentioned in connection with portfolios were Chiume as minister of education, and Chisiza as parliamentary secretary to the ministry of finance. Both were northerners. Chipembere was still in gaol. Now he spoke of the two seats to be allocated to upper roll members. Although he had previously said he wanted Cameron as minister of labour, he now wished him to be minister of works and transport. Although, too, he had earlier said he wanted Surtee as minister without portfolio, he now wished Mkandawire to fill that post. He was reluctant to discuss Chirwa and was a little anxious about taking him out of private practice by bringing him, the only African barrister in the country, into a ministry. It may be that in suggesting a separate ministry of justice he had Cameron, rather than Chirwa, in mind, though he did not say so. He would discuss the question with Chirwa and others and would then talk to Jones about it again. Although he was the founder and caretaker of the MCP during Banda's detention, Chirwa may have been suspect politically, having forsaken Congress to form a new party in 1953. Like Chiume and Chisiza, Chirwa was a northerner.

Finally Banda turned to the portfolio he himself wanted, and Jones found the doctor's wishes in this respect difficult:

> The biggest 'rub' arose over the question of his own portfolio ... He wants the joint portfolios of Natural Resources *and* Local Government but made it clear that the latter was more for the sake of appearances

and he did not want responsibility for the Law and Order side of the functions of Native Authorities ... I suggested to him that a portfolio comprising both Natural Resources *and* Local Government would be too big. Banda replied that the cooperation of the people would not be forthcoming if he himself had a portfolio which comprised the same range of subjects as that formerly in the hands of Mr. Ingham [secretary for African affairs].

Jones thought there might be room for manoeuvre over Banda's wish to control the two portfolios, 'but not much'. In the course of the discussion, the doctor said that in addition to Kettlewell being minister for land and mines – rather than secretary for natural resources as previously – the second nominated official minister, Ingham, should be responsible for the portfolio of works – this was before he suggested Cameron – rather than for local government as previously. He was, in effect, moving these two senior officials out of their previous major responsibilities and was taking them over himself.

If Banda's wishes regarding individual ministries had been acceded to, there would have been the three led by ex officio members of council specified in the constitution and seven ministries led by non-official members: natural resources and lands; justice; development; trade, commerce and industry; education; works and transport; and labour and social development. Since the number of non-official ministers under the constitution could not exceed five, there would have to be a combination of ministries in not more than five pairs of hands. It is likely that Banda, aware of this, deliberately inflated the number of ministries so as to lessen the objection to his combining ministries in his own hands. Jones's insistence on a separate ministry of land and mines in practice supported Banda in this strategy. It also provided a temporary ministry for one of the nominated officials.

As to who should be ministers, Banda made it quite clear that he personally would decide which Africans would be available for the Governor to appoint to executive council. 'He was quite dictatorial about this' and said, 'They either take what I say or go!' The Governor may have had some say in which posts were to exist but none in who among the Africans was to fill them. Jones detected that Banda was jealous of Chisiza, and saw him as 'better material for leadership'.[58]

On 4 September 1961, less than three weeks after the elections, Banda was appointed minister of natural resources and minister of local government; Bwanausi minister of labour and social development; Cameron minister of works and transport; Chiume minister of education and Mkandawire minister without portfolio. Chirwa and Chisiza were appointed parliamentary secretaries.[59] Of these, four were from the northern region, one from the central region, one from the southern region and one was a European. The ex officio members of executive council were the chief secretary, Foster; the attorney-general, Pine; and the financial secretary, Phillips. In addition there were two nominated official members: Kettlewell, minister of land and mines, and Ingham, minister of urban development.

A number of senior members of the MCP believed that Chiume had been influential in their not being appointed ministers. These included Dunduzu Chisiza and Chirwa, who were made only parliamentary secretaries and not members of executive council, and Yatuta Chisiza, to whom no government post was given despite the constitution providing for a third parliamentary secretaryship which he could have filled. Chiume has said that these allegations 'were completely baseless and without foundation', and this is confirmed by the available papers dealing with the way the portfolios were decided. Chiume also recalled that none of the ministers was consulted or given a choice over to which ministries they should be appointed; 'there was no discussion at all'.[60]

Two of the four ministers and two parliamentary secretaries, whose appointment Banda had secured, had not previously been particularly prominent publicly in active party politics: Bwanausi and Cameron. Augustine Bwanausi had taken an interest, and had participated in a mild way, in Nyasaland politics since 1951, but even his joining Chipembere and Chiume in their speech-making tour the previous December did not unduly attract the authorities' attention. It had never been his ambition to become a professional politician: he liked being a teacher. He claimed that he did nothing to put himself forward or draw attention to himself, but it is likely he was recommended to the doctor by Chiume, who knew his calibre and enthusiasm from the December 1960 tour. Banda specifically asked him to stand for election to the legislature and to accept ministerial office. As Bwanausi recalled:

> I told him that, while that would give me joy, I would probably find the job very difficult because I had never been a Member of Parliament before and to jump from outside straight into the Cabinet the task might become difficult. But the [doctor] assured me that he would do everything he could to help me ... He lent me books; he gave me lectures ... he did everything to help me.[61]

The candidature of Colin Cameron, a young Scottish solicitor, for election was also at Banda's specific request, and the doctor made it clear at the time that he wanted him as a minister. Initially Banda wished him to challenge Blackwood in the Blantyre constituency, but Cameron pointed out that he wanted a real chance of succeeding and consequently selected the Soche constituency. Banda observed that this was the constituency for which Sacranie, the Asian leader, hoped to stand. When Cameron explained the situation to him, Sacranie accepted it and promised full support throughout the Asian community in the country. Cameron, like Chiume, recalled that none of the ministers was consulted over, or given any choice in, which ministries they should head. He recalled, too, his car journey from Blantyre to Zomba with Chiume, Mkandawire, Bwanausi, Chirwa and Chisiza to be appointed and the way in which they 'speculated and joked about it, rather like excited schoolboys': 'the whole journey ... was one of hilarious speculation'.[62]

A number of points emerge from Banda's discussions with Jones about portfolios. First, from an early stage Banda was clear that he wanted Chiume as a minister and Chisiza as a parliamentary secretary. In Chisiza's case he may have been predominantly keen for him to secure a thorough apprenticeship in finance under an experienced expatriate minister. Alternatively, while availing himself of Chisiza's economics expertise, he may have been keen not to have him in executive council itself, especially if Jones was correct in believing Banda to be jealous of him. Second, although for a short period he considered having two non-Africans as ministers – Cameron and Surtee – he soon reduced this to one, Cameron, and was keen to have him in his cabinet in one capacity or another. He may have had in mind that the European community required more reassurance than the Coloured community, represented by Surtee, to stay in Malawi to contribute to its financial and economic stability, and hoped that Cameron's appointment would secure this. Third, he had some doubts over appointing Chirwa, though it is unlikely he was significantly disturbed by the prospect of removing from private practice the only African lawyer in the country. Fourth, he does not seem to have been bothered at this stage about a balanced regional representation in the government: four of the five African colleagues he appointed were from the north of the country. Fifth, by giving the two nominated official ministers trivial portfolios he was making it more certain that major functions would have to be combined in other hands – his own – and that he was not creating important ministries to which his more ambitious colleagues might lay claim when the time came to replace the nominated officials by non-officials. Sixth, by not pushing his claims that the district administration, chiefs, native authorities and African courts should be placed in elected hands, he ensured that they remained in official hands and beyond the grasp of his political colleagues. This may also have been the case with his not making a bid to control the police, law and order. Seventh, by having leading, specialist and well-trained colleagues with a record of competence behind them – which the apppointment of parliamentary secretaries to the minister of finance and the attorney-general would provide – it would be easier for him to argue, in due course, that they should replace two of the three official ministers: finance and justice. Chisiza had long been recognized as Congress's economist, and Chirwa as Congress's lawyer. Eighth, none of the 'three Cs' who were with him in Gwelo, where he had been able to learn a good deal about them, was appointed to executive council. Ninth, Yatuta Chisiza was given no government post. He had not been included in the discussions about a future cabinet that Banda had with his other colleagues in Gwelo gaol, and his name was not mentioned by either Banda or Jones during their recent discussions. Tenth, he secured in his own hands two major ministries:

> From the beginning I wanted to have responsibility for Natural Resources and Local Government, the first because our future as an independent country was, to a large extent, dependent on how we identified and used all of those resources, and the second because of the great importance of local or grass roots government.[63]

Finally, and of greatest importance, it was he, and not the Governor, who decided which Africans became ministers and parliamentary secretaries. His power of patronage over African appointments in government had become total – as it was already in the MCP. Furthermore, on several occasions he emphasized to Jones and Foster that he was personally and solely responsible for MCP policy and the policy to be adopted by the elected ministers in government. This was an early indication of the way he saw the party and the government as much the same thing. He emphasized, too, that he laid down the policy without consulting any of them. 'If they do not like it they can either lump it or sack me but I have made it quite plain right from the start that I impose my own policy on the party.' Jones recognized that while this attitude bore the long-term dangers inherent in any dictatorship, it could nevertheless be advantageous in the short term, particularly when the doctor was 'in a cooperative frame of mind and willing to "smack down" people like Chiume when they become particularly difficult'. He was, however, privately under no illusions as to the potential end result and 'not unmindful of the possibility that it could lead ultimately to Dr. Banda's downfall': he would be obeyed so long as his policies were popular, but once he tried to impose an unpopular policy 'his dictatorial methods could sink him'.[64]

Jones shortly wrote to Macleod about the first business meeting of the new executive council:

> This was a protracted and difficult meeting in which Chiume tested the patience of us all. I fancy he will be a difficult customer to deal with ... Dr. Banda seems anxious to keep the proceedings of Executive Council

as friendly and happy as possible. He has admitted to me both in writing and verbally that he will do as much business as possible by means of informal discussions with me and his colleagues, leaving the minimum of essential stuff to formal meetings of Executive Council. He and the other elected Ministers are very anxious that as many decisions as possible will be taken by the ministers themselves without reference to Executive Council and of course I will do my best to meet them on this within the possible limits.[65]

It is likely that, even at this stage, the elected ministers were more keen than was Banda that decisions should genuinely be taken by ministers themselves – they certainly were later on.

The twelve months following the Lancaster House agreement on a new constitution saw a substantial consolidation and expansion of Banda's personal power. In respect of Jones, he proved that by threatening to return to Gwelo – and thereby return the country to the impasse which the emergency had created in 1959 – he could induce the Governor to accede to his demands to release the final hard-core detainees, Jones's profound fears that Chipembere and the Chisiza brothers would 'revert to their known bitter and violent tendencies' notwithstanding. He achieved this without giving anything in return except guarantees and solemn undertakings – on which he almost immediately showed he could not or would not deliver – to control people like Chipembere. The violence and intimidation, especially, but by no means solely, in Visanza, were not only other examples of his failure to ensure peace and good behaviour by his people, but by intimidating and attacking political opponents it also furthered the MCP's – and thereby his own – hold over the country. He contrived that the release of the detainees was effected in such a way as to bring greatest kudos to himself. In not resisting Chipembere's prosecution and imprisonment, he ensured that his most militant lieutenant – and his greatest competitor for the admiration and following of the people – was behind bars for an extended period. The conviction may well have served to warn others to behave themselves and do as he told them. By personally selecting all the MCP candidates, he virtually guaranteed their loyalty to himself personally and ensured his dominance of the legislature. The election itself, with a high turnout and a 99 per cent vote for the MCP on the lower roll, strengthened still further the MCP's dominant position in the country and his own position as the leader of the party. By effectively refusing to form any sort of coalition with the UFP in executive council he increased the MCP's – and his own – power in government. He was adamant that he, exclusively, would decide who among his MCP colleagues should be appointed to council or made parliamentary secretaries. His power of patronage in this respect was complete.

Banda may have appeared ambivalent about delegating responsibilities to his colleagues. After his return from the Accra conference in December 1958, he privately recorded, as we have seen, that it was his policy to give his colleagues 'as much work and responsibilities as possible' and to teach those who would succeed him one day by 'allowing them to do things and share responsibilities' with him now as much as possible.[66] By September 1961 he both decided to control the major ministries personally and wished to have as many decisions as possible made by the ministers themselves without reference to executive council. The beneficial impact of this wish was, however, removed before it took effect. To being solely responsible for deciding the policy of the MCP, he now added that he personally would decide the lines his colleagues were to follow in executive council. In effect, the advice the elected members of council gave the Governor was to be Banda's advice. By insisting on being made responsible for a wide and important range of functions in his own portfolio, he substantially enhanced his personal position in executive council. Although by 'without reference to Executive Council' he gave the impression that decisions would be made in the ministries, where official support and advice could be brought to bear, he knew that in practice they would be made in MCP headquarters – by himself. Indeed, he required each of his non-official ministers to meet him weekly to report on their activities and receive their orders from him. The Governor's ready willingness to allow all this to happen, despite its manifest dangers, meant that from the outset executive council was deprived of the moderating influence that experienced official ministers could bring to bear in council and increased the personal influence Banda was able to exert in government, through the party machinery. It not only fell well short of being a sound training for the exercise of collective responsibility in the future, but it again potentially exacerbated the doctor's dictatorial inclinations, blurred the boundary between party and government and was accepted by the Governor without comment. Given these factors, from that point onwards, Banda and not Jones was de facto governing the country.

CHAPTER 4

In Government: September 1961 to February 1963

THE elected ministers were determined to throw themselves into their departmental work immediately and to keep up the pace of constitutional progress. They wanted this both in its own right and also to show their followers they were continuing the pressure on Britain to secure further, and rapid, advances. This they did by pressing two points. The first was an appropriate title for Banda – which, as they well knew, could have implications for the distribution of some of the important responsibilities currently entrusted to the chief secretary. The second was replacing the two nominated official members of executive council by elected members.

Within a few days of being appointed, the elected ministers – other than Banda – and the two parliamentary secretaries spoke with the Governor.[1] Chiume opened the discussion by saying they wished to accord Banda a title more appropriate to his position and the support he commanded in the country: the time had come to recognize him as chief minister. Chisiza emphasized that Banda himself did not wish to press the claim, because he was a modest man. Nevertheless, he was confident they were expressing the views of their electorate. Jones pointed out that the custom in other British territories had been to accord the title of chief minister at a slightly later stage than that currently reached in Nyasaland. He explained that the chief secretary was the Governor's deputy when occasion demanded and this made it essential that he take precedence over other ministers. Banda's position had been recognized by giving him special precedence after the chief secretary and before the attorney-general and the financial secretary. This, together with the title of leader of the majority party, had been given careful thought and had Banda's agreement. He would carefully consider the matter, would require time and would consult the secretary of state. Chiume, who opened the meeting, also had the last word: 'constitutionally he could not see any objection to ... having both a Chief Secretary and a Chief Minister at the same time; the latter, after all, was not a Prime Minister'.

This same group met Maudling, the new secretary of state, during his visit to Nyasaland at the end of November 1961. Chiume again opened the discusssion, saying they had been in office three months and had amply demonstrated their preparedness to work the constitution. As the key figure in this, Banda should be recognized by the title of chief minister. Other ministers said they had to be careful that their followers did not become disillusioned. Chirwa, building on an explanation and objection Jones had given at their previous meeting, would like to see the chief secretary made deputy Governor, who would take the place of the Governor in his absence but would otherwise move out of the political arena and have some of his responsibilities transferred to the doctor.[2]

Privately, Jones saw granting the title of chief minister as a means of reducing Banda's 'predeliction to accumulating a multiplicity of portfolios to himself':

> We may be able to resolve this difficulty if we ... give him the title of Chief Minister. It could perhaps be represented that as Chief Minister he has the right to control the work of all the unofficial ministries. If we could get this across, we might perhaps get him to agree to a fairer distribution of work within the ministries.[3]

It may have been the ministers' motive, as well as Jones's hope, in seeking to make Banda chief minister, that he would reduce the scope of his portfolios, and Chiume was careful to introduce the safeguarding point that granting the title would not make Banda the prime minister. By 'a fairer distribution of work' Jones probably meant a more equal distribution and implied that he was rather more concerned with this than he was with other considerations, such as the politics of the situation and Banda's motives for accumulating portfolios. Later, the doctor confessed that he did not trust any of his ministers to handle the more vital responsibilities.

Maudling, who felt there was a strong case for conferring the title, thought the change would not materially affect Banda, since all ministers had direct access to the Governor. The ministers did not, in practice, avail themselves of this direct access. Cameron has said the ministers' contacts with Jones were strictly limited and most of their dealings were directly with Banda.[4] Chiume shared this view, scarcely ever seeing Jones outside executive council.[5] Maudling did not think the title would confer authority over other ministers and empower the doctor to control their work. Jones, on the other hand, thought the change might be represented as indeed conferring that right on Banda, and he hoped it *would* materially affect him by leading to a decrease in the subjects in his portfolio.

With little real pressure, Maudling and Jones, despite not having coordinated their approach particularly well, were keen to accede to the request, the difficulties they foresaw notwithstanding. They paid little regard to the fact that Banda himself was not especially in favour of the idea. Furthermore, neither they nor the elected ministers seemed concerned about the significantly increased personal dominance the change would confer on Banda, especially if Jones were correct: that as chief minister he would have the right to control the work of the other ministers. The elected ministers must have been impressed at this stage by the effectiveness of their united approach – a strength they were to use a few years later – though they should have spotted that they might be playing into Banda's hands by risking his exercising control over their ministries, a matter about which they were to complain a few years later.

The second point they urged was replacing the two nominated official members of executive council by elected members. They pressed the point with Maudling. At the Lancaster House conference, they had, they reminded him, been strongly opposed to having nominated members, but had compromised. From their point of view, although they did not express it, the replacement would add two to their number who could, should the occasion arise, join them in a united front against whomsoever they wished to influence.[6]

Maudling discussed with the official ministers, too, replacing the nominated members.[7] Foster made the point that the replacement would be a far greater gain for the MCP than they could reasonably expect. He did not expand, but his point was profoundly important. The replacement would be a major step forward in the country's constitutional progress, for it would alter the balance in the executive from the parity of five official and five elected councillors to three official and seven elected councillors. Not only would this give Banda a substantial majority in the executive, but it would also give him significantly increased scope to arrange the greater part of the subject matter of government as he wished and to distribute it to whom he wished. It would increase the power of the MCP generally in government and also considerably increase his personal power both in the MCP and in the government. Furthermore, it would completely undo what Macleod had said he was aiming at, and which he had considered vital – indeed the whole point behind the Lancaster House agreement: the retention of real power in the hands of officials.

The officials' advice was clear. They should not rush into the replacements – although they could not long be delayed – and they should recognize that they were ignoring the fundamental basis of the Lancaster House agreement. Despite these clear reservations – shared by the British high commissioner to the Federation – Jones told Banda on 6 December that the two nominated official members of executive council were to be replaced: Ingham at the end of January and Kettlewell at the end of March. The doctor was pleased because he had been 'under much pressure' from his party to find out when it would happen – and Chipembere had urged it from the outset. Without, once again, having to exert a great deal of pressure, the ministers had, with a united front, secured a major constitutional advance, the effects of which were far-reaching.

In considering the changes he would make when Ingham and Kettlewell left the government, Jones did not assume that the current parliamentary secretaries would necessarily become full ministers – the contrary intention of the Lancaster House agreement notwithstanding.[8] He envisaged 'a fair degree of reshuffling' of subjects between the ministries and thought Chisiza, but not Chirwa, would be a good choice for one of the new ministries. If he appointed Chisiza as a minister, he could appoint a new parliamentary secretary to a ministry other than the treasury, probably Banda's ministry, 'which covers a wide field and lacks adequate ministerial attention due to Dr. Banda's other preoccupations'.[9] This was a major objective in Jones's mind. He had already formed the view that Chisiza was better leadership material than Banda, who was jealous of him,[10] and though he did not say so, wider experience would make him a formidable member of executive council – a point no doubt not lost on Banda. As it transpired, Jones may have been doing Chisiza no favour by recommending his promotion to executive council.

Banda ignored the Governor's views on the composition of the new government, particularly those relating to 'a fair degree of reshuffling', making Chisiza a minister, appointing a new parliamentary secretary and reducing the span of the doctor's ministerial responsibilities. When the nominated official ministers left, their places were taken by Willie Chokani as minister of labour, and John Msonthi as minister of trade and industry. Bwanausi became minister of internal affairs; his labour responsibilities were transferred to Chokani and his social development responsibilities to Chiume.[11] Apart from Banda, Chiume was the only member whose range of responsibilities was increased. The doctor had considered appointing Gwanda Chakuamba rather than Chokani; both were southerners. Although Jones did not mention his views to Banda, he was pleased Chokani was appointed because he felt Chakuamba was 'a young man of no marked abilities'. On the other hand, he saw Msonthi and Chokani as 'men of good calibre'.[12] All ministers with a portfolio and both parliamentary secretaries now had a university or college education – though Chiume and Chisiza did not have a degree – and five were former schoolmasters.[13] Of the African members of executive council, two ministers came from each of the three regions, though both parliamentary secretaries came from the north. It may be that Banda was beginning to see advantages in a regional balance in council.

About the middle of January 1962, Chiume left Nyasaland to attend a Commonwealth education conference.[14] From New Delhi he wrote to Banda a letter which reveals a number of important aspects of his political thinking at the time:

> Unity and solidarity – yes, this is what is keeping this country intact otherwise India would have fallen apart or fallen a prey to Communism ... However much I was convinced upon solidarity and unity when I was at home and after travels all over Africa, I have been made aware even more now that our problems will actually start when we are free ... We in Nyasaland [are] extremely lucky that God gave us your leadership. If for nothing else all of us must dedicate ourselves to serve you and follow you to death in order to save the Nation from the chaos which can easily result when the country is exposed to intrigue and machinations by foreigners. 'To serve Kamuzu to death' must be the motto of every sane nationalist in the country ... the real battle starts when you begin to manage your own affairs and therefore it is now more than any time before that your leadership is vital and indispensable if we want to keep Nyasaland intact ...
>
> You would be glad to learn that you are the hero of this conference among African nationalists. The policies pursued in Tanganyika as regards [multi-racial] citizenship have caused disgust and resentment among Africans, and the development of tribalism in Kenya and Uganda have made those countries as lost to the cause of African nationalism ... Uganda students [are] begging me to tell you to keep up your 'extremism' even if only for the sake of saving East Africa from what they call 'bogus multi-racialism' ...
>
> Britain has been insisting on the Commonwealth Scholarship and Fellowship Plan being restricted to postgraduate studies. We opposed this because it virtually meant that we would not benefit by the plan at all [having as yet very few graduates] and we will continue to depend upon expatriates from the UK.
>
> It was a pity ... Ghana and Nigeria were and are being used [through bilateral deals to support Britain over entry to the Common Market] to block the way of us in the colonial territories but you can rest assured that the fight is going on. It is disgraceful how Africa can be used to beat Africa.[15]

If one leaves aside the flattering references to Banda, the essence of Chiume's belief is the importance he attaches to the country remaining 'intact' and not disintegrating under the influence, first, of internal schisms such as tribalism; second, of external pressures such as the activities of foreigners, whether expatriate civil servants, other countries or the Commonwealth; and, third, external doctrines such as Communism and 'bogus multi-racialism'. This could be achieved only if Africa fended off attempts to divide the continent and if Nyasaland itself remained unified – which could be accomplished only by Banda's leadership. Hence solidarity and unity became vitally important. He foresaw that the country's problems would really start when it achieved independence, but in order to reach independence the country must unite behind the doctor. He implies that Banda has an international role to play, at least in East Africa. He sees 'African nationalism' as black nationalism, shunning multi-racialism, tribalism and alien influences, and keeping the nation intact under a strong leader.

From April 1962, Special Branch reports began to warn of two dangerous trends. First, they pointed to the growing, all-embracing power of the MCP:

> By exploiting the public fear by intimidation, the Party continues to endeavour to ensure that its members will control all aspects of public affairs. Thus party members have so far succeeded in taking all non-official places in district councils, the Farmers' Marketing Board liaison committees and cooperative societies.[16]

Second, they warned of Chiume's unpopularity and of a widening gulf in private between Chiume on the one hand and Dunduzu Chisiza, Chirwa and Aleke Banda on the other, despite all four being northerners. Additionally, there was hostilty between southerners and northerners in general and towards Chiume in particular. The southerners' dislike was increased by Chiume taking over social development responsibilities from Bwanausi, a southerner. Seventeen months earlier, Special Branch had reported on splits between Chirwa and Aleke Banda, and between Banda on the one hand and Chiume and Chipembere on the other, with Chisiza 'as yet uncommitted'.[17] Chirwa and Aleke Banda seem to have patched up their differences, and Chisiza had joined them, at least in opposition to Chiume. On the other hand, Chipembere was in gaol and Chiume was 'now probably the only Party executive who [had] the ear of Dr. Banda'.[18] Chisiza may have lost ground to Chiume over the preceding year, for in April 1961 a normally shrewd American observer had remarked that Chisiza was then 'perhaps Dr Banda's closest lieutenant'.[19] Be that as it may, certainly Chiume was normally treated well by the doctor. When, in June 1962, Banda visited Britain, Chiume went with him and was accommodated in the same hotel, occupying rooms of the same grade as those of the doctor.[20]

There were rumblings, too, accompanying a large international economics symposium held in Blantyre from 18 to 28 July, conceived and organized by Chisiza. He may have upset Banda, not so much by the success of the event as the danger that economics might be considered more important than politics in his fight for secession: 'Despite [the] weight of expert opinion, Dr Banda ... rejected all economic arguments and reiterated that he was determined to pull Nyasaland out of the Federation whatever the economic consequences.'[21] In his own paper, 'The Temper, Aspirations and Problems of Contemporary Africa' – the ideas for which he had formulated in a draft book written in Gwelo – [22] Chisiza dealt with a number of political aspects and wrote of 'the problem of initiative':

> If a nationalist movement is to achieve the goal of independence, it is vitally important that one of the leaders should be elevated well above the others; that his former equals should look upon themselves as his juniors; that they should accept his decision as final; and that they should pledge loyalty to his leadership. But once independence has been achieved, the problem of reconciling submissiveness to the top leader and individual initiative on the part of the second-level leaders arises. To a man who has been surrounded by submissive associates for a long time, the exercise of initiative by his asssociates is easily misconstrued as a sign of rivalry and disloyalty.[23]

While he and his colleagues were in agreement with the first half of this passage, the second half was open to several interpretations. At the least it was an indication that he expected to exercise his individual initiative after independence and a plea that Banda should not interpret this as rivalry and disloyalty.

Chisiza's success with the symposium may also have roused the envy of Chiume, who saw himself as Nyasaland's leading figure on the international scene and as the future minister of foreign affairs. Additionally, a projected imminent visit by Chisiza to Salisbury was interpreted by some as a form of potential defection. Shortly, the minister of finance explained its real nature:

> In the *Rhodesia Herald* ... there appears an article by Alan Hart which has as its principal theme a proposed visit by ... Mr. Dunduzu Chisiza during which it was said that he was to see the Federal Prime Minister ... In fairness to him and in the interests of accuracy I should like to state the facts ... Mr. Chisiza conceived the idea of going to Salisbury for the sole purpose of following up on a personal basis with an accredited diplomatic representative certain economic matters which had arisen during the former's visit to Europe earlier in the year. At no time did Mr. Chisiza suggest that he intended to see anyone else. He asked that all arrangements for his visit be made through the British High Commissioner's

office ... Shortly afterwards, and only a day or two before [3 September] Mr. Chisiza decided not to go.[24]

There was a further matter that may have roused suspicions and envy against Chisiza in some sections of the party. Many years after the event, Andrew Ross recorded:

> Both Chisizas had close connections with Kenneth Kaunda, the leader of UNIP in Northern Rhodesia, while Yatuta Chisiza was a close friend of Julius Nyerere of the future Tanzania. The Chisizas became involved in confidential negotiations with both men about a possible future federation of the territories which were to become Zambia, Malawi and Tanzania. Dunduzu ... believed such negotiations must be completed before independence was achieved, for once three separate states were established then there would be soon too many invested interests in the way of any kind of union. The Chisizas, Kaunda and Nyerere felt that their three territories could develop better together than separately ...
>
> With firm agreement from Kaunda and Nyerere that they were willing to enter into formal negotiations, the Chisizas approached Banda with the idea. He refused adamantly to have anything to do with it. Dunduzu and Yatuta ... could do nothing in public about this, because it involved the leaders of two other territories who did not want such a rebuff made public and because of the need for public unity in the drive towards secession and independence.[25]

Dunduzu and his colleagues had recently had discussions with the secretary of state's advisers on the implications of secession, were it to be granted.[26] He would have realized how keen the British government was that a new type of association between states should be formed, and he may have surmised that if he could come up with one, Britain would readily dissolve the existing Central African Federation. If the new association included Northern Rhodesia, Nyasaland would have far fewer financial worries and this also would help Britain to agree to Nyasaland's independence. In this way the two main objectives of Congress could be accomplished with relative ease: secession and independence. His negotiations would, however, fundamentally undermine Banda's tactic of consistently and adamantly refusing to consider any new form of association until the old one was abolished. He adhered to this immovable stance with absolute tenacity, and it assisted him in securing other concessions from the British government. It is virtually inconceivable that Banda had asked Chisiza to enter on these clandestine negotiations. Learning of them would have incensed him because they gravely impaired his tactic, were behind his back and came from what he may have realized was one of his principal competitors for leadership. It is clear that Dunduzu was heading for trouble of one sort or another.

Late in July a 'feud' emerged between Cameron, minister of works and transport, and Chiume, minister of education, over implementing the secondary schools building programme in the development plan.[27] Shortly, Cameron, Chisiza, Bwanausi, Chokani, Msonthi and Mkandawire met at Chisiza's house and discussed their dissatisfaction with Chiume, with whom they were thoroughly fed up because he was interfering with the work of their ministries and undermining Banda's trust in them. He was 'virtually decrying the other Ministers' efforts [and] lauding Dr. Banda even more than others were doing'.[28] It was not said, but the Chisizas' negotiations with Nyerere and Kaunda would have been seen by Chiume as *them* poaching in *his* preserve of external relations, and he may have been keen that they should progress no further. They talked for some time but came to no conclusion or agreement, principally because most of them thought there was no chance of success in taking any action. They then left for their own homes, but soon after Cameron got into his car, he began to ponder the matter and quickly decided it was wrong to take no action. The matter was serious and he ought to do something about it. He returned to Chisiza's house to tell him his feelings, and on the way met Mkandawire who, himself uncomfortable about taking no action, returned with him. When Cameron told them his views and that he intended to see Banda, Chisiza and Mkandawire – both northerners – said they shared his opinion and would go with him. Bwanausi, Chokani and Msonthi – from the south or centre of the country – declined to accompany them.[29]

Cameron's house was next door to Banda's – the African ministers preferred not to live so close to him – and that evening Cameron, Mkandawire and Chisiza went to see the doctor. They told him about Chiume's behaviour and the dangers involved in allowing it to continue. They alleged that Chiume was using his good standing with the doctor to frustrate their schemes and to influence him against them. They felt he was 'gradually obtaining for himself the position of chief adviser and crony to Dr. Banda'.[30] 'The meeting ... was heated and all three ... took part but there is no doubt that Dunduzu Chisiza was the most powerful of the speakers, but nevertheless what [all three] said fell on deaf ears.' Banda seemed not to believe what they told him and he refused to do anything about it. They did not take any further action at this stage because they wanted to preserve government and party unity. They told Banda that for this reason they would support him until independence, but made it clear that once independence was achieved they would not automatically support him.[31] Chipembere may have had this meeting in mind when he recalled that Banda 'after listening carefully to each side ... walked away from both groups, uttering not a word aimed at bringing about a reconciliation'.[32] This disconcerting technique of walking away from an interview was one which Banda used to considerable effect on other occasions.³³ Chipembere later remarked of Banda's approach to differences among party colleagues that: 'He seemed to delight in any internal clashes among us.'³⁴ If this were so, Banda would have done little to remove the friction between northerners and southerners and among northerners that Special Branch was reporting.

There was a second meeting of the ministers with Banda, on 1 August, as Chiume recalled:

> In July–August 1962, the feud between me and Colin Cameron arose out of the development plan. The sum allocated to building secondary schools was welcomed by Cameron but I found it grossly insufficient especially since it was intended to build only three schools. I ... came up with the idea of having a large number of day secondary schools supported by local self-help activities and contributions. One of the headmen in the ... Cholo district was against a school being built in his area and organising the self-help contributions. I went to the area and after a great deal of hard work won over the headman and the people. I collected a large sum of money and many presents, mainly eggs. I was very pleased with the success of this mission and went to call on Banda to tell him about it, hand over the money and give him the gifts. When I got to Banda's house I found there Cameron, Dunduzu Chisiza, Mkandawire, Bwanausi, Chokani and, representing the MCP, Yatuta Chisiza. Banda told me that the others present had made complaints against me, and, in his usual confrontational way, asked them to repeat their complaints in my presence. This they did, and Dunduzu took the leading part, accusing me of overly influencing Banda and being responsible for him and Orton Chirwa not being made full ministers but only parliamentary secretaries. Yatuta was vicious and said I was very unpopular in many areas and, for example, if I went to the Cholo district I would be chased out. Fortunately I had just come from Cholo with money and gifts and I pointed out this success. Yatuta was angry because he had not been given a ministerial post and blamed me for this. Banda did not decide who was right and who was wrong. Neither Chirwa nor Chipembere – who was in prison – was present. Dunduzu tendered his resignation at that time.³⁵

The day after this meeting, Chiume wrote to Banda.³⁶ He addressed the doctor as 'Dear Father' and ended 'Your son'. He wished to assure him that,

> in spite of the many false accusations which were showered on me yesterday including the threat of my being beaten up by my friend Chisiza, I bear no ill feeling against my friends and will do all I can to maintain unity to assist you in the difficult tasks that lie ahead. It is not the first

time that allegations of this nature have been falsely made on me. Nevertheless, when I entered politics I was aware that the task of liberating a nation and maintaining it intact is not an easy one; and I have travelled enough to realize that our worst problems have not yet started.

He continued, saying that he had tried to find out what the 'dangerous rumours' were which Chisiza said were circulating, and had discovered they were that he, Chiume, was the person blocking Chipembere's release from prison. He had never heard 'such a fantastic rumour' in all his life, but was glad that it was being taken as 'a huge joke' by the people who knew well 'how dear Chip is to me and how dear I to him'. It was not a rumour the doctor should be worried about, and he felt he need not go into details as to who was spreading the rumour – presumably one of the Chisiza brothers. He was puzzled by Bwanausi's apparent change of friendship with him and enclosed a friendly letter which Bwanausi had written to him while he was in London with the doctor early in July.[37] Chiume ended his letter:

> Again I assure you that as far as I am concerned yesterday's ugly performance against me is now ancient history and as always I pledge to work together with all your boys for the good of Malawi. May our Heavenly Father shower His blessings on you so that you lead us and teach us the tasks of holding intact a nation when we are so surrounded around Nyasaland by political vultures.

While Chiume was composing this letter, Cameron, Mkandawire, Bwanausi and Chisiza went to see the Governor to complain that they 'had not received a very sympathetic hearing' from the doctor. Chokani did not accompany them on this occasion. Cameron, Mkandawire and Chisiza – but not Bwanausi – tendered their resignations from the legislative council and in the case of the first two from executive council. Jones declined to accept the resignations and had a meeting with Banda:

> I was able to convince him that the complainants appeared to me to have reasonable grounds for complaint and ... while the Cabinet changes did not necessarily imply that the Majority Party was experiencing serious internal disorders, nevertheless a change at this point of time would make it difficult for Dr. Banda to represent ... that all had gone well since the election last year.

He added 'in no uncertain terms' that Chiume was also making things difficult for him, Jones. Banda took this in good part and was pleased that all the complainants had 'expressed their complete loyalty and devotion to [him] personally'. He agreed that Jones should ask them to reconsider their resignations in the interests of party unity.[38]

The Governor then saw the complainants and after a 'long and frank discussion' they agreed to withdraw their resignations and accept Jones's advice that they show more courage in future dealings with Chiume and insist on Banda taking them more into his confidence. He did not think that any of them really wanted to resign, but thought the threat of resignation would bring things satisfactorily to a head.

Chisiza – thought by many to be one of the most able and promising, and by some *the* most able and promising, African politician in Nyasaland – did not let matters rest where Banda and Jones had left them. In a letter of 4 August to Jones he set out the nature of his concerns, and said that Chiume was

> indulging in activities which make the work and life of his elected colleagues ... impossible and [also] I am satisfied that Dr. H. Kamuzu Banda ... is for some inexplicable reason not prepared to see that Mr. Chiume is engaging in activities which are harmful to teamwork on the Ministerial level, dangerous to the morale and cohesion of the Party (MCP), and unfortunate for the country.
>
> Specifically speaking, Mr. Chiume has launched a campaign of undermining the confidence which the Doctor has in other Malawi Ministers and MLCs [members of legislative council]. He is casting suspicion on innocent people; he is questioning the integrity and loyalty of men who have willingly suffered for the Doctor, the Party, and the Country; and he is subjecting his colleagues to a feeling of alienation [and] the Doctor to a feeling of insecurity by making the Doctor believe that some of his followers and aides are undermining his prestige and authority when God knows not a single soul in this country is guilty of such an offence. He is also making the Doctor believe that other elected Ministers are being run by the permanent officials and that only he is able to control his Permanent Secretary. He would have the Doctor believe that the judgement of everyone except Mr. Chiume must be held in serious doubt. And most unfortunate of all, he has established such a relationship with the Doctor, that he is able to kill out of sheer jealousy schemes and proposals from other Elected Ministers by setting the Doctor against the proposals.

He had seventeen specific cases to establish his allegations and, although he would not tell Jones what they were, he had told Banda about them. The remainder of his letter was taken up in emphasizing his admiration of and loyalty to Banda: 'Without Dr. Banda's leadership this country would go to the dogs. It is no exaggeration to say that Doctor Banda is the most important asset of this country.' He ended with a thinly veiled offer to oust Chiume:

> I would like to assure the Doctor also that if there is anyone who poses serious opposition to him and the Party ... he has only to send for me

and in collaboration with his other soldiers I will make sure that his opponents are defeated. I offer myself for service now as I did in 1958 when he sent for me. Unlike some people I am prepared to go to jail again with him if need be in order that Malawi should be independent in the minimum of time.[39]

The words 'unlike some people' clearly referred to Chiume. Ousting him would, of course, lead to a vacancy in executive council with Chisiza himself as the most obvious candidate to fill it.

Two years after the events, Yatuta Chisiza told friends that Banda insisted his meeting with Cameron, Dunduzu and Mkandawire should be in Jones's presence and that two weeks later Dunduzu saw Banda again, this time alone, and forcefully expressed his antipathy to the doctor's style of leadership.[40] Yatuta's claim appears false. The evidence is that on no occasion did Banda see the three complainants in Jones's presence, nor ask that this should be so, and the claim of Dunduzu's expressed antipathy conflicts with his written avowals of loyalty. It would have been folly to avow loyalty in writing to Jones, and antipathy orally to Banda.

It is extremely unlikely that Banda was ever told of Chisiza's offer to oust Chiume or that he would have accepted the offer had it been made known to him. Even if Chisiza was in effect asking Jones to tell Banda of the offer, the Governor would have believed this to be no time to allow a split to appear in the party. Banda would have shared this view and it may be that he preferred continued internal frictions to oustings that would reduce the number of factions he could exploit in a *divide et impera* policy. It may have been in Banda's interests to have friction among his lieutenants – provided it did not lead to a public rift in the lead up to secession, self-government and independence – because with interpersonal differences they had to rely on him, Banda, for recognition and support, and divisions would provide useful sources of tell-tale information. Chipembere later expressed the view that:

> [Banda] always declared that he did not want to see the development of cliques or factions among the leaders immediately below him. While one must concede that as far as the party generally was concerned he did admirable work in maintaining unity and authorised stern action against any evidence of nascent factionalism, the same cannot be said about his attitude towards members of his cabinet ... There was much evidence of the all-too-familiar pitting of us one against another. [Banda's] desire to arouse mutual jealousy among us became clearly discernible ... For a long time we believed that any act of disfavor by [him] towards one of us was the result of intrigue by one or more of our colleagues, and [he] did nothing to discourage this feeling.[41]

Chisiza's role in the events of late July and early August 1962 is interesting. The meeting he had with Cameron, Bwanausi, Chokani, Msonthi and Mkandawire was held in his house and was concerned with Chiume interfering with the work of their ministries. But Chisiza did not have a ministry. He was parliamentary secretary to the expatriate minister of finance, and it is inconceivable that the minister, Phillips, would have allowed any interference with his ministry. Nor did Mkandawire have a ministry: he was minister without portfolio. Furthermore, the initial dispute was between Chiume and Cameron, in which Chisiza was not involved. It appears that he seized the opportunity presented by the dispute – hijacked the feud – to achieve three related ends. First, he was sore about Chiume outdoing his colleagues in lauding Banda, and receiving the rewards of that lauding: Banda's confidence. By complaining to Banda and denigrating Chiume, he may have hoped to weaken that confidence and reduce Chiume's influence with the doctor. Second, while in Gwelo gaol, Chisiza had discussed with Banda and Chipembere – but not Chiume, who was not there – the cabinet that would be formed when Africans joined executive council. He would have assumed that he would be a member of that cabinet. Yet he was not made a minister when the council was reconstituted in September 1961, nor when the nominated officials were replaced in March 1962, despite his own advocacy for their replacement. He had twice been passed over, and the opportunity for Banda to secure additional seats on council – one of which he could fill – was unlikely to occur for some considerable time. If Chiume – whom he blamed for his not having been made a minister, and whom he knew to be widely unpopular – were ousted, his seat would become available. Third, these steps may be seen as a determined bid by Chisiza to become the party deuteragonist, the informal but influential deputy leader, which Chiume had in effect been up to this point. His ability to gain the support of all the non-official ministers in complaining to Banda indicates the potential of his bid.

A possibly connected matter surfaced at about this time, the second half of August. At Banda's request, Jones asked the secretary of state, now Butler, to agree to Yatuta Chisiza being sent to the Bramshill Police College 'A' course in Britain to prepare him for the commissionership of police. Yatuta enjoyed the fairly wide reputation that he had been a senior police officer in Tanganyika[42] but in fact he had risen at most to the rank of assistant inspector and was far from being qualified to attend the 'A' course.[43] Butler's official advisers were alarmed by the request. They asked for an assessment of Yatuta's personal temperament and asked, 'Is he likely to turn out a "Dunduzu" rather than a "Chiume"?' It is clear that the Colonial Office thought more highly of Dunduzu Chisiza, his reputation there as a man of violence notwithstanding, than they did of Chiume. Jones's precise reply is not known, but he continued his advocacy of Yatuta and the matter was taken up personally by the secretary of state, who said that his entry into the police force would involve him, Butler, in tacitly endorsing Banda's selection of him as a potential future commissioner of police and he naturally had doubts about doing this in view of his political record and because of the effect it would have on serving officers. Nevertheless, he agreed that they should accept the situation and do their best to 'turn Chisiza into a capable policeman in the time likely to be available' to them. It may be that Banda was concerned, for whatever reason, not simply to turn Yatuta into an acceptable senior police officer, but also to have him out of the country for a while, either generally or at this particular time. In the event the matter was not pursued because he shortly entered the legislature and a police service career became irrelevant.[44]

A related matter about which a number of the elected members of government approached the Governor at this time was Chipembere's release from gaol. They were probably the same as those who had made the representations about Chiume, and certainly included Bwanausi, Chokani and Dunduzu Chisiza. They claimed that if Chipembere were released fairly soon – before the November 1962 constitutional conference – 'he would be bound to break the present influence being exerted by Chiume over Dr. Banda'. Jones received this argument 'with some reserve' because his Special Branch reports consistently showed that Chipembere and Chiume had been close friends and each had supported the other's extremism.[45] As part of the Chiume–Chipembere faction, Bwanausi's advocacy of Chipembere's release was more likely to have been as an ally than as a counterbalance to Chiume. He and Chiume, 'with the help of friendly militant African prison warders, had been in daily contact with Chipembere in jail and sent messages to keep him informed about developments in Zomba and the country'.[46] They were the principal means of his staying in touch with the outside world.

Jones privately thought Chipembere was 'almost as widely popular as Dr. Banda, very intelligent and capable of bitter extremism'. In the past he had been known as 'violent and irrresponsible, as an able speaker but a rabble-rouser'. He thought that an alliance between Chipembere and Chisiza might have acted as a salutary influence on Chiume, but now there was 'a distinct possibility of a link-up between Chiume and Chipembere, in which case the outlook would not be good'.[47] Nevertheless, he advocated early release to the secretary of state: 'Some gesture of leniency may make a favouurable impression on him. If he were to return to the scene in a mood of bitterness, he could cause untold harm.'[48]

After the elected members of government spoke to him at the beginning of August, Jones told Banda he intended to see Chiume, who was away travelling in the north of the country, and tell him 'in no uncertain terms' that his conduct could lead to a political crisis. He hoped to convince him that 'he must be a good deal more cooperative with us all in the future'. The doctor did not attempt to dissuade him. Maybe he guessed that Chiume would not be amenable to Jones's wishes and was confident that the Governor's efforts would not harm his own divide-and-rule policy. Jones told Banda that Chiume's colleagues were 'very angry' and would not 'put up with any more nonsense from him', although they recognized his competence and did not wish to see him leave the government.[49] They may have felt, as Lyndon B. Johnson felt of J. Edgar Hoover, that he would be more dangerous outside the tent,[50] and they would have been reluctant to make public a split in MCP ranks. While solutions short of removal from ministerial office might be kept out of public knowledge, expulsion from the government could not. Jones hoped that on the whole 'this letting-off of steam' would have done some good.

It is unlikely that Jones did speak to Chiume about his behaviour, because a tragedy intervened, one that caused the loss of Dunduzu Chisiza's services in a much more catastrophic and final way than could ever have been envisaged from the possibility of his resignation. Late in the evening of Saturday, 2 September, exactly a year after he was appointed parliamentary secretary, he left Limbe to return to Zomba. Just after midnight, some ten miles south of the capital, his car crashed and he was killed. The crash occurred just over a year after the similar accident at Ncheu, in which he had been seriously injured with a suspected fracture of the skull.[51]

The police were quick to investigate, and the officer in charge at Zomba recalled:

He was travelling back to Zomba from Limbe at night. He had not been drinking but probably lost concentration or even dozed off. As a result, his car ... veered to the left off the tarmac. His left-hand wheels went into a drainage ditch as it approached a bridge over a stream near Ntondwe. The car followed the ditch thereby missing the bridge and went over to the other side of the stream where it hit the bank and fell back into the stream. Dunduzu was flung forward in the impact and struck his head on the bodywork above the windscreen. He sustained a severe impacted skull break and must have died instantly ... I went out to the scene myself and with the traffic officer made an examination of the car and surroundings. The body of Mr. Chisiza had been taken to Zomba African Hospital shortly before I arrived at Ntondwe. I left the traffic officer at the scene and instructed that a guard should be put on the area until further notice. I also later asked for the Provincial Traffic Officer to examine the accident. I went to Zomba African Hospital that night and saw the body of Mr. Chisiza. I realised rumours of all kinds may arise from this accident. I made absolutely certain from a police point of view that it was covered in every detail. It was, I am certain, a most unfortunate accident, caused as I described above. There were some wild rumours later that he may have been forced off the road by another vehicle but we were able to satisfy leading Congress members of the true facts. The rumours soon died down.[52]

On the other hand, the provincial traffic officer who was asked to examine the accident did so and later said: 'The injuries he received could just as easily have been manufactured as [in later cases] ... There were no witnesses to Chisiza's death so we may never know whether his was the forerunner of many others.'[53] The senior police photographer took numerous photographs of the vehicle and the scene of the crash and later wrote:

> The accident (if it was an accident!) presented some curious features. We all discussed it at the time and puzzled over it ... the photographs show that the road from Blantyre took a fairly sharp right-hand bend and then ran downhill for about two hundred yards to the scene of the accident. Essentially, the car had dropped its nearside wheels into the storm drain at the side of the road, and of course once that happened Chisiza was trapped – he was in effect running along a railway line, and was stuck on his course until he got to the bottom, and ran into the culvert.
>
> Our first thought was that he had fallen asleep at the wheel ... But if he had dozed off, why had he not 'run out of road' at the top of the hill – he must have been wide awake to negotiate the bend. Therefore did he perhaps take the bend a little too fast and did not straighten up quite quickly enough to avoid running into the drain?
>
> The 'conspiracy theory' is very intriguing, but as the motor vehicle examiner said at the time – if the accident was 'arranged', it was done very cleverly. However it was done, there was no question of mechanical tampering with the car.[54]

Like most of their uniformed colleagues, the Special Branch found nothing sinister in his death: 'A few mischief makers have suggested there may have been something sinister in the manner of Chisiza's death. MCP leaders, however, have not pursued this line and have not questioned the coroner's verdict of accidental death.'

Chisiza was in the habit of driving at excessive speeds. At the time he was known to have been working at high pressure and to have been fatigued. It is considered that in these circumstances he probably fell asleep at the wheel while travelling at a speed reliably estimated at 80 miles per hour. He was alone in the car and no other vehicle was involved.⁵⁵

Chisiza had spent part of the day before he was killed in Limbe discussing his resignation with a European businessman and close friend, who recalled that Chisiza was 'very frightened and worried'. Chisiza said there was something wrong with the brakes of his car, and his brother, Yatuta, had them fixed at the MCP headquarters. The businessman suggested that Chisiza should spend the night with him and his wife but he declined and returned to Zomba, being killed on the way. He attended Dunduzu's funeral at Karonga and was convinced that Yatuta acted like a guilty man. He was certain he had been deliberately killed.⁵⁶

Soon after Dunduzu's death Banda sent Chiume to London for two months to make a thorough study of intelligence-gathering and security matters.⁵⁷ He remained puzzled for many years about this assignment. It may have been designed to ensure that he was out of the way during a period when there may have been a backlash following Dunduzu's death. It is unclear whether, if this were so, Banda's intention was to prevent Chiume exploiting a difficult situation, or to protect him during one.

Following Dunduzu's death, the vacated legislative council seat at Karonga was filled, unopposed, by his brother, Yatuta. This removed any problems there might have been in his proposed rapid advance to the commissionership of the police force. Also, the position of parliamentary secretary to the ministry of finance was, after a while, filled by John Tembo, the uncle of Cecilia Kadzamira, for many decades Banda's nurse and his official hostess. Aleke Banda was appointed to succeed Dunduzu as secretary-general of the party.⁵⁸ In these ways Banda was beginning to instal a group of new men, working alongside the more established senior members of Congress. The old guard had disappeared two years earlier and he was now promoting new lieutenants to the new guard.

Chisiza's death caused widespread shock in the country and gave rise, as the police anticipated, to numerous rumours as to its circumstances – which many were convinced were not accidental – and attributed political motives to the death.⁵⁹ The ministers who had been with him so recently to complain to Banda about Chiume's behaviour must have been especially horrified and worried. The tragedy seems particularly to have affected Bwanausi. One of the senior officers in his ministry later recalled:

> My Minister was Bwanausi, the nicest and most gentle of people. I saw a lot of him as he would often ask me to remain late when others had gone home. He wanted me to explain documents and papers to him as he was afraid that he did not understand backgrounds etc. Also he was terrified of Dr. Banda and this I realised one day. It happened weekly ... that Ministers had to go and see Dr. Banda and report on their activities

and receive their orders. Usually, he was briefed by [the permanent secretary] but one Friday he was away and I was asked to officiate. Bwanausi asked me to go with him to the secretariat. I agreed of course and as we got into the car I noticed that he was trembling and had gone quite grey. Then he held my hand. When we arrived he said that I should accompany him upstairs. I went to the door and more or less pushed him into the inner sanctum. Then Banda began to shout and the hangers on shuffled off. Banda rang his bell but nobody came and then he appeared at the door and I was ordered to enter. Bwanausi had collapsed into a chair. Banda pushed a piece of paper at me and read out a list of instructions that Bwanausi had to follow. I replied that I was unable to oblige as I was a civil servant and the interview was a political matter. Banda roared with laughter and asked me if I was staying on [after independence]. It was then that he ... offered my wife and myself jobs in Lilongwe.[60]

There are a number of interesting aspects of the Dunduzu Chisiza affair in addition to his direct dispute with Chiume. There is no doubt that the economics symposium was a considerable success for him. First, Nyasaland had never before mounted an international event on this scale, attracting so many distinguished academic and other contributors. It required much careful planning and organization to gather together so many people and ensure that the proceedings were smoothly conducted. Second, it involved a good deal of negotiation and coordination with the federal authorities, who were responsible for immigration approval and for external affairs. Chisiza did not conduct these negotiations personally, but he was responsible for seeing that they were done. In some cases this was achieved against the opposition of the federal government, who were not overly impressed with the political allegience of some of the overseas participants. These inevitable, albeit indirect, contacts with the federal government, and particularly his projected visit to Salisbury at a time when the official policy of the party was rigorously to shun all things federal, was fated to rouse the gravest suspicions among those who did not know the nature of his dealings and among those who wished to exploit them. In particular, the MCP was adamantly opposed to the implementation of the Nkula Falls hydro-electricity scheme because it was a federal project. This strong opposition existed despite the fact that the power that would have been generated was crucial to implementing the 1962–65 development plan, a plan for which Chisiza was responsible. There were suspicions that Banda and Chisiza would have compromised with the federal government but were dissuaded by their colleagues. Third, establishing himself as an international figure was likely to fan the embers of any envy that existed among his colleagues in the MCP and particularly those who might see this as nudging Chiume from the limelight on the African international stage. Fourth, there was the danger Banda might fear that economic factors would be thought more important than political factors in considering the country's constitutional progress. This would play into the hands of those who argued that the country could not survive outside the Federation as an independent state. Also it would be a fundamental shift from the path he had consistently taken, following Nkrumah's doctrine 'Seek ye first the political kingdom', and going against statements such as 'I would rather see Nyasaland starve than accept federal aid'. Indeed, only two months earlier the doctor had said, 'Get political power first and then you can manipulate the economic situation.'[61]

Next, there was the matter of Dunduzu and Yatuta having discussions with the Northern Rhodesia and Tanganyika leaders about forming a new federation. This would not only have been seen as meddling in pan-African affairs – Chiume's domain – but it would gravely have upset Banda, not simply because much of it was done behind his back, but particularly because it ran the risk of destroying the effectiveness of his tactic not under any circumstances to discuss future arrangements until secession from the existing Federation had been achieved. These reported activities of the Chisiza brothers do not fit comfortably with Dunduzu's published views on regional cooperation: that independence should be attained first – which was Banda's stance – that there should then be vigorous modernization of the internal economy, that this should be followed by encouraging regional economic cooperation and regional consciousness, and only then and lastly, political regrouping of neighbouring countries.[62]

There were a number of lessons, or indicators for the future, in the events of August 1962. *All* the elected ministers joined Chisiza in criticizing Chiume and complaining about him to Banda, though not Chirwa – a parliamentary secretary – whose name does not crop up at all. They used the initial feud between Cameron and Chiume to express far wider concerns about him, and they united in making their representations. Taking an issue and using it to express broader worries, and doing so with a united front were tactics they were to use again in the future. Those sufficiently courageous to approach Banda and risk incurring his wrath – Chisiza, Cameron and Mkandawire – saw the others – Bwanausi, Chokani and Msonthi – as insufficiently bold. It may have been not timidity but a lacking in full sympathy with the others that induced them, especially Bwanausi, to hold back. Alternatively, they may have been more realistic in their assessment of the efficacy of representations to the doctor. In any event, once their solidarity melted their case was lost. When they tendered their resignations Jones declined to accept them. They were to learn later that this in no way created a precedent to be followed in future cases. Jones advised them to insist on Banda taking them more into his confidence – though he had no advice as to how to do it – and this was to become an even more important issue later on. Among Chisiza's objections was Chiume's making Banda believe that the other ministers were being controlled by their expatriate permanent officials – another matter that was to crop up again later.

Banda's responses to these events are also interesting. He professed not to believe what the ministers told him about Chiume, and he did nothing overtly about their complaints. He 'walked away from both groups' and declined to mediate between them, although he did expose both sides to his usual method of face-to-face confrontation, which in itself added to the effectiveness of his divide-and-rule tactics. Contrary to the complainants' hopes, he did not seek to have Chipembere released from gaol so that he could act as a counter-influence to Chiume. Perhaps he believed the result would be the opposite of their hopes and simply add to any danger Chiume presented. He would not have overlooked the fact that Jones agreed with the complaints and personally criticized Chiume, though he apparently took the agreement and criticism in good part. He was particularly gratified that the complainants said they were completely loyal and devoted to him personally. Professions of loyalty were important to him. It would not have escaped his notice, however, that only Chiume actually conveyed to him an assurance of loyalty and he did so in writing. Dunduzu committed his avowal to writing, but only in a letter to Jones, not to Banda. Indeed, he told Banda that he could count on his loyalty only until independence was achieved. In respect of the other ministers, Banda had only Jones's word that they said they were loyal.

Yatuta Chisiza had been the doctor's personal bodyguard and in charge of his party guard since his return to Nyasaland in 1958. It may be that Banda's steps to have him groomed for the commissionership of police were designed in part as a warning to Chiume and others that he intended to strengthen still further Yatuta's personal protective role and add the executive role of the commissioner, which included control of the whole force, including the PMF, and supervision of the Special Branch. On the other hand, sending Chiume to London to study intelligence-gathering and security matters may have been designed not only to get him out of the way during a potentially difficult period, but for another purpose. Coming at about the same time as the proposal that Yatuta be groomed for the commissionership, it may be that Banda was looking ahead to the time when control of the police and intelligence services would be taken from official hands and passed to an elected member of the government. He may have wished either to ensure that these functions, under his own control, were operationally in hands upon which he could rely, or alternatively – and possibly additionally – to have two opposing sets of hands managing them so that neither became overly influential in what was to be a vital and potentially dangerous area.

The Chisiza affair in August 1962, two years before independence, was capable of quickly becoming a deeply worrying government crisis. There was a real danger that Banda might lose the two ministers – Cameron and Mkandawire – elected on the upper roll, and a parliamentary secretary. Disposing of a parliamentary secretary elected on the lower roll would not have caused a constitutional difficulty – though it might have caused other difficulties in this particular case – but losing two ministers elected on the upper roll was a different matter. By-elections for the upper roll seats might not result in another win for MCP candidates. Banda would not have wanted to run the risk of losing these upper roll seats and having to form a coalition executive council with two UFP ministers. This would have lost the significant advantages of party and personal dominance in council and his own patronage, which he had secured a year earlier. He certainly would not have wanted the alternative of going into opposition, because this would have brought government to a halt and he was keen to keep things moving towards his goals of self-government, secession and independence. Even in the case of Dunduzu Chisiza, whose resignation would have incurred a by-election only on the lower roll and therefore not have involved a coalition, Banda would have wished to avoid a publicly known split in the party in the short period before the Marlborough House conference to decide on self-government. He would have wished to avoid this, even if he were prepared, as he almost certainly would have been, to sacrifice Chisiza, in spite of – and possibly because of – his recently acquired status in international eyes after the symposium. Nevertheless, he could undoubtedly have weathered any crisis that might have arisen from resignations. He still had Surtee on the upper roll, to whom he could offer a ministerial post, and it is likely that he could have persuaded Mkandawire to remain in office.

We have noted how a number of elected members of the government had approached Jones to release Chipembere from prison before the Marlborough House conference in November 1962. At that conference, a full cabinet system was introduced, the leader of the majority party became the prime minister, the chief secretary became the Deputy Governor and the only ex officio cabinet post was that of the minister of finance.[63] Although Jones had contemplated release as early as August, Banda had not pressed him on the issue, but when Butler raised the matter privately during the conference, Banda said he hoped the sentence could be curtailed and Chipembere released after the conference. Almost exactly a year earlier, Banda had held a press conference with Chiume in the chair. When he was asked, 'Have you any plans for Mr Chipembere?' he replied, 'He is a Minister where he is. I know his portfolio. So far as I am concerned he is a Minister now ... There will be no doubt when Chipembere comes out he will be a Minister.'[64]

About a fortnight after Banda returned from the Marlborough House conference, he received a letter from Chipembere.[65] Dated 19 Decenber 1962, it began 'My beloved Father and Master' and ended 'Your affectionate son and servant, Masauko Chipembere'.

> I have now come to the end of my prison sentence which ... has been reduced to two years in accordance with a prison law which grants remission of sentence for good behaviour. You will be proud to learn that the good conduct which has earned me this remission of sentence stems directly from the impact of your wise admonition given to me and my colleagues in Gwelo Prison in 1959. In that piece of advice you enjoined that a political prisoner must not give any trouble to the prison authorities and must make no fuss of any kind, so as to demonstrate his willingness to suffer for his country; and you set an admirable example for us to imitate by keeping absolutely quiet and not complaining about this or that amenity. I have endeavoured to live up to this ideal throughout my stay here. As a result I will be released in a few weeks time, probably on 9th February.

A number of other MCP members who were convicted at about the same time as Chipembere had not shown the same restraint, and consequently were given an extra month to three months' imprisonment before being released.[66] He continued his letter, saying that he longed to see the doctor again – 'you who have become more than merely my leader and are now my veritable father'. He intended once more to place himself at Banda's disposal so that if he thought he could be of any use to the doctor or the country, 'you may freely assign any duties to me either in our party or in our Government'. The content and tone of this letter suggest that by this time Chipembere had given up all hope of an early release – a matter for Jones, advised by Banda – other than for good behaviour – a matter for the prison authorities – and was by no means certain that Banda would restore him to ministerial office.

Jones already had in mind freeing him about Christmas time and cancelling his period on licence, which would have barred him from membership of the legislature. Butler, however – presumably believing that the longer Banda and politics in Nyasaland were free of Chipembere's direct influence, the better – was markedly doubtful: 'I cannot help feeling some doubt about an early release ... and I should be grateful if you would let me know how you see the advantages of this course so that I can offset them against my general anxieties.' These anxieties existed despite Banda's expressed confidence that he could control Chipembere. Possibly because of them, Jones – who probably thought that a week or two one way or the other was of little consequence – changed his proposed date of release to 31 January 1963, but this date still worried the secretary of state, who was due to visit Nyasaland a few days before then:

> I think that release on 31 January i.e. the day following my departure from Zomba will be bound to be linked with my visit, and ... I should have thought that it might be embarrassing to yourself if there were any suggestion that I had been brought into the matter. If release is to take place, it seems to me that the best time might be [before I arrive in Nyasaland].[67]

As it happened, the day before Butler expressed these views, Banda had told the Governor he hoped Chipembere could be released before the secretary of state's visit. This coincidence of opinion induced Jones to change his mind again and agree to release on 15 January, which

> would allow Chipembere to go to his home in the Fort Johnston District before attending Dr. Banda's swearing in [as prime minister] ... In all the circumstances, and having regard to the fact that I have staved this one off for a long time I feel inclined to release him on the 15th thus hoping to gain from him some good will for the future when he becomes a minister.[68]

Jones was overdoing the 'staving off' piece. Banda had not in fact pressed him, and the pressure, such as it was, had come in August from some of the ministers, including Chisiza, who hoped to acquire a counter-balance to Chiume. The Governor had seen advantage in early release but thereafter Chisiza had been killed and the others had not pursued it. Being somewhat unsettled by the death of one of their number so soon after raising the question, they may have considered it prudent to let the matter rest a while.

Chipembere was released from prison, and his period on licence cancelled, during the late evening of 15 January 1963, though it was not announced until the following day.[69] He had served fractionally less than two years of his three-year sentence. It has been suggested that Banda asked for this slightly early release in order 'to forestall a massive demonstration of support being planned by the Party' to press for an early release.[70] If this was so, the planning was almost certainly Chiume's. Immediately he was released he was driven to Blantyre by Special Branch officers and taken to see Banda, where 'his attitude was one of servility'. He was then driven to his home at Malindi, and the officers with him reported an apparently marked change for the better in his general demeanour compared with that before his imprisonment. The next day he told press reporters,

> There will be a noticeable change in my behaviour, not because of my prison experience but because there is nothing now to be violent about. When I went to prison Nyasaland was a slave state. As I come out of it it is a free country. So I lay down my arms and I abandon my hostility to Europeans and join Dr. Banda in extending a hand of welcome to them as long as they are prepared to accept Dr. Banda as the indisputable master of Nyasaland.

This, of course, was a diplomatic and prudent impression to create – he had made similar remarks when he was released from detention just over two years previously – but there were signs also that he was dissatisfied with a number of matters. He told a friend that he understood Banda was to offer him the ministry of local government, but he hoped to persuade him – in the event unsuccessfully – to make him minister of the interior for nine months or a year. He wanted this post because he felt Bwanausi, the current incumbent, was 'too mild to deal with the white settlers', European government officers and the police who had taken action against Congress during the emergency. He was dissatisfied, too, with the slow pace of Africanization. The friend gained the impression that he was 'as bitterly anti-European as ever'. Special Branch believed that in the south there was a general feeling that Chipembere's release would put an end to the 'favouritism' being shown to those from the north and centre of the country.[71]

> Chipembere's return was welcomed with all the enthusiasm accorded to a long lost son. Banda gave a cocktail party to celebrate his release and vigorously defended his earlier militancy. Shortly afterwards, on his instructions, Archdeacon Chipembere resigned his seat in the legislature to make way for his son. Within the Party Chipembere was re-instated as Treasurer-General.[72]

Immediately after Chipembere had seen Banda on the day of his release, the doctor wrote him a letter in which he indicated that he intended to offer him ministerial office but warned that he expected diligent and sustained hard work from him. Chipembere thanked him in a letter written on 19 January.[73] He had been told many times by Chiume about the standards of work the doctor expected from him, and he was 'now psychologically prepared for it and [bore] it in mind constantly'. It would be an honour and a source of joy: 'I look forward to it, and will call any time you send for me.' To reassure Banda that he was behaving himself, he concluded:

I am doing what resting is possible with so many friends flocking in to see me. I have actually 'detained' myself in my house and have not yet moved even fifty yards away from it, in order to work up strength for the tasks ahead. I have forbidden excessive drumming, shouting etc., not only because I want to rest but also to assure local Europeans that I mean to be a man of 'peace and calm' now. In order not to kill or discourage national enthusiasm I have allowed quiet singing and drumming.

He was manifestly delighted to be back home and free, and was keen for Banda to be assured that he was looking forward to returning to active ministerial life, would work diligently and in the meantime was behaving himself and restraining his followers' enthusiasm – subject to a little quiet singing and drumming!

The seventeen-month life of the Lancaster House government, which drew to a close at the time of Chipembere's release, was characterized by a further consolidation of Banda's personal power. He was not bothered about being made chief minister, because he was content, as leader of the majority party, with his de facto position of being solely responsible for who were to be ministers, and who not, and for dictating MCP policy not only in the party but also in executive council. The replacement of the nominated officials increased the power of the MCP generally in government and substantially increased his personal power, both in the party and in government. He did nothing to reduce, indeed he fostered and exploited, the growing friction among his principal lieutenants as a means of dividing and ruling. In the country at large the factionalism was revealed as a split between the north and the south, and within the government as opposition to Chiume. At one stage all Chiume's elected executive council colleagues, with one of the two parliamentary secretaries, complained about him to Banda; they also complained to the Governor, who agreed with them. Dunduzu Chisiza took the leading part in voicing this dissatisfaction, but to little effect. Banda took no action, despite their tendered resignations, which were capable of bringing about a constitutional crisis and revealing to the world schisms that would have weakened Britain's confidence in his unifying leadership, upon which they were relying for further constitutional progress.

The thrust of the opposition was not overtly against Banda, but was directed at Chiume. Although the parts played by individuals varied, and although the nature of their complaints differed with individuals, they were all – save for Chirwa, who did not get involved – united in their objections to Chiume. It is probable that Chiume was using Chipembere's absence to establish or confirm his position as the senior lieutenant and, in effect, Banda's deputy. He attempted this, they claimed, by criticizing, belittling and frustrating the work of other African members of the government and by exulting Banda. Chisiza's hijacking of the Cameron–Chiume feud may be seen as a challenge for the leadership under Banda by ousting Chiume and placing himself in a strong position to succeed the doctor when the time came for him to leave office. The challenge failed. Rivalry between contenders for future leadership is often to the advantage of the existing leader.

When Banda did nothing about their representations, the leading complainants told him that while they would maintain a united party front until independence, their cooperation would not automatically be forthcoming thereafter. This early warning would have served to put Banda on his guard. It also mutedly indicated deeper concerns: that the executive should be collectively responsible for the decisions of government; that if the leader wanted their collegiate support he had to earn it and would not be able to rely on his colleagues blindly following him irrespective of the merits of the course he was pursuing; that while they were quite content that Banda should be *primus* they were clear that this should be *inter pares* and no one of them should be considered other than the equal of the others. They were, in effect, tinkling in Banda's ear some of the bells of the Westminster model of government.

CHAPTER 5

Self-government: February 1963 to July 1964

ON 1 February 1963 Banda was sworn in as Nyasaland's first – and, as it turned out, only – prime minister. Chipembere became a member of the cabinet as minister of local government. Indeed, Banda referred to him and Chiume as his 'inner cabinet ... the people who had been primarily responsible for his return'. Shortly, Banda sent the two of them away for an extended study tour of the USA, 'to allow the excitement at his return to die down'. Banda later claimed that during this tour Chipembere and Chiume began to plan to oust him, and that thereafter he watched them closely.[1]

A fortnight after Banda became prime minister, the MCP unanimously adopted the report of a committee of the central executive, chaired by Chirwa, which had inquired into party discipline so as to 'improve the management of the Party as the sole ruler of [the] country'.[2] In adopting the report, the party yet again greatly increased Banda's status and furthered his powers as life president, not only over the lowly ordinary members of the MCP but also over its more highly placed senior members:

> The Life President, as the Supreme Leader and Symbol of the Supremacy of the Party, must be respected, honoured and revered by every member of the Party, high or low, and Party Members, high and low, are expected to conduct themselves in a courteous and respectful manner in his presence. Any member of the Party ... who contravenes any of these rules and regulations ... shall be dealt with in such manner as the President in his absolute discretion may think fit.

These discipline regulations also restricted the use of certain slogans to praise only the president, and prohibited the encouragement of 'tribalism, regionalism, sectionalism, parochialism, division or disunity, and the forming of personal cliques within the Party'. In an early indication that the party and the government were, in Congress eyes, much the same thing, the regulations also forbade ministers issuing policy statements without Banda's prior approval.

In April Banda appointed Yatuta Chisiza parliamentary secretary to the ministry of labour, and Albert Muwalo suceeded him as administrative secretary of the party.

It may be that part of Banda's motive in sending Chipembere to the USA with Chiume was to avoid him making speeches that might whip up his audiences to create disturbances. If this was so, the benefit was short lived. About the middle of June, now well settled into his ministry, Chipembere made speeches in Port Herald and Chikwawa districts, where he had made the speeches two and a half years earlier that resulted in his conviction and imprisonment. During this new tour, as Special Branch reported, he

> said that Capricorns and 'stooges' could not be tolerated and that action should be taken against them. Following this visit a number of incidents [of abuse of the police, assault, boycott of stores and closure of shops] were reported, 'sweeps' checking MCP cards, an assault on the [Portuguese] stationmaster at Port Herald, and other cases of assault on individuals ... In Chikwawa district a local court clerk was beaten up and dismissed when he complained to the police. [Chipembere] is reported as saying ... that he is to be regarded as 'Minister of Violence' and that the activities of 'stooges' and Capricorns are to be reported to him so that he could issue orders for dealing with them.[3]

Since February 1963 Banda had regularly received the monthly intelligence reports, and consequently he was aware of these and other reported activities of Chipembere. He showed them to none of his colleagues.[4]

The doctor was away from 21 August to 17 October 1963 on an overseas trip with Tembo, Cecilia Kadzamira and her sister. While he was away Chirwa was made responsible natural resources and the cabinet office, Chiume for health and Jones for public order.[5] Banda and those accompanying him first visited Ghana, where he impolitely ignored the attempts by the British high commissioner to welcome him and offer assistance.[6] He may have been somewhat apprehensive in returning with these particular companions to the country where he had lived earlier with Margaret French. It was noted that he 'spoke somewhat condescendingly of Dr. Nkrumah, whom he described without exception as "Kwame" and on one occasion as "Young Kwame"'. He also visited Liberia, where President Tubman gave 'a men's dinner party', probably of freemasons.[7] It may be that Tembo also attended this function. He then went to Germany, where he 'hoped for some quiet days to make certain medical arrangements for one of the Miss Kadzamiras'. The German foreign ministry found him 'very tiresome over the arrangements for his stay and indeed at one stage [the foreign minister said] Dr. Banda was the most troublesome African who had ever visited the Federal Republic'. On the other hand, he pleased his hosts by his 'wide knowledge of German history which he drew on to good effect'.[8] His next stop was Britain, where he had a number of meetings with Butler and Jones.[9]

Banda's final visit was to the USA, where he narrowly missed an embarrassing encounter when it was realized he had been booked into the same hotel as had Welensky, the prime minister of the Federation, who was also visiting America. While there he had a 'sentimental reunion [with] three negro ladies who many years before had been his teachers at Wilberforce High School in Ohio and the memories of which encouraged Dr. Banda to make some extremely gracious remarks about his debt to America [which] provided him with the groundwork of an education'.[10] The whole of this overseas trip, which was tiring and at times emotional, was private, almost a family holiday, and the arrangements were made – not always clearly and efficiently – by Tembo. Although generally a private trip, the London component dealt with the important issues of Nyasaland's future financing and a date for independence. Negotiations on these important issues were conducted on Nyasaland's behalf entirely by Banda without his involving any of his cabinet colleagues, which could hardly have escaped incurring their displeasure.

Not all had gone well in Nyasaland while Banda was away. The intelligence committee report which he saw on his return alerted him:

> A freer attitude among the rank and file of the ruling party has become noticeable in many parts of the country towards the discussion, even criticism, of Government policies and personalities. Inevitably, tribal and provincial prejudices tend to be expressed in this context, and would, were it not for the unifying influence of the Prime Minister, create the likelihood of rival factions developing in the ruling party.[11]

Additionally, as soon as he arrived back, Yatuta Chisiza 'presented [him] with an indictment of Chipembere, Chiume and Bwanausi', alleging that these three were 'ganging up' against Chokani and Chisiza himself.[12]

There was another occasion on which Chisiza made damaging accusations against Chipembere, Chiume and Bwanausi. Taking a break from their work, Chiume and Bwanausi had gone to shoot duck one Sunday morning and returned with thirty-eight duck, some of which they saved to give to the doctor. When they arrived at his house they discovered Chisiza and Rose Chibambo there, accusing them of having been to Lake Chirwa the previous day, staying overnight and returning on the Sunday, having procured medicine with which to poison Banda so that

Chipembere could take over. The doctor challenged Chisiza and Rose Chibambo to repeat the accusation in Chiume's and Bwanausi's presence and thereby 'defused an ugly situation'.[13]

The state of affairs facing Banda on his return from his overseas visits in October 1963 put him generally ill at ease. Most untypically, he 'lost his temper with Rowland his expatriate permanent secretary, was rude, loud, nearly incoherent and said things to [him] about Bwanausi that were highly objectionable. He got up, went out and slammed the door while Rowland was in the middle of a sentence.'[14] The specific nature of the indictment and the precise matter over which Banda lost his temper are not known, but there were allegations – later dismissed by Chiume, who said he was framed by Chidzanja, MCP chairman of the central region – that Chiume 'was seeking to enhance his popularity by having laudatory articles inserted in the government newspaper and that he was trying to form a personal power base in the newly created young pioneer movement'.[15] Neither of these, as Chidzanja and others well knew, was a matter to which Banda would take kindly. Almost immediately, he removed education and social development from Chiume's portfolio, took over the latter himself, gave the former to Chipembere and appointed Aleke Banda as commander of the young pioneers.[16] Chiume was now responsible for 'the rather strange Ministry of Information and Independence Celebrations'.[17] As the doctor explained a year later:

> I deliberately demoted, took away some of the Ministries of Chiume ... because I knew what he was doing. He didn't know that I knew but I knew. You know what he was trying to do with the Youth League when I was away in Europe ... Yes, Sir, that's why, when I came back, I dismissed the Council [of which Chiume was chairman] and took over the Youth League myself. I knew everything, but I didn't let them know that I knew what was going on. That's how I do things. Give them a long rope with which to hang themselves.[18]

His use of the word 'them' rather than 'him' suggests that he suspected others of being implicated in 'what was going on'. By giving some of Chiume's responsibilities to Chipembere, he not only demoted the former but also increased the potential for driving a wedge between the two of them by simultaneously promoting the latter – a continuation of his divide-and-rule tactic. He also deprived Chiume of the potentially powerful position of chairman of the young pioneers' council and elevated Aleke Banda to command that body. Officials in the Central Africa Office in London quickly saw a connection between these changes and the Special Branch reports – which Banda saw – of 'dissident factions within the MCP'.[19]

Banda's irritation with his ministers surfaced publicly on 27 October, ten days after his return from America, when the freedom of the city of Blantyre was conferred on him. In his speech of thanks, he made it abundantly clear that 'he was the boss': 'No other minister need think of undermining me.' Phillips, who was present, was sufficiently struck by this to record it in his private diary and add, 'I think he distrusts his ministers and that includes Kanyama Chiume.'[20] Seven years later, Chipembere recalled the occasion. He said that Banda had 'never been lacking in frankness in his dealings with those ... who worked close to him' and he had never been slow in criticizing or rebuking his ministers when he thought them to be in error, but his criticism hitherto had always been in private.

> But to everyone's surprise, towards the end of 1963, he developed the habit of doing so in public, and the tone and content of his remarks were often so belligerent as to constitute an attack, challenge, or denunciation of his own cabinet. The first of these open attacks was made ... during a ceremony at a party rally held in the city of Blantyre's Central Stadium. The Municipal Council of Blantyre was honouring Dr. Banda by granting him 'the Freedom of the City' ... On this occasion, Prime Minister Banda devoted only a few minutes to matters concerning the city and spent nearly two hours attacking his own cabinet ministers. We were at a loss to know what had caused this outburst which was later relayed in full by Malawi Radio.[21]

Two of Chipembere's closest friends in the cabinet, probably Chiume and Bwanausi, suggested that the outburst had been caused by his absence from a recent rally, which Banda may have seen as a boycott. It is more likely that the outburst reflected wider concerns about his ministers than just the absence of one from a rally.

A few weeks later, Chipembere and Chiume visited Tanganyika and were told by 'intelligence sources' that British officers in Malawi, fearful of the security of their positions in the civil service, were deliberately playing on Banda's feeling of insecurity and were 'systematically sowing seeds of suspicion in Dr. Banda's mind' about the probable communist sympathies of his radical ministers. They were told that the intelligence reports submitted by British officers to Banda were written in such a way as to make him believe that the ministers were 'building themselves up' at his expense. Chipembere and Chiume were convinced of the accuracy of these allegations. 'That the Prime Minister was receiving distorted reports on his ministers became more apparent during the months that followed, as he stepped up his campaign to get his own cabinet [members] discredited in the eyes of the public.'[22] Officials in Chipembere's ministry noticed at this time that he employed in the headquarters office what they believed to be 'a girl spy' and began to make false and damaging allegations about some of his expatriate officials.[23]

Later, Banda explained why he had spoken as he did when receiving the freedom of the city of Blantyre and on another occasion at Liwonde. He believed that Chiume and Chipembere had begun to plot against him: 'but I kept quiet. That is why ... once in a while I used to say something [indirectly about it.]'[24]

The end of October 1963 was something of a turning point in Banda's relations, at least in public, with his ministers, and after that date they deteriorated. Subsequently, Chiume referred to the ministers being 'not happy with the way [Banda] had elected to do things' from about that time onwards.[25] Banda had accomplished virtually all he had initially set out to achieve in returning to Nyasaland: the country was self-governing, federation had been abolished and independence had been agreed, though a date had not yet been set. He did not want any of his ministers jeopardizing his final achievement of sovereign status, nor manoeuvring themselves into positions where they could hinder the way he wished to run the country after independence.

Banda not only took over control of the paramilitary young pioneers but, looking to the future, he also took steps to ensure his position in relation to the army. The first battalion of the King's African Rifles reverted to the Nyasaland government from the Federal government at the end of December 1963. Less than a month later he told Jones that it was important that the conditions of service for soldiers should be fair, 'otherwise there would be dissatisfaction which could be used by unscrupulous politicians'. At independence he himself would take responsibility for the army and 'no other minister would have anything to do with it whatsoever'.[26]

Chipembere later commented on Banda's public denunciations. He felt that the increased tendency in late 1963 and 1964 to discredit his ministers was particularly aimed at himself because he commanded a substantial following in the country, especially in the south.

> Since his arrival and election to leadership in 1958, he had always seen us not as his colleagues or as loyal followers, but as actual or potential rivals and had consistently striven to strengthen his own position in relation to us. Some of his public attacks were part of an attempt to 'cut us down to size.'[27]

Towards the end of 1963 the violence foreshadowed six months previously by Chipembere's speeches in the Lower River emerged on a much more worrying scale. In November the Special Branch correctly forecast 'a disturbing manifestation of pre-election violence'. The troubles focused on the main opposition party, Mbadwa, and were deeply alarming. Early in December Mbadwa announced that they would contest all seats in the forthcoming general election.[28] On 15 December a petrol bomb destroyed the Blantyre house of Pondeponde, who had been recently named – against his will[29] – as the parliamentary secretary in the Mbadwa shadow cabinet. The next day Chief Chikowi – who had for many years shown great loyalty to the colonial government but who had recently been deprived of his chiefdomship by Jones at Banda's behest – together with a member of Mbadwa travelling with him, were assaulted, and the chief's car was badly damaged. The following day the house of another Mbadwa member in Lilongwe was burned down, and that same night an African former federal MP was grievously assaulted with an axe and hospitalized with severe head wounds. There were attacks on individuals in the Port Herald area led, it was alleged, by Gwanda Chakuamba. Two days before Christmas, Pondeponde was hacked to death and his body dumped near the entrance to the chief justice's official residence in Blantyre. He was a prominent member of the Catholic community and attended the same church as Sir Edgar Unsworth, the chief justice. Unsworth 'gathered from reliable sources that the murder had been committed by members of Banda's bodyguard'.[30] No prosecution was brought. Two days after Christmas the house, maize mill and two cars belonging to a member of Mbadwa in Mlanje were severely damaged. The following day the house of yet another Mbadwa member was wrecked in Chikwawa. In every case the crimes were carried out by 'gangs of young men allegedly members of the League of Malawi Youth'. The Governor, with no great perspicacity, believed they were part of ' a planned policy to prevent any African opposition party from contesting seats in the May election'. There were reports of 'special action squads' being formed among members of the LMY and being responsible for some of the violent incidents in Blantyre, Port Herald and Zomba districts. Special Branch reported that in the central and southern regions those who carried out the attacks believed their actions had the tacit approval of the MCP. By early January the leaders of Mbadwa had fled Nyasaland for Salisbury and Lusaka.[31]

With the opening on 30 December of registrations for the forthcoming general election, the country entered upon a further and particularly disturbing period of political violence. There was dissatisfaction, especially in the northern region, that the MCP had decided that candidates should continue to be selected personally by Banda.[32] Already there had been a number of murders and a worrying number of other cases of severe violence, including the use of petrol bombs.[33] During the early stages of registration there were a few incidents where members of parties in opposition to the MCP were prevented from registering, but

> As time went on the number of incidents multiplied. They took the form

of bands of young thugs usually identified with the Malawi Party going about slashing crops, burning houses, assaulting and threatening people, mainly Jehovah's Witnesses because they decline to register as voters. By the close of the [three-week] period of registration on 19th January there had been some 420 such incidents reported to the police, including two more violent deaths.

At a public meeting held ... in Chikwawa district [a member of the legislature] said that any person who failed to to register should have his house destroyed, his crops uprooted and be made to suffer personal injury. [Two days later he] made a further speech in which he encouraged his listeners to assault and burn the houses of those who were opposed in any way to the MCP and threatened dismissal of any policeman who endeavoured to make a proper investigation ...

On one occasion the MLA for Lilongwe South, Mr. Chidzanja, approached the officer in charge of police about some malicious damage cases. He said that the police must stop interfering in these cases as they were political matters and that unless the charges were dropped there would be more trouble. On a second occasion the police officer approached the MLA to discuss generally the wave of violent incidents in the region ... He was informed that the cases were political and nothing to do with the police force [who] should not interfere as it was a matter for the politicians.[34]

The Governor hoped that with the close of registration and thereby the 'removal of the cause of the incidents of violence', as he saw it, the country would quieten down, but this was not to be. In the last two weeks of January 1964 a further 369 cases of violence – mainly concerned with refusals to have registered – were reported, bringing the total at the end of January to 789. Many others were not reported.[35]

The police kept Banda informed of what was going on, including the continuation of violence, the murders, arson, intimidation of Jehovah's Witnesses and Mbadwa members, the activities of certain MLAs – who were also senior members of the MCP – the role of the youth league and the special action squads and the belief that the violence had the approval of the MCP. At the same time he was receiving information from his own party sources that general peace and calm prevailed.

The Governor, deeply disturbed by the violence, which was causing him 'very serious disquiet indeed', wrote to Banda on 8 February asking him to appeal for peace and calm. Despite his protestations of exaggeration and fabrication in reports of violent breaches of the law, Banda addressed a large public meeting in Zomba two weeks later and said no trouble should be caused to anyone. Nevertheless, the intelligence committee's report for February said that, particularly in the Mlanje district, gangs were 'slow to respond'. The action taken by party officials to comply with his instructions 'varied considerably' in different areas. In some cases they were not obeyed at all and in others their colleagues, 'by contrary advice and activities, frustrated their efforts'. The report made sorry reading. The total number of crimes reported during February was twice that of January: 1,204 as against 619. Nearly a thousand of the complainants were members of religious groups, and a further sixty were opponents of the government.

> The central region was the most seriously affected ... four murders occurring in the Dowa district alone ... On 19 February, [a very senior member of the MCP, a protege of Banda's] addressed gatherings [there] ... the people addressed understood him to indicate that they should carry on damaging the crops and taking offensive action against 'Capricorns' and Jehovah's Witnesses and that by doing so these people must learn that the MCP demands cooperation. A particularly savage murder occurred in the Mponela area of the Dowa district [the same day] when a gang of youths ordered three families of Jehovah's Witnesses to leave the area. All the families left with the exception of three men who were not prepared to move. They were attacked in daylight by youths who hacked them to death with pangas.[36]

Two days later in the Mlanje district a Jehovah's Witness was trussed up and buried up to his neck. He was rescued by the village headman in the nick of time before his face was completely covered with earth.[37] In March the number of violent incidents reported during the month dropped to 237.[38] Either Banda's plea was at last taking effect or, more likely, what those behind the violence hoped to achieve had largely been accomplished.

The police were having a difficult time. So far they had sent 322 cases – each usually involving several accused – to the director of public prosecutions, Colonel R. F. L. Gulliver, but he had authorized prosecutions in only nine cases and had rejected seven; the other 306 cases were still pending a decision. The problem stemmed from the constitutional requirement that the director should consult the attorney-general in cases where there might be a political element. This inevitably slowed down the pace, but the situation was exacerbated by Gulliver's difficulty in securing regular or early access to the attorney-general to consult him. Chirwa was 'very often away and [was] a highly evasive person when it [came] to something he [did] not care for'.[39] The Governor suspected him of using the constitution to stifle prosecutions against members of the MCP even in cases of extreme violence. He wrote a number of letters to Chirwa and then had a meeting with him. He sincerely trusted Chirwa would consider cases of murder, serious assault, arson and crop destruction as 'straightforward cases of unjustifiable violence which should be prosecuted with the utmost vigour regardless of whether they have political content or not'.[40] Chirwa, having discussed the matter with Banda, insisted that each case had to be dealt with on its individual merits, denied that the constitution was being used in the stifling way Jones feared,[41] insisted that he must be fully consulted in all cases with a political flavour[42] and claimed that some of the reports were exaggerated, fabricated or the outcome of provocation by Jehovah's Witnesses. Nevertheless, he promised to go into the outstanding cases and consider each with a view to authorizing prosecutions in appropriate cases.[43]

Amiable, accommodating and reassuring as Chirwa was, the problem persisted and Jones had to write to him again three weeks later. Banda was away and the Governor expressed himself concisely and unequivocally. The police had told him earlier that day about the still large number of cases in which the attorney-general's instructions had not been received.

> Having regard to my overall responsibility for public order and public safety ... I shall have no alternative but to bring the whole matter to the attention of the Prime Minister immediately on his return. Meanwhile, however, I ... ask you, as Attorney-General, to express your views ... so that the Director of Public Prosecutions can, without further delay, exercise his powers under the Constitution. With this in view, I am requesting the Director of Public Prosecutions to contact you in person as soon as possible so that he may, as agreed between you and me at our last meeting, go ahead with the prosecution of the serious offences involving violence.[44]

This letter provoked an irate response from Chirwa. He rounded on Jones and vented two major resentments. First, he resented that Jones should have availed himself of advice either from the police 'or from any person other than your Prime Minister or myself or other Minister' over matters for which they were fully responsible in a self-governing state. Second, he resented being 'pushed around'.

> The Director of Public Prosecutions, whom I met [recently], spoke about his powers under the Constitution to go ahead with the prosecution of political cases ... [It] is not yet possible for any person other than myself, as the representative of Dr. Banda and the Malawi Congress Party, to mount any major political arrests. I have, therefore, told the Director of Public Prosecutions that if he persists with the prosecution of political cases without my knowledge and support he will not make the slightest progress, and such arrests will be vigorously resisted in every corner of this country. May I also add that we resent being pushed around by any

person, for we have been pushed about far too much in this country. Nor should we be hurried into doing foolish things because certain people within or without this country are clamouring for action. These may well be the same people who have given us little or no support throughout our political struggle.

He concluded by saying that he had received a letter from the director, in which, 'after a vehement attack on my professional and political integrity', he said he had no option but to resign.

> As he feels so strongly ... we have come to the conclusion that it is better for him to leave us in peace as soon as arrangements can be made for his repatriation. We would like to have someone who is not so wide-mouthed about his constitutional powers which, in our view, are non-existent ... because we hold that the ultimate power belongs to the people of Malawi, of whom I have the honour to be one of their representatives.[45]

Jones was not cowed. He wrote straight back. He was aware that he had no powers in relation to mounting prosecutions, though he could not escape his ultimate responsibility for public order and safety, despite the fact that he had currently assigned responsibility to the prime minister. He would not exercise this responsibility in a way that overrode Banda's opinions. Nevertheless, he had the right to tender advice with the object of serving the best interests of Nyasaland and its people. He hoped that giving such advice would not be construed by Chirwa as pushing him about. He hoped, too, that arrangements could quickly be made so that there was continuity in the functions of the director of public prosecutions.[46]

There are a number of interesting elements in this Jones–Chirwa exchange. Jones expressed himself firmly and critically with Chirwa in a way that he never did with Banda. Chirwa also expressed himself firmly: he insisted on treating each case on its merits, as he saw them, and on being consulted in political cases. Although Chirwa had discussed the matter with Banda, the prime minister appears not to have intervened, nor did Jones ask him to intervene. Perhaps the doctor was content to tolerate delay in prosecutions for offences against his opponents and to allow Chirwa to fight this particular battle with the Governor. Jones, on his side, may have felt that he was more likely through Chirwa to achieve the result he was seeking. Chirwa insinuated that Jones was pushing him around and made it clear that he was not going to put up with it or be bulldozed into hasty decisions. His frequent use of the word 'we' suggests that he had consulted his colleagues and was, in effect, expressing their joint opinion, including Banda's. Unsworth's view was that Chirwa, with whom he had 'a happy relationship', was 'very much under the control of Banda on matters of policy'.[47]

80 · *Revolt of the Ministers*

For whatever reason, the position began to improve. By the end of May, the figure for complaints involving injury to persons or property since registration opened in December stood at 2,693. There were still sporadic outbursts of violence against Jehovah's Witnesses, but their seriousness had declined. The police had sent 391 dockets to the DPP seeking permission to prosecute and this was approved in 209 cases; 164 cases were still being considered. Prosecutions were now approved in all cases involving death where evidence was available, save in one case that was still being considered.[48] Throughout the five months of political violence the government rigorously suppressed all news of the incidents,[49] and the extent and nature of the violence were not widely known then or later, though it is clear that the Governor, prime minister and others were abundantly aware of what was going on.

Once the registration for the elections was completed, Banda's mind turned to the structure and composition of the cabinet he wished to form after the elections, ready for independence. This was a matter on which Jones offered his advice. The ministry of finance was clearly a crucial ministry, not only because of the role it played in the internal public finances and development of Nyasaland, but also because of the budgetary support Britain would continue to give for some time. Special arrangements had been made to retain Phillips as minister of finance until independence. Jones told Banda that Phillips had on occasion to resist 'demands and blandishments' from the other ministers, who naturally wished to further their own projects enthusiastically.

> I know that you have been grooming young John Tembo to be Phillips' successor and I have no doubt that he has the intellectual qualities required for the job. I ask you however, with respect, to consider whether John is yet strong enough and mature enough to take on the onerous task of Minister of Finance at the present time ... I would like to draw your attention to a possibility which you may already have examined – that is, that for the time being you should consider Bwanausi for the post of Minister of Finance and John Tembo for the post of Minister of Development where he will obtain further valuable training for the post of Minister of Finance in the future.[50]

A few days later, without intervening discussion, Banda reached decisions on the ministers he wished to have following the recent elections – in which no seats were contested: Chirwa, justice; Chiume, independence and information, and after independence, external affairs; Chipembere, education; Chokani, labour; Msonthi, transport and communications; Bwanausi, development and housing; Cameron, public works; Phillips, finance, until independence when Tembo would take over; Yatuta Chisiza, home affairs, which included local government, formerly part of Chipembere's responsibilities. The three parliamentary secretaries – Chirwa, Tembo and Chisiza – were promoted to full ministerial rank. Mkandawire was dropped from the cabinet at his own request so that he could further his education. There were no newcomers to the government. Banda himself was prime minister, minister of trade and industry, minister of health and minister of natural resources, surveys and social development. Jones had tried hard to get him to retain Cameron in transport and communications. Cameron had told Banda he wished to continue with that portfolio. The Governor had tried hard, too, to get the doctor to agree that Bwanausi should become minister of finance, that Tembo should become minister of development and that the doctor should restrict the number of his own portfolios. In all cases 'there was no give' and Banda ignored or rejected Jones's advice.[51]

As early as April Banda had asked the Governor to tell Cameron he wished to appoint him as a minister in the independence cabinet, but he made it clear that he 'expected him to observe the same conditions as all other ministers ... namely that he should take no decision on any matter of policy without prior reference' to the prime minister. This condition does not seem to have disturbed Cameron, who replied that 'he and his wife were devoted to the service of Malawi and would serve [him] as Prime Minister as long as [he] desired in any position that [he] directed'.[52]

Chiume's position during the period leading up to independence is interesting. As we have seen, he was instrumental, with Chipembere, in Banda returning to Nyasaland. He created a most favourable impression on the doctor at the very outset when he and his wife accommodated and entertained him during the Nkhata Bay conference. At that conference he was appointed to the influential post of publicity secretary. He seems to have induced Banda to shun European social contact. At the Accra conference he reinforced the favourable impression the doctor had of him. He did a great deal of overseas travelling and built up for himself an international reputation, at least in Africa. He was in Britain during Banda's detention and kept the fire of Congress alight overseas. For six months after Banda's release from Gwelo gaol, he was the only one of his principal lieutenants, save for Chirwa, who was free and able to work closely with the doctor; the others were still in detention. He was a delegate and political adviser at the Lancaster House conference. One of Banda's arguments for releasing the final hard-core detainees was that Chipembere and Chiume should be restored to their seats in the legislature – and, presumably, be available for appointment to executive council. He put significant pressure on Banda to secure the release of the final detainees. He was in charge of the organization of the Kota Kota conference which, with the detainees' release, was a significant feather in Banda's cap and therefore, albeit to a lesser extent, also

Chiume's. He joined Chipembere in his first post-detention tour and made speeches rousing the people and resulting in Chipembere's conviction – which ensured that Chiume, who escaped prosecution, effectively became Banda's senior lieutenant, uneclipsed by Chipembere's presence for the next two years. He was the first person to be named by Banda for a portfolio in the 1961 executive council. Others believed that it was his influence which deprived them of a seat in council. It is probable that it was he who drew Banda's attention to Bwanausi, who did become a member of that council. That he irritated Jones – as he had Armitage – and probably a number of others at the early council meetings, does not detract from the fact that he took an immediate and active part in their deliberations; he may have thought that his African colleagues – Banda, Bwanausi and Mkandawire – were unlikely to keep the revolutionary spirit sufficiently ablaze. He may in any case have found it difficult to alter the firebrand approach he had used in the legislature before Banda returned to Nyasaland. He took the leading part in pressing for the title of chief minister to be conferred on Banda, although he made it clear that a chief minister was not a prime minister. He took a similar leading part in pressing for the early replacement of the nominated official members of council – thereby opening the door for two more colleagues to join council. He was then given the additional responsibility of social development. Only Banda also held two major ministerial responsibilities. By mid-1962 he was thought by Special Branch to be probably the only leading member of the MCP to have the ear of Banda. Despite the criticism of all his elected colleagues in government, save Chirwa, their representations to the Governor and to Banda, and Chisiza's offer to oust him, no overt action was taken against him, and indeed Banda walked out of the confrontation meeting without agreeing with either side. He was seen by expatriate permanent secretaries as being an energetic, if a somewhat uncouth person who antagonized many people working in his ministry. His European lady secretary found him to be a phenomenally hard worker.[53] A fellow minister believed there was always a close relationship between Banda and Chiume:

> Banda found Chiume extremely useful to him as he would not counter him in any way ... For instance, some of Chiume's proposals with regard to the Education Ministry and indeed his proposals for the Independence Celebrations, Banda seemed to accept without too much thought and certainly countered any criticisms in the Cabinet or the Executive Council that others raised.[54]

There was, however, the opposite side of Chiume's progress. Banda was prepared to 'slap him down' in council if he became too difficult. Chiume was not detained with Banda and did not share the benefits – of getting to know him better and being part of the Gwelo team planning Nysaland's future – that Chipembere and Dunduzu Chisiza had. Not being detained also deprived him of the great political honour of being a 'prison graduate' and, even more important, a 'camp finalist'. Armitage thought him of insufficient consequence to be prosecuted, once Chipembere was out of the way, despite having enough evidence to do so. Banda was critical of Chiume for not paying money from Nasser into his personal account. The doctor kept him waiting outside like a schoolboy during his visit to Salazar and the foreign minister of Portugal. The Deputy Governor, a man of great experience, recalled how Banda insisted on his being present when he reprimanded Chiume so severely that it was the 'biggest rocket' he had ever seen anyone receive in the whole of his career.[55]

By May 1962 there were warnings of Chiume's unpopularity in the country and of 'a widening gulf' between him on the one hand and Chisiza, Chirwa and Aleke Banda on the other. It may be that Banda's attempts at that time to have Yatuta Chisiza trained to become the commissioner of police was in part designed as a warning, or future counter-balance, to Chiume. The Colonial Office hoped that Yatuta would be a 'Dunduzu' rather than a 'Chiume'. His relations with his colleagues had deteriorated sufficiently by August 1962 that, save for Chirwa, they all complained to the Governor and directly to Banda. In October 1963 Yatuta Chisiza handed Banda an indictment alleging that Chiume, with Chipembere and Bwanausi, was 'ganging up' against him and Chokani. It seems, too, that Chiume had tried to take over control of the young pioneers. Almost immediately after this Banda 'deliberately demoted' him, took education and social development from him, split the portfolio between himself and Chipembere, gave him 'the rather strange Ministry of Information and Independence Celebrations' and took over from him control of the young pioneers.

At the end of April 1964 Banda addressed the Zomba Debating Society, which met regularly under Chipembere's chairmanship and included most of the cabinet. He criticized Communism and warned that after independence the country would receive foreign ambassadors who would 'speak a very very sweet language' and 'brain-wash you so that your minds will follow their ideas'.[56] By this time, although he did not say so until later, he was convinced that Chiume, despite earlier objections to Communism, which he communicated to the doctor, had come under its influence. The Chinese ambassador in Dar es Salaam, he later asserted, was 'deliberately inciting dissension and ... had promised Chiume Malawi would receive [very substantial sums] in aid'. Chiume had already brought the ambassador to see him twice that year. The ambassador threatened, argued and pleaded with Banda to recognize Peking China. He offered

£6m. and then raised it to £12m. and then to £18m.⁵⁷ Relationships were deteriorating fast, and Chiume was seriously considering, with others, not standing as MCP candidates for election to the legislature.

The period from Banda's return to Nyasaland in July 1958 to the achievement of independence in July 1964 contained, as we have seen, many elements that established and increased his personal power. He got off to an important start when, less than a month after his arrival, he was made president-general of Congress with sole power to appoint office-bearers and members of the central executive. When he was released from detention in April 1960 his principal lieutenants stayed in gaol and this gave him an unimpeded opportunity personally to deal with the secretary of state and the Governor, including – save for the presence of Chiume and, less importantly, Chirwa and Akeke Banda – reaching constitutional agreements at Lancaster House. He was responsible for having the the hard-core detainees eventually released, and in practice their continued freedom depended upon him – as Chipembere soon discovered when Banda decided not to oppose his prosecution. The government did not fear returning any of the others to incarceration: only he, Banda, held and could successfully play the Gwelo card. This gave him an extraordinarily powerful weapon against the Governor and the Colonial Secretary, to use virtually as he pleased. The Kota Kota conference, at which he produced the camp finalists to the unsuspecting crowd, was another major coup that raised still further his status as leader of the party, demonstrably able and prepared to obtain major concessions from the Governor, and he extracted every personal advantage from it. The gratitude of the released detainees was manifest – Dunduzu Chisiza announced that the doctor was now the life president of the party, thereby further entrenching his personal power. When the self-government executive council was being formed Banda ensured that it had, save for the officials whose numbers he matched, exclusively an MCP membership. His power of patronage over his colleagues, made total within the party at Nkata Bay, was now made total in the government: he alone decided who should and who should not be ministers and parliamentary secretaries. He furthered his personal dominant position by insisting on heading two major ministries himself. The replacement of the two nominated official members of executive council widened his power of patronage, gave him a majority over officials in council and placed him in a still firmer position to have his own way. Factions within the party made it easier for him to employ a policy of divide and rule. Dunduzu Chisiza's representations in August 1962 were criticisms not of Banda's great and growing power – indeed he clearly professed his loyalty to the doctor – but of Chiume's growing power. Any attempt, from whatever source, to diminish the power of others was to Banda's advantage. Even Dunduzu's death was used to bring into the government one of the doctor's strongest allies – Tembo; to bring into the legislature, and thereby into a position shortly to be made a parliamentary secretary, Yatuta Chisiza, a person who had been close to him as his personal bodyguard for several years; and to make his young protégé, Aleke Banda, secretary-general of the party. The rumours surrounding the death made some colleagues fearful of crossing Banda and consequently added to his power. Over a longer period the violence and intimidation in the country both removed effective opposition and generally, as with the rumours surrounding Chisiza's death, made dissent less likely. He used the 'indictment' that Yatuta Chisiza presented to him late in 1963 as a means of constricting Chiume's ministerial powers and removing him from the chairmanship of the young pioneers council, which he took over directly himself, while making Aleke Banda commander. He made it clear to Cameron, as was already clear to other members of the cabinet, that if he wished to remain a minister he could not take any policy decision without his prior approval. Coupled with all of this, his insistence on personally nominating all MCP candidates for election, and the violence perpetrated against his political opponents, ensured that by May 1964 all seats were uncontested and the party reigned supreme with Banda ruling over it.

There were two other factors that added to Banda's power and personal supremacy. The first came into play during the the eighteen months prior to independence. When he became prime minister he was routinely given copies of the monthly intelligence reports. This added a particularly important source of information to that which came to him from party and personal sources, and enabled him to be closely aware of reactions in the country and the activities of his lieutenants and other Congress leaders. Although he could show these reports to his ministerial colleagues, he never did. Whether or not he believed them – and the chances are that he did – they contained warnings of the behaviour of some of his colleagues and of other dangers. The April 1963 report spoke of the increased Communist literature entering the country. In June 1963 Chipembere's speeches in the Lower River, which provoked violence, were reported. In August 1963 the tendencies towards tribalism and provincialism were highlighted. Violence in the Lower River and Chakuamba's activities were reported in January 1964, as were Chidzanja's attempts to stifle police action in 'political' crimes. The speeches of another young MCP leader and the subsequent appalling deaths in the Dowa district were dealt with in February 1964. A claim by the LMY that Banda had been 'wrongly advised' by the disciplinary committee of the party, especially Aleke Banda, Chirwa and Chisiza, was recorded in the March 1964 report. In June 1964, the intelligence committee produced for Banda a paper on reactions to the Skinner report – which recommended severe economies in the local civil service. Reactions were 'extremely critical' but in the immediate future the committee expected little more than general grumbling, especially when the end of July pay packets were received. 'There is no doubt, however, that at some later date if any measure is introduced which is unpopular, particularly among civil servants, reaction to it will be reinforced by reintroducing complaints about the Skinner report.'[58] The Governor had long held the opinion that Banda's policies would be obeyed while they were popular with the people, but once he tried to impose an unpopular policy 'his dictatorial methods could sink him'.

The other factor adding to Banda's power existed throughout the whole period from 1960 onwards: the Governor's invariable and immense support of the doctor, his conviction that he was the only person capable of bringing the country peacefully to independence and prosperity, and his determination to keep him in power, whatever the cost. This support contributed mightily to Banda's power and reinforced all the other factors.

Chiume traced Banda's accumulation of power to the time he took over leadership of the party. Previously it had been the custom to ask questions at every rally, but Banda stopped this on the pretext that the battle for freedom was so formidable that allowing questions would enable enemy agents to disrupt the unity of the movement:[59] 'Banda gave me the impression right from the day he arrived in Malawi and certainly at the Nkhata Bay Conference at which he took over the Nyasaland African Congress leadership, that he wanted nothing short of absolute power at first under his guise, that only then could we have defeated the federation.'[60] Chipembere, also, wrote of Banda's autocratic methods of adding to his personal power and the way he 'quite blatantly rejected the principle of consultation'. In several public pronouncements he 'declared that he made and would always make all the decisions'. 'He said that consultation merely confused a man: you listened to many conflicting opinions and often ended up more confused than you had been before. Thus, decisions affecting our ministries were sometimes made without consulting us and often behind our backs.'[61] Roberts, too, spoke of Banda's personal decision-making tendency, saying he was a man who, 'if he was going to heed advice, certainly did not readily acknowledge the fact, and it took a long time for the advice of others significantly to produce any real change in the directions in which [he] had set himself.'[62]

Whatever the fears of Banda's considerable personal powers – both those conferred upon him by the party and the constitution and those he assumed and developed with the Governor's help – and whatever the frictions between him and his colleagues on the one hand and between his colleagues on the other, up to independence little about them became public knowledge. It was in the interests of all that the public image should be unquestionably one of a solidly united party and government, devoid of frictions, utterly loyal and devoted to the president of the party and the prime minister.

CHAPTER 6

The Revolt: July–August 1964

THE situation in Malawi at the time of independence, as it appeared on the surface and to outsiders – and many insiders – was described by the British high commissioner, David Cole:

> Politically the country was under the firm paternally despotic control of Dr. Banda. Politics here had gained a certain monolithic appearance that suggested security and permanence. There was no real opposition. The Malawi Congress Party seemed popular and deeply-rooted ... Stability, moderation, realism and firm leadership seemed to be Malawi's distinguishing characteristics. The ... Government of Dr. Banda ... seemed to promise stability, anti-communism, realism and moderation in foreign policy, and slow but sensible progress in its internal political development.[1]

Banda's position seemed to Cole to be 'beyond challenge' and his ministers 'scurried about from place to place to perform his most menial behests'. The whole political system revolved around the doctor and it 'was almost inconceivable that it could ever change'.[2]

Roberts painted a similar picture:

> throughout the fight against British colonialism and the fight to break up the Federation, Dr. Banda had achieved a remarkable degree of unity throughout the nation; and in July 1964 there was no question of [him] or anybody else in a prominent position, representing or recognising any threat to the unity which had distinguished the Malawi Congress Party in its fight for independence.[3]

The impression that Cole and Roberts had was shared by Clyde Sanger, a journalist of considerable repute, well acquainted with Malawi and its politics. Making an assessment in August 1964, he wrote:

> The degree to which Malawi had achieved national unity before independence ... has few parallels in Africa ... Malawians are remarkably of one mind ... [Chiume, Chipembere, Chisiza] and other young ministers and

party officials, comprise as well-balanced and cohesive a team of leaders to be found nearly anywhere in Africa ... No dramatic changes seem likely in Malawi's internal administration. [Since 1960] Malawi has been working its way through calm water ... and the calm water seems to stretch ahead out of sight.⁴

From within the cabinet, too, Cameron wrote publicly in July: 'the country has been united as never before' and its unity was 'second-to-none in East and Central Africa'.⁵ Phillips, expatriate minister of finance until independence, wrote a month earlier that 'If national unity, stability and purpose were alone the principal ingredients for social and economic progress, there have been few counties approaching independence better equipped than Nyasaland ... Under the leadership of the Prime Minister ... the unity of the country is beyond challenge.' Chipembere, too, said later that 'unity and goodwill prevailed'.⁶

Jones, who became Governor-General at independence, and who over the preceding three years had repeatedly told Banda that he had one hundred per cent following in the country, recalled that at independence: 'All seemed set fair for a happy and prosperous future.'⁷

Cole, however, without in any way drawing back from his view that the country was stable, firmly united behind Banda and unlikely to experience any changes in these respects, added that his ministers 'had from time to time been brought to the verge of resignation and revolt by Dr. Banda's refusal to accord them either respect or responsibility'. In fact, although no doubt some of the ministers seethed inwardly about the way Banda treated them, the only evidence that they had been brought to the verge of resignation was the readily withdrawn offer to resign by Dunduzu Chisiza, Mkandawire and Cameron two years previously – which was aimed at Chiume rather than Banda – and Chiume's, Chipembere's and Bwanausi's temptation earlier in 1964 not to stand for election as MCP candidates – about which Cole knew nothing – which *was* aimed at Banda.⁸ There is no other evidence that before independence they had been brought to the verge of revolt. Indeed, the ministers complaining about Chiume had made their loyalty to Banda clear. But, Cole continued,

> as the fireworks went up in the Stadium at midnight on 5th July, the situation was not as it outwardly appeared. The Ministers around Dr. Banda, who had previously restrained themselves in a commendable determination not to 'rock the boat' before independence, were already saying to themselves, 'After tomorrow all will be different: Malawi will become an African country: we shall become real Ministers: and Kamuzu will treat us with respect.'⁹

Cameron observed that during a large garden party at Government House during the independence celebrations 'all the ministers, apart from Chiume, were moving around from one to the other, seething with anger about Dr. Banda's dictatorial behaviour. It was as clear as daylight at that time that there was trouble ahead and serious trouble at that.'[10] Andrew Ross, too, recalled that:

> in the weeks in the run up to the independence celebrations, the ministers began to express openly to friends their uneasiness about Banda's leadership. They showed that they felt threatened in a way they had not before. [What they] all talked of was vague, but always included phrases like 'difficult times ahead', 'grave difficulties to overcome' and it was clear that they were not talking about the situation of the economy nor of international relations ... they were clear that the style of Dr Banda's leadership was central to all of this.[11]

In ignorance of, or more likely choosing to ignore, these portents, Banda left for London a few days after independence day, to attend the Commonwealth prime ministers' conference, and then travelled to Cairo for the OAU summit of heads of state. The Cairo conference had been delayed for two months – at Chiume's instigation – to allow Banda to attend as prime minister of an independent nation. Before he left Malawi, Cole called on him. The high commissioner had privately noticed, with surprise, that in none of Banda's nine or ten speeches at the independence celebrations did he mention 'the politics and ideals of African unity'. In the course of their conversation Cole said he thought Banda would be under many pressures from the OAU, and he received the reply 'simply that no one was going to push him around'.[12] The Ghanaian delegation to the independence celebrations also commented on the absence of African unity in Banda's speeches. They feared he was 'not well grounded ideologically' and attributed his contrary emphasis on the Commonwealth and the United Nations to Chiume. They seem to have had little understanding of either Banda or Chiume.[13]

While in London Banda had two meetings with Kenneth Neale of the Commonwealth Relations Office, who had been closely involved in dealings with Nyasaland over the past several years.[14] He found the doctor relaxed, having enjoyed his attendance at the prime ministers' conference. Banda felt he had not played as full a part in the conference as he would have wished, but was conscious of 'the need to feel his way forward in Commonwealth circles'. By and large, he was satisfied he had acquitted himself 'tolerably well'. They discussed the forthcoming financial talks that the Malawi government would have with the British treasury, and Banda revealed his intention to start moving the capital from Zomba to Lilongwe the following year so as to leave the Zomba premises free for the new university. He gave Neale this information in the strictest confidence, since – though he did not say so – he had not yet told his cabinet colleagues. On only one matter did Banda appear 'a little tetchy': a meeting the previous evening with the directors of Lonrho:

> They had told him that certain of his Ministers (in particular Bwanausi, the Minister of Development) and senior officials were openly accepting an attitude of extreme suspicion towards the company. This, they felt, seriously inhibited their proposals for further investment. [Banda] was irritated that such attitudes should be struck as they cut across his own position. His position seems to be that he is fully aware of the drawbacks of dealing with Lonrho but he does not feel able to do anything which might deter them or other investors ... There is no doubt that certain of his Ministers (particularly Cameron) have something of a feud against Lonrho but the indications are that he intends to take strong action about this. He has called a cabinet for Wednesday morning which is to be followed by a meeting of Permanent Secretaries. I strongly suspect that they are to be told to 'pipe down' on this subject and there may well be further changes.

It is clear that already, a few days after independence, Banda was dissatisfied with the attitudes of some of his ministers, particularly Bwanausi and Cameron, towards major commercial companies whose investment he saw as vital to the country's economic future. This dissatisfaction was sufficiently expressed to Neale for him to feel that Banda might make changes in his cabinet. There had already been one change. On 10 July a *Gazette* notice announcing the distribution of portfolios did not metion Msonthi's name. Instead, the portfolio of transport and communications was added to Banda's responsibilities.[15]

While Banda was away, Chirwa called on Lomax, the new head of Special Branch, and urged him to talk with Chisiza, who 'speaks for all of us', referring to himself, Chiume and Chipembere, which suggests that there was already some sort of coalition between the factions in the cabinet. When Lomax went to see Chisiza – whom he regarded highly on grounds of 'ability, moderation and courage'[16] – the minister spoke of his political anxieties. While, he said, completely loyal to Banda, he and his colleagues were concerned on a number of counts:

> Why had Mr. Msonthi been dismissed? Surely a reason should have been given? Much speculation on this followed. How could Ministers have any confidence if they were liable to be dismissed without explanation? The country really needed Dr. Banda. He was the only man who could lead it. But he would kill himself running six Ministries and taking all the decisions. [He] had promised that when independence came the Malawi

people would run their own country. But in fact they were not. If [he] tried to run six Ministries, the only possible consequence was that those Ministries were run, after independence, as they were before, by British civil servants. Dr. Banda used to say that the only way to learn to swim was to go straight into the water; but in fact he was not allowing his Ministers even to wet their feet.

Chisiza was also upset by the slow rate of Africanization and the recent promotions of many African clerical officers instead of 'some of the younger men of real quality whom the country needed'. He felt Banda might lose touch with reality and be told only what was agreeable to him. Lomax formed the view that Chisiza was trying to discover why Msonthi had been removed and to induce him to put something of these matters into his monthly intelligence report, 'in the hope that he would convey a warning of impending crisis to the Prime Minister'.[17] Presumably, Chisiza and his colleagues at this stage preferred this indirect approach to the alternative of directly confronting the doctor. He had already broached the promotion issue with Banda and 'got his head bitten off and been accused of disloyalty'. It is significant that even at this stage Chisiza was speaking in terms of 'impending crisis'. He also spoke to Jones about his worries, but it is probable that if Jones intended to mention them to Banda he would have picked his time and done so only indirectly and partially.

The Special Branch view at this time, well within a fortnight of independence, was that there was a feeling of disillusion in the country about independence not having produced many material benefits but rather that costs, for example of hospital attendance, were increasing and few were getting the jobs they had anticipated. This was not thought to be a grave feeling nor a threat to security, but it was worrying. Banda, Special Branch thought, did not seem to recognize the unrest among his ministers.[18]

All this took place while Banda was away in London and Cairo. His speech at the OAU summit was seen by Short as 'one of the most thoughtful and convincing' he had ever made. There was little of the 'repetitious woolliness which marred many of his public statements, and each point was made lucidly and forcefully, but without bombast'. In the course of a carefully worded, restrainedly defiant and forthright speech on Malawi's foreign policy he said:

> The independence of Malawi will be meaningless as long as there is an inch of African soil under colonialism and imperialism. I share the view ... that all independent African states and all African leaders must do everything possible in their power to help those countries which are still under the imperial yoke. [But] not all independent African states are in

the same position to help [and while] I am just as anxious as anyone in this conference to help our brothers and sisters still under colonial rule ... the geographical position of Malawi makes it impossible for me and my country to sever all ties, diplomatic, economic and cultural, with a certain power still controlling great portions of our continent.

As Short said, Banda's explanations were accepted and no one disputed his courage in stating these unpopular views or protested when he abstained from voting on a boycott of South Africa.[19] Four months earlier, he had 'cleared with Kenyatta, Nasser, Nkrumah and Haille Selassie his present policy of friendship and cooperation with Portugal which is dictated by the facts of Nyasaland's geographical position'.[20] Chipembere later acknowledged that Banda secured support and sympathy in the OAU for the views he stated in Cairo, and that Malawi had to 'soft pedal' in its relations with other southern African states.[21]

When Chiume, who was with him in Cairo but did not return with him, tried to persuade Banda to be more positive in condemning the Portuguese in Mozambique, the doctor became angry and refused to speak with him for the remainder of the summit.[22] Indeed, he was still angry when he arrived back in Malawi on 26 July.[23] In a speech echoing some of what he had said at the Zomba Debating Society, he told the crowd welcoming him at Chileka airport – which included the cabinet and the diplomatic corps – to 'Watch everybody! Even Ministers' and if they did things the people thought were not good for the MCP they were to report them to him.

> It is your job to see that nothing injures or destroys the Party. Ministers are human beings, you know. [We will] have strange funny people here very soon, Ambassador from this country, Ambassador from that country, and they will be trying to corrupt people in the Party, and they will be starting with Ministers and Members of the National Assembly. So I want you to be vigilant. One Party, one leader, one government, and no nonsense about it.[24]

Journalists observed that when Banda mentioned 'spies' being everywhere and sought the women's help in smelling them out, he 'waved his famous fly-whisk in an all-embracing gesture that seemed to take in the restive cabinet ministers'.[25]

Chipembere saw this speech as 'intended to sow distrust, contempt and dislike for the ministers among the people', and he claimed that although a few youths applauded, most of the audience were sad and remained silent; older people thought it in bad taste for Banda to insult his ministers in the presence of guests and foreigners.[26]

Youens, who was present, recalled that the ministers were placed just below Banda on the rostrum, 'sitting down at his feet almost prepared to applaud' when he delivered this part of his speech and the 'look of absolute astonishment' on their faces when they realized what he was saying. When Banda came down from the rostrum and went into the terminal building, Youens remarked to him, 'That was a very interesting but rather injudicious speech, wasn't it?' In reply he grinned and said, 'You know, Mr Youens, you are really rather naïve. I know what I am doing.'[27]

Chiume claimed that Banda's performance in Cairo was a dismal failure and he 'knew that the ambitious mission to build himself into an impressive African figure had failed. As Mr Bwanausi put it, the great *Ngwazi* had become a wounded buffalo. The big fish had failed to leap from the small pond into a larger one.' He also claimed that Banda, disappointed in the small crowd welcoming his return to Malawi, assumed his ministers had deliberately sabotaged his reception.[28]

These two July 1964 speeches, the one at Cairo, the other at Chileka, gravely upset Banda's ministers, and the extent of their displeasure, coupled with deeper concerns, was soon to be made known to him. Chiume – who saw the Chileka speech as the beginning of a 'bitter tussle'- recalled:

> The Ministers and party leaders were shocked and infuriated. We had been divided for a long time but this was the first occasion on which my colleagues saw the storm clouds in the sky. They realized to their horror all that this meant for the future. Those who had been divided were united overnight and determined to restore the dignity of Africa and of themselves as people. They knew that their authority among the people must have been grossly undermined and it would be difficult to regain that lost ground ... We had become a section to be reported on personally to the Prime Minister by any member of the Women's League or the Youth League at any time.
>
> My colleagues summoned an urgent meeting and each group – and there were two factions in the cabinet – confessed its 'sins'. They discovered that a detention bill had been in preparation for the last four or five months without their knowledge! They agreed to bury their differences; it had become a question of surviving or perishing together.[29]

The ministers were, however, anxious about whether Chiume would join them. They would have recalled that in 1962 when all the elected ministers had criticized him, Banda had done nothing about it. Having him on their side this time was vital, so they sent Chokani, who was not in Chiume's faction, to meet him at the airport. Chokani told him of the newfound unity among ministers – there were, as we have seen, already signs of a coalition between factions – and was greatly relieved when he agreed to join them. Chiume saw this agreement as less a matter of principle than 'a marriage of convenience'.[30] It may be that whereas Chiume had been able successfully to stand alone against his colleagues in 1962 when Chipembere was in prison, he realized he might not be able to do so in 1964 now that Chipembere was free and either had joined them or was likely to join them. He could withstand united opposition that did not include Chipembere, but not opposition that did include him.

Having agreed to join them, he then met with the other ministers at Chirwa's house, a house he had not entered until then because Chirwa also had not been in Chiume's grouping. The view was held by others that 'Chiume, at the very end, was opportunistic and when the chips were down and Banda was isolated he switched sides and became the strongest of the rebel ministers in his denouncing of Banda'.[31] The fact that Chiume was persuaded to join his colleagues as soon as he returned from Cairo indicates that he switched sides before, though not long before, the doctor became isolated. It could be argued that his switching sides brought about the isolation.

Two days after Banda made his Chileka speech, Tembo was sworn in as minister of finance. A little later in the day Banda visited Jones.[32] They spoke first of the recent expulsion of Msonthi from the cabinet because, it was thought, of accusations of disloyalty.

> The Prime Minister told me it was not so much an expulsion as a suspension from duty. He had received reports that Msonthi's behaviour was bringing the Government into disrepute and he wished to have these reports thoroughly investigated. If he subsequently found that they were unfounded he would ask Msonthi to rejoin the Government. He was not very explicit but I gathered that ... Msonthi was rather too talkative in his cups and ... there was a question of his relations with women. We have known from Special Branch for some time of Msonthi's weakness in these respects. Possibly [he has] also [been] accepting presents from commercial people.

Writing later of Msonthi and of Banda's motive in suspending him, Chipembere explained that 'he was quite a favorite of the Prime Minister, but he tended to incur his master's displeasure on all sorts of petty matters, some of them purely personal'.[33]

> It was also alleged that as Minister of Trade and Industry, he had been implicated in a scandal over the grant of trading licenses to Asian traders ... We believed that the Prime Minister's aim in dismissing him was to drop a hint of what he wanted to do to the rest of us. Msonthi was a kind of guinea pig; Dr. Banda was trying to gauge the likely consequences of dismissing a minister.[34]

If Chipembere was correct, then shortly before independence Banda must have contemplated dismissing other ministers, because he had decided to remove Msonthi before independence but had delayed it until after the celebrations, specifically at Msonthi's request. Within a few days of independence, Neale, as we have seen, understood that Banda would probably be making changes in his cabinet.

Having dealt with the Msonthi matter, Jones then – probably following Chisiza's representations to him, though it was a longstanding concern of his own – raised the question of Banda's heavy responsibilities and asked if he could not shed some of them, especially in view of his external commitments in the Commonwealth, the United Nations and the OAU, now that Malawi was independent. He thought the prime minister should restrict his internal responsibilities to law and order, defence and external affairs.

> However, I was not very successful in my approach because he told me what he has often told me before – that he finds it tolerably easy to manage his multifarious activities including the important functions of being the controller and watchdog of the Party – and that he was quite happy to carry on provided he was served by efficient civil servants. Moreover, he could not contemplate ... delegating portfolios such as agriculture, trade and industry to Ministers because he could trust none of them to withstand the advances that would be made to them by a certain class of Indian and European who he knew was quite prepared to bribe Ministers to obtain licences to grow certain crops and to conduct industries ... he could trust none of his Ministers to stand up to bribery.[35]

Banda's references to being controller and watchdog of the party and to ministers not being trusted to stand up to bribery were clearly related to his speech at Chileka. He repeated that he still had in mind making Malawi a republic on 1 April 1965 if legislation could be prepared before then. Jones got the impression, however, that he could be moved off this date if a good reason could be put forward.

The following day Banda held the usual Wednesday cabinet meeting – on 29 July at 9.30 a.m.[36] It was this meeting to which Neale had referred, and it may be that Banda did tell his ministers to 'pipe down' over opposing Lonrho. In any case, one of the items discussed, which Banda 'casually announced',[37] was his proposal to reintroduce detention without trial in the absence of a state of emergency. This was a proposal against which Jones had spoken to him exactly a year previously and the doctor had then agreed to delay its introduction.[38] Now, unshackled by any delaying or prohibiting steps the British government might take, he brought it forward again – at the first meeting of independent Malawi's cabinet. As the secretary to the cabinet recalled:

Cameron made it clear that he was not going to go along with that suggestion. He said that Banda was introducing the things which he, Cameron, had been highly critical of in the British Administration, and he was adopting the sort of worst practices taught him by the British and that he was not prepared to be associated with it and he got up from his chair in the cabinet and took his leave and said he was off. After he had gone Banda said, 'Anybody else want to go?' At that stage there were no volunteers.[39]

In view of his remark a few days earlier about knowing what he was doing, this question of Banda's suggests that he was deliberately inviting, or provoking, or challenging his ministers to come into the open and disagree with him.

Cameron has given his own account of what happened:[40]

> I had, along with the others, received my Cabinet Papers a few days before the meeting and was more than surprised to find 'Detention without Trial' on the Agenda with the legislation all drafted. I then went round all the Ministers with a view to assessing their position and to let my own position be known before the meeting.

He said that 'approval of the amendment would constitute the thin end of the wedge'. He asked his colleagues, 'What could Ministers do if, one morning, they walked into parliament and found the security bill on the order paper? The bill would be passed and the Ministers detained before they could get out of town.'[41] Cameron told them this was not a matter on which he could compromise. His account continued:

> At the Cabinet meeting all the business had been done in the normal way until it reached 'Detention Without Trial'. Ministers made comments for and against and I indicated that this was a situation where I felt that Dr. Banda as Prime Minister would know I, as a lawyer, could not accept, and I indicated that if this was to be pursued I would resign. Dr. Banda made no comment, one way or the other, but merely nodded his head. I stayed in the Cabinet Room while the debate went on on this matter, and it was clear all the Ministers were apprehensive, apart from Chiume, but were prepared to acquiesce and do what they could to minimise the effect later. The Cabinet then adjourned for coffee outside the Cabinet Room and I stayed for coffee with my colleagues, and when they returned to the Cabinet Room, I merely went downstairs, was picked up by my driver, returned to the Permanent Secretary and told him that I had resigned and the reason.

Phillips, former minister of finance, had moved out of his office at independence, but did not leave the country until a little later. He was therefore in close touch with Youens and Jones. His personal diary for 29 July recorded Cameron's resignation: 'there was quite a scene ... the other ministers were upset – probably getting a bit rebellious'.[42] He was right.

Chipembere's account of Cameron's resignation – which he saw as 'a symptom of the deteriorating political situation in the country' – was:

> Dr. Banda had had a Preventive Detention Bill in draft for some time, ready to get it passed by the cabinet and subsequently by Parliament at an opportune moment. It was an instrument to enable him to jail without trial any persons he considered dangerous to the security of Malawi ... When Dr. Banda introduced the draft of the Detention Bill, which was no doubt for detaining the now critical and therefore, to him, 'dangerous' ministers, Cameron severely criticised it. Dr. Banda declared that he was determined to go ahead with it, and that those who did not like it could resign; Cameron ... declared that he had spent the last few years fighting this very type of injustice committed by his own British people on the people of Malawi. He could not support it when it was perpetrated on the Malawi people by their own government. He was resigning. With those words he left the cabinet chamber.[43]

The important longer-term significance of this cabinet meeting was not so much Cameron's resignation, important as it was, but, first, that knowledge of the 'impending crisis', to which Chisiza had referred a week or so earlier, could no longer be kept within the cabinet – Phillips, for example, noted it in his diary, and ministerial changes had to be gazetted – and, second, the emboldening effect it had on the other ministers. Cameron recalled 'that the Ministers felt this was not a resignation matter but something they could change during the Cabinet and when the Regulations were brought into force'.[44] Chipembere later explained why the remaining members of the cabinet did not there and then force a showdown over this 'tricky and delicate issue'.[45] The people were still bitter about a number of leading Malawians – politicians and chiefs – who were considered traitors for having supported the colonial regime during Congress's struggle for freedom, and there were widespread demands that they should be punished. Banda privately had said he would detain them after independence. If the ministers had opposed the detention bill, Banda would have 'gone to the people to denounce [the ministers] for interfering with his intention to make the country safe by punishing the ... pro-colonial men'. They were sure Banda would have won that battle and the ministers would then have lost the chance to confront him on issues more favourable to their success. They confined themselves, therefore, merely to securing from the doctor a temporary withdrawal of the bill 'so that the more harsh parts of it could be studied thoroughly and if necessary amended', which is what they had told Cameron they preferred to do. It may be that the belief that Banda would defeat them in a head-on collision extended beyond the detention bill, at least in Chipembere's estimation, and was not the best strategy for getting him to change his ways generally.[46] Chipembere nevertheless saw this temporary withdrawal of the detention bill as a victory for the ministers – never before had they managed to get the doctor to hold back on a measure about which he felt strongly – and this further encouraged them in their determination to get him to change his policies.

During the afternoon of his resignation Cameron was visited by Chirwa and Chisiza. Ross also was there. The ministers described what had happened after Cameron left the cabinet meeting: 'Chiume alone had welcomed the legislation enthusiastically and derided Cameron's scruples which had led to his resignation.' They reluctantly agreed with Cameron when he pointed out that, since there was no real opposition to the MCP in the country, the legislation 'could only be aimed at them if they stepped out of line'.[47] If indeed Chisiza and Chirwa were giving an accurate account in saying that Chiume expressed enthusiasm for the legislation – and, supporting this, we have seen that Cameron noticed the obvious apprehension of all the ministers, *apart from Chiume* – then either he was deliberately giving Banda a false impression of enthusiasm, or he had not genuinely thrown in his lot with his colleagues. The former is the more likely, though the reason is unclear.

Chiume's account, possibly telescoping two meetings, of this cabinet meeting and what happened thereafter was:

> Our confrontation with Banda took place ... at the first cabinet meeting after his return from London and Cairo.[48] On the agenda of that meeting was a proposed constitutional change which would permit preventative detention without the declaration of a state of emergency ... We seized upon the opportunity to tell the Prime Minister that we were not happy with the way he had elected to do things just before and after independence ... In that stormy cabinet meeting, the constitutional amendment was approved, but the bill itself was shelved. Dr. Banda had, for the first time, been opposed and beaten ... Within forty-eight hours of Cameron's resignation, the reasons for it were known among all the civil servants of Blantyre and Zomba, many of whom knew the bill was meant for them too.[49]

Almost immediately after the cabinet meeting Cameron saw Jones and told him he had resigned because of the proposed detention legislation.[50] The Governor-General suggested Cameron should go to Banda to see if it was possible to reach a compromise. Even if this were not possible, he thought it would be a good idea to have 'a quiet candid conversation' to ensure that they retained cordial relations. Cameron did as Jones suggested and then came back to see him again, in the early evening:

> [He had] a very cordial and frank discussion with Dr. Banda[51] ... The Prime Minister is adamant that ... the Constitution must be altered [but] has decided at this stage merely to introduce an enabling clause ... and does not propose to introduce the Public Safety Preservation Bill at least until after he has been to America and possibly discussed the matter with someone in the United Nations.[52]
>
> Cameron went on to say that ... the other Ministers are very concerned about this legislation because they feel that it is unneccessary and ... they themselves may in the future be victims of it. They are also ... becoming more and more dissatisfied because Dr. Banda treats them as small boys and publicly belittles them ...
>
> Cameron ... would not retreat from the position he had adopted and there was no possibility of Dr. Banda climbing down.[53]

Cameron had told Banda he considered that his refusal to repose trust in his ministers 'would lead to future trouble'. The doctor, however, was convinced that 'there was a strong bond between himself and the people and that none of the Ministers could stand without his support'. Cameron did not believe this and thought Banda would have 'no support in the Fort Johnston district if Chipembere were removed from the Cabinet, or in the Karonga district if Chisiza were removed'. Three and a half years earlier the head of Special Branch had thought Chipembere's following so strong that to remand him in custody might 'set the country alight' and to prosecute him would 'ignite a powder train'.

The British government was relaxed about Banda's wish that Malawi should become a republic, though they felt that with 1 April 1965 in mind 'it does come rather hard on the heels of independence, particularly having regard to the position of the Crown', and preferred Banda's previous date of November 1965.[54] Banda – egged on by Blackwood, who wanted an early announcement[55] – continued for a while to insist on making the announcement in parliament on 2 September. He would send a message to the Queen to this effect and would, reluctantly, give advance notice to other Commonwealth countries. This reluctance stemmed from his fear of a leak, especially in Kenya and Ghana.[56] Presumably he did not want his ministers to learn about it and the additional powers it would give him, before he announced it in public.

Neither Banda nor his ministers left things where they were after Cameron's resignation. On 31 July, Banda met Jones again and although the doctor would not change his mind on detention without trial, there was no ill feeling between him and Cameron, who he hoped would stay and have a successful career in Malawi. They had agreed there would be no official announcement, and any press enquiries should be directed to Cameron, who would simply say he had resigned because of a difference of principle.[57] Banda was keen to appoint another European to the cabinet in Cameron's place. They discussed a number of possibilities, but all were already 'satisfactorily employed'. Finally, Banda suggested Major Peter Moxon as a possibility for the portfolio of public works, and asked Jones to 'make enquiries as to his present mode of life, and if such enquiries revealed that Moxon was leading a sober and respectable life the Prime Minister might within the next ten days nominate him' as a minister. A week later Banda asked Jones to see Moxon again – he had seen him on 1 August[58] – and tell him he was being considered as a replacement for Cameron.[59] They agreed that Moxon was not an ideal candidate, but he did have good qualities and was 'liked by many Africans and some Europeans'. Jones was also asked to tell him the reason for Cameron's resignation and that if Banda decided to appoint him it 'would be on the strict understanding that he would give loyal support to Government's policy in regard to changing the constitution to permit detention without trial'. If Moxon shared Cameron's objections there would be no point in offering him the post. If he could find a suitable European to accept a ministerial post, Banda would like him to be in the cabinet 'indefinitely'. At their meeting on 11 August, Jones suggested that Morgan, the European member of parliament for Lilongwe 'would feel able to accept a cabinet post without much trouble', but the prime minister quickly said Morgan was 'entirely unacceptable'. They agreed that there would be difficulty in finding an acceptable European for a cabinet post:

> Any white person acceptable to Dr Banda and the majority of the Africans would inevitably be a person who would feel unable to agree with the preventive detention proposals while ... any white person who felt able to accept these proposals would be unacceptable to the Prime Minister and the majority of the Africans.[60]

Jones saw Cameron and Moxon on 12 August and Cameron alone the following day.[61] Cameron recalled: 'Banda offered Peter Moxon my Portfolio but he refused on the ground that he would not take my place and, secondly, he would not agree to detention without trial either.'[62] While these grounds were undoubtedly valid, it was also the case that Moxon was disappointed in the post offered. Some months earlier he had told Jones that because he was in financial difficulty with his business, he would like to be given a government post:

> We talked about the possibility of my rejoining the army and agreed that

if I did so it would be certain that before long I should become Commander of the Malawi Army with particular responsibility for training the new African officers ... to a position where they could be fitted for high rank in the shortest possible time. Another possibility was that I should become 'Chief of Staff' acting as a professional link between the Prime Minister (who would hold the defence portfolio) and the commander, a post for which he thought my professional training combined with my political record made me particularly well fitted. [Jones] said he would discuss this with Dr Banda and General Lea, temporarily in command of all forces in Northern Rhodesia and Malawi.[63]

When Jones told Banda that Moxon had asked to be commissioned in the Nyasaland Army, the doctor 'did not think this would be a good thing' since Moxon would expect to stay in post when the other white officers left and 'indeed become the commanding officer'. Banda did, however, recognize that Moxon needed a job, and promised to try and find him one, possibly with the farmers' marketing board.[64] Jones almost certainly expected this response and was doing no more with Moxon than simply 'tagging him along'. He must have known that there was no possibility that Banda would have agreed to his being a member, still less a senior member, of his military forces. His military experience was well in the past and his political record, to Banda, was suspect. To have entrusted the army to him would have been even more dangerous for the doctor than to have entrusted the police to Yatuta Chisiza.

Several years later, Chipembere, looking back on the events following the Chileka speech, said:

> Now Dr. Banda had gone too far, and we decided to have a meeting to discuss what action should be taken to bring to an end these public attacks. We found ourselves to be unanimous in our feeling that the Prime Minister was wrong in thinking that these attacks did harm only to the political image of his ministers; the damage was, we felt, being done to the reputation of Malawi as a whole and to its government in particular ... We were unanimous that the Prime Minister's attacks on us would adversely affect discipline in our departments and in the party ... We decided to seek an immediate audience with the Prime Minister.[65]

Chiume also recalled the decision unitedly to confront Banda and, in addition to the Chileka speech, placed emphasis on the effect of Cameron's resignation, which made it quite clear that unless they fought vigorously, they would all land up in detention. 'We therefore had a meeting to take stock of the situation. We were determined to finally sink our differences in the face of a common danger. We met again on the 6th [August] for the same purpose.'[66]

The date of the confrontation meeting with Banda is unclear. Although the ministers had agreed among themselves, probably on 27 or 28 July, to confront Banda, they decided not to do so at the cabinet meeting of 29 July when Cameron resigned. Instead they met just after the cabinet meeting and again the following day, 30 July, to decide what to do. The confrontation could not have been before then. Chiume said the ministers 'met again on the 6th' which indicates the earliest date as being 6 August. There was a cabinet meeting on 12 August,[67] and had the confrontation taken place in cabinet Youens and Jones would immediately have known about it. In writing on 11 August about a meeting he had with Banda the previous day, Jones said, 'I know that Cabinet Ministers are dissatisfied, both about the preventive detention proposals and also about the Prime Minister's refusal to delegate powers, and that they have made complaints to him on both these subjects.'[68] This knowledge indicates that the representations, including the question of delegation, had been made before 11 August. When Chirwa met Jones on 24 and 25 August, he said the meeting had taken place about two weeks previously.[69] Given Chiume's known propensity not to be present when trouble was brewing, it is likely that he was not at the meeting. Although Chirwa told Jones that all the ministers were present, Short says Chiume was in Dar es Salaam and did not attend the meeting,[70] and Ross says that when ministers went to confront Banda they 'deliberately choose to go only after Chiume had left the country on an overseas visit'.[71] He left for East Africa on or about 10 August. It is likely that the meeting took place on 10 August 1964.[72]

At this meeting,[73] the ministers complained to Banda about, first, his 'slighting references' to them in his public speeches and, second, his keeping too many government functions in his own hands. He initially gave vent to a display of anger but then gave them a patient three-hour hearing, at the end of which they were left with the impression that he promised to give attention to their complaints and to 'reform his ways'.

> He was extremely reluctant to see us as a group and suggested that we come one by one. His eternal fear of people 'ganging together' manifested itself once more. When he finally agreed to see us we were frank and courageous. We pointed out to him all the implications and likely consequences of the type of speech he had made at Chileka Airport on his return from Cairo. After much prevarication, he said that although he did not agree that he had been wrong to make that type of speech, since we had objected to it he promised that he would not make such a speech again in future.[74]

It is probable that by giving the impression he intended to reform his ways, Banda was diverting them, raising their confidence in the possibility of change – and so making them over-confident – and giving himself time to decide how to handle them. He may have had the same motives when he temporarily withdrew the detention proposal. The day following this meeting he told Jones he had now 'firmly decided that Malawi should become a republic on 1 April 1965 and would wish to announce this somewhat earlier than he had originally intended', that is, before 2 September.[75]

Chipembere saw this meeting as another turning point, both in their relations with Banda and in the history of the country. First, they discovered that it was possible for the ministers to overcome their differences and rivalries, which Banda had fostered, and unite on a matter of principle. Second, they discovered, they thought, that if they were united in pressing him he would in fact change his methods and policies. Third, their fear of a violent outburst disappeared. To their surprise, the doctor seemed to lose his poise in the face of their 'barrage of arguments and objections against his Chileka speech' and at times became incoherent – but not enraged. The success of their united approach induced them to resolve not to allow Banda or anyone else – a possible reference to the Governor-General – or any issue to divide them, and in order to ensure lasting unity, they agreed that all decisions would be made only after discussion by them all. They also agreed that because their own 'excessive praising and glorifying of the Prime Minister had contributed in no small way to his feeling that he knew everything and need not consult anyone', in future they would tone down their praise. They decided, too, to capitalize on the gains they believed they had made, and use their 'new strong position and psychological victory' to press him to change certain aspects of his domestic and external policies.[76]

At his meeting with Banda on 11 August Jones brought up the question of the prime minister's relationships with members of his cabinet, but 'he was not very forthcoming on this subject. [He] continues to show every appearance of being quite relaxed and happy with the present situation.'[77] The Governor-General hoped that 'even at the eleventh hour' the doctor would feel able to change his mind about the detention legislation, but he was 'quite obdurate', and Jones got the impression that Blackwood had told him he would support the measure.[78]

There was a lull in the fortnight following the ministers' meeting with Banda on 10 August. Jones was away at Gorongoza viewing game from 15 to 19 August. Chiume went off to Tanzania and was shortly joined by Bwanausi and Chisiza for a tour of game parks there and in Kenya and Zambia, where they adopted what they called 'the Momela resolution which stressed the need for a change in Banda's attitude to make him fall in line with the rest of Africa in respecting his people and their aspirations'. They agreed that they were prepared to be 'sacked and locked up rather than be a party to the betrayal of the people of Malawi and Africa'. On 19 August Chipembere went off to a conference in Canada. Save for Chipembere, they were all back by 23 August.[79]

On 19 August the Governor-General told the British high commissioner that all ministers except Tembo were opposing Banda on two fundamental points: his refusal to transfer authority to them, and his publicly insulting them. Cameron told Jones that all the ministers had sent a joint letter to Banda, but he doubted this because he had detected no change in the prime minister's attitude. It is possible that they were contemplating writing a joint letter setting out their complaints, either as an alternative to, or in addition to, a further confrontation meeting. Jones was less optimistic than he had been and feared that, at the very worst, Banda would at some stage declare a state of emergency 'lock up all his Ministers and replace them with stooges'. Youens saw no change at cabinet meetings and this made Cole wonder whether the ministers had 'the guts to press the issue with Banda'. He thought the only one of them who might do so was Chisiza, whom he found 'friendly, moderate, intelligent and forceful'. Cole, feeling twinges that he may have been mistaken about the country's solidarity and stability, now held the view that:

> A number of his Ministers, e.g. Mr. Chipembere, are extremely popular. Indeed, Dr. Banda probably has no idea of the extent to which his own position depends on the popularity of his Ministers. There could, therefore, in these circumstances – and I repeat the word 'could' – be rumblings among the police and soldiers and elsewhere in the country. No doubt under present conditions the situation could be contained if only because so much of the machinery of Government, including the police and army, is still under expatriate direction ... On the other hand, Dr. Banda and his Ministers might perhaps patch up this quarrel and then all would be well. If they do not do so, it looks as if the prospects ... are rather worrying.[80]

On Monday 24 August Chirwa secretly visited the Governor-General.[81] He told him about the meeting he and his colleagues had had with Banda two weeks earlier, and added that the ministers had decided they could no longer tolerate the doctor's conduct. He was becoming increasingly dictatorial and was making important decisions without consulting his cabinet. Chirwa instanced the recent appointment of Jardim as Malawi's honorary consul in Beira and the trade agreement with Portugal. His appointment of Aleke Banda as head of community development was deeply resented. A feeling of great insecurity had been created in the ministers by Msonthi's expulsion from the cabinet with no reasons given. Furthermore, Banda's acceptance of the Skinner report was most unpopular, and the continuing power of expatriate civil servants was much criticized. The people were accusing the ministers of simply being 'yes men'. Their morale was 'rock bottom'.

Chirwa continued that since their meeting with the prime minister there had not, contrary to their expectations, been any reforming of Banda's ways. They were now in determined mood and were about to tackle him again. The Governor-General should not be surprised if he received Banda's resignation during the next forty-eight hours. He asked Jones to take no action other than give Banda tactful 'Queen's advice' about delegating responsibilities to his ministers. Chirwa and his colleagues looked forward to Jones staying in Malawi for 'at least a year after independence', to which he replied he was 'not sure about that' and advised him to ask the prime minister at an early date whether he had formed any view on the matter. It seems that Chirwa – fearing the power of an executive president – was 'fishing' for information on Banda's proposals for republican status and that Jones was encouraging him to tackle the doctor on it and bring his intentions out into the open. He knew that Banda had 1 April 1965 in mind and that he intended to make an early announcement about it. Chirwa went on to say that Banda placed so little confidence in his ministers because the top civil servants were undermining them. Jones strongly rejected this view. Chipembere later said he also believed British officials were feeding Banda with false reports on them, in order to maintain their own positions.[82]

Jones told Chirwa that he appreciated the ministers' feelings that they were being slighted, belittled and deprived of the opportunity to exercise their full responsibilities as members of the cabinet, where the principle of collective responsibility should be observed. He in effect told Chirwa he agreed with the substance of their complaints. Chipembere later said the Governor-General told Banda that, at least on the question of consultation, the ministers 'were quite right',[83] and Chiume received the impression from Chirwa that 'Jones felt that some of the grievances [they] voiced against Banda were genuine and needed redress'.[84] To that extent the Governor-General was encouraging the ministers in their confrontation with the prime minister. Chirwa repeatedly told Jones that Malawi must not be allowed to become 'a dictatorship like Ghana'. He was worried about the country becoming a republic, although he did not see this happening for some time. It seems that at this time

> the nearest thing to a plan that [the ministers, as opposed to Banda, had] was the suggestion that when a republican constitution was created, as was planned [by them] for the future, it would include a very honourable but essentially non-executive presidency which Banda would be forced into. The country would then be run by a cabinet led by a prime minister.[85]

Jones told Chirwa he could not intervene and – strangely, in view of the possible resignation of the prime minister – did not give him any advice as to how he should proceed save to see Banda, which he agreed to do that evening.[86] Chirwa called on Jones again the following day and presumably he reported either on a visit to Banda the previous evening or, more likely, that a visit had not taken place.

Soon after Chirwa left him on 24 August, the Governor-General told Cole about their meeting and said that when all the ministers – except Tembo – went to see Banda, on 10 August, he had 'immediately offered to resign, warning Cabinet however that in that event all external aid to Malawi would cease'. The ministers said they had no wish for him to resign. Since their meeting, Banda had been much more agreeable towards his ministers, but was giving them no greater authority than previously. Rather, the increasing authority of Aleke Banda outside the cabinet was deeply resented.[87] Cole reported that Jones also told him the ministers had spoken 'individually on various occasions to [him] and asked him to intervene with the Prime Minister',[88] but this is inconsistent with Chirwa, on their behalf, asking him *not* to take any action other than to give advice, and there is no evidence in Jones's papers that other ministers did approach him at this stage.

Whether or not the ministers really wished or intended to induce Banda to resign, and whether or nor he went so far as offering to resign, they seem to have accepted in mid-August 1964 that this was a possible outcome of their representations. Chipembere later said:

> It is true that by the beginning of 1964 we were already unhappy with his policies and his increasingly authoritarian methods, but we hoped to be able to persuade him to change, and it was only after failing to get him to change and after the final parting of the ways, which came in September 1964, that we began to think in terms of getting him removed from power.[89]

Chirwa's references to the ministers being about to tackle Banda again and to a possible resignation during the coming forty-eight hours indicate that they intended to provoke a situation at the latest at the cabinet meeting two days later, on 26 August, in which Banda would either agree to reform his ways or, as they believed was more likely, would offer to resign. Chiume, too, said, 'We decided ... to confront Banda, together with other colleagues, at the cabinet meeting on August 26th.'[90] Since Chirwa was addressing Jones in secrecy, the request that he do nothing except tender tactful advice implies that he wanted Jones not to tell Banda about their meeting and neither to accept nor reject his resignation but simply give advice, presumably to mend his ways. If this is so, then the ministers probably hoped that, in the absence of being able themselves to persuade Banda to reform, they could provoke him to the point where he would feel he should offer his resignation, would go to Jones to do so, the Governor-General would add his view supporting the ministers and advise him not to resign but instead to reform his ways, whereupon he would withdraw his tendered resignation and all thereafter would be well, with the ministers enjoying more ministerial autonomy and greater collective cabinet responsibility.

The day following Chirwa's second meeting with Jones, there was a long meeting of the cabinet, from 9.30 a.m. to 2.45 p.m.[91] Banda, Chiume, Chirwa, Tembo, Bwanausi, Chokani and Chisiza were present. Cameron had resigned, Chipembere was still in Canada and Msonthi was not currently a member of the cabinet.[92] Youens, secretary to the cabinet, with David Ellams, clerk to the cabinet, were in attendance. The early items on the agenda were dealt with fairly amicably, although even in these there were signs of trouble.[93]

The first item on the agenda of this meeting, on Wednesday 26 August, was a proposal to alter the constitution to allow for the appointment of ministers who would not be members of the cabinet.[94] This stemmed from the appointment on 14 August of the three regional chairmen of the MCP – McKinley Chibambo, Richard Chidzanja and Gomile Kumtumanji – as regional ministers, in order to give them appropriate political status.[95] The constitution allowed the appointment of ministers without restriction of numbers but it also provided that all ministers should be members of the cabinet.[96] Strictly speaking – though this was not said – they were already members of the cabinet. This was not what Banda wished at the time and consequently he was seeking to have the constitution altered.[97] The cabinet ministers should have been relieved that the regional ministers were not also to be members of the cabinet, but they did not let the opportunity pass to say they hoped the regional ministers would not be allowed to interfere in the work of their ministries. Chiume, who had himself been accused of interfering in the work of other ministers, in 1962, said he had already had to warn the central regional minister – Chidzanja – about this and added that regional ministers should respect the seniority and superior status of cabinet ministers: Chidzanja was 'notable for his failure to show such respect'. Banda replied that he would correct this defect in the regional ministers.

Possibly with the intention of drawing out the ministers, Banda went on to say that civil servants, too, especially African civil servants, should show proper respect to ministers. Many civil servants were inclined to take advantage of their earlier acquaintance with ministers and 'treat them with undue familiarity'. This point, which it was not strictly necessary for the prime minister to raise, gave Chirwa and Chiume the opportunity, while agreeing, to point the finger at European civil servants and say that they also were at fault. Banda himself had not found

European officers lacking in respect, but Chiume – long a severe and open critic of expatriate civil servants – said some of them were using the prime minister's name to issue instructions purporting to come from him but which in fact did not represent his wishes. A number of European officers had inflated ideas of their importance and powers. The secretary to the prime minister, Youens, was particularly at fault. He appeared to labour under the delusion that he was the deputy prime minister.[98] Chiume, Chisiza, Chirwa and Tembo gave examples of the actions of top European civil servants to which they objected. They were in effect attacking Banda's main political and administrative supports – the regional ministers and the expatriate permanent secretaries. With this, albeit for the present limited, ventilation of their grievances, the ministers then agreed to the proposed amendment to the constitution.

If Banda at this stage had wanted to ensure the presence of people on his side in the cabinet he could easily have had the new ministers there. Maybe he really wanted the cabinet ministers to revolt as a group so that he could deal with them together rather than piecemeal. It is extremely unlikely that he feared the regional ministers would be won over to the rebels' side. They were tough MCP leaders, known to be loyal to Banda, and were older and less well educated than the cabinet ministers. He appointed them as regional ministers only four days after the initial confrontation meeting. In this way he would get them on his side, strengthen his authority in the regions, put a warning shot across the bows of the cabinet ministers and show them the importance he attached to the party, as opposed to the cabinet. He may also have been showing the new ministers that he had confidence in them and would reward them. Perhaps, too, he had already detected the antagonism between the cabinet ministers and the regional ministers that Chiume had just expressed, and wished to use it to his own advantage.

The cabinet turned next to the second item on its agenda, a bill to set up a provisional council for the proposed University of Malawi. Banda introduced this item and said the post of vice-chancellor had been offered to a European academic. Both Banda and Chipembere had been impressed when they met him recently. Chiume opened the discussion by saying that, while the establishment of a university would be widely welcomed, he was concerned about the appointment of an expatriate vice-chancellor and he urged that a Malawian understudy be appointed at an early date. Banda, in general agreement with appointing understudies eventually to take over, pointed to the ability of high-calibre expatriate staff to attract outside investment into the university. This also was not a strictly necessary remark and may have been designed further to draw out the ministers. Whether or not this was Banda's intention, it certainly had that effect. Chiume countered: 'Many countries of the world were not impressed by Europeans who purported to speak for African nations. The time had now come when Africans should speak for themselves.' Banda's response was gentle and measured. He was in general agreement with this view but 'those Europeans who had contacts with, and some influence over, sources of financial aid, were thereby better placed than some to obtain such assistance'. Chiume returned to his point and maintained that experience in East Africa showed that 'Africans could speak for themselves', and their own leaders had secured substantially greater help from Britain at independence than had the expatriates from Malawi. Tembo agreed with Chiume that indigenous representatives were more likely than expatriate negotiators to receive favourable hearings when seeking external aid. He thought, too, that borrowing money from Eastern Bloc countries would not, as had been suggested, deter Western investment. Chiume believed they should not allow themselves to be taken for granted by the Western powers; he would like permission to lead Malawi missions to Moscow and Peking and thought Eastern technicians could be used to help develop the country's natural resources.

Once more Banda's reply to these points was gentle as he explained that the British support of Kenya, unlike Malawi, contained little new money. There were particular circumstances in Malawi that required them to depend on Britain for financial support for some time to come. He had always made it clear that Malawi was committed to neither the East nor the West. He did not object to the missions Chiume had suggested, but he warned that Eastern aid was often tied to conditions that might be inimical to the recipient country's interest. He did not challenge the assertion that Communist aid would not deter Western investment, though he probably believed it would.

Chirwa intervened to agree that it was necessary to maintain British support for some time to come and desirable to retain the services of some expatriates. 'There were, however, dangers in this. When the people of Malawi saw many Europeans ... holding high official posts, they felt that they were still being ruled by the Europeans.' Although Banda undoubtedly saw the danger signs in this point – since it undermined his basic intention that Africanizing official posts should be gradual and only when suitable Malawians were trained and experienced sufficiently to take over – his response continued to be restrained. It was essential that the country should not be seen as anti-European but rather should find a balance. Malawians must be given the opportunity to acquire experience and expertise and in the meantime expatriates would 'impart their experience within the country and engender confidence outside it'.

Banda rounded off the discussion by telling his colleagues that 'already the greater proportion of the money needed for the Development Plan had been promised' and, though he did not highlight the point, promised from Western sources. Ministers then agreed that the draft bill should be published and introduced into the next session of parliament.

So far in the meeting, the criticisms of Banda's policies and methods of operating, though only thinly veiled, *were* none the less veiled, and he had responded reasonably and patiently, explaining his rationale for the views he was taking and giving ministers rather fuller information than they already possessed. By giving these explanations, and to that extent sharing his views and taking his colleagues into his confidence somewhat more than previously, he may have hoped his ministers would feel he had taken to heart the points they had made to him two weeks previously and that he was indeed beginning to reform his ways. Whether or not this was his intention, he had been able fairly amicably to bring discussion to a close and to secure agreement to the two items so far dealt with. This was not to last.

After a minor item about subsidiary factories legislation, Chokani, minister of labour, introduced a paper about an agreement with the Witwatersrand Native Labour Association (WNLA), which had been entered into by the colonial government some time previously. Thirty thousand Malawians were recruited each year under this agreement for work in the South African mines. Since one of the association's directors was shortly to visit Malawi, he thought this was an appropriate time to negotiate a new agreement to 'reflect the constitutional changes which had recently taken place'. The proposed changes in themselves ought to have been uncontroversial and, if accepted, would lead to increased revenue for the government and continued employment for many thousands of its citizens. The agreement could in any case be terminated on a year's notice. It is likely that Chokani, with his colleagues' encouragement, had this apparently innocuous item placed on the agenda deliberately to provide an opening for ministers to launch an attack on Banda, his policies and his methods of operating as prime minister. It is possible, too, that the ministers had not intended to use the earlier items on the agenda for this purpose, although some of them had been unable to resist the opportunity to have a preliminary go at him. In any event, they had not pushed Banda so far that he had reacted intemperately. Chiume was ready to lead the attack by harking back to his disagreement with Banda's foreign policy statement at the Cairo summit:

> Malawi had been accused of refusing to make sacrifices in the cause of African freedom. He agreed that the country was in a most difficult position with regard to its neighbours to the South, but there was, nevertheless, an undercurrent of feeling that Malawi was not truly sympathetic to African aspirations ... He advised most strongly against the signing of a new Agreement. Should African countries turn their face against Malawi the economic progress of the country would be gravely impeded. [He]

agreed that it might be undesirable to stop the flow of workmen to South Africa, but questioned whether it was essential to continue to accept the annual grant of £120,000 [which WNLA paid to the government]. He thought that it might be sensible to cancel the agreement while continuing to allow the Association to operate.

Chiume was understandably opposed in principle to the Malawi government having dealings with South Africa, but his most immediate objection was to bringing the world's attention, especially the attention of other African counties, to the matter by entering into a new agreement.

Chirwa had additional concerns. Under the proposed changes to the agreement, the Mozambique government had agreed that Africans from that country could be recruited in Malawi. He felt 'some concern' that ministers had not been told in advance that the prime minister was negotiating with, and intended to visit, Mozambique. The price Malawi would be asked to pay for its friendship with Mozambique was too high and its dealings with Portugal were earning the country 'a bad name throughout Africa'. Momentarily forgetting the recent pact of unity between the factions in the cabinet, he was critical of Chiume's 'two-faced approach' that the agreement be cancelled but the association be allowed to continue to operate. Bwanausi thought it wrong to seek to obtain more money from South Africa, and Tembo, while saying that the money involved was 'of considerable importance', believed the political costs of a new agreement were serious. Chokani agreed with his colleagues' political objections but said the country had a serious unemployment problem. Not only would terminating the agreement lose a good deal of money for the country – in the form of grants, family remittances and emigrant worker savings – a point Tembo supported, but he anticipated it would bring serious internal labour unrest, a point Bwanausi supported.

Throughout the whole of the discussion so far on the WNLA agreement, Banda had spoken only once, and then briefly, to say that the Commonwealth prime ministers' conference had doubted whether boycotting South Africa would in fact serve the purposes prompting it. Now, probably with the intention of bringing discussion to a close as he had, successfully, with that on the university, he said

> He had allowed a long discussion on this subject because of the important matters of principle which it raised. He was aware that a campaign against Malawi was being mounted by her ill-wishers ... Nevertheless there was another side to the picture. He referred to the delegation from the Economic Commission for Africa which [had recently visited the country]. In their discussion with him the delegation emphasised that there was new thought in the Economic Commission and the Organisation of African

Unity as a result of what he had said in Cairo. The leader of the delegation had explained that African statesmen well understood the problems which faced Malawi. The indication was that he had been able to convince African leaders that his policies were based on a realistic appreciation of certain inescapable factors. It would be to the country's ultimate advantage for its leaders to be seen as mature men who were prepared to face the realities which confronted them and to deal with them on the basis of what was in the best interests of the people as a whole.

This last remark implied that he did not think his colleagues were behaving in a mature, realistic fashion with the country's best interests in mind. He believed the annual financial grant from the association was less important than the problem of unemployment. If workers went to South Africa other than through the association, they risked being imprisoned. 'The plain fact was that a decision to terminate the activities of WNLA must be expected to give rise to considerable labour unrest in Malawi [and] there would be an upheaval in Malawi.' Although he did not say so explicitly, he was much more concerned with the effect of the cabinet's decisions on the people of Malawi – from whom his support came – than he was with the country's external reputation. He probably also thought he might have enough trouble handling an escalating conflict with his ministers without having difficulties with labour unrest.

If Banda had hoped these remarks would bring discussion to a close, he was mistaken, for Chiume, Chirwa and Chisiza came back at him, which reinforces the probability that this item had been put on the agenda to give the opportunity to ministers more fully to ventilate their grievances.

Chiume, referring to what Banda had said about the Economic Commission for Africa delegation, claimed that many people visiting Malawi said one thing to the prime minister's face and another behind his back when they left. He would do well to recognize that many of the people who worked for international organizations were 'political rejects in their own country'.

Chirwa said the international campaign against South Africa and Portugal was sincere and, returning to the point he had made earlier, he hoped ministers would be kept informed of proposed visits by the prime minister and others to Mozambique. This 'and others' was probably a reference to Jones having spent part of the previous week in Mozambique as a guest of Jardim. No doubt recalling the Governor-General's advice two days previously, he added: 'The constitutional principle of collective responsibility was involved. It was difficult for Ministers to defend the Prime Minister's action if they were not consulted in advance on what he intended to do.'

Chisiza, who so far had said nothing – and who, it will be recalled, Cole considered the only minister likely to 'have the guts' to press the issues firmly with Banda and who, too, was the first to speak of an impending crisis – now intervened:

> In all sincerity he must speak out at this point. The Prime Minister had allowed him to travel extensively and hitherto he had been highly respected as one of the Prime Minister's men. On his recent visit to East Africa he had found this situation drastically changed. Whereas Malawi had ranked high in world esteem, the reverse was now true. It was said that Malawi was a traitor to the cause of Africa. He had, together with [Chiume], tried to refute the criticisms directed against Malawi, but had not been able to do so effectively. It appeared that the Prime Minister trusted his European civil servants more than his own Ministers, and yet he must know that Ministers were more loyal than the expatriate civil servants. The Prime Minister had too many ministries; he could not possibly devote sufficient time to [them] and it appeared that the Government was still controlled by expatriate European civil servants. These men came between the Prime Minister and his Ministers. These were the people who had put the Prime Minister, himself and others, in prison. These officers, such as the Secretary to the Prime Minister, were the enemies of the country. It was a dangerous and disgraceful situation.[99]

This was the last shot in the particular skirmish arising out of the WNLA agreement. The list of grievances had grown substantially from that reported to Jones by Chirwa as having been the subject of the ministers' original discussion with Banda: his slighting references to them and his personal retention of too many portfolios. Chiume, having already criticized the attitudes of the regional ministers, the appointment of a European vice-chancellor and the power of expatriate officials, had now emphasized the dangers of Malawi's pro-South Africa, pro-Portugal, exclusively pro-West external relations policies and had doubted Banda's judgement as to the quality of those who worked for international organizations. Chirwa, having already criticized the appointment of expatriates to high office and the apparent continued rule by European civil servants, had now emphasized Banda's failure to consult and give information to his cabinet colleagues, and the importance of collective responsibility. Tembo, having already criticized the reliance on expatriates, the exclusive dependency on Western aid and the shunning of Communist Bloc help, now spoke of the political costs of accepting South African money, though he realized its considerable financial value. Bwanausi, who recognized the unemployment and labour unrest potentialities of shunning South Africa, now said he believed it would be wrong to seek further money from that country. Chokani, restrained by the fact that it was he who brought the WNLA agreement proposal to cabinet and by the fact that as minister of labour he wished to resist any move that would threaten employment and increase labour unrest, none the less agreed with his colleagues about the political objections. Chisiza, as if to make sure none of their rehearsed points was omitted, had gathered other grievances together: Malawi's rapid fall in world esteem, Banda's reposing more trust in European civil servants than in his ministers, his personal retention of too many ministries, his failure to delegate and his continued employment of expatriate officers who stood between the prime minister and his ministers. Of the points Chirwa had mentioned to Jones two days earlier, they had not so far in the present cabinet meeting raised the questions of Aleke Banda's appointment, Msonthi's expulsion from the cabinet, slighting references to the ministers, accusations that the ministers were simply yes men and the Skinner report.

Finally returning to the specific agenda item, the cabinet agreed that the minister of labour should not for the time being negotiate a new agreement with WNLA. Instead, Chokani, Tembo, Bwanausi and Chiume should give further consideration to whether an agreement would be in Malawi's best interests, and bring the matter back to the cabinet.

The ministers had not yet fired their last salvos of the day, however, for Chiume – to be followed by each of the other ministers except Chisiza – reopened the campaign by telling his colleagues about his recent visit to Northern Rhodesia. They added nothing new but took the opportunity to repeat, emphasize and reinforce the points they had already made. Chiume said of his visit:

> He had been there to try and negotiate between the rival African political parties of Southern Rhodesia. He had been unable to do so effectively because of the recent visit [to Malawi] of the prime minister of Southern Rhodesia [Smith]. Nationalists from Southern Rhodesia had alleged that Malawi was a friend of Portugal and a traitor to African nationalists in the southern part of the continent [and] throughout Tanganyika and Kenya he had found a mounting hostility towards Malawi. He was sure that the real friends of this country were the free African countries. The decision by [President Nyerere of Tanganyika to cancel his proposed state visit to Malawi] had come as no surprise to him ... There was much criticism of European civil servants ... The Prime Minister had allowed himself to be dominated by his European Permanent Secretaries who had sought to persuade him that he could not trust his Ministers.

Bwanausi, following Chiume's lead, added that it was the duty of ministers to defend Malawi's foreign policy and they must, therefore, be consulted in the formation of that policy.

The Prime Minister had failed to place confidence in his Ministers, and had forced through a number of measures which the Ministers had been unable to discuss fully and with which they were not always in agreement. He referred particularly to the proposals contained in the Skinner Report which, he said, had been bulldozed through the Cabinet.

Chokani then spoke of the effect Banda's foreign policy was having in Southern Rhodesia on Malawians living there. They were encountering 'bitter hostility' from the Southern Rhodesia Africans. Furthermore, the Skinner report was having 'a most serious effect' on the civil service, and his own ministry's representations that consultative machinery be set up before the Skinner proposals were implemented had been rejected by the prime minister's office. In a verbal sideways swipe at Youens, he doubted whether Banda had been properly informed of his representations. Chokani was also 'unhappy about the development of institutions which were not under the control of Parliament and a Minister': recent proposals for community development and placing Aleke Banda in charge, a point Chirwa had mentioned to Jones as causing resentment.

Chirwa emphasized that 'apathy and criticism of the Government' were growing and one cause was Banda's failure to inform, consult and make proper use of his cabinet ministers. He repeated that the principle of collective responsibility needed to be observed. Banda should place more trust in his ministers and rely less on expatriate civil servants.

Tembo also spoke critically and said that when, recently, he held a number of meetings to encourage prompt payment of taxes, he met with a great deal of criticism of the government.

> The people felt that there was no sign of the improvements which they had expected to see once Independence had been achieved. Africans in the civil service had suffered as a result of the Skinner recommendations. Most of them were prepared to accept the changes ... but compared their own conditions with the recent rise in expatriate officers' salaries [and] complained bitterly of the series of promotions of European officers which had followed so soon upon Independence.

The question of hospital charges, which was also causing concern, was not raised at this meeting. Phillips, until recently minister of finance, was surprised by the introduction of hospital charges because he had previously not heard anything about them. Youens, too, had not heard of the proposal, which must have been introduced without reference to the cabinet. Most other matters, including the Skinner report, had been discussed in cabinet and agreed.[100] The ministers' subsequent opposition to the measures suggests either that they were reluctant to challenge them before independence or before they were ready to take on Banda, or that the ministers having agreed to them, Banda pushed them further than they had expected or could accept.

By this time, Youens – who had been openly and repeatedly insulted – and Ellams 'felt they could take no more' and asked to be allowed to withdraw.[101] Banda, possibly embarrassed by the criticisms voiced by his ministers in front of these two officials – including the most senior of all officials, the head of the civil service and secretary to the prime minister and cabinet – and possibly, too, glad of a break in the flow of criticism, if only temporarily, permitted them to leave. Before they did so, however, and repeating a point he had made earlier in the meeting, he made it clear that European civil servants had never tried to come between him and his ministers or to warn him that he could not trust his cabinet colleagues. Indeed, he had often instructed them that unless he gave his specific authority, his name was not to be used, or orders issued purporting to come from him.

After Youens and Ellams left, the cabinet members continued their discussion until 4 p.m. Banda 'kept quiet, merely saying from time to time, 'Has any other minister any complaints to make?'[102] He listened patiently and 'in exceptional silence' to all the complaints which they made,[103] and then told them: 'If my present policies are disapproved by you I should go now. You need not fear my political ghost for I shall return to medical practice either in Britain or in Ghana.' The ministers, Banda told Jones the following day,[104] were shocked at this – which suggests that it was the first time the question of resigning had been raised, contrary to what Jones had told Cole two days earlier. Although what Banda now said began with the conditional 'if' and fell well short of actually offering to do so, they begged him not to resign. Probably correct from the point of view of political practicalities but not necessarily constitutionally accurate, he insisted that a prime minister could not continue in office if all his ministers disapproved of his policies. In effect, he was saying that either they agreed to his policies or he would go.

At this stage Chirwa intervened to say the meeting had probably gone on long enough and they should leave matters as they stood, take time to rest, reflect and then meet again the following morning. This may have been an error of tactical judgement, for had they continued the momentum of their attack it is conceivable that Banda might in fact have offered to resign. This failure to seize the initiative and immediately find a successor has been seen as evidence that the ministers' dispute with Banda was personal and not ideological.[105] Chirwa may have felt that having got Banda to the point where he himself mentioned resignation, now was the time to pause and, rather than jeopardizing what they had so far gained and risking his actual resignation – which neither he nor they wanted – hope he would agree that the only alternative was to mend his ways. This was not the way Banda looked at it. For Chirwa the alternative to Banda's resignation was his reforming his ways. The alternative for Banda was that the ministers should change their minds and approve his policies – or, presumably, resign. Chirwa and his colleagues may also have felt that Banda had chaired this meeting in a more restrained and open way than ever before and that they were making progress with him, progress that if they pushed him any further at this juncture might be reversed. It seems they genuinely did not want him to resign but simply to reform his methods of operating. Maybe each individual, or each alliance of individuals, was looking to the future when one or other of their colleagues would take over the prime ministership and when each of them would want a new pattern of operating to have been well established and accepted as the norm. It was bad enough having Banda behave as he did, without wanting his successor, whoever it might be, to behave in a similar fashion. It is likely, too, that the individual ambitions of some – perhaps most – of the ministers dissuaded them from pressing for Banda's resignation because each feared that another of their colleagues, rather than they themselves, would replace him, and they each preferred Banda as prime minister to any of their colleagues. Possibly, too, at this stage they did not wish to push for a successor in Chipembere's absence. On the other hand, it is possible that Banda precipitated the rebellion and allowed or encouraged the matter to be brought to a head in Chipembere's absence, knowing that none of the ministers would readily accept the premiership in his absence because he might oust them on his return.

Youens, who worked closely with Banda over a much longer period and knew him better than any other expatriate official, including Jones, was convinced that Banda never had any intention of resigning. He firmly believed it would have been quite out of character for him to have done so.[106] On the other hand, Roberts, who was secretary for justice at the time and closely involved in the top levels of administration – though not then as closely as Youens, said:

> I think the position was that the ... dissident ministers ... roundly and spontaneously and unexpectedly told Dr. Banda that his leadership was now at an end. He had fulfilled the task for which he had been required, which was to unify the nation in a struggle for independence against colonial rule, and now when this had been achieved was the time for him to stand down. I think this came as a complete shock to him and, perhaps temporarily, he was minded to heed it and accept it, and resigned himself to it.[107]

Being minded to do something, especially temporarily, however, is different from actually doing it, and again Roberts does not say that Banda either resigned or offered to do so.

Chiume later gave his recollections of the cabinet meeting on 26 August:

> Dr. Banda was shocked to be confronted by our united stand, after all his concerted and carefully calculated plans to divide us. He declared that the people appeared to have lost confidence in him and that the only honourable course was to resign. He would leave Malawi so that his political ghost would not haunt his successor. We asked him to reconsider and to wait for twenty-four hours before coming to a decision. He agreed. That evening, Dr. Banda saw the Governor-General and told him of the criticism levelled against him.[108] Sir Glyn said that they were probably justified but that Banda should stay on, moderating his position. The next day Banda was still prepared to quit, if that was the will of the people.[109]

Banda shortly told parliament of his feelings when the ministers attacked him in cabinet. He was shocked because he was 'isolated, deserted by every one of my Ministers. No one tried to support [or] defend me ... I could not believe it was my Ministers speaking to Kamuzu. I just couldn't believe it.'[110] By 'shocked' he almost certainly meant 'astonished at their temerity and insolence' rather than 'taken by surprise at what they were doing'. The ministers had tackled him about his belittling remarks and failure to consult them, at their meeting two weeks previously, so he had ample warning, and it must have occurred to him that they were united and prepared to tackle him, though possibly not so disrespectfully.

He continued: 'It was that draft Bill to create the University of Malawi that sparked off the smouldering embers of disunity, disloyalty, indiscipline, disobedience, which I have noticed on my return from Cairo.' It was not, in fact, discussion on the university bill that sparked off the attack, but he may have felt that the popular topic of creating a university provided him with safer ground on which to stand in parliament than the topic that did spark it off: the unpopular question of relations with South Africa.

> As soon as I began talking of that paper my Ministers began to attack me ... viciously, violently and most disrespectfully ... Although the paper was on education, it was not education we were discussing at all. My Ministers turned it into a general discussion on my policies since we became self-governing and particularly since we became independent ... I am not always so sweet but that morning I tried my best to be sweet, to be calm. I let them have their way ... I said to my Ministers, 'All right,

you say I am wrong ... Then it means I have failed as a Prime Minister. In Britain, the only honest, sensible and honourable thing as a Prime Minister who is a failure is to resign.' So I said, 'I resign now. I am going up to Government House to advise ... the Governor-General, to send for you Kanyama. If you cannot form a new Government, Kanyama, then I will advise His Excellency to send for you, Ching'oli Chirwa. If you, Ching'oli Chirwa cannot form a new Government, then you, Bwanausi or Yatuta Chisiza and on down along the list.' To my surprise, they said, 'No, we didn't mean that.' I said, 'Yes, what did you mean by attacking me? I take your attack on me as ... an implied vote of no confidence and, therefore, I have no intention of standing here against anybody's will ... My job is done. Why should I hang on to power when my job is done and when people have no confidence in me? That is not my style. I came here by the will of the people and if the people do not want me ... then I am going back where I came from.' Yes, I told them I was ready to go back to Ghana, Britain or the United States of America.'[111]

Immediately he left the cabinet meeting Youens told Jones what had happened while he was present. His recollection a few years later was:

The young men had obviously decided ... to make their stand and there was long and fierce argument in the cabinet, where they criticised Banda for his external policy, his willingness to accept and exploit the friendship of the Portuguese, his reliance ... on expatriate officials who they said Banda used as spies to report on their activities to him, his practice of going over their heads to their own Permanent Secretaries and giving them instructions which didn't accord with the instructions already given them by the Ministers, his refusal to adopt a policy of speedy Africanisation of his civil service and particularly ... his police force and his army.[112]

In reporting what he had learned from Jones – who had learned it from Youens, Banda and other ministers – Cole wrote that the meeting ended with Banda saying he 'would consult the Governor-General about the position generally, making it clear that it was cabinet's wish that he should if possible stay'. The high commissioner thought the proceedings in cabinet 'may have been a pre-arranged plan by ministers, Chirwa having been to the Governor-General ... previously to explain the anxieties of the rest of the cabinet'.[113]

A little later that evening, 26 August, Chirwa called on Jones to tell him there was a crisis in the cabinet and repeated what he had said earlier, but now more imminently, that the Governor-General might receive the prime minister's resignation 'at any moment'. He added that the ministers did not want Banda to resign but merely to 'mend his ways' by delegating more responsibilities to them. Referring to the attacks made in cabinet on senior civil servants, particularly Youens, he said too much weight should not be attached to them since they were made with the intention of 'letting the Prime Minister down gently in the form of an oblique attack on him personally'. He asked Jones to tell Youens the ministers appreciated that the permanent secretaries were 'doing a very fine job' and it was not their fault Banda placed more trust in them than in his ministers. Few of the other attacks on Banda had been oblique or calculated to let him down lightly, and perhaps Chirwa realized that while Jones might well agree with many of the other criticisms, he was extremely unlikely to accept these of senior civil servants. The Governor-General indeed thought them 'grossly unfair' and was sorry the ministers lacked sufficient courage to make their complaints in a forthright fashion. In his view the ministers had damaged what was a fairly legitimate case by 'such unpleasant remarks'.[114]

Jones tried to see Banda that same evening. The doctor excused himself, saying he was tired, but asked to call on him the following evening.[115]

The next morning, Thursday 27 August, Banda met his ministers and they covered the same ground as the previous day.[116] He told Jones that he again threatened to resign and contemplated sending Chiume or Chirwa to him to be appointed prime minister. Having listened once more to their 'earnest plea', however, he told them he would 'put the question to the Governor-General who would decide whether it was in Malawi's best interests that he should remain as Prime Minister'. This was a good deal clearer than Cole's report that Banda 'would consult the Governor-General about the position generally'. The ministers agreed and asked Banda to tell Jones they unanimously wished him to remain in office. Banda and the ministers knew his question to Jones would be rhetorical and the answer a foregone conclusion. The Governor-General could have appointed Chiume, Chirwa or any of the others only if he was sure one of them commanded majority support in parliament. He, Banda and the ministers must have known no one else could command this support, save possibly Chipembere, who had a substantial personal following in the country, though much less so in parliament, but was in Canada and scheduled to be away for at least another fortnight. Again, what Jones recorded the doctor as telling him he had said to the ministers fell short of offering to resign, and he said nothing about agreeing to accept Jones's view.[117]

A quarter of an hour before Banda arrived at Government House for an evening meeting with Jones on 27 August, he was preceded, somewhat to the Governor-General's surprise, by Msonthi and a priest, who said they had been instructed to await Banda's arrival.[118] Jones recorded the odd proceedings that then took place:

At 6.15 p.m. the Prime Minister arrived and after the usual courtesies had been exchanged he asked if he could bring the Father and Msonthi into my office. When they came he delivered a homily on the evils of drink, particularly its tongue-loosening effects, and hinted that Msonthi had been guilty of indiscreet talk on various occasions of a kind calculated to bring not only himself but the whole Government of Malawi into disrepute. He had decided to 'suspend' him from his duties and would have done so prior to 6th July but for Msonthi's earnest entreaties that he be allowed to be present at the celebrations as a Minister. He took advice after Independence and for the past two months Msonthi had been at his home in Visanza living quietly and giving no information to his many questioners. During this period the Prime Minister had investigated allegations made against Msonthi which he did not particularize. He had come to the conclusion that Msonthi had been guilty of no more than 'indiscreet talk in his cups in mixed company'. He had decided to have a talk with [the] Father who he knew was Msonthi's friend and confessor, and during the course of this he had asked that Msonthi should be taken before the Bishop at Lilongwe and admonished for his insobriety and indiscreet behaviour. This process had been duly carried out and Msonthi [was told that he] must drink in his own house and go to bed afterwards. The Prime Minister had later seen the priest and Msonthi together to tell them that he would in their presence advise me to offer Msonthi ministerial responsibility again for Transport and Communications. This was the purpose of the present meeting and I had great pleasure in congratulating Msonthi and asking him to come to be sworn in at Government House the next day. The priest with great difficulty concealed his mirth at this truly strange performance and I must confess to having to exercise considerable restraint myself.

The reason for Msonthi's temporary removal from the cabinet was, and remained, a well-kept secret. Jones had not previously known the reason and it is probable that the other ministers never learned of it. Perhaps Banda deliberately kept them in the dark to induce the sense of insecurity to which Chirwa referred.

It is likely that Banda, having been attacked the previous day by the whole of his cabinet, save for Chipembere who was overseas, was anxious to secure Msonthi's support and to have that support in the cabinet itself. He may also have hoped Msonthi might influence the other ministers in portraying him in a more favourable light than that in which they currently saw him. Msonthi was the only member of the cabinet – including Tembo and Chipembere – who, though temporarily 'suspended', had not voiced criticism of him. Perhaps, too, Banda had been doing some political arithmetic and calculated that with six ministers having spoken out against him, he might be able to swing the balance with Chipembere, the three regional ministers and Msonthi, who might also bring Tembo – Miss Kadzamira's uncle, and a close friend of Msonthi from the central region – over to his side. Cole described Msonthi's reinstatement as a gesture of reconciliation by Banda, 'the single concession made by him throughout the whole period of the crisis'.[119] There is no evidence that Banda treated this as a concession or a gesture of reconciliation. Had he have done so he would undoubtedly have made greater play of it, whereas in fact he rarely if ever mentioned it in public.

However this may have been, as soon as Msonthi and the priest left, Jones turned to the doctor and, possibly a little miffed that he had not mentioned the dispute to him before now, said, 'Now Dr. Banda, I must be frank and say that I have heard rumours of a serious difference of opinion between Ministers and yourself.' This could not have surprised Banda because he would have been sure that Youens had told the Governor-General about the cabinet meeting, although he probably did not know that Chirwa had told him about it and their other meetings. As soon as Jones said this, Banda cut him short and said that the purpose of his coming to see him was to tell him 'frankly what [had] happened during the past two days'. His account differed little in detail and not at all in general from that given by Youens covering the period while he was present, and he went on to describe what had happened after he had left.

When he was told of Banda's reference to resigning and his colleagues' reaction to this, Jones 'told him without hesitation that he should retain the office of prime minister in the general interests of the people of Malawi'. Banda was pleased with this response and 'his tail rose appreciably'. There was no persuading on Jones's part nor the need for it. Indeed one of his own accounts makes this clear:

> It came to the point where Dr. Banda felt that he had lost the confidence of his cabinet ministers, and perhaps of the country at large, and there was a stage when he felt inclined to resign ... I did not dissuade him from resigning, so much as give him advice as to why he need not resign.[120]

Again, 'feeling inclined' to resign is different from offering or threatening to resign. Some eighteen months later, Jones addressed the staff of the University of Malawi and he specifically altered the drafted text of his talk from 'Eventually I persuaded the Prime Minister' to 'The Prime Minister was persuaded', followed by 'that under the constitution his only recourse was to summon Parliament to ascertain if he still retained the support of the majority of the members.'

With the question of Banda's immediate future so quickly out of the way, the Governor-General and the prime minister talked of ways in which they could make the ministers feel happier than they had felt since independence day. Jones urged him to treat them with respect, not make important decisions without consulting them, not appear to be reposing more trust in expatriate civil servants than in the ministers, and delegate more responsibilities to them. In this way, without – save in one respect – giving specific examples or going into detailed recommendations, he gave precisely the advice that the ministers had, less amicably and helpfully, tried to give him the previous day and, to some extent, a fortnight earlier. He did, however, go further and was more precise in respect of Banda delegating some of his responsibilities to ministers, a matter that had long concerned him. All his previous attempts to get the doctor to reduce the scope of his ministerial responsibilities and to allocate portfolios to named individuals had completely and routinely failed. Nevertheless, he now suggested that Banda should shed the ministries of health and of natural resources, and he recommended giving Chisiza the latter. He should retain defence, law and order and the public service, although later, 'as he saw a convenient opportunity', he might take external affairs and appoint a parliamentary secretary to do most of the travelling involved. Jones's motivation for these redistribution suggestions is unclear, but they would have slightly weakened representation in the cabinet from the north of the country while retaining the balance in the centre and in the south. More importantly, in personal terms, Chisiza would have been elevated – by taking over a vital ministry from the prime minister – and Chiume made less powerful – by losing a prestigious ministry to the prime minister. He did not go into the effect, intended or otherwise, this might have on Chiume or Chisiza, but it must have been clear that the political ramifications of such changes in their personal fortunes and in the balance of power between the factions, might well be considerable.

They then turned from what in essence was Banda's style of governing to discuss the policy areas agitating the ministers. He would not alter his foreign policy because it was based on the realities of Malawi's landlocked location and was conceived in the best interests of the country.[121] Similarly, he would not alter his policy of gradual Africanization and the retention of expatriates who were 'essential for the administration of Malawi'. Jones must have recognized, after four years of dealing with Banda, that these were points on which no amount of persuasion would shift him. His advice, therefore, was that, 'without being Machiavellian', the prime minister could 'play the present situation carefully', conceding some points but not in fact altering his basic policy on important matters. For example, Jones suggested that his foreign policy might not have been as well presented as it could have been and perhaps Banda should pay more attention to the actual presentation of this, and other, policy areas, and 'above all consult his ministers before making decisions'.

Jones moved on to talk about a deeply important policy matter and an example of the need for Banda to consult his ministers: republican status for Malawi, about which Chirwa had fished three days earlier:

> I referred to his intention to announce [in the legislature in six days' time] his decision that Malawi should become a republic on 1st April 1965. This would come as a considerable surprise to the House, the Cabinet and the people since it was clear he had consulted no one about it except Blackwood. While I would not attempt to push him off 1st April 1965 I thought it inadvisable that the announcement should be made so soon.

Banda listened carefully, and no doubt feeling he already had enough trouble on his plate, decided not to make an announcement about republican status the following week. To have done so might have driven his ministers to flash-point and he was not yet ready to have them provoked that far in public.

As Banda was about to leave, the Governor-General gave him 'a secret warning'. Jones had shown signs of disliking Chiume from the earliest days of knowing him, and he now said he was not loyal to the doctor. This was probably what he had in mind when he suggested that at some stage the prime minister might take over external affairs himself. Banda's reply was simply that he 'quite understood what [Jones] was getting at'.

It would not have escaped Banda's notice – though it passed without his commenting – that, however he expressed it, Jones was in principle agreeing with the ministers and siding with them, while not withdrawing his support from the prime minister. He had made a similar response two years earlier when he had agreed with the ministers' complaints against Chiume. Then Banda had taken no overt action. Now, save for slightly postponing the announcement of republican status, he ignored all of Jones's advice.

Cole, to whom Jones gave details, quickly reported this meeting to the Commonwealth Relations Office:

> Banda came to see the Governor-General last night [and] described the previous day's events. He said that he had come back to Malawi to lead the country out of federation and into independence. This had been achieved and if the people wanted him to go he would go. What did the Governor-General think? The Governor-General advised Banda against resigning though he said he fully respected the principles on which Banda said he must stand. He felt, however, that the real trouble was that Banda was not giving his ministers enough to do. Banda should divest himself

of some of his portfolios. Ministers here were not by African standards a bad lot, and had capability to do far more. If they were busier they would stop grousing and stop feeling inferior to expatriate officers. Banda, who appeared severely shaken, left in much better heart. Question of republic never came up in Cabinet. Banda still clearly has his eye on 1st April but will presumably now move more cautiously towards it, discussing with ministers first.[122]

This is an interesting account. First, Banda said that if the people – he did not say the ministers or parliament – wanted him to go, he would go. Second, the words 'What did the Governor-General think?' are far removed from specifically seeking his advice – as opposed to his opinion – on resigning. They are even further removed from actually offering to resign. Third, Jones's saying he fully respected the principles on which Banda said he must stand, in the context in which they were said, could be taken to imply that if he stuck to those principles then maybe he should go. Fourth, Jones used the practical argument that the ministers had not got enough to do to keep them out of mischief, as an argument for Banda handing over some of his own work to them. This avoided him having to rely on principle – collective responsibility – to try and persuade Banda to divest himself of some of his portfolios, in the face of a great deal of evidence that the ministers were in fact working extremely hard. The real grounds for wishing him to hand over some of his responsibilities were to reduce his personal domination and control of government affairs. This, together with reducing the extent to which he relied on expatriate civil servants, was precisely what the ministers were seeking and, as Jones well knew, they were arguments it would have been unwise for him to deploy with Banda, especially since his own repeated attempts to persuade the doctor to reduce the breadth of his responsibilities had so consistently failed. Cole presumed that the discussion Banda had with Jones would lead the prime minister to consult his cabinet colleagues over Malawi becoming a republic. Plainly, he thought Banda was on the point of reforming his ways.

Later that evening the prime minister briefly met with his ministers again. He told them he had accepted Jones's view and would not resign. He did not say with what alacrity he had accepted this view, still less did he indicate the high probability that he never seriously intended actually resigning, but he may have left the impression with his ministers – shared by many others later – that the Governor-General had to press him hard and at length not to resign. This indeed may have been the impression he wished to leave with them. Being pressed hard not to resign may be interpreted not as a determined intention to resign but as demonstrating strong support. The greater the persuasion needed, the stronger that support. It was important to Banda that the public should know of the Governor-General's belief that his continuing in office was extremely important – even indispensable – to Malawi and its people. Jones was unlikely to make this belief known publicly, but the impression left in the ministers' minds and many other minds was capable of having the same effect. Believing that Jones had to press the doctor long and hard not to resign also served to concentrate the ministers' minds on the prospect that he might leave them to face the masses, the party, the probable administrative mess and the internecine and bloody manoeuvrings for power that would undoubtedly follow. There seems to have been no further discussion with the ministers on this occasion, and the differences between them had moved no closer to being resolved.

The possibility that Banda may have wished to create in the minds of his ministers the impression that he was seriously intending to resign and was dissuaded only after sustained and great pressure from the Governor-General is accompanied by the similar possibility that this is the impression Jones also wished to create – and for the same reasons: to demonstrate the strength of the belief, held personally by the Governor-General, that Banda's continuing in office was vital to the welfare of the people of Malawi; and to concentrate the minds of the ministers. A prominent expatriate businessman claimed that Jones told him:

> Dr. Banda was quite prepared, indeed anxious, to resign and to return to Britain to practise medicine: he had secured independence for Malawi and had smashed the Federation – his job was done. Glyn Jones, with great difficulty, persuaded Banda that he must stay, no one else could do the job and it was essential for Malawi for him to stay.[123]

Assuredly, the firm impression left in many minds was that Banda required great persuasion from Jones not to resign, but this is far from what Jones's own papers show to be the case. Youens, who worked more closely with Banda and over a longer period than anyone else, was, and remained, convinced that the doctor never had any intention of resigning and consequently would not have required persuading to stay in office. Indeed, when the idea that Banda had sought Jones's advice on resigning, and that Jones had 'strengthened him against it', was put to Youens some years later, he replied, 'I never knew that. I must admit I never knew. I find it hard to believe that he would ever think of resigning.'[124] Nowhere in his two speeches to parliament, in which he gave detailed accounts of what had happened, did Banda mention having sought the advice of the Governor-General over resigning, still less that Jones had expended much energy in dissuading him. In one of those speeches he said, 'I wanted to make it quite clear to them that I would consider concessions, compromises, accommodation, only if I could do so with honesty to myself ... Otherwise I prefer to go, I prefer to resign.' Again there is the conditional 'if', and the words 'prefer to resign' once more fall well short of offering to resign. Roberts's account mentions that Banda consulted Jones, but does not say that the Governor-General had any difficulty in persuading him to stay; indeed he does not say that Jones gave him any advice.

Chiume's account of the meeting was recorded later:

> A special cabinet meeting was held on the 27th. [It was more likely a meeting of cabinet ministers.] We decided to present to him all the grievances developed in the two meetings we had had ... Dr. Banda was taken aback and asked for all our demands to be given to him in writing. We met [again] on August 28th, joined by Msonthi who had been reinstated, at the Kuchawe Inn on the Zomba plateau and wrote our complaints and demands in a document called the Kuchawe manifesto. We insisted that our full set of demands should be met by the beginning of the next session of parliament, scheduled for September 3rd, only six days away.[125]

During that day, too, Friday 27 August, Banda saw Muwalo, administrative secretary of the MCP. He also saw Aleke Banda, who said that news of the ministerial differences had leaked in Blantyre and members of the women's and youth leagues 'were very angry' that the prime minister was being opposed. Separately, Banda also had a forty-five-minute discussion with Chisiza. No details of this latter discussion are available; unfortunately so, because the other meetings were all with non-minister party stalwarts. While the doctor was meeting Chisiza, Youens received a telephone message from Chirwa asking him to tell Chisiza to attend a meeting of ministers at Chiume's house. At the subsequent meeting – which was adjourned to the inn on Zomba plateau – the ministers drew up a formal list to be presented to Banda, headed 'Matters on Which Ministers Want Immediate Action Taken'. This was the Kuchawe manifesto. It was probably intended by the ministers to be the ultimate debilitating series of blows in their contest with the prime minister. It contained eight major demands with numerous subsidiary demands. Since the meeting was convened at Chiume's house it may well be that he was the instigating force behind committing the demands to writing – and adding a few more.[126]

The ministers' first demands were about moving the capital from Zomba to Lilongwe and locating the university in Zomba:

> Malawi is a poor country and therefore cannot afford the luxury of unplanned economy. The Government must therefore use all existing facilities and where possible must avoid creating new projects that will

duplicate existing facilities or create an extra burden on the taxpayer in the form of recurrent expenditure. The Government must thus revise the plan of changing the capital and thus the site of the University. The capital must remain in Zomba and the Soche Hill College [in Blantyre] should be the seat of the University of Malawi. The country cannot afford the financial burden of changing the capital at this stage and indeed the decision to do so must be carried out after a carefully planned survey and examination of the facts including the fact that some foreign countries have already started investing money into the [present] capital in the form of buildings ... The decision to change the capital even in the future must be made after the approval of the Cabinet.

Their second representation, a clear personal attack on Banda, was that 'Government must not be or appear to be the personal property of an individual'. Government, they said, was the people's instrument not only for the administration of the country but also for economic and social change. 'Such practices as are or appear to be a reflection of this practice must stop.' Among these practices, they alleged, were the arbitrary awarding of excessively high salaries to Tembo's female relatives including Cecilia Kadzamira, and the giving of land bought with public funds to Tembo and Aleke Banda as political gifts.

Turning to the Skinner report, the ministers insisted that the severe economies on African civil service salaries and other conditions of service should be scrapped immediately. The report had caused 'wide and uncalled for hardship' to the African people, both in the civil service and among those who depended on the purchasing power of the civil servants. It had also caused 'the jubilation and consequent contempt of the white civil servants on the African people and owners of Malawi'.

> With the scrapping of Skinner, the Department of Establishments must be Africanised immediately so that Africans cease to be onlookers and observers in their own country while foreigners boast to be enjoying it ... A Minister must be appointed to be in charge of the Public Service Commission in order to bring about immediate Africanisation of the Civil Service.

Their fourth demand was that the three-pence hospital charges must be removed, because they were an unnecessary financial burden on the people, were annoying them and causing apathy in the country and open hostility to the government. They went further and said that the European permanent secretary for health should be sacked and immediately replaced by a Malawian doctor, otherwise people would feel that the ministers had cheated them when they told them 'Independence will open the gates for them to increased responsibilities and to better life in their country.'

The list of complaints and demands continued – in confused wording – with what they saw as favouritism and nepotism. Again they singled out Tembo, his relations and Aleke Banda.

> Favouritism and nepotism, intended or apparent, e.g. the Tembo family is favoured, must stop for the good of the country and of the Government. Public denunciation or public expression of favours in the public must stop. Extra-Parliamentary institutions which tend to dilute the powers and functions of the Cabinet must be abolished. Equally, people like Aleke Banda must not be treated not only as the favoured pets of the Prime Minister but also Ministers must not be treated as if they are mentally the inferior of such people.

Under their sixth heading, the ministers gathered together a number of concerns. They said that government housing – on which Skinner had placed increased rents – should be free for everybody and must be considered as the property of the people of Malawi. These houses should be the responsibility of the minister of housing and not of the prime minister, 'as it is very bad taste that a Prime Minister should be distributing housing'. They insisted that permanent secretaries should not have direct access to the prime minister to discuss matters concerning their ministries unless the prime minister was in charge of the ministry concerned or the full knowledge and consent of the minister concerned had been obtained.

They next turned to the operation of the cabinet system and stated that cabinet government must be 'respected and restored'. They wished ministries to be 'properly distributed' and felt strongly that the prime minister should 'not be bogged down with petty things like the distribution of houses or the scrutinizing of a list of students going to Israel etc.' There had to be 'real Cabinet Government', and ministers should be given real power:

> Once the Cabinet has decided on the general policy, Ministers must feel free to execute that policy without having to take small and petty matters to the Prime Minister for checking [which gave] the appearance of Ministers as spineless puppets ... Puppetry must be avoided in distributing Ministries. Careful consideration of the standing of the individual in the society must be considered before a key Ministry is given to him. There must be full consultation before Ministries are distributed.

In order that the cabinet system should work properly, they demanded that 'security reports and information must be shared between Ministers so that Ministers can know the state of things in the country'. For this reason they should have telephone scramblers in their homes so that they could be in direct contact with each other and the prime minister.

Furthermore, the Special Branch should be immediately Africanized. In fact, for many years most Special Branch officers had been Malawians, but the senior posts were still held by Europeans.

Other matters included as being necessary for the proper operation of the cabinet system included 'real and full consultation between Ministers and the Prime Minister before any decision is taken'; forbidding permanent secretaries to use cars intended for ministers because 'this has a bad effect on the people as it gives the impression that white civil servants are still ruling the country'; and the demand that the development plan be 'vigorously implemented' with no changes or arbitrary alterations being made without the full agreement of the cabinet. This last was a reference to moving the capital to Lilongwe and allocating the vacated premises in Zomba to the university.

Finally they turned – and at length – to foreign policy. Malawi, they believed, could not afford to be in the pocket of any country. This belief had to be reflected in Malawi's foreign policy 'which must be such that Malawi does not inherit the enemies of other countries, whatever the price'. Malawi must 'recognise and accept the realities of the African and world situation', and so far as China was concerned:

> Malawi cannot afford to antagonize such major powers as the People's Republic of China in preference to defunct states such as Formosa [and] must take the only logical step without fear and decide to recognize the People's Republic of China and ignore Formosa which in the long run will not only be a liability but will bring us unnecessary trouble.

They were highly critical of the appointment of European officers as members of Malawi's diplomatic missions and were clear that 'whites cannot be the representatives of Malawi abroad' because their presence unnecessarily increased the financial burden on the taxpayer; damaged Malawi's reputation in the outside world; and brought contempt on the nation. Furthermore, it was resented by the rest of Africa, as implying the acceptance of African inferiority, and by Malawians, who felt that 'having fought for their country they are entitled to represent her here and abroad'. Appointing Europeans to represent them overseas destroyed the standing of the Malawi minister of external affairs at home and abroad: at home 'because all those whites who have been chosen to go abroad are diehards who beat or killed our people in 1959, and abroad, because it gives a bad reflection to the effect that Malawi still has slave mentality'. The Europeans in question should be withdrawn immediately and replaced by Africans. They were emphatic that 'Malawi Embassies and the Malawi Ministry of External Affairs must be used for all affairs concerning the external world. Private or dealings unknown to the Ministry make a mockery of the very existence of the Ministry itself.'

Their last foreign policy point was that an intensified campaign to raise funds for the country's development must be launched. They insisted that funds should be raised from 'any part of the world as long as there are no strings attached'. High-powered delegations should be sent to 'all parts of the world' to negotiate loans, and the ministers who led these missions must be given 'full powers to negotiate effectively on behalf of the Malawi Governmen'.

The Kuchawe manifesto was not a well-written or well-thought-out document. It shows signs of having been drafted in a hurry. In essence the ministers had six substantive areas of concern: the prime minister's failure to use the cabinet in the way they wished, foreign policy, moving the capital, Africanization, the Skinner report and the hospital charges. Indeed, the last five of these could be subsumed under the first: if the cabinet were used to arrive at collectively agreed policies then the other problems would not arise. Two of the eight sections were personal attacks on Banda's style and practice of government – treating government as personal property, and favouritism and nepotism – but even these were separated and not put under a single heading, though both were concerned with criticisms of Banda's support of the Tembo family – especially Cecilia Kadzamira – and Aleke Banda. There were good and telling points in the paper, but they were not gathered together: the need for economy and careful planning, the politically dangerous hardship caused by the Skinner report and the hospital charges, and, particularly, the effects of Malawi's foreign policy. Not unnaturally, the counter-arguments were not put.

The ministers must have known which parts of the paper in particular would not be well received – the policy areas of Africanization and foreign relations, the procedural areas of consultation and collective responsibility, and the personal areas of treating government as personal property, favouritism, nepotism, the disposition of government land and of financial gifts from foreign governments, and 'bad taste' – but they did nothing to move carefully, rationally and persuasively into these areas. Similarly, they must have known which parts of their paper would immediately rouse Banda's deep suspicions of their real motives: opposition to moving the capital to the central region, Banda's home area; rewarding those who had fought for their country, regardless of other merit; appointing a minister for the civil service; ministerial access to security reports; scrambler telephones in their homes and Africanizing the security department. Yet they did nothing to avoid rousing these suspicions or to allay them. Instead, with no preamble, they produced a document that mixed substantive policies with procedural and personal matters and that was blatantly abusive in parts. The document was an unsigned, joint, 'collective responsibility' sort of paper, but most of it shows signs of having 'almost certainly [been] written by Chiume'.[127] It was manifestly an ultimatum, ill judged and, despite its length, peremptory. The word 'must' was used sixty-six times out of a total of 1,728 words. Banda did not take kindly to it – or to its authors.

Although Chipembere was not present when this list was drawn up, he was certainly in sympathy with its main points, and a few years later wrote of them and the way in which, while the cabinet recognized the problems, he felt Banda pushed his policies to unnecessary extremes:[128]

> It was agreed that if we were to develop Malawi, a certain amount of sacrifice ... was necessary. We [the ministers] had supported the introduction of a graduated tax based on incomes, and we were ourselves paying the highest taxes among the African people. The Prime Minister had suggested a 25% reduction in our salaries and we had accepted that. We had gone further and demanded that we cease having free housing and must, therefore, pay rent and at a higher rate than that paid by our people in the civil service. But the Prime Minister had gone even further. He had decided on a drastic reduction of the salaries of all African civil servants ... The Skinner Commission was a farce. It 'recommended' what the Prime Minister had already told us he was going to do! ... But what caused even greater resentment among us and the African civil servants was the fact that the salaries of the European civil servants had been raised just a few months before.

Chipembere wrote also of the hospital fees that Banda introduced. The people had 'throughout the colonial era never been made to pay for government health services'. Although the amount charged was small, when one considered the low per capita income and the long distances most of them had to walk to the nearest hospital or dispensary, 'the three-Malawi-penny fee was a heavy burden which prevented many people from taking their fever-striken children to a dispensary'. He then turned to Africanization:

> It was unanimously recognised that ... there were not enough Africans with the skill and experience to replace all European officials as soon as we took over the government. But Dr. Banda had himself often said that the best way to train a man to do something is to let him do it, 'even if he burns his fingers' in the process ... So it had been agreed that we would Africanise all those posts for which able Africans were available; we had begun to do so gradually, but steadily. Suddenly, Dr. Banda changed his mind and was beginning to prefer extensive retention of British colonial officers, many of whom were, to say the least, hostile to the very concept of African independence and sought every opportunity to frustrate our national aspirations.

He dealt, too, with Malawi's external relations, and said Banda had gradually begun to abandon the non-alignment policy that they had agreed. Before independence the doctor had not caused particular concern in this respect: 'Indeed, he had begun to establish contacts with Communist China through the Chinese Embassy in Tanzania to neutralise the effects of Malawi's too strong history-rooted western links.' After independence, however, the balance was no longer maintained, and Banda leaned more and more to the West.

> What also caused concern was his growing friendship with the segregationalist minority regimes of South Africa, Rhodesia and Mozambique. Malawi's geographical position necessitated a certain amount of caution in our relations with these regimes, but it was not necessary for Malawi to become a political or military ally of these enemies of Africa ... It is true that thousands of her people go to South Africa and Rhodesia to seek work. But it is a mutual benefit set-up.

It soon became clear to Chipembere and his colleagues that Banda was 'too much of a European in his outlook to keep away from the white company that Southern Africa had to offer'. During his more than forty years' absence, he had 'ceased to be an African in everything but his skin color'.

> This was confirmed by his attitude to the Organisation for African Unity and to the other African states. He had the greatest contempt for them ... No black African state [in 1970] has any embassy in Malawi, while there are embassies from practically every west European country and the United States. Besides, South Africa, Portugal, Nationalist China, Israel, and Japan have embassies in Malawi; but no African state has.

Clearly, Chipembere shared the views on which his colleagues confronted Banda, and they were confident that they were speaking also on behalf of Chipembere.

At 5 p.m. the day they drew up their written demands, 28 August, Chirwa called on the doctor and handed him the list that they wished to discuss with him the next morning, Saturday.[129] Chirwa told him the document was not complete because they wished to add something to it – what this was is not clear. He then began to read his own copy to Banda. We do not know whether he read the whole of the 'Bill of indictment', as the doctor called it, but it is unlikely that he would have been allowed to do so. Banda probably made no immediate response but read the document fully as soon as Chirwa left. During this meeting the prime minister made up his mind not to give in to the ministers' demands until he had consulted parliament and 'the people'.[130]

An hour and a half later, Banda went to see Jones, who asked him how things had gone the previous evening when he met the ministers.[131] Initially, the doctor was in an excitable mood – undoubtedly incensed by the list of demands Chirwa had just handed him – but as their discussion proceeded he 'showed more confidence and became more his old self'. He said things had gone tolerably well and he had told them he was not going to resign. He added that he had not asked the ministers to see Jones, as they had arranged, because he wanted to keep the Governor-General out of the business. He said he felt confident he could handle it himself. These remarks suggest that he was concerned about Jones siding with the ministers in principle. He did not mention the written demands – another example of his not keeping Jones informed of what was going on – and it is probable that the allegations of treating government as private property, the disposition of land and of foreign financial gifts, nepotism and favouritism so hurt and embarrassed him that he did not wish the Governor-General to know of them yet. Although he would be happy to explain and justify his policy decisions, it would be much more difficult to explain, justify or, possibly, refute these more personal accusations. It was these particular complaints and allegations that seem most to hurt, and probably were intended most to hurt, him. Banda continued that not only had the news of the ministerial conflict leaked in Blantyre, but it was also known in the central province where, he said, 'If Chiume puts his head into Lilongwe he will be killed.' Although the prime minister himself did not raise the question at this meeting – indeed he made it clear he had already told the ministers he did not intend to resign – Jones recorded that he reiterated his opinion that Banda should not resign, and the doctor shared this view. He nevertheless added that it might not be a bad thing to let them 'run their own show themselves for a bit and see how they get on', presumably by giving them some of the responsibility for which they asked, and letting this and the consequences be known to the public. He implied that they would make a dismal failure of it. Again Jones advised restraint and steps in the ministers' direction:

> I advised him to play it cool. He could agree to certain modifications to Skinner. He could delegate more responsibilities. He could play down his foreign policy so far as Portugal and Southern Rhodesia were concerned. In short, he could go some way with his ministers without having to go the whole way. He said the crucial thing for him [in his relations with Portugal] was the Nacala rail link with its significance for the pulp industry [which he proposed to develop in the north of the country]. He would resign rather than give way over this.

So far as his policy over the Skinner report was concerned, Banda, most untypically, tried to excuse himself by saying the application of new conditions of service to existing civil servants was done at Phillips's insistence. Jones knew this to be 'quite wrong' because Phillips had tried hard to get the report watered down, but without success. It was out of character for Banda to place blame on others, but he now did so in respect of Phillips over the Skinner report and he blamed Chirwa for advocating the detention bill.[132] It was, of course, the case that the British government had been insistent that Nyasaland should economize as much as possible before it agreed to grant independence. The Skinner proposals were part of this and no doubt Phillips tried to reduce the political impact of them.

Just before he left the Governor-General, Banda referred to their final comments the previous evening. He was fully aware that Chiume was 'the spearhead of the attack and was organizing the Africans in the civil service against [him]'. The longer period of access to formal education in the north of the country had resulted in a large proportion of the civil service coming from the north, and this may have made it easier for Chiume, also from the north, to secure their following.[133]

Early in the evening of the following day, Saturday 29 August, Banda met the ministers yet again to discuss their demands, with a number of which he found it difficult to agree.[134] For example, he was already committed in principle to the Nacala rail link. Also, despite great criticism by the ministers of the European permanent secretaries, he would not agree to dismiss any of them. He also stuck to his plans to transfer the capital from Zomba to Lilongwe. There were signs, however, that he might be prepared, as Jones had suggested, to move on some issues while not basically changing his policy. He was willing to shift a little on the Skinner report by a compromise that helped existing civil servants. He told them he had changed his mind over making an announcement about republican status. He was prepared to play down the appointment of Jardim as Malawi's honorary consul in Beira: 'He may continue to come here but his visits are not to be advertised. He is a very understanding man.' Even on the rail link he said, without elaborating, 'We will get round Nacala somehow.' The allegations of nepotism and favouritism were not touched on. It is unlikely that the ministers were particularly satisfied with the responses Banda was making to their concerns, but they may have thought they detected a mild shift in their direction. Indeed, two days later Chirwa told Jones he thought they had made some progress.

Banda shortly gave his own account of the progress they were making and of his attitude towards some of the points:

> At a certain stage we had almost reached agreement. I had told them that I was quite willing to consider their points. 'Tickey [the three-penny hospital charge], what was a tickey?' I said to them. 'Skinner, I could go

into that but ... Skinner will require tact.' I could not just scrap Skinner, when I asked the British Government to help us with our Budget on the understanding that we, in our turn, would do our best to help ourselves, by effecting certain economies, and one of the means of effecting economies was the Skinner Report. I couldn't say 'We drop that' before I had studied ... ways of effecting changes in the Skinner Report ... I have a sense of honour, a sense of honesty and a sense of responsibility. I am not going to move an inch from my point. I am not going to break my faith with the British Government, by scrapping the Skinner Report ... And this is not because I do not want to do something about the Skinner Report. Of course I will do something about it. But I have to do something about [it] in my own way, and not in the way forced upon me by someone.[135]

Cole's account of the 29 August meeting said that Banda had conceded some points and held out on others. 'Orton Chirwa on his side is reported to have said that though some difficulties remain, things are going well ... Though ministers are clearly determined to establish permanent changes in their relations with Banda, spirit of compromise seems to be in the air.'[136]

Chiume said of the meeting, and the progress they were making, that Banda called the ministers to discuss their 'extended list of demands'. Banda, he added, acceded to all their demands but pleaded that they could not be met by 3 September. Consequently he proposed to alter the date of the next meeting of the legislature to 6 October, by which time he should have complied with all the demands.[137]

It appears from these accounts that Banda was indeed prepared to move somewhat on the Skinner report and hospital charges – though not on other contested matters, save possibly marginally. The ministers, however, were encouraged by the fact that he was at least discussing the issues with them, and may have thought he was agreeing to go further. For example, Cole understood that 'Banda had moved some distance towards compromise [and] seemed prepared to give up two or three portfolios and to agree to bring major policy issues up for discussion in Cabinet.'[138] Chiume's claim that Banda said he intended to delay the next meeting of parliament so that he could comply with the demands is interesting. Since he had decided the previous day not to give in to the ministers, at least until he had consulted parliament and the people – although they did not know this – the postponement must have been a device to lull them into thinking that he was prepared to move further in their direction than was in fact his intention, and consequently they had no need for the present to press him further or to mobilize support for their cause in the country.

The Commomwealth Relations Office view at this time was that, provided a final breach could be avoided, some good might come in the long run. They thought Malawi would become less independent of pan-African influences but some dependence was probably inevitable. They hoped Banda's 'realistic approach', for example to relations with Portugal and Southern Rhodesia, would 'not be too rapidly or drastically undermined'.[139]

Special Branch's view was that there was no immediate security threat and Banda had a comfortable majority of members of parliament on his side. They believed that Chiume – who was now demanding that Communist China be allowed to open an embassy in Malawi – though leader of the revolt, was not popular and Chipembere was still the man to watch.[140] Home, the British Foreign Secretary, advised Macmillan that 'there would be great advantage in pinning responsibility [for the trouble in Malawi] on Chinese subversion'. He thought that every other African leader would then 'feel his seat in danger'. He hoped that British newspaper editors could be 'warned of the situation and invited to write accordingly'.[141]

The American ambassador sent long cables to his government, reporting what he described as Banda's 'capitulation after a week long cabinet crisis'. The British embassy in Washington, to whom the cables were shown, concluded from the list of points on which Gilstrap said Banda had given way, that 'capitulation' was an apt word to use.[142] It is probable that the main American sources of information were the dissident ministers – who overstated the progress being made – and a few Europeans sympathetic to their cause. Rumours of Banda's capitulation were believed by some of the ministers, for Chokani contacted Cameron and told him that Banda had resigned and that a new government, including Cameron, was to be sworn in the next day. Though not all the ministers wanted Cameron back in the cabinet, Chokani and his colleagues felt that even for a short period it would be helpful to them if Cameron could be seen to join them in a united front. The following mornng, Cameron, dressed in his dark suit, was about to leave for Zomba when he heard on the radio that Banda was to remain in power as prime minister. Consequently he cancelled his journey to Zomba. It was, and remained, Cameron's understanding that Banda had resigned and then withdrawn his resignation.[143]

The prime minister went straight from his meeting with the ministers on 29 August to visit the Governor-General.[144] Perhaps not surprisingly, Jones found him 'still pensive and rather unwilling to talk. [He] had to drag information from him.' Clearly, the written list of demands had deeply disturbed him, though he still did not mention it. He told Jones about the meeting that had just ended and went on to give an assessment of his ministers. Chirwa was 'impressionable and changeable'. Chokani 'followed the others'. Chisiza seemed to be 'something of an enigma'. Bwanausi was 'the most sound and solid'. 'Chiume's being Vice-President of the OAU Committee of Nine is probably at the bottom of all the trouble.' He did not on this occasion say anything about Tembo or Chipembere. It is probable that after the cabinet meeting of 26 August Tembo did not attend any other meetings of the ministers. Chipembere later said that Tembo 'had withdrawn from the growing controversy at an early stage and was a staunch supporter of the Prime Minister'.[145] While this was undoubtedly true, it overlooked the intriguing fact that Tembo had sided with his colleagues and spoken out against Banda at the cabinet meeting on 26 August. Banda had made no arrangements for another meeting with his ministers and he thought nothing was likely to happen over the remainder of the weekend.

The position, then, on 29 August, so far as the ministers were concerned, was that they had made their complaints clear to Banda at the cabinet meeeting three days previously and they had reinforced their views by presenting him with the Kuchawe manifesto. They believed that they were making progress and that Banda was beginning to compromise and shift in their direction. He said he would postpone the next meeting of parliament in order to move even more in their direction. It is likely that he was playing for time while he decided more precisely what to do and while he rallied support. He was probably also deliberately lulling the ministers into a false sense of security so that they did not yet take any steps to rally their own support or push him harder. They did not know that when he had received the list of demands from Chirwa he had decided not to give in to them until he had consulted parliament and the people. Indeed, their impression that he was shifting his ground in their favour, and the rumours of capitulation, would have led them to conclude that this was not what he had decided.

CHAPTER 7

Banda's Retaliation: September 1964 to January 1965

BANDA'S pensiveness and unwillingness to talk when he visited Jones during the evening of Saturday 29 August indicated that he had much on his mind. During the previous afternoon – the day Chirwa delivered the Kuchawe manifesto – he began to receive anonymous letters saying his ministers were stirring up trouble against him and it was not true that there was the widespread unrest, resentment and bitterness in the country, that they claimed. Further, on the Saturday, a number of people called personally to see him, concerned that he had not appeared in public for the past few days, and implored him – as had the anonymous letters – not to resign.[1] Though long aware of the divisions and individual ambitions within the cabinet, Banda had not until now accepted the rumours he heard about the ministers conspiring against him. Now, however, he began to believe them. The letters, coupled with the new and surprising unity between his ministers, caused him to conclude that they were in fact conspiring against him. He also had a number of meetings with 'Muwalo and other party stalwarts' who, 'for obvious reasons ... strongly advised him not to resign and instead to expel the ministers'.[2] Furthermore, the rumours circulating in Blantyre – emanating at least partly from the American embassy – that Banda had surrendered to his ministers, infuriated him.[3] These five factors – the Kuchawe manifesto, the anonymous letters, the visits from his supporters, the advice of the party stalwarts and the rumour of capitulation – made him even more determined not to resign, 'come what may', and any progress he might have begun to make with his ministers notwithstanding.[4] A major turning point had been reached.

Chirwa saw Banda's receipt of the anonymous letters in this light:

> [Dr Banda said the hospital fees] can go tomorrow. It is going. Don't worry ... We will look into the Skinner Report, and everything else, even foreign policy ... and as far as we were concerned the matter was finished

... it was not until Sunday [30 August] that we were told that the Prime Minister had received certain letters, information that we were planning to overthrow him, to plot, and when we saw him for the second time afterwards he was different.[5]

Chiume also saw the anonymous letters as a turning point: 'This business was almost solved, until certain people began to tell him stories [and] began to write anonymous letters ... that we were conspiring ... to overthrow the Prime Minister.'[6] Bwanausi, too, saw it as a turning point: 'At one stage we almost reached agreement, but agreement spoiled by outside influence, when people started writing letters to the Prime Minister, telling him that we were plotting.'[7]

Banda's mind had begun to turn to how he was going to handle the crisis from now on. He had already decided not to give up the premiership. The ministers said repeatedly said they did not want him to resign, supporters implored him not to resign, Jones saw no reason why he should resign, and it is unlikely that he had ever seriously considered resigning. His tactic so far was to shift – or appear to shift – marginally on some points without changing his basic policies, and to give the impression that he might be prepared to move on others. In his own mind he had formed an outline of the important characteristics of his dissenting ministers and he was convinced now that they were conspiring against him. He had decided that the scheduled 2 September meeting of the legislature should be postponed till 6 October 'to let tempers die down'. He was contemplating asking the Governor-General to dissolve parliament so that he could tour the country to see what support he had. He told Jones, 'The ministers are getting no sleep and the thought of my possible resignation troubles them.' This suggests that he now believed he was winning the battle with the ministers and could afford to take the initiative himself.[8]

Over the weekend, probably on the Sunday, Banda took further 'stock of his standing in the party', by consulting Aleke Banda, Chidzanja, Muwalo, Nyasulu and Kumtumanji.[9] These party colleagues came from all regions of the country and included the secretary-general and the administrative secretary of the party, the Speaker of the National Assmebly and two of the regional ministers – the third was in Britain. Banda had already observed the friction between members of the cabinet and the regional ministers, especially Chiume's antagonism towards Chidzanja. These party colleagues assured him that the MCP was fully behind him. The consultation did away with the need for parliament to be dissolved so that he could undertake a nation-wide tour to assess his support in the country, and no more was heard of the proposal. The consultation was Banda's first parrying blow to the ministers' written attack.

Chipembere has written of the significance and influence of these stalwarts, 'the strata of party leadership immediately below' the ministers:

> They had been active in the struggle for self-rule [and] were generally a little older than [the other ministers] but they had not been appointed to the cabinet because they lacked education [and] some of the men who had been left out of the cabinet were disgruntled. They believed that we had kept them out. Of course they wielded much power within the party ... They all had direct access to the Prime Minister. Since they knew the Prime Minister's fears and anxieties about his ministers, and wanted to ingratiate themselves to him with a view to promotion, they tended to tell him what they knew he wanted to hear about us. They told the Prime Minister grave distortions of our speeches.[10]

After the weekend, on Monday 31 August, Chirwa asked to see Jones urgently.[11] They spent an hour and a quarter together in the early afternoon. Chirwa explained that the purpose of the visit was for the ministers to 'maintain contact' with the Governor-General. They knew Jones agreed with their complaints and were no doubt puzzled by his not intervening by asking to see them, since they did not know this was at Banda's request. Chirwa seemed 'quietly confident but not perky', as Jones had sometimes found him to be. All the ministers, Chirwa said, were united in their determination to ensure that the principle of cabinet responsibility operated. He briefly summed up the meeting they had had on Saturday evening – which he referred to as 'round five' – with Banda at which he, like Chiume, felt the ministers had made progress. 'Round six' would take place during the coming week and they all hoped it would be a 'hand-shaking meeting'. He and his colleagues seemed to look upon the contest as a boxing match in which they hoped to deliver a number of debilitating blows, falling short of a knockout, that would weaken the prime minister and force him to recognize their rights and strength and be reluctant ever again to humiliate, belittle and ignore them.

Chirwa went on to refer to the Nacala rail link – one of the issues on which Banda would not move – about which the ministers were seriously concerned because of the close relations that it formed between Malawi and Mozambique. 'This', he said, 'makes us look ridiculous in the eyes of our African nationalist friends.' The ministers would have nothing to do with the removal of the capital to Lilongwe. They would not rush into converting Malawi into a republic: 'We do not want a Ghana here. We will not tolerate an executive president.' He did not say so, but what the ministers hoped for was 'a republic with a vice-president and a prime minister'.[12] Finally, Jones warned Chirwa that the ministers should 'not go too far and drive the Prime Minister over the edge'. They would be doing well for the time being if they got Banda to agree to delegate more functions to them. Policy differences could then be thrashed out in detail.

Chirwa's optimism that they were approaching a 'hand-shaking session' was gravely misplaced – it turned out to be more of a fist-shaking affair! He was unaware of the cumulative adverse effect on Banda of the list of complaints from the ministers, the visits by his supporters, the anonymous letters, the advice of the party stalwarts and the rumours of capitulation, which had already driven him over the edge.

A few hours after Chirwa saw the Governor-General, Banda also asked to see him. In advance of their meeting, at 5 p.m., the doctor saw Youens and said 'he was going to teach a political lesson to the Cabinet that they would not forget'. They were not going to 'Nyererize' him. Banda then went on to Government House. Gone was the reflective mood and reticence of the previous Saturday evening. Now he was in an excitable mood, his speech was staccato, he often repeated himself and left sentences unfinished. He spoke of the soundings he had taken over the weekend. Confident now of his following in the country, he was 'not going to suffer the same fate as Nyerere at the hands of his Ministers'. Now was 'the time to be firm, to be tough'. In order to clear the air, he proposed to resign, not for good but momentarily so that he could instantaneously be reappointed and could then form a new cabinet without sacking the cabinet ministers. His resignation would, he said, mean that all present cabinet ministers would be out of office unless and until they were reappointed. He intended to advise Jones to reappoint all except Chiume, Chisiza and Chipembere, and to appoint Chidzanja, Chakuamba, Muwalo and Nyasalu to the cabinet. His discussions with the present cabinet ministers could go no further. The ministers had gone too far.[13]

Banda shortly explained his references to Nyerere, and Chiume's role in the crisis:

> The crisis was planned by Chiume [who] was following the footsteps of his friend Kambona. It was not of his own free will that Nyerere left the premiership to organise the party. It was the first round in a Kambona-inspired conspiracy to oust him from the party leadership. Something similar was planned for Malawi ... Chiume was an ambitious friend of Kambona and he followed Kambona's footsteps in the conspiracy to oust [the Malawi prime minister].[14]

As soon as Banda left, Jones asked Youens and Roberts to see him, and together they tried to arrive at a plan of action.[15] This was not a straightforward matter, because although Youens and Roberts were clear and consistent, Jones was not, because 'he was up against a man who at the present moment was mad with rage; in these circumstances a solution amenable to a person in such a frame of mind was necessary'. An acceptable solution was difficult to reach. Roberts's role in advising Jones – and thereby Banda – was crucial.

> [Jones] had suggested to the Prime Minister that he might do well to retain the support of the four ministers that were with him and to sack those that were against him.[16] He reminded him that he could dissolve Parliament ... on the advice of the Prime Minister. This would be followed by a General Election. Mr. Roberts raised the point that if there was a General Election in a single party State, it would be problematical who would nominate the MPs. A wise course would appear to be to ask the Governor-General to declare vacant ... certain Ministers' posts rather than dissolve Parliament

Roberts said the constitution did not cater for a split in the cabinet between the prime minister and the ministers: the cabinet was collectively responsible to the National Assembly. In Britain the situation would be thrashed out at a party caucus from which would emerge the new leader. He made it clear that Banda could not say he was going to resign on condition that the Governor-General would reappoint him. The basic condition of his appointment as prime minister was that he enjoyed the majority support of parliament. Resignation was quite inconsistent with that condition. Jones acknowledged the logic of Roberts's advice, but thought it might be better to let things simmer until October, when parliament was to meet, and to have the matter thrashed out then. Youens disagreed and did not think it would be possible to leave things that long.

> [The Governor-General] would like to see the enemy Ministers (or Minister) sacked and Mr. Youens confirmed that the Prime Minister had said he wanted to sack them all and then to call Parliament. [Jones], however, stressed that the Prime Minister had it firmly in his mind to resign [momentarily] and then appoint Ministers ...
>
> [Jones] said the Prime Minister baulked at the idea of resignation without an immediate re-appointment ... If [he] accepted his resignation and re-appointment, Dr. Banda would have time to reassemble his ministries and give general confidence to the community. [He] felt that he must first test the opinion of the National Assembly if he was to consider re-appointing the Prime Minister and assure himself that he commanded the support of the majority of the members of the majority party in the Assembly.

It appears that Banda may have been giving Youens and Jones different versions of his intentions. He told Youens that he wished to sack all his ministers and then call a meeting of parliament. He told Jones he wanted to resign momentarily and then reappoint certain ministers. This is more likely to have been the result of uncertainty and a degree of confusion – stemming from a lack of clear advice from the Governor-General – rather than of deviousness.

Jones considered Banda's intention to resign to be irrational in view of the country's morale. 'There must be a reason for his resignation – this could be that there was a majority against him in the Cabinet.' He thought that if the ringleaders were to be sacked, then the others would either come to heel or resign. Youens had the impression that the whole cabinet was united solidly against Banda, and added, 'Once they came apart the Prime Minister would be ruthless with them.' The solution that Roberts advised was simple: ask the members of parliament whether they supported Banda. He thought it might be advisable to have such a meeting first and if the prime minister had the support of the majority of the members, there would be no reason why he should resign. Members could be consulted individually or in groups at Government House and not necessarily all together. Roberts was clear that the ministers need not be consulted because they had already told him they wanted Banda as prime minister.

The next evening, Tuesday, 1 September, Banda called on Jones and they discussed the plan to consult members of parliament.[17] When Jones said he would go ahead and see them all before the end of the week, Banda impatiently retorted that this was far too long and he wanted it done immediately. He felt, it seems, that the battle was going his way and he did not want his progress hampered by any delay. They eventually agreed that the Governor-General should see all or most of the members before Banda resigned and was reappointed to form a new cabinet – which was still what he wanted to do. Jones promised to see some of the members in Zomba, some in Blantyre and others in Lilongwe and Mzimba, which would mean his undertaking a good deal of travelling at short notice.

Banda went on to indicate the membership he had in mind for his new cabinet. Chiume and Chisiza, as he had indicated earlier, would not be members. He might recall Chipembere, but Msonthi was more doubtful. This was odd because he had reappointed Msonthi only five days previously, which implies that the reappointment was simply a tactical move to secure temporary support, or to wrong-foot the ministers, or to give the impression of making a concession. He would reappoint Bwanausi to the ministry of natural resources, which he had controlled personally up to now, and Chokani if they agreed to serve. He would probably have Muwalo as minister of health. Jones was able to dissuade him, for the present, from appointing Chakuamba a cabinet minister – Banda agreed that he was unpopular – but he failed to dissuade him from having Chidzanja, who Banda agreed was a drunkard but said, 'Churchill also was a heavy drinker and Chidzanja is a very good worker.' When asked, Jones said he had no objections to Chibambo being in the cabinet. At the close of their meeting, everything was set for the plan – that Jones should consult parliamentarians – to be implemented.

Early the following morning, Wednesday 2 September, Miss Kadzamira phoned Jones and said the prime minister wished to speak to him. His private secretary held the line for ten minutes but Miss Kadzamira was unable to 'raise' Banda. The doctor shortly phoned to say that he had changed his mind and wanted to take action straight away.[18] Jones's plan would take too long. He now intended to tell the ministers when he met them later that morning that he was sending Chiume to Jones to be appointed prime minister. Jones was alarmed by this change of mind and new intention, and insisted on seeing him before the meeting with the ministers. Time was desperately short and he offered to go to the ministry to see him if this would save time, but Banda said he would come at once to Government House. Two minutes later Banda phoned once more and said he had again changed his mind and the plan for consultation should stand. He still favoured the original idea of resignation followed by reappointment. Indeed, save for this early-morning momentary abberation, he had never dropped the idea, although he had entertained coupling it with prior soundings of members of the legislature. In response to being asked to be as quick as he could, Jones promised to proceed with all possible speed. It is possible that by threatening to send Chiume to the Governor-General Banda was selecting the minister least likely to command the support of other ministers, who would then reinforce their plea that he should remain prime minister. At the very least, it was likely to test, and probably break, the ministers' united front and isolate Chiume. It is most likely that this threat, not only to resign but to propose Chiume as his successor, was designed to alarm Jones and force him to get a move on. He did not say that he *would* send Chiume to Jones to be made prime minister, but simply that he would *tell* the ministers he would do so. Alternatively, he may simply have been behaving irrationally: his unusually early-morning wish to speak to Jones, his inability then to be 'raised' and his subsequent changes of mind give the appearance of dithering, and his suggestion to send Chiume to the Governor-General was extraordinary.

Banda met his ministers at 10 a.m.[19] He showed no sign whatsoever of meeting their representations, but 'merely lectured them' and the meeting 'ended in chaos'. His mood was one of 'cold resolution and hostility'.[20] At the end Banda called in Youens and asked him to see the ministers out, saying to them, 'You will not make a Nyerere out of me. You can shoot me. I will not be Nyererized.' When Chiume asked Banda if he had asked Youens in, he replied, 'Yes, because I want him to hear what I have to say.' The prime minister then rose and walked out in anger, leaving the ministers sitting in his office. The meeting had lasted fifty-two minutes. When, a little later, Banda not having returned, they left and walked through Youens's office on their way out, they neither spoke to nor looked at him. By asking Youens in to hear what he was saying, and knowing that he would tell the Governor-General, Banda ensured that Jones, despite his efforts to get him to meet the essence of the ministers' complaints, would be left in no doubt that he had no intention of giving in to them. Youens recalled:

> All ministers were in Banda's office, there were noisy shouts coming [to me] outside it and eventually Banda rang the bell and I went in and he said, 'Mr Youens, I have finished with these gentlemen, see them out.' Well, there was a dead silence and Chiume it was who said, 'But wait one moment, Mr Prime Minister, we have not yet finished with you.' And Banda said,' 'Well, I am not going to sit here and listen to you any further. If you are not going to leave the room immediately, I am going to leave it.' Which he did do, he withdrew and then the meeting broke up.[21]

As soon as he learned of this, and realizing that a dangerous impasse had been reached, Jones tried to get Banda to come and see him, but Miss Kadzamira excused him, saying he was not feeling well and would like to see Jones at 5.30 p.m. Again, he was in no hurry to bring the Governor-General up to date. He was handling things his own way, he had already told Jones that he did not want him to intervene and now, via Youens, he had made it clear to him that he would not adjust to the ministers' demands. Jones immediately once more sought the advice of Youens and Roberts:

> Because of the disastrous meeting and Chiume's change of plan [he had, unbeknown to Banda at this stage, decided not to leave to visit Addis Ababa for an OAU meeting as previously arranged] and because of the difficulty of [Jones's] own position, Roberts advised that the plan [for Jones to ascertain the feelings of parliamentarians] should not be carried out. It would be far better to advise the Prime Minister himself to meet his MPs altogether [*sic*] and explain the position fully to them and endeavour to obtain their support to his continuing to be Prime Minister. To sack Chiume at this stage would probably lead to the resignation of the majority of the other ministers and the need to appoint new ministers. This would entail the Prime Minister having to obtain at some time a mandate from the party and the MPs and he would then have his position

undermined by the ousted Ministers who would feel free to criticise him forcibly and work against him in all sorts of ways. Roberts also said that for [Jones] to canvass opinions of MPs on whether they would want the Prime Minister to be re-appointed before he had resigned would be a sterile performance. MPs would feel they were being led into a trap and if it transpired that the Prime Minister fell and some other person succeeded him [the Governor-General's] intervention in this respect could be viewed with great suspicion if not hostility.[22]

The meeting was brief, and ten minutes later Roberts called on Banda – which suggests that the doctor's not feeling well had been an excuse for not visiting Jones. It is most likely that he explained to the prime minister the difficulties and lack of necessity of resigning and being reappointed, and the reasons for advising that all he need do for the present was to ascertain the feelings of members of parliament. His verbal skill – indeed eloquence – clear thinking, simplicity and logic of argument and his forthrightness of approach undoubtedly appealed to Banda, and his advice was quickly accepted.

On the surface, it had so far been a bad day for Banda. He had rung Jones early in the morning; then he could not be raised – presumably would not come to the telephone; he had told Jones his astonishing proposal to tell the ministers he was going to send Chiume to become prime minister; two minutes later, having profoundly alarmed Jones, he had changed his mind; he had stormed out of his meeting with the ministers; he said he did not feel well – not surprisingly – and declined to see Jones; now he had changed his mind again and would not resign even momentarily but would simply determine his support among parliamentarians. And it was not yet noon! On the other hand, these rapid apparent meanderings could be seen as deliberate on his part, designed more acutely to concentrate the Governor-General's mind and produce from him clear, supportive, advice – which indeed emerged from Roberts just before lunch.

In the meantime, having left Banda's office, the ministers repaired to Chirwa's house. Here they reaffirmed their solidarity and concluded that, after Banda's rebuff at the morning meeting, he should be forced to resign and Chirwa should take his place as prime minister, leaving Chipembere out of the cabinet, possibly at the suggestion of Chisiza.[23] Chirwa was probably seen by the more extreme members as the most likely colleague not to resist their wishes and to be more acceptable to the Governor-General than they were. During the course of the ministers' meeting, Jones sent a message asking Chirwa to see him.[24] Presumably, since Banda would not come to see him, Jones wanted to find out from Chirwa what had happened at the morning meeting – no officials had been present and Youens had heard from his office only noisy shouts.

At Government House Chirwa described what had taken place in the morning. He went on to say – contrary to what they had just decided – that although the ministers still hoped Banda would not resign, there was a growing feeling that it would not be a bad thing if he did; one of the other ministers could easily form a cabinet. He became 'thoughtful' when Jones pointed out that a prime minister was chosen as the person who appeared to him to command the support of the majority of the legislature – not simply of the cabinet. As minister of justice, this ought not to have come as a surprise to him. No doubt he was beginning to see that his chances of becoming prime minister were not as strong as he had been thinking. When Chirwa again asked him to tell senior civil servants the ministers were not really attacking them, Jones said he would consider it. Chirwa was despondent and thought stalemate had been reached, especially when Jones told him the ministers had pushed the matter too far and Banda was now unlikely to concede anything. He had warned him earlier not to 'go too far and drive the Prime Minister over the edge'. The Governor-General found this meeting 'rather dreary and unproductive'. He was probably beginning to lose patience with them and felt they had played their cards badly and had made matters much worse.

Later, at 5.30 p.m., Banda, now 'well, confident and cheerful', went to see Jones.[25] The ground having been prepared by Roberts, the Governor-General advised that the plan they had worked out earlier – that Jones would see the members of parliament and determine their views – should no longer be implemented. He urged the doctor to seek an early opportunity to put the members of parliament 'fully in the picture as to what had been happening' and 'to give them his version of the discussions within the cabinet'. Jones's information was that the cabinet crisis, but not the reasons underlying it, was widely known. He continued by telling Banda that speculation and rumour were rife and he believed the people wanted to know from the prime minister himself what was happening. He therefore urged him to summon the members of parliament for a private meeting in Zomba as soon as possible. He should not contemplate resigning at this stage.

> The Prime Minister said his information agreed with mine. People were angry and many from Port Herald were contemplating 'marching on Zomba' to demand an explanation of what was happening. He said he still believed he commanded the support of the great majority of the people and had himself come to the conclusion that it would be wise and advantageous for him to summon MPs to Zomba and have an unofficial

meeting. He decided to have the meeting [on] Sunday September 6th. [The] messages [were] not to be sent out until sometime on Friday 4th. He then reiterated his determination not to be Nyererised. He must be allowed to govern with authority. The other ministers were not fully responsible people[26] ... The contents of the Skinner Report were being distorted by Ministers. The three pence hospital fee was not being put across by them in a fair way. They were using these decisions, to which they had agreed, to denigrate him. He would Africanise at a reasonable pace ... He was clearly in [a] fighting mood.

If he had previously been inclined to make any concessions to the ministers' demands, it is clear that he now intended to do nothing of the sort, but to dig his toes in still further – which makes Jones's advice, which Banda did not seek, that he should not contemplate resigning at this stage, puzzling. Delaying sending notices of the meeting until 4 September, the day Chiume was due to leave for Addis Ababa, was presumably designed to exclude him, to allow only just sufficient time for the members to travel to Zomba, and too little for any serious attempts to be made to dissuade them from supporting the prime minister. Banda said Chiume had been conciliatory during his meeting with him the previous day, though, it seems, insufficiently so because he had told Jones that Chiume would not be a member of the new cabinet. The doctor did not yet know of Chiume's change of mind about leaving for Addis Ababa. He and Jones then asked Youens in to discuss arrangements for calling the members of parliament to Zomba, the way forward with which they now both agreed.

During the afternoon, between Chirwa's and Banda's visits, the British high commissioner spent almost two hours with Jones, Youens and Roberts. He visited the Governor-General again in the evening, with Youens present.[27] The evening meeting was called to bring Cole up to date with what was going on. Jones explained that he had told Banda the present plan – that he, Jones, should seek the feelings of parliamentarians in various parts of the country – was now inadvisable because of the 'unfortunate Cabinet meeting' that morning. The true reason was not the cabinet meeting but, as Roberts pointed out, directly and personally ascertaining the views of parliamentarians was an inappropriate task for a Governor-General to undertake. Additionally, and crucially, Jones continued, in the meantime Chiume had decided not to leave for Addis Ababa in the afternoon. Jones thought there might be 60 per cent support for Banda from the members of parliament but Youens estimated it at only 50 per cent because the ministers were 'sticking' on points which would 'command fairly wide and influential support'. Given that neither he nor Youens thought the ministers were in a majority, and concluding that 'there now seemed to be no possibility of compromise', Jones came down firmly on Banda's side. This may well have been what Banda hoped to achieve when he asked Youens in to hear him tell the ministers he would not give in to them.

Messages were sent to the divisional officers in charge of police who, in at least the case of the northern division, sent 'an officer around the division in a Land Rover, picking up all the M.P.s and ordering them down to Zomba forthwith'.[28] Chipembere later wrote of the summoning of members of parliament:

> Malawi at this stage still had a British Governor-General representing the Queen. His functions were purely ceremonial and his powers purely advisory. The man who then filled the post was Sir Glyn Jones. He had been a liberal and had played a part in hastening the coming of self-rule. He was a much respected man among the people, but was now ineffectual. He disagreed with Dr. Banda's dictatorial ways and had himself on several occasions been treated by Dr. Banda rather like a junior officer ... What the Governor-General did not realise was that the Parliament in Malawi was a rubber stamp of the Prime Minister. As head of the Malawi Congress Party, he had nominated all that party's candidates for election to Parliament ... Since the opposition parties had all disbanded, and the Malawi Congress Party candidates had all been elected unopposed, Parliament was full of members who owed their seats to Dr. Banda. They could not conceivably pass a vote of no confidence in him; they were too grateful to him and were looking forward to the day when their loyalty would be rewarded with elevation to the cabinet.[29]

Chipembere was correct in saying that Jones did not realize the extent to which parliament was 'a rubber stamp': he had estimated only 60 per cent support for the doctor in parliament and this proved a gross underestimate.

The next morning, Thursday, 3 September, at 9.15 a.m., Miss Kadzamira phoned the Governor-General to ask if the doctor could see him at 6.45 p.m. A little later she rang again, said she had made a mistake and asked if he could see him at 11 a.m.[30] Their eleven o'clock meeting lasted only ten minutes. Banda was convinced that at the meeting with his ministers the previous day he had taken the right course in 'smacking them down'. Up to that point there had been reports spread by them that he would concede all their demands, but since then he had heard nothing of that sort. This suggested to him that they were demoralized. As Jones recorded:

> His idea is to get Cameron as Minister of Justice with Chirwa as Attorney-General with ministerial status. He said the detention without trial

legislation would not be passed and this would help Cameron. 'This Bill was entirely Orton's proposal'!! ... He had a lot more of interest ... which he would tell me in the evening.'

In toying with the idea of Chirwa being attorney-general with ministerial status, Banda may have been seeking to get him out of the cabinet without getting shot of him completely. He may have realized how desperately Chirwa wished to retain a distinguished public service post, and have hoped that by offering him the attorney-generalship he could split the rebel ministers' ranks. Retrieving Cameron might encourage Chirwa to accept and would have widened the split. It had been the threat of detention legislation which had helped bring about the ministers' solidarity, and removing the threat might take with it part of the solidarity. In any case, by not going ahead with the legislation, Banda must have decided that he could handle the ministers without it.

During the morning, Chirwa went to his office in the ministry of justice and asked Roberts a number of questions about the constitution 'of which he appeared to have poor knowledge':[31] 'What happens if the Prime Minister has a difference of opinion with cabinet colleagues?' – 'He could get rid of the ministers concerned.' 'But if he won't do that?' – 'The ministers could resign.' 'But if they won't resign?' – 'The Prime Minister could resign.' 'But if he won't resign?' – 'Stalemate.' Chirwa, thinking that at the present stage Banda would not sack any ministers and that none would resign, was probably wondering whether there was any way they could constitutionally oblige Banda to resign. He seemed lost as to what to do. The previous day he had told Jones they had reached stalemate and now Roberts's replies confirmed this position. No doubt, he could see his chances of succeeding Banda as prime minister – an aspiration Chiume believed had existed since 1959[32] – were now negligible.

Banda called on the Governor-General, as Miss Kadzamira had originally arranged, early that evening.[33] He said he would like to have Cameron as a minister or – presumably if he turned it down – alternatively Sacranie, an Asian lawyer, but Jones advised him to see what happened at Sunday's proposed meeting with the members of parliament before offering Cameron ministerial office. Banda agreed with this. When Jones told him he had heard that Chiume had decided not to go to Addis Ababa as he had planned, the doctor said he understood the reasons but it would not deter him from carrying on and summoning the members of parliament to Zomba. 'If I had carried on while he was [out of the country] he might have become a martyr.'[34] Chiume had decided not to go to Addis Ababa, immediately after the meeting when Banda walked out on them, but he also probably got wind of the meeting with members of parliament proposed for two days after he was expecting to leave. He had a reputation for not being where perhaps he should have been, especially when trouble was looming,[35] but on this occasion he would not have wanted to be out of the country at a time that might well determine the whole of his political future, for good or ill, martyrdom or not. Cole's view of Chiume, 'as leader of Ministerial revolt', and the part he was playing, was:

> Chiume ... had discussions with Chinese Ambassador in Dar es Salaam about Chinese aid, urged Cabinet to send delegation to Moscow and Peking and to secure aid from both East and West ... My own contacts with Chiume suggest he is well indoctrinated in more dangerous forms of African Nationalism. Although it is by no means certain that Chiume could personally win enough Party support to become Prime Minister, his role is strong and sinister one.[36]

Banda's close party advisers, he told Jones, said the people of Mlanje – like those of Port Herald – were angry and wanted to march on Zomba to find out what was happening.[37] He was 'holding [the people of Zomba] back from the ministers' throats'. Now convinced that it would be a blunder to 'attempt to detach any of the ministers from the clique', he was determined not to do so. He was surprised the ministers had not resigned, and he seemed to hope they would do so. He was convinced, as he had told Jones that morning, that his meeting with them the previous day, when he had walked out on them, was a success for him, and the ministers were cowed by it. Certainly Chirwa was despondent and Chiume was sufficiently worried not to leave the country despite his penchant for international travel. He gave his present assessment of his non-cabinet colleagues – upon whom, presumably, he now realized he would have to depend since he was intent on getting shot of all the rebel ministers. He was seeing a good deal of Muwalo, Aleke Banda and Nyasulu, and was sure of their support. He knew Rose Chibambo was against him and McKinley Chibambo, her brother-in-law, definitely for him. He was doubtful of Kumtumanji's loyalty, and this possibly accounts for his support of Chakuamba. Though he did not say so, he knew he could always rely on the people of Port Herald, led by Chakuamba, to cause trouble for his opponents. He had no doubt he would gain overwhelming support at the meeting of members of parliament proposed for the coming Sunday, and he asked for a formal meeting of parliament the following day or the day after. 'Finally he said that [the Governor-General's] servants had been instructed to listen in to [their] conversations and for this reason he has on the last few occasions insisted on all the windows in [the Governor-General's] office being closed.'

This conversation, with its paranoiac suggestions, gave the first indication that Banda intended to hold a formal meeting of parliament, following the proposed informal meeting. The first meeting – which Cole thought was to be 'a trial of strength'[38] – would show the extent of Banda's support and be an easier forum in which to ensure that support; thereafter success at the formal meeting would be a foregone conclusion.

The prime minister was up and about early the next morning, Friday 4 September, and called on Jones, again for only ten minutes, just before 8.30 a.m.[39] He was convinced he had the support of the great majority of the chiefs. Although support in parliament was where he would stand or fall in the immediate term, it appears that Banda had his eye on the longer term and was also looking for support in the country as a whole, including among the traditional leaders. His confidence in the support of the chiefs is interesting. During the preceding three years or so, he had repeatedly and heavily criticized many of them and, with Jones's help, he had deposed some of them and radically curbed the powers of all of them. Now he was confidently looking to them for support. Presumably, he was hoping they would see him – despite his Western experience and attitudes – as an older, traditionally minded, African leader, deeply knowledgeable about, and respectful of, Malawian history and culture, who would side with them against the young politicians.

The doctor now believed he had Mlanje, Port Herald and Zomba districts on his side. He could no doubt rely also on support in his home area of the central region. Cole reported that he was currently 'seeing virtually nobody except Aleke Banda and Muwalo'.[40] He had the support of leading non-cabinet senior members of the party in addition to Aleke Banda and Muwalo: Chibambo, Chidzanja, Nyasulu, Kumtumanji and Chakuamba. He produced a letter from Chipembere, written from Canada, which said Banda 'was liked and respected in many countries including Canada, Australia, India and Ghana' in which nations people 'claimed him as their own'. When asked if he thought the letter sounded genuine in what it said, Jones – who could hardly do otherwise – replied that he did, although a few days later he told Chokani that Malawi was 'the laughing stock of the world'. 'Well,' continued Banda, probably hoping that Chipembere was unlikely to side with Chiume at least over foreign affairs, 'this disproves what Chiume says [about] my foreign policy making me unpopular everywhere.' The doctor's parting words as he left were defiant: 'I'm going to hit them hard.'

Cameron had lunch with Jones that day and was 'surprised and disappointed to hear that Chiume was making so much of the running'.[41] He was convinced Chiume was hated by all the other ministers and by most of the people in the country. The ministers, especially Chisiza, had been talking freely over the past few days. When Jones mentioned a possible ministerial offer, Cameron said he would seriously consider accepting reappointment provided the constitution was not changed to allow for detention without trial in the absence of a state of emergency and provided, too, that he was given the real responsibilities of a minister. Banda had already told Jones that he would not proceed with the former of these provisos. The latter was one of the points that bothered all the ministers and there were no real signs that the doctor was moving in their direction over it, though he might well have been prepared to give Cameron himself more autonomy and responsibility.

The prime minister had another meeting with the Governor-General that evening and, for the first time, showed him a copy of the demands made in writing by the ministers a week earlier.[42] He said Chiume, Chirwa and Rose Chibambo 'must go at once' but, 'if he came through' – which, surprisingly, may have indicated an element of doubt – he was prepared to keep Chisiza and the other ministers. Jones advised him to stay his hand until after the meeting with parliamentarians before sacking anyone. Banda repeated that he would want Cameron or Sacranie as attorney-general[43] and Jones told him he thought Sacranie would cause trouble. The prime minister said he proposed to move the meeting of parliamentarians from Sunday afternoon, 6 September, to Monday morning, 7 September. Given the short notice, he may have been unsure whether all the members would reach Zomba in time for a meeting on 6 September, and he would have wanted as full an attendance as possible.

Chiume sent a 'distraught telegram' to Chipembere, asking him to return straight away to Malawi.[44] This may have been sent personally by Chiume and not on behalf of his colleagues, because if they had decided that Chirwa should take over from Banda and that Chipembere should be excluded from the cabinet, they would hardly have wished him to return at this stage. If, as seems to have been the case, Chipembere had warned his colleagues before he left for Canada that it would be unwise to challenge Banda head on generally, and not simply over the detention bill, because he would beat them, Chiume would have realised that in Chipembere's absence they had done precisely that against which he had advised and he would have wanted him back in the country as quickly as possible. Immediately, rumours began to circulate in Blantyre that he would arrive back on Sunday, 6 September. Lomax had become less confident of Banda's chances of success, fearing his opponents were gaining ground, and having some doubts about the youth league's loyalty to him. There was anxiety that anti-Banda crowds would be marshalled outside the parliament building when the parliamentarians met and that a fracas would develop between opposing factions. The police were taking precautions, and secret arrangements were being made for a company of troops to be on instant call. The high commissioner warned the Commonwealth Relations Office that if 'things turned nasty' British officers might be involved and there was no existing directive to cover this eventuality.[45] The situation, clearly, was tense.

The cable to Chipembere was probably sent on Friday, 4 September and it would have taken him at least two days to return from Ottawa, via London, Nairobi and Dar es Salaam to Chileka.[46] It could not have gone into much, if any, detail of the crisis, because Chipembere did not learn until he reached East Africa that 'there were exchanges of bitter words' in Malawi and that some ministers had been dismissed and others had resigned.[47]

On Sunday morning, 6 September, Banda called at Government House again.[48] He had little to say and seemed to Jones to be 'preoccupied and unwilling to be drawn'. This unwillingness may have been part of the general reticence that manifested itself in his not invariably bringing the Governor-General up to date with what was happening and in asking Jones not to intervene but to leave Banda himself to deal with the revolt. No doubt his mind was still on the list of complaints, the anonymous letters, the advice of the party stalwarts, the rumours of capitulation and particularly the meeting of members of parliament rescheduled for the following day upon which so much would depend. He was pleased that Jones had arranged for Archdeacon Chipembere, Henry's father, to come to Zomba to see him, Banda, and it is likely that he hoped the archdeacon would influence his son to side with him.

> He said he thought Chipembere was not really in the plot which had been hatched when Chiume, Chisiza and Bwanausi were on the Nyika Plateau [in August]. They had pledged themselves to stick together and when they returned they had got hold of Chirwa and the others. It was a rebellion and [he] would like to have them prosecuted for sedition. Could [he] not seize their passports?

When Jones again advised him to await the outcome of the parliamentarians' meeting the next day, he 'quietly agreed'. Jones may have been hoping that some form of reconciliation would result from that meeting. He had advised Banda both not to offer Cameron a ministerial post and not to sack anyone before the meeting. Now he advised him not to take any action against those he considered guilty of sedition. Banda contemplated the morrow's meeting and assumed that Nyasulu, the Speaker, would take the chair and he himself would give the members a full explanation of what had been happening. Despite his mildly doubtful remark about 'coming through', he was quite confident he would be victorious. At most, three members, other than the ministers, would be against him and he felt that the ministers themselves would want to keep him because 'they could get nowhere without [his] name'. They simply wanted him as 'a puppet, a Nyerere. But this he would not be.' His mood now was that Chiume, Chisiza, Chirwa and Bwanausi would have to go and Chokani, Msonthi, Tembo and probably Chipembere could stay. Some time during the day the ministers, or at least Chisiza, Chokani and Msonthi, tried to see Banda but he refused to see them.

Cole was not convinced that Banda would be victorious and he thought the outcome of the meeting was 'quite unpredictable, but [the] general feeling is that it will be a close thing'. The fact that the ministers, 'who are already jading members of the party', had accepted this trial of strength suggested that they, like Banda, were confident of success. He thought, too, that the ministers had already decided on who was to be Banda's successor, though he did not indicate who he thought it was.[49]

At about this time, probably on 6 September, Banda took the precaution of summoning back to Malawi, Chibambo – recently promoted regional minister for the north – who was accompanying a party of chiefs visiting Britain: 'Please make arrangement return Malawi immediately repeat immediately by fastest route ... your presence here is imperative.' Chibambo returned immediately via Dar es Salaam.[50]

The following morning, Monday, 7 September, Banda, ignoring the advice Jones had so recently given him not to take any important action before the meeting of members of parliament, rang the Governor-General and formally advised him that the offices of the ministers of justice (Chirwa), external affairs (Chiume), and works, development and housing (Bwanausi) together with the parliamentary secretaryship for natural resources (Rose Chibambo) should immediately be declared vacant. The three ministers were those who he had told Jones just before and during the weekend 'must go at once'. If arrangements could be made soon enough, the radio would make an announcement to this effect on the lunchtime news; if not, it would be made in the evening. The doctor said he would not be attending the informal meeting of members of parliament, adding, 'It is not necessary.' Plainly, he did not share Cole's lack of confidence as to the outcome of the trial of strength. He said he would call on Jones later in the day.[51]

While this telephone call was being made, the informal meeting was taking place of members of parliament, including ministers, but not Banda. Chipembere and Chibambo had not yet returned to the country. Those present at the meeting were told by Nyasulu that a formal meeting of parliament would take place the next day to debate a motion of confidence in the prime minister. They demanded to see the agenda, and the motion of confidence was read to them. The backbenchers, as the Speaker almost immediately told Jones and Youens by telephone, showed 'enthusiastic support' for the motion, but the ministers 'sat dejected'. The meeting seems to have been quite short. It was unlikely to have started before 9.30 a.m. and was over by 10.30 a.m.[52] Cole's account was:

'Speaker says there was much enthusiasm for Banda at meeting and that ministers looked uncomfortable. Latest Special Branch report is that substantial majority of MPs are in favour of Banda. Banda will talk privately to them this afternoon.' He added that there were no demonstrations outside the legislature, and that Banda was 'supremely confident and impatient of advice even from Governor-General'.[53]

Of the private afternoon meetings, Chiume said that Banda summoned the other members behind the ministers' backs, 'talked earnestly to them and demanded a statement of loyalty from each of them'.

> The members of parliament were put in a very difficult situation. Apart from those who saw in our departure their opportunity to step into our shoes, quite a number of them could not understand how we, who had been so divided, could now put up such a united front. We lost quite a number of supporters whose suspicions were aroused in that way.[54]

It is likely that Banda went forward with the motion of confidence to bring matters to a head, to demonstrate the overwhelming support for him, to humiliate and embarrass the ministers in public, to stir up the members of parliament against the ministers and in support of himself, to ensure that the members returned to their constituencies and spread their support for Banda, and to provide justification for getting rid of the most troublesome ministers.

The prime minister rang Jones soon after the informal meeting ended and said he would not come to see him that day, but he would come the following evening.[55] Although he did not say so, much of the afternoon was to be taken up in speaking privately and individually to the members of parliament. He added that if he lost the vote of confidence he would advise dissolution of parliament and fresh elections. It is clear that even a defeat in the house would not be the end of the matter. He had not been able to win over the cabinet, and now, if he could not win over parliament, he would go to the country. As life-president of the MCP he would nominate all the party's candidates, and the rebel ministers would be forced either not to stand for election or to stand in opposition to the MCP and do so with insufficient time to organize any party machinery of their own. When Jones took the opportunity to question the wisdom of sacking Bwanausi, Banda became impatient and said, 'I know what I am doing. I want this thing done as quickly as possible – with as little delay as possible.' An hour or so later he rang again, apologized for 'thumping the table' when he spoke earlier, and asked if Jones was sure he had got correctly the names of those being sacked. Jones repeated them: Chirwa, Chiume, Bwanausi and Rose Chibambo – which was correct.

Immediately after receiving Banda's telephone call, the Governor-

General saw the three ministers who were about to be dismissed, at half-hour intervals, and handed them the letters of removal from office. Indeed the first was delayed for five minutes while the call was being made. The first minister to be dealt with was Chirwa, and Jones recalled:[56]

> I told him the news and he accepted it with calm and dignity. He considered the Prime Minister had done the right thing ... and would win his motion of confidence tomorrow. 'Most of the MPs do not understand the issues at stake, but they will learn eventually. They do not have the same principles as we have.' Ministers did not wish to criticize the Prime Minister publicly and would not do so in tomorrow's debate unless provoked, 'but I suppose we shall be provoked'. I handed him the letter and he expressed the hope that he would be given a day or two to settle his affairs. I told him that the Prime Minister appeared to be hurt and angry about the written demands that had been made of him. Chirwa said he in his profession could not agree to the methods of the Prime Minister. He thought he had done the best for his country by making a stand with the others. He thought he had been picked out for dismissal because he had opposed the detention bill ... Finally, Chirwa assured me that he had nothing whatsoever against the Prime Minister personally and that he had enjoyed working with me.

Jones recalled that the next to come in was Chiume, who also was 'calm and dignified' and showed no surprise when he received his letter of dismissal. 'I make no apology for what I have done. The Prime Minister has been managing the affairs of four million people without seeking advice from anyone. This is a very undignified form of independence.' Like Chirwa, he said he had nothing personal against Banda and also that he had enjoyed working with the Governor-General. His own account of this interview was:

> At about three thirty it was my turn. 'I am sorry, Mr. Chiume,' began the Governor-General, 'the Prime Minister has advised me to revoke my appointment of you as Minister of Foreign Affairs.' 'I expected it, your Excellency,' I replied calmly. 'What do you plan to do?' he asked. I paused for a moment. I knew that this man had asked for my expulsion from the cabinet in 1963 because he alleged that I had called him an imperialist and, in 1962, he must have been instrumental in preventing me from becoming the first Minister of the Interior in Malawi [a post which Chipembere had also coveted]. I thought it was none of his business to ask me what I was going to do in the future and I told him so. He then signed the letter of termination of my appointment, we shook hands and I proudly walked out of his office for the last time. I got into my car [to return to Chirwa's house] with a clear conscience that what had happened

was part of the sacrifice that some of us had to make for Africa. My friends cheered wildly when I joined them.[57]

Chiume had indeed called Jones an imperialist, a view to which he strongly adhered ever thereafter, but he was wrong about Jones being instrumental in his not becoming minister of the interior.[58]

The third minister to appear was Bwanausi, who also 'received the news in calm and dignified fashion'.

> He understood the Prime Minister's position: 'He does not need men of my calibre. He needs people who will just endorse his policy. I can do more for the country outside politics. I don't like politics and will be glad to get out.' He said ministers had probably only themselves to thank in that they had built up Dr. Banda as a Messiah and it was probably very difficult for him to face opposition now.

The three dismissed ministers were not the only members of the cabinet to call on the Governor-General that afternoon. When it became clear to them that only three were being sacked, Chisiza drew Chirwa's typewriter towards him and 'with a confident smile' typed out his own resignation, insisting that they must all 'sink together'. Chokani and then, 'not without some hesitation', Msonthi followed suit.[59] Within half an hour of Bwanausi's departure from Government House, Chisiza, Chokani and Msonthi arrived and handed in their letters of resignation.

> Chisiza was bitter and said he would never withdraw what had been said in their letter of complaint. He would continue to say it again and again. It would be hypocritical for them to remain after their colleagues had been sacked. There was no difference between them. Chokani was not bitter but said he supported the others and could not remain a minister after the others had been sacked. He did not agree with the way the country was being run by the Prime Minister. Msonthi said he had been out of all this, since he had only recently been reappointed. 'But how can I stay on by myself?' All said they truly understood [Jones's] position and had enjoyed working with [him]. They wished the Prime Minister well and would not work against him. They declined to try and see the Prime Minister which [Jones] suggested they do. They had tried yesterday and he had refused to see them.

Chisiza's letter gave no explanation for his resignation, nor did it refer to solidarity with his dismissed colleagues, but simply informed Jones that his office was now vacant. Chokani's letter explained that he had decided to resign because of 'the recent developments in the country and [he] sincerely [felt he could] not continue as minister'. Msonthi's letter said that 'under the circumstances [he felt he could] not remain in office alone'.[60]

Chokani later gave his account of the resignation meeting, which differs somewhat from Jones's: 'Sir Glyn ... pleaded with me to reconsider my position and withdraw the resignation. He emphasised that Dr Banda had nothing against me. Sir Glyn was definitely unhappy about my resignation.'[61] From this account, though not from Jones's, it is clear the Governor-General was still desperately trying to retain at least Chokani in the cabinet. In his own account, Jones made no effort to decline the tendered resignations, whereas in 1962 he had refused to accept any of them.

Some time during that day Msonthi rang Philip Howard, a businessman, to seek his advice, and when Howard asked what it was about, Msonthi was reluctant to say because it was about politics. Howard declined to discuss it because he had always refused to give political advice. He recalled:

> Msonthi said he was desperate and must discuss the matter with me. He then said he had to decide whether to stay as minister and support Dr. Banda or join the other ministers and leave government. I said that only Msonthi could decide this but he must think very carefully indeed about it, but implied that he should stay. He said 'thank you', but I had the feeling he was not alone. I asked if someone else was there and he said yes, it was John Tembo. When I asked what Tembo was intending to do he said Tembo was going to stay in the cabinet but would act as liaison with the rebels.[62]

It is not clear what intended objective this liaison had, nor whether Tembo's proposed role was at Banda's request rather than on his own initiative, nor how he proposed to conduct the liaison. Youens was convinced that Cecilia Kadzamira 'saved Tembo's bacon when she persuaded him to come off the fence at the time of the cabinet crisis and come onto Kamuzu's side'.[63] He had sided with his colleagues at the 26 August cabinet meeting.

In Jones's account of the dismissals and resignations it is noticeable that the ministers who were sacked and those three who resigned all said they had enjoyed working with him. Many years later, Chiume, whose memory of the events long remained detailed and clear, could not recall having said he had enjoyed working with Jones and thought it most unlikely that he, and some of his colleagues, had said so, because, at least in his own case, it was not true.[64] Indeed, given his views on Jones as an imperialist, it would have been strange if he had told him he enjoyed working with him. Chiume was never a man to flatter anyone other than Banda. Maybe the others wished Jones to understand that they would be happy to work under him again if events proved this to be possible, either if Banda changed his mind or if, for whatever reason, he left office. They could, of course, do this only if Jones were Governor-General, and this would be the case only if Malawi did not become a republic – a prospect they strongly wished to avoid because of the increased executive powers it would give the head of state.

Banda later gave one of the reasons why he sacked the ministers – in which term he included those who had resigned:

> I have stated more than once that my main business ... is to maintain in this country a stable Government, an efficient, honest and incorruptible administration, and if to do this I have to sack Ministers, I will not hesitate. That is why, among other things I sacked Chiume, sacked Chirwa, sacked Chisiza, Bwanausi, Chipembere, Chokani, because they wanted me to do things that are being done in other countries, which, in my view, no Prime Minister with a spine would permit ... Here I must have a stable Government, an efficient, honest and incorruptible administration. People must come here when they have money to invest, get a licence without putting so many pounds in the pocket of a certain Minister first. Not here.[65]

Immediately after Chisiza, Chokani and Msonthi left Government House, Jones rang Banda and told him of their resignations. The doctor's only reaction was to say that he would see them after the meeting of parliament the next day, though they had told Jones, who had suggested a meeting to them, that they would not do so. The prime minister said he did not wish the resignations to be given publicity through government channels, only the four dismissals.[66]

Early on the morning following the 7 September dismissals and resignations, at twenty minutes past seven, Msonthi rang Jones from Blantyre to say he wished to see him urgently to withdraw his resignation. He had tried to telephone the doctor the previous evening – presumably after consulting Tembo and Howard – but had failed. Jones told him to drive over to Zomba straight away. He must have driven quickly, because less than an hour later he arrived at Government House. He said he had reconsidered his resignation and wished to withdraw it. He reminded the Governor-General that he had said the previous day he was resigning only because he was 'all alone'. Jones asked him to wait in another room because the prime minister was due to arrive only moments later. When told of Msonthi's change of heart, Banda 'expressed great pleasure' and immediately accepted the withdrawal. Msonthi was called in and Jones left them alone for about five minutes. After Msonthi left, Jones spent a few more minutes with Banda and advised him to 'let magnanimity and calmness be the motifs of his speech' in parliament when he spoke on the motion of confidence that morning. Banda agreed and thanked Jones for his moral support during the past few days.[67]

During the remainder of that and the following day, parliament debated a motion, drafted for Banda by Roberts,[68] that the house supported the MCP policy of unity, loyalty, discipline and obedience; supported the policies of the prime minister on domestic and external affairs; and reaffirmed its confidence in the prime minister.[69] In this single formula Roberts sought for Banda the necessary mandate of both the party and parliament to which he had referred earlier. The UN representative in Malawi, Gordon Menzies, privately reported what he saw from his 'little office ... quite close to Parliament House':

> The atmosphere was somewhat electric ... Crowds gathered outside the House from early morning, cheering the Members as they arrived, and there were interludes of singing, until the meeting started. Loudspeakers broadcast the Parliamentary proceedings and the crowds waited all day, very orderly and good humoured. A somewhat smaller crowd gathered on the second day of the meeting, when there was no broadcast of the proceedings.[70]

Cole described the occasion as 'dramatic and historic', and spoke mainly of what went on inside the building:

> The House was packed and ... Dr. Banda, supported by only Messrs. Tembo and Msonthi, proposed the motion of confidence in a remarkable speech which lasted for an hour and a half. He described in detail the Cabinet proceedings and skilfully built up a picture of a Ministerial conspiracy against him, steering clear of the underlying issue of collective responsibility and claiming that his colleagues had tried to create popular antipathy to his policies ... He said that the Ministers were motivated by ambition and avarice, and by the sinister enticements of Red China ... he deduced a 'Chinese plot' to overthrow him. At one stage he alleged that the Ministers would have murdered him if they thought they could get away with it. Dr. Banda received an overwhelming ovation from M.P.s, and it was clear from that moment that the vote of confidence would be carried without any difficulty ... The crowds outside parliament, who had occasionally been noisy and aggressive, dispersed in good humour.[71]

Chiume wrote of what went on both inside and outside the parliament building, where they 'found hundreds of people waiting outside'.

> They cheered us tremendously as we arrived. It was quite obvious that we were representing their feelings ... As Dr. Banda drove to parliament, he did not stop to wave to the people as was his custom ... the employees of the government press came out in full force to cheer us. Banda was furious and, as he entered parliament, he was shocked to find that ... the masses booed him and openly called him *chisilu* (traitor). For one and a

half hours that morning he denounced us savagely. The charges were disunity, disloyalty, disobedience, avarice, ambition, bribery, favouritism and treason; he exposed, as it were, every skeleton in the political cupboard. Loudspeakers carried his word to a growing crowd outside but, curiously, as he dealt with each of the critical issues ... there was an ambivalent reaction. The MPs in the chamber howled their support for him; the people outside roared for us.

On the morning of Wednesday, September 9th, the loudspeakers were therefore removed but the crowd remained. *Hansard*, which carried the verbatim report of the parliamentary debate, had to be withdrawn from circulation and revised because it contained too many mentions of applause for us.[72]

Banda was reported by some of the press to have punctuated his speech with 'shouting and dancing [as he] denounced the sacked and those who had resigned'.[73] Short referred to the 'standing ovation' he received at the end of his speech: 'It was a magnificent performance.' He added that to the ministers it was clear the day had gone against them – 'a conviction which grew stronger as the hours passed and member after member rose to denounce them as "traitors", "conspirators" and "power hungry maniacs"'.[74]

Chipembere and Chibambo arrived back in Malawi early in the afternoon of 8 September. Throughout the journey from Dar es Salaam, Chibambo pleaded with Chipembere: 'Go and do your best and make sure that the Prime Minister and his Ministers can come to some understanding.' He beseeched Chipembere to 'be the bridge between Ngwazi and the Ministers' since he was the best person to do this. Chipembere pondered these words and Chibambo thought he had convinced him to attempt a reconciliation. Kumtumanji was at Chileka to meet them. He handed Chipembere a letter from Banda asking him to remain in the cabinet,[75] and 'in a mood that was almost in tears said, "Look, Chip, you have been outside. You have every chance of making a contribution which will bring about an understanding and unity between the Prime Minister and his Ministers."'[76] The letter must have been written before parliament began its deliberations, before, that is, Banda knew how much support he would command. Chipembere refused to discuss the matter with Kumtumanji and he 'brushed aside newsmen and drove to Zomba'.[77] He refused to do so in a ministerial car, presumably so that Kumtumanji would not be able to press him.[78] On reaching the capital, Chibambo wanted to join the meeting of parliament – which adjourned at 5.30 p.m. – but was dissuaded from doing so. He told his parliamentary colleagues the next day: 'I went to see the Ngwazi. I met nobody except my son ... I didn't want anyone to come and speak with me. I wanted to have

Ngwazi's word ... and he told me the story, then I dashed off and slept far away from this town.'[79] Clearly, he was not going to give the ex-ministers a chance to try and influence him: speaking with Banda and 'having his word' was sufficient for Chibambo.

At 8.20 p.m. Chipembere – with whom a number of his friends on his arrival in Zomba had pleaded that he should attempt a reconciliation[80] – went to see Jones, having been sent there by Banda.[81] To his surprise, Jones was not expecting him. It is likely that the prime minister refused to see him – the only minister not yet to have declared his hand – and simply told him to go and see the Governor-General. By this stage, Banda had no intention of trying to effect a reconciliation, whether or not Chipembere was on his side. It is probable that he considered that the first day of the debate on the motion of confidence had gone so well for him that he did not need Chipembere's support on the second day. Chipembere was gravely concerned by the 'tragic situation' that had arisen while he was away. This suggests that when he left for Canada, there was no intention – at least not one including him – or no indication that things would deteriorate as much as they did. He had advised him against confrontation. His permanent secretary, who was with him in Canada, was sure that the cable asking him to return to Malawi came as a complete surprise.[82] Chipembere asked why it had been necessary to sack the ministers. Perhaps it was the sackings – which may have been unintended on their part – and not the confrontation in itself – which they intended – that, to Chipembere, was the 'tragic situation'. Jones recalled:

> I told him that things seemed to be going fairly well until ministers put their demands in writing to the Prime Minister. In my view they had carried what was originally a good case much too far. He then said he had not made up his mind what side to take. Before taking a final decision he would like to satisfy his conscience that he had done everything within his power to get a reconciliation between the Prime Minister and the Ministers. Was there still a chance of his doing this ... ? I said I thought that if the Ministers were prepared to make a gesture there might still be a chance. He said he would be prepared to try and get the Ministers to make an approach if I would ascertain whether Dr. Banda would be prepared to receive one. I then telephoned the Prime Minister ... When I put the proposition to him he at first said he would be prepared to receive an approach only after the debate had been concluded. I said Chipembere very much hoped to have a meeting before the debate was resumed. The Prime Minister said he would consider it but showed very little enthusiasm. I phoned Chipembere and said the Prime Minister was considering the matter and I would be prepared to approach him again tomorrow

morning if he could get the Ministers to go along with him. I said I thought the Prime Minister would not agree to postponing the resumption of the debate to enable the discussion to take place; therefore it would be necessary for the discussion, if agreed to, to take place before 9.30 am. ... Later he phoned to say he had contacted all the ex-Ministers and they were in agreement. He asked that the meeting should take place in Government House in my presence since I was 'the most neutral of all'.[83]

Chipembere's account of his meeting with Jones was:

I went on the advice of the Prime Minister himself, to see if I could get the Governor-General to be a kind of mediator between the Prime Minister and us, his Ministers. I made a specific request that some sort of discussion should take place, that the Prime Minister and us, his Ministers, should come together at Government House where we could at least make a beginning, in an attempt to solve the differences that have sprung up. And I was particularly keen that the discussion should take place in the morning before we came to the House, because I felt that in this House the situation would deteriorate as a result of the exchanges which are made ... The Prime Minister indicated that he was prepared to have some sort of discussion and informed us, through ... the Governor-General, that he had an open mind on this matter and that he would be prepared to discuss the possibility of a settlement.[84]

Having apparently made this important progress, Chipembere left Government House and met late into the night with the ex-ministers.

Early the next morning, Wednesday, 9 September, Jones rang Banda at a quarter to eight.[85] 'He was not in a happy mood' and was incensed that Chipembere had suggested that resuming the debate should be postponed. He 'absolutely declined' to meet the ministers until after the debate. 'He was angrily emphatic about this.' The first day in parliament had gone well for the prime minister and he was anxious that the second day should not go wrong. He was keen now to get things over and done with. Banda's account of Jones's telephone call and his own reaction, as he told parliament, was:

This morning ... the Governor-General rang me to come over. 'Oh,' I said, 'What is up?' 'I have someone here. He thinks you should postpone the session until the situation is settled and see what reconciliation can be effected.' I said that is not my way of doing things at all. We started yesterday. If we stopped in the middle of the debate, people will think that I am afraid, and I am not afraid of this debate. I want to see the end of it, that's all. I was not going to stop a debate which had been started without reaching a decision. No ... We must finish the debate to-day. And, therefore, no tea break, no lunch. That is how I work. A decision one way or the other, no two ways about it.[86]

Jones immediately told Chipembere of Banda's decision and received the response that he and his colleagues felt that no useful purpose would be served by meeting Banda after the debate because strong attitudes would by then have been adopted from which people would find it difficult to retreat.[87] It sounds as if at least some of the former ministers were with Chipembere when he received this telephone call, that they had agreed that if there were to be a meeting it would have to be before the debate resumed, and that Banda's refusal to see them then made Chipembere decide to join his colleagues. Half an hour later Jones told Banda of Chipembere's reply and the doctor simply said, 'That's all right.' At 9.15 a.m., at Banda's request, the Governor-General swore in Chibambo as regional minister – he had been in Britain when Kumtumanji and Chidzanja had been sworn in. Five minutes later he received Chipembere's resignation.[88] Chipembere then drove to parliament in his ministerial car and as he walked into the chamber he hesitated at the front bench. Then, with a wave of his arm, he joined his colleagues on the back bench. It was a dramatic gesture which, coupled with his arrival in the ministerial car, gave the impression that only when reaching the front bench did he decide to resign.

It is possible that Banda deliberately rescheduled the parliamentary meeting to a date before Chipembere was due to return so as to get it all cleared up in his own favour in his absence. This would then have left it open to Chipembere to join him rather than the rebel ministers, and the letter he sent via Kumtumanji, together with his meeting with Archdeacon Chipembere, was designed to achieve this. Chipembere's early return and his attempts to effect a reconciliation rather than automatically join Banda would have turned the doctor against him. It was victory, not reconciliation, that Banda wanted, and after the first day's debate victory was virtually his. He was not going to have Chipembere ease it from his grasp: he either unequivocally joined him or left the government.

Moxon, who was present in the chamber on 9 September, gave an account of the early stages of the morning's proceedings after Banda arrived. Though overly colourful and grossly exaggerated, it does illustrate that Banda, as Jones had observed, 'was not in a happy mood':

> There followed a most extraordinary scene. There in front of the entire house, in which were present the whole of the Corps Diplomatique, the Prime Minister leapt to his feet, hurled his fly whisk down on the cushions and, raising his arms above his head, he started to scream. He stamped and raved up the 'aisle', his face twisted with fury ... Executing the most grotesque contortions he hopped and bounded up to the Clerk's desk and waved his arms in his face, yelling 'Who organised those people

outside?' ... 'I've made a decision. I've made a decision', he screamed, 'No tea, no lunch, nothing – until we reach a conclusion.' Then, exhausted, he hurled himself into his chair. Up again after a few seconds he again threw down his fly whisk and cavorted round yelling once more. At any minute I expected him to fall down and start biting the plastic tiles. He hurled himself into his seat, however, breathing heavily. It was like a monstrously exaggerated caricature of a wilful child denied his bag of sweets. The ex-ministers on the back bench sat looking on impassively.[89]

No doubt the doctor was upset by Chipembere's attempts to delay the resumption of parliament's business, his failure to side with him and his resignation, and by the pro-rebel crowd outside the chamber. The house did in fact sit without break all day, and 'the former ministers put their arguments not only apologetically but without a grain of socialistic argument' – much to the disappointment of those who had hoped for a more revolutionary approach.[90] At 8.10 p.m. parliament unanimously gave Banda the vote of confidence he had sought.

At the close of the second day of the debate, despite the late hour, the former ministers met 'to assess the situation'. They agreed it was their duty to return to their constituencies and explain why they were no longer in the government. 'The battle had to be taken to the people themslves who would be the judges in the final analysis.' They discussed their strategy thoroughly and decided to meet again in Blantyre on 28 September, three weeks thence, 'to compare notes and launch a new party'. One of them was so impressed with the crowd behaviour outside parliament that he was confident he and his colleagues would be back in government within three weeks.[91] The nature of the battle they intended to take to their constituents soon became known to the doctor.

Late the following morning, Banda called on Jones.[92] He was pleased with the support he had received in the House and he hoped Chisiza and Chokani – two of the three, excluding Msonthi, who had resigned and not been sacked – might one day return to the cabinet. Chiume, Bwanausi, Chirwa and Chipembere, in that order, were 'quite unacceptable' and he was convinced from reports he was now receiving that these four had been contemplating his resignation and had been canvassing people in Zomba to ascertain whether Chirwa would be acceptable as president and Chipembere as prime minister. Chipembere's exclusion now from Banda's list of those who had resigned and might one day return to his cabinet, and his placement – albeit last – on the list with those he had dismissed, who were quite unacceptable, is interesting. During the second day of the debate, when Chipembere had said, 'I hope nobody will call me a traitor by resigning,' Banda – his displeasure notwithstanding – had interjected, 'You, no.'[93] Now, twenty-four hours later, the prime minister was treating Chipembere as one of, or on a par with, the traitors. This overnight change came about when he learned that they were taking steps in Zomba, where many Malawian civil servants were known to be disillusioned with Banda, to see if he, Chipembere, would be acceptable as prime minister. This was the battle the former ministers intended to take to the people.

Chiume was particularly cautious over his departure from Zomba to return to his constituency in the north of the country. When he had finished discussing plans with his colleagues during the evening after the debate, he began to pack his belongings, and, as he recalled:

> Suddenly there was a knock on the door and my ... personal secretary came in. She apologised for coming at such a late hour ... I took her to the verandah of the house where she asked me, sobbing, when I would be leaving. 'Why?' I asked. 'Do they want to chase us out of these houses immediately?' 'No,' she said, 'it is more sinister than that. They are planning road accidents.' There was no mistaking the seriousness of her warning. She knew what she was talking about. Her husband had just come from a meeting of senior police and army officers. I realised at once what she meant ... She said goodbye and left in her husband's car.[94]

The personal secretary acted entirely of her own individual volition. Her husband, a police officer, was not in any way involved, save to drive her to Chiume's house. She had 'gathered information from careless conversations [by other people] and realised that it was time to move Kanyama quickly'. She remained clear many years later that there was a real danger to Chiume.[95] After she had left, Chiume pondered their conversation and recalled a remark made by Banda at a meeting of the MCP central committee: 'To those who oppose us, accidents happen.' He recalled, too, Pondeponde's murder, which was followed by neither inquest nor prosecution – 'The Governor had apparently been prevailed over by Banda.' He thought a good deal about Dunduzu's fatal car crash, and the physical attack Chakuamba had attempted on him outside the parliament building just before the debate. The following evening, without warning and in the dark, he left Zomba for the north.[96]

Over the previous week or so the British government, not unnaturally, had taken a close interest in events in Malawi and were beginning to contemplate their future relations with the country. Cole kept them informed of what was going on, and the Commonwealth Relations Office sought his opinion on a number of points. He agreed with their view that it was in Britain's current interests that Banda should remain in power, 'though one fears that unless his survival is accompanied by some concessions he may be heading for a greater fall later on'. Any alternative to Banda seemed to Cole to 'vary from worse to very bad indeed':

Almost any successor Government imaginable would be much more 'African' and 'non'aligned', would court popularity in dangerous ways and would speed up Africanisation with damaging consequences. With Chiume these processes would be very rapid with consequences which could be disastrous. With people like Chipembere a more gradual move in this direction would seem probable. Immediate chaos seems unlikely and ... in any case the Governor-General and expatriates in police, army and civil service can to some extent still hold the ring ... My guess is that at present army and police will obey orders of their senior officers – all British – who will be loyal to properly constituted Malawi Government – whoever may be heading it.[97]

Immediately the debate was concluded and its outcome known, the Commonwealth Relations Secretary sent an emergency cable – already in draft – to Cole asking him to pass on to Banda his 'congratulations on the impressive vote of confidence which [he had] received from the Malawi Parliament':

I fully realise that this episode must have caused you much personal distress but I trust that you will be encouraged by the love and respect which has been manifested by your people. Your many friends in this country have admired the courage and resolution with which you have met this challenge to your authority and the policies on which the future prosperity and safety of Malawi so greatly depend.

He hoped that Cole could contrive that theirs should be the first expression of congratulations that Banda received.[98]

At their meeting on Thursday, 10 September, Banda asked Jones to swear in Nyasulu as minister for natural resources, Muwalo as minister of information, Chakuamba as minister for community and social development, Chidzanja as minister of works and transport and Roberts as attorney-general. He himself took over the portfolios of justice and external affairs.[99] He also appointed the four new cabinet ministers and Kumtumanji to the MCP central executive, which now included all three regional ministers. Later that day he held a press conference at which he said the country was peaceful and calm, because he had given instructions that it was to be so. He described the troubles as 'just a family squabble' and explained that he had left the cabinet seats of the resigned ministers vacant because he was 'quite certain, if not all, some of them will come back and I'll take them back when they come'.[100] Cole pointed out that 'this bait had little attraction when viewed alongside the general inflexibility of Dr. Banda's attitude'.[101]

Banda and most of the ex-ministers – who were still members of parliament representing their own constituencies – separately spent the weekend holding public meetings in various parts of the country to try and win support for their respective points of view. Banda gave instructions to his party members that 'there was to be no rough stuff'.[102] Bwanausi called on Jones to say goodbye.[103] Chokani, too, seemed to be in the process of bowing out quietly. The Special Branch was 'uneasy' and was watching events closely.[104] Chiume left Zomba the day after the meeting of the legislature and drove to Nkhata Bay. With Chirwa and Chisiza, who also went to the north, he addressed meetings at Mzuzu and Nkata Bay that were reported to be attended by only 200 to 300 people. Chiume's later account was:

> The meeting at Mzuzu filled us with encouragement. It was well attended by civil servants and businessmen who pledged loyalty for our case. At Nkata Bay the mass meeting expressed its determination to oppose the establishment of a black dictatorship in Malawi ... We met with similar success at Rumpi, but at Karonga our plans were very nearly disrupted. Here the attitude of the people had been affected by earlier divisions in our ranks; they were suspicious. But when at last we were able to hold the meeting, we knew that we had won over this area too. The same was the case [elsewhere in the north]. The wisdom of starting a new party, which some of the former ministers were contemplating, had been confirmed by the reaction of the people.[105]

Chiume addressed several other meetings and a particularly large one at Livingstonia despite the efforts of Chibambo, sent by Banda, to dissuade people from attending. Shortly, the junior college and the secondary school at Livingstonia were closed down and the headmaster dismissed by the government because they had given refuge to Chiume.[106]

In the south, Chipembere's meeting on Saturday at Fort Johnston was larger, but not as large as he had hoped, because Chief Mponda had told his people not to attend. Even though the door had been left ajar for him to return to the cabinet, the firm exclusion of his closest colleagues, Chiume and Bwanausi, made him take a fairly hard-hitting line in his speech. He spoke to foreign press reporters and was still confident of eventual success.[107] Banda's own meeting on Sunday was at a mass meeting at Palombe where he had a 'large and enthusiastic' audience.

Information about these meetings was given to Jones by Banda on the Monday afternoon, when they met at the Governor-General's lodge in Blantyre.[108] They discussed the situation in which Banda now found himself:

> The Prime Minister agreed that he would be in a stronger position if he could get back the ministers who had resigned [as opposed to those he had sacked]. He said [Jones] could contact Chokani and Chisiza right

away so long as [he] did not let it appear the approach was coming from him. Chipembere should be seen later. [Banda] was still very angry with Chiume, Chirwa and Bwanausi – latter almost most of all.

Banda rang the Governor-General the following evening to say that he 'had it on good authority' that Chisiza, Chokani and Bwanausi would be prepared to rejoin him if approached.[109] He asked Jones to contact them – including Bwanausi, with whom he had been so angry the previous day – and 'see what he could do', but to do so 'behind the scenes'. He did not mention Chipembere. It may be that he was doubtful of disposing of Chisiza, who had been both in charge of MCP security and his personal bodyguard, and would as a consequence be particularly dangerous in any attempt forcefully to oust him.

During the course of the next few days, Jones had a number of meetings designed to try and repair some of the deep damage caused over the past few weeks. Cole reported that Chipembere also 'made considerable efforts both during and immediately after the Parliamentary debate to bring Dr. Banda and the other Ministers together', but there is little evidence that he made much effort.[110] Indeed, his nocturnal discussions with his colleagues to 'take the battle to the people' and form a new party suggest the contrary.

The morning after Banda asked him to 'see what he could do behind the scenes', the Governor-General had a long discussion, on Wednesday, 16 September, at his invitation, with Chokani, who hoped that Jones would 'promote a reconciliation between the Prime Minister and the ex-Ministers this week before the attitudes had hardened beyond recall'.[111] Jones was not confident he could get Banda to accept Chiume and Chirwa and asked how important Chipembere was. The tactic of dividing the ex-ministers, originally attempted by Banda to get rid of some of them, was now used by Jones in an effort to get some of them back. As Jones recorded:

> [Chokani] said no reconciliation could take place without Chipembere. The [ex] ministers would press for all to be taken back. I said that if they adopted an 'all or nothing' attitude the prospects of getting things back to normal were very slight indeed. The possibilities were either (a) all except Chiume and Chirwa to come back, or (b) the others come back first and Chiume and Chirwa later. Chokani said this [latter] would be all right if they could get some sort of guarantee. Finally, I said there might be a possibility that the thing could be solved if all except Chiume came back. Chiume might be given a job outside the Government. Chokani said, 'If Chiume as Minister of External Affairs is unacceptable why could he not go back to Education or Information?'

Jones was trying to work within the constraints Banda had set and to draw up lists of 'next best options'. Under no existing circumstances – and probably under no future circumstances – would the prime minister have Chiume back in his government, but Chokani does not seem to have grasped this point. He seems to have thought the trouble was confined to external affairs and not to have recognized that it was wider than this. Chirwa was almost in the same category as Chiume. The position of neither Bwanausi, of whom Banda was very doubtful, nor Chisiza, whom he would be willing – possibly even anxious – to have back, was discussed by Jones and Chokani. The key figure was Chipembere. Without him no others would return, even if invited. Banda said he should be approached but later than Chokani and Chisiza. Jones asked how important the others felt his return to be, and Chokani said it was indispensable to a reconciliation.

The Governor-General was at pains to explain to Chokani that he was acting without having secured Banda's agreement, that he had no authority to make any concessions and that any argument and bargaining would have to take place directly between Banda and the ex-ministers: he could take no part in it. He then spoke in pointed terms, which reveal how deeply disturbing he believed the position to be and which explain why he had gone, and was continuing to go, to such lengths to heal the rifts and bring about a return of stable government. He almost certainly intended his words, their tone and his view of the profound seriousness of the situation to be conveyed to the other ex-ministers:

> Malawi was now disunited and the laughing stock of the world. If I could not promote a reconciliation I would have to go. The situation could go from bad to worse and civil war on a Congo scale could happen. The ex-Ministers ... had over the past three years conceded full power to the Prime Minister; he had got them what they wanted; they could not, having regard to his very authoritative methods, get him in one fell swoop to reverse all his policies and decisions. They must be prepared to met him half way. All was going well in their negotiations until the memorandum of demands was drawn up. That document was in my view disastrous.

It is unclear why Jones said he would have to leave if he could not secure a reconciliation, nor is it clear how extensive that reconciliation would have to be for him to stay. It may be that having learned from Banda, over the years – and more recently – the efficacy of threatened resignation, he was applying the same tactic. Perhaps he hoped Chokani and at least some his colleagues believed they needed him as Governor-General – he claimed they all said how much they had enjoyed working with him and Chirwa had said he looked forward to him staying for some time.

Perhaps a threat to go might pull them round? On the other hand, Chipembere believed that by now Jones had become ineffectual and Banda treated him as a junior officer. Perhaps, too, the prospect of remaining in ill favour with Banda without having Jones to turn to for advice and support, would induce a greater willingness to attempt a reconciliation. Most importantly, if he resigned, either he would be replaced or, more likely, Malawi would become a republic. The prospect of having either an unknown person in his place, or an executive president, would not have appealed to them. In the event he neither promoted a reconciliation, nor did he go.

Chokani agreed that Jones should try to get Chisiza and Bwanausi, together with himself – the three Banda had asked him to see – and Chipembere, for a meeting on Friday 18 September, two days hence. Jones immediately sent messages through the police radio network to Chisiza in the north asking him to fly to Zomba, prepared to see Banda 'immediately on arrival', and to Chipembere – whom Banda had asked Jones to delay seeing – in Fort Johnston, asking him also to go to Zomba but to meet him, Jones, and be prepared to stay over to Saturday 19 September.[112] It appears from these preparations that he was at least somewhat hopeful that a meeting and a reconciliation were possible between these ex-ministers and Banda. Bwanausi and Chokani both lived in Blantyre and were easier to contact. His task was not helped that evening when, at a special meeting of the executive committee of the MCP, all the ex-ministers and Rose Chibambo had been suspended from the party for making damaging speeches.[113] This deprived them of the benefit of the party organizing their meetings and it banned members from attending their meetings, while leaving Banda unrestricted use of party organization and unrivalled attendance at his own meetings.[114] As the press observed, 'While he controls the party, Dr Banda will control the country.'[115]

During the day following this meeting with Chokani, Jones met with Youens and Roberts to 'discuss the general situation'.[116] He asked Youens to see Banda and tell him that when he had asked Chipembere to come and see him Chipembere had replied, 'At the present stage I cannot see [the Governor-General] by myself alone. I can only see him together with [my] colleagues, the former ministers who are likely to be in Zomba and Blantyre at the end of this month' – which was two weeks away.[117] Banda knew the former ministers were seeking support in the country for their plans to form a new party and replace him by Chipembere as prime minister, and would have concluded that the delay was to give them time to further their plans. Youens was also asked to tell Banda that Jones had seen Chokani and he, too, stressed that he would not come back alone but only with his colleagues, although he was in a cooperative mood. Further, Youens was asked to say that Jones had invited Chisiza to fly down to Zomba to see the Governor-General, but so far there had been no reply. If Chisiza accepted the invitation, Jones expected to see him, Chokani and Bwanausi. He wanted Youens to ask Banda what effect the suspension from the MCP would have on the ex-ministers and what effect it had been designed to have. When Youens put this question to the prime minister he received the reply that he did not expect any effect. 'They will stick together. I shall demonstrate that they are not indispensable.'

The next day, 18 September, Banda appointed nine new parliamentary secretaries to assist the ministers. Six of the nine came from the central region of the country.[118] They, together with the 'seven close supporters' whom he appointed to the central executive,[119] strengthened still further his personal control over the government and the party. During the course of that day Jones saw Chokani, Chisiza and Bwanausi.[120] Chokani phoned him in the morning and was strangely guarded in his phraseology, asking, 'Is the gentleman from the north coming down?', to which Jones, taking this to refer to Chisiza, answered that he had not received a reply but he might be on his way. Chokani then said, 'Augustine and I have spoken to the one who refused your invitation for yesterday [Chipembere]. He says he will join us if the man from the north comes down. Then there will be four of us.' This would exclude Chiume and Chirwa.

Chisiza arrived at Government House early that afternoon and talked for about an hour with Jones:

> He admitted that the Prime Minister had pockets of support all over the country particularly in the central region and even in the north but it was shallow support which would not survive a real crisis. The ex-ministers were gaining a lot of support and he said that any of the new ministers going north would be attacked. Orton [Chirwa] was in control of the whole of Nkata Bay and Chiume of the greater part of Rumpi. He only came to see me in my personal capacity and not as Governor-General. He agreed to come with Chipembere, Chokani and Bwanausi at 6.30 p.m. [He] promised to do all in his power to remedy the very difficult situation that had arisen by all means short of abandoning his principles. He said the situation was 'not beyond repair' ... I said I thought the memorandum deplorable: it had a disastrous effect on the Prime Minister.

Chisiza's remark about Banda's support not surviving a real crisis carried the implication that he did not think they had yet faced a real crisis and that he expected more to come. It was, of course, Chisiza who first – and shortly after independence day – spoke to Lomax about an impending crisis, and Chipembere later claimed that Chisiza, and not Chiume, was the instigator of the revolt.

At seven o'clock that evening, Chisiza – who was 'slightly tight' – together with Chokani and Bwanausi, saw the Governor-General, but Chipembere did not join them. His colleagues excused him on the ground that 'he did not know there was to be a meeting'. Jones recorded:

> [They] all spoke saying they were willing to do what was possible to heal the breach. There could be compromise but [they] strongly felt the doctor should see all the ex-ministers. I said I doubted if the Prime Minister could agree to that. Why could not those whom he would agree to, go and see him in the first place? I said that though I had no mandate from the Prime Minister and no proposals I sensed that at present Chiume and Chirwa were unlikely to be received by the Prime Minister. Chisiza ... said 'We all know that the Prime Minister thinks just as badly of us as he does the others. He wants to divide us. But we shall stick together and must be loyal to our friends.' I said they might conceive a loyalty greater even than that – to the country and the people. I said the Prime Minister [was] a man of strong heart and spirit. They could not expect him to reverse his policies. Their document had been an arrogantly worded ultimatum probably unique in history.

The Governor-General continued by telling them that if they secured four cardinal principles of cabinet government they should be satisfied: the prime minister should back them up, particularly in public; should delegate functions as much as possible; should take his ministers into his confidence in all important matters of state and certainly before important decisions were taken; and should accept collective responsibility to parliament – this was laid down in the constitution. All these points were directed at Banda reforming his method of governing and none of the substantive policy issues was mentioned. While capable of meeting all the ex-ministers' demands, Jones must have known that there was absolutely no chance of them being accepted by Banda. It is clear that the Governor-General still agreed fully with the demands. The three ex-ministers were 'grave, not very happy and occasionally boastful'. They finally promised to reconsider their decision not to meet Banda unless all the ex-ministers were present. They agreed to meet again the following evening at Blantyre before Jones's meeting with the prime minister.

Jones repeatedly and almost obsessively told the ministers about the damaging effect of the memorandum containing their list of complaints. He did not, however, at any stage suggest that they withdraw it. Indeed, quite the contrary. Perhaps he felt the damage done by the memorandum had already become irreparable and withdrawing it would not help. More likely, he felt withdrawal would have been too much to ask of the ministers, especially since they knew he agreed with much of what it contained.

Chisiza, Chokani and Bwanausi met at the Governor-General's lodge in Blantyre, as agreed, the following evening.[121] Again Chipembere was not present, and his colleagues again excused him, this time by saying he was 'on his way but had probably had a puncture or something'. They would see him later in the evening. On this occasion Bwanausi was the spokesman. They had considered what Jones had said to them the previous evening and, in the interests of the country and the people, they had decided to try and see Banda without insisting on all the ex-ministers being present. They seemed 'more cheerful' than they had the previous evening. It was left that Jones should suggest to the prime minister that he meet Chisiza, Chokani, Bwanausi and Chipembere sometime during the following Monday. In the meantime Jones would 'try and create as friendly an atmosphere as possible for the meeting'.

Soon after the ex-ministers had left, Banda arrived at the lodge in a 'very confident and, from the point of view of the purpose in hand, very difficult mood'.[122]

> He was going to teach the ex-ministers a lesson they would never forget. They had picked on the wrong man to try and 'Nyererise'. 'But for the fact that [he was] telling the people to exercise restraint some of them would be dead and under the ground by now.' All the people were solidly behind him even in the north. Messages of loyalty had come to him from Karonga where Chisiza had been 'chased away' when he had tried to hold a meeting at his own home in Deep Bay.

This made it extremely difficult for Jones to create a friendly atmosphere in which the former ministers could meet the prime minister. He told Banda of his two meetings with Chisiza, Chokani and Bwanausi, and said that they and Chipembere wished to see him without asking for Chirwa and Chiume to be present. Banda was 'very lukewarm about it, saying, "I cannot see them until I have finished all my meetings throughout the country. They have been having meetings; I must now be allowed to have mine."' When Jones protested that this left him in a most awkward position, Banda agreed to meet the four sometime on Monday 'but only to shake hands with them, not to talk business. We will talk after I have had my meetings.'

> He was ... in a mood of rather devastating confidence and quite unshakable. He thought Chisiza was treacherous and wondered why Chipembere should wish to see him in view of what he had said about [him, Banda] at his meetings in Fort Johnston ... Many people were trying to promote reconciliation between him and the former ministers, and Cameron had been to see him with this object in view.

Cameron recalled that when he raised the matter with him 'Banda went berserk, pulled off his jacket and started to tug at his braces. Had Banda been a bigger man, [Cameron is] convinced that he would have attacked [him], so incensed was he.'[123] Others able to observe Banda at close quarters commented on other occasions on how, when angered, he would show signs of having a fit and froth at the mouth.[124] His facial tic, which became noticeably worse in anger, was well known.

The likelihood of a meeting between the prime minister and any of the ex-ministers, limited as it already was, faded significantly when, having left the Governor-General that evening, Chokani, Chisiza and Bwanausi joined Chipembere and held what they claimed was a cocktail party in Blantyre to which MCP members and the press were invited.[125] They claimed they were still loyal to Banda and were not engaged in attempts to oust him. On the other hand, they criticized his policies, particularly on external affairs, Africanization and hospital charges, and vowed they would return to the government only if he changed those policies. The 200 or so people present gave them a 'standing ovation'.

The following day, Sunday, 20 September, Banda addressed a crowd of about 5,000 at Ngabu in the Lower River area. The massive organization of the MCP was behind this meeting: dozens of lorries, fully loaded with flag-waving and song-singing members, travelled from Blantyre to Ngabu, and the meeting was given great publicity.[126] He denounced the ex-ministers, accusing them of 'criminal irresponsibility' and of stirring up unrest against him.[127] He showed no sign of changing his policies, save that he announced, as he had at Palombe,[128] that he would not levy the three-pence hospital fee on those who could not afford to pay – thereby doing away with the one complaint in which his audience and the rural peasant population generally was likely to be interested. Banda had told Jones he would hold his own public meetings before talking with the former ministers. He had been confident that by then he would be in an even stronger position and they in a weaker position. Ngabu would have reinforced this confidence.

Listening to the radio account of the Saturday 'cocktail party' meeting in Blantyre and to Banda's tape recorded speech at Ngabu, Jones believed the doctor knew the former had been arranged when he spoke with him the previous evening and was 'so difficult'. He also believed that when Chipembere 'probably had a puncture or something' he was in fact arranging that meeting.[129] What was said at the cocktail party and at Ngabu persuaded him to reconsider the appropriateness of the proposed meeting between the ex-ministers and Banda. Consequently, well before eight o'clock the next morning, Monday 21 September, he met with Youens and Roberts and they quickly decided it would be advisable to ask Banda if he now felt any helpful purpose would be served by meeting simply to shake hands.[130] Youens rang later in the morning to say that,

1. (left) Dr Kamuzu Banda, Chikela Airport, 6 July 1958.
2. (below) Dunduzu Chisiza, 1958.

3. (above) Henry Chipembere and Dunduzu Chisiza, Gwelo Prison, 1959.
4. (below) Orton Chirwa, Dr Kamuzu Banda and Dunduzu Chisiza, Federal Review Conference, London, December 1960.

5. (above) The Governor, elected ministers and parliamentary secretaries, September 1961. Left to right: D. Chisiza, C. Cameron, A. Bwanausi, Sir Glyn Jones, Dr Kamuzu Banda, K. Chiume, M. Mkandawire, O. Chirwa.

6. (below) Executive Council, September 1961. Left to right: K. Chiume, H. Phillips, J. Ingham, Dr Kamuzu Banda, R. Kettlewell, Sir Glyn Jones, R. Foster, J. Pine, C. Cameron, M. Mkandawire.

7. (above) Legislative Council, September 1961.
8. (below) Kanyama Chiume, 1962.

9. (left) Kanyama Chiume, Dr Kamuzu Banda and Henry Chipembere, 1963.
10. (below) The Governor, Sir Glyn Jones, and the Prime Minister, Dr Kamuzu Banda, 1963.

11. (above) Kanyama Chiume and Henry Chipembere, on tour, 1963.
12. (right) Dr Banda, 1963.

13. (above) Legislative Council, 1963.
14. (below) Henry Chipembere, in hiding in the bush, January 1965.

15. (above) Henry Chipembere's house at Malindi, destroyed by security forces, February 1965.
16. (below) The Fort Johnston Ferry, February 1965.

when asked, Banda said there would be no point in a meeting with the former ministers 'at the present time'. It was almost certainly as a result of the Blantyre cocktail party meeting – which he described as a 'secret meeting' – that Banda concluded he should not meet them.[131] He had, of course, already said he would not meet them, save to shake their hands, until he had held his series of meetings throughout the country, and Ngabu was just the beginning. Having received Banda's response, Jones rang Chokani and asked him to tell his colleagues that although Banda had reluctantly agreed on Saturday to meet them, he now felt that a meeting would be pointless. He added that he was sorry his efforts had failed. Chokani was sympathetic, but sounded as if he were relieved by Banda's decision.[132] Even remote possibilities of a reconciliation had now disappeared. At this point Banda appointed Msonthi minister of education, Chipembere's former post. Shortly, too, he appointed Alfred Chiwanda minister of labour, Chokani's former post.[133] All the ministerial posts formerly occupied by the rebel ministers were now filled.

Jones would have been justified in wondering if either the former ministers or Banda had been completely open and honest with him, or whether they were simply using him, toying with him and playing for time, not seriously intent on a reconciliation. The three ex-ministers had given manifestly implausible excuses for Chipembere not joining them in meetings with him. Jones had only Chisiza's, Chokani's and Bwanausi's word for it that Chipembere – who, it seems, was avoiding Jones – would go with them to see Banda. Chisiza was 'slightly tight' at one of the meetings and the three of them were in a 'cheerful' mood before going off, immediately after leaving him, to the cocktail party meeting. It is clear that they knew about the party but did not mention it to Jones, who believed that Banda also knew of it in advance but did not mention it. Banda had told him he knew the rebels were considering setting up a new party and making Chipembere the prime minister. Unless Jones disbelieved him, he ought to have expected neither side to be genuinely interested in reconciliation.

There was something of a hiatus following these events on the Monday, though Chipembere told reporters he was under pressure to form a new political party, pressure he was resisting in the interests of national unity.[134] Jones held vespers – a secret meeting with the heads of the security forces, the attorney-general, the head of the civil service and the head of Special Branch – in the early evening of Monday 21 September. There was a meeting of the new cabinet on 23 September, when, too, Malawi's ambassadors called on Jones.[135] The purpose of their visit is not clear, but it may have been 'to test their own allegiances and to work for a settlement', though nothing came of it.[136]

On Friday morning, 25 September, Banda visited the Governor-

General in Blantyre.

He seemed very fit and was confident that his tour of the central and northern provinces would go off well. He was still quite adamant that he would accept no ministers back on the 'all or nothing basis'. If that was their stand then he would chose nothing. Nevertheless he was willing to have some back on his own terms – Chokani, Bwanausi and even Chirwa. I told him Chirwa had asked to see me and he said he hoped I would agree. I received the impression that the Prime Minister would be very glad indeed to have the three of them back. But 'never Chiume and probably never Chipembere: possibly never Chisiza'. Chipembere, Banda avowed, was mentally deranged. 'There is insanity in the family; his sister is mentally deranged.' Furthermore, he [said] 'Chisiza is a much more treacherous man than you think, Your Excellency.'[137]

Chirwa, who, shortly after the vote of confidence, had gone to Northern Rhodesia to see his wife off by air to London, went to see the Governor-General on Saturday morning, 26 September.[138] He had attended a meeting of the Northern Rhodesia legislative council and was saddened to note the marked contrast of the proceedings there with those in Malawi: the order and dignity, the politeness even when angry, 'so different from our own meetings where violent speeches were made and bad language used and [the] Speaker had no control of the proceedings and was ignorant of the rules'. He was shocked to learn of the contempt in which the people of Northern Rhodesia now held Malawi and he would like to do something to reduce the tension before it was too late. Jones told him that Chokani, Bwanausi and probably he himself could get back their ministerial jobs, but certainly not Chiume and Chipembere and possibly not Chisiza. Chirwa doubted if he personally could get a polite word out of the doctor. The last time he had tried to contact him by telephone – about a Ghanaian deportee – Banda had 'blown him off the phone'. He thought perhaps he should write to Banda, and Jones encouraged him to do so and to continue to think in terms of 'more friendly overtures' to him. Two days earlier, in Lusaka, he made the first friendly approach when, in a press statement, he said, 'We like Dr. Banda. We like him to lead us, and we wish him well. We realise the greatness of his achievements.'[139] He blamed the 'imperialists and colonialists' for 'deliberately dividing Banda from his ministers'. He described the trouble as a domestic affair that 'would soon be settled'.[140] Chirwa believed that the prime minister held it against him because he had been the one chosen to hand to him the written list of demands. Jones, repeating the point he made so often, told him 'what he thought of the document: arrogant and peremptory in tone, smacking of an ultimatum'.

That same morning, Banda rang Jones from Blantyre on the open line just before departing on a tour of the central and northern regions. He said, 'Chipembere's thugs have beaten up Kumtumanji and Lali Lubani at Fort Johnston.' He understood that Chipembere's 'gang' was going to Blantyre to organize a meeting the next day, and he was adamant that the meeting should not be allowed to take place 'because it would lead to violence'. Indeed, he published regulations banning public meetings and processions in the southern region without police permission.

> If necessary, force must be used to stop it taking place. If necessary people must be shot and I mean that the Police must shoot to kill. You are in charge of public order, Your Excellency, while I am away in the North. The maintenance of public order and security is paramount at this time. One person cannot be allowed to endanger the security of the whole state.[141]

This was not the first time Banda had instructed that people should be shot. Early in August he learned that violence had broken out among Lumpa Church followers on the Malawi border with Northern Rhodesia and 'it seemed possible that an armed gang had already crossed into Malawi'. He gave orders that strong measures should be taken to capture any armed people causing trouble in Malawi, even if they had to be shot in order to be captured.[142] Nor was it the last. Several years later, a senior army officer 'referred to an operation he had mounted in the Lower River area against rebels, and Banda told him he wanted thirty shot in the first minutes of the operation'. On a further occasion, as another senior army officer recalled, 'there was a good deal of trouble in the Mlanje district ... Banda called me in and told me to sort it out. When I asked what I was expected to do, Banda replied, "Kill them."'[143]

The meeting Banda understood Chipembere intended to organize was probably connected with the decision to set up a new political party. It fell to Chipembere to try and arrange the meeting. Chiume was still in the north where 'the screws were apparently being tightened on everything and everybody by Chibambo'. He was afraid of travelling south to Blantyre because he would have to drive through Kasungu, Banda's home district, where 'tribalism had been fanned to such an extent ... that the consequences of deliberately passing through that area would have resulted' in tragedy.[144] Banda was about to visit the area and this increased the danger. Chiume – like Chisiza who had returned home after his meeting with Jones – was effectively marooned in the north. Chirwa had been away in Lusaka. Bwanausi and Chokani were making arrangements for their imminent departure for Northern Rhodesia: they left on 29 September by car, arrived in Lusaka the following day and stayed at the homes of government ministers.[145]

Youens was concerned about the prime minister leaving the capital to tour the central and northern regions. He suggested it would be better for him not to travel away from Zomba and the south of the country. Rather, he 'had better stay and see this one out', but Banda disagreed.[146] The police estimated that the motorcade that accompanied him from Blantyre to Lilongwe grew from the original twelve vehicles to 300 en route. The doctor arranged for a chartered aircraft to take the diplomatic corps to Lilongwe for a party that weekend, presumably so that they could be left in no doubt about his support, at least in the central region.[147] He was away on tour in the north until early October and then, when trouble broke out in the south, he moved closer – but not too close – by going to Kasungu, his home area, where he could be more easily in touch – and presumably safer.

On the same day that Banda left Zomba, Saturday, 26 September, a number of ugly clashes occurred. Two hundred members of the youth league arrived in Limbe in an attempt to stop people attending Chipembere's meeting scheduled for the following day. Local residents resented their presence, fighting broke out and some twenty people were injured.

> The following afternoon Mr. Chipembere was to have held his meeting at Soche, an African residential area between Blantyre and Limbe, but it was banned on the grounds that the necessary Police permission had not been obtained. Nevertheless Mr. Chipembere did put in an appearance and spoke for a few minutes to a well-ordered crowd of some 300, who gathered outside the house where he was staying. He told them that he could not hold his meeting but would do so the following Sunday and he gave them a pointed résumé of what he would then say. As he finished speaking, gangs of pro-Banda Malawi Youth arrived in Government lorries, heavily armed with clubs and iron bars, and attacked the audience. They had rather the worst of it in a bloody affray, and there were again about twenty casualties. The riot act was read by a police officer and the crowd dispersed.[148]

Meanwhile, at Ntondwe, on the Blantyre road ten miles south of Zomba, near a young pioneer training base, at the place where Dunduzu Chisiza had suffered his fatal car crash two years previously, a large tree had been felled across the road by a team of some 170 youth leaguers, who manned this roadblock from the early hours of Sunday in order to prevent Chipembere, other former ministers and his supporters reaching Blantyre for the banned meeting.

> All vehicles were stopped, and although a few police were present under a young European officer with a radio car, they made no attempt to

intervene. No Europeans were however prevented from driving through ... But in the evening there were some violent incidents in which two cars were burned, one of them belonging to Mr. Orton Chirwa, the ex-Minister of Justice, and Mr. Chirwa himself was chased in the darkness into the bush where he was fortunate to escape with his life.[149]

It seems that Chirwa arranged to see Banda in Blantyre after leaving Government House that morning, in response to Jones's encouragement to make 'more friendly overtures' to him, and as a follow-up to the friendly approach he had started in Lusaka. It was while travelling quickly to Blantyre to see the doctor that Chirwa was attacked and his car destroyed.[150]

When Chirwa escaped into the bush, he made his way on foot to Zomba – a distance of about ten miles – and to Government House, where he found the army commander with the Governor-General. He arrived, 'very shaken, with a cut face and torn clothing. He said Government House was the only safe haven in Zomba.'[151] His whereabouts after escaping from Ntondwe were not known publicly for some time and the press assumed that he had 'taken to the bush'.[152] Chirwa's colleagues and most others long remained unaware of the fact that he had escaped through the bush to Government House.[153] After leaving Jones he went secretly, with the help of the Chiradzulu former district chairman of the MCP, to Malindi, where he stayed, until at least 8 October, in a house next door to Chipembere's.[154]

The next day, Sunday, 27 September, Jones held vespers twice in the evening. Kumtumanji, minister for the south – who would not have taken a gentle approach to affairs after his recent beating at Fort Johnston – and Muwalo attended the second meeting. This was the first time any African, including the prime minister, had attended vespers.

The following week was deeply troubled. It opened on the Monday with rioting between the youth league and civil servants in Zomba.

> [During the night] a party of Malawi Youth, some of them from the road block, moved into Zomba and stayed at the Malawi Congress Party headquarters ... In the morning they tried to eject the traders from the market and to intimidate the reputedly pro-Chipembere civil servants on their way to work ... The civil servants reacted sharply and armed themselves with sticks [bicycle chains, bottles] and iron bars. Open clashes resulted, the Congress Party headquarters and the store of the local MCP chairman were burned down, the Malawi flag was torn down in two places [the district commissioner's office and the district council office] and burned, and two of the new ministers, Messrs Muwalo and Chakuamba, were attacked, the latter being seriously injured ... Two of the leaders of the Youth League were also nearly killed. The police, including the Mobile

Force (riot squad) were frequently engaged, but no arrests were made. [Chief Chikowi's house was burned down.]¹⁵⁵

The attack on Muwalo and Chakuamba occurred during a fracas at the African hospital, where a number of Banda supporters were pursued and heavily beaten. Chakuamba, and possibly Muwalo, hid under a hospital bed in one of the smaller wards. When a European police officer found Chakuamba there he sent him, semi-conscious, to the Blantyre hospital, where he was admittted to the maternity wing for his own safety. He complained of being roughly treated by the police but wrote a kind letter of thanks to the sister in charge – the wife of the police officer who had sent him there.¹⁵⁶

At lunchtime on Tuesday, 29 September a rumour spread that the youth league and young pioneers were coming to Zomba to attack the civil servants' families in the residential 'lines'. Immediately, the civil servants left their work, rushed to the lines and armed themselves with 'every sort of cudgel', pangas, pick handles, steel bars and bricks. Here they were joined by a pro-Chipembere faction and there was a clash in which a man was killed.¹⁵⁷

During the afternoon Jones received a 'calm but verbose' telephone call from Chipembere.¹⁵⁸ In this 'long and repetitive' call Chipembere made two points. First, he said the people were expecting the Governor-General to take some action to 'remedy the present unfortunate situation in the country'. Jones said he had made several attempts to effect a reconciliation, but they had been unsuccessful. Even so, he was willing to make further attempts if he got a lead from the ex-ministers, as he had told Chirwa the previous Saturday.

> Chipembere said that for his part he would be very willing to try and heal the breach but the trouble was that Doctor kept on in his speeches making very serious allegations about him and the other Ministers and that made reconciliation rather difficult. It also made it imperative for him to reply to these speeches and defend himself against allegations which were being made, not only against him but against the other Ministers.

When Jones, seeking to continue to be helpful, said he would convey these views to Banda, Chipembere asked him not to, because he was speaking only for himself. He said he would ring Banda in two days' time 'if he was still alive'. This last remark, which referred to Chipembere, did not seem to startle Jones, who said that if he stayed where he was – he had discovered from the post office that the call came from Fort Johnston – he should be quite safe. The Governor-General added that although Banda was properly exercising his right to put his own case to the country, he saw no point in the ex-ministers putting their case before the public because they had done so in parliament and Hansard was available for all to read. Chipembere did not point out, as he might have done, that Banda had also put his case in parliament and all could read it. Chipembere later alleged that the unrevised edition of Hansard covering the 8–9 September debate was 'rare' and implied that it had been significantly revised for publication.[159] Additionally, the *New York Times* correspondent claimed that Banda ordered the recovery and destruction of all 8,000 copies of the first day of Hansard, because 'they showed that Mr Chiume's speech had been interrupted by outside cheers', and that a parcel of Hansards had been stopped at Chileka airport to prevent copies getting out of the country.[160]

Chipembere told Jones he would like to keep quiet and he would do so, with the others, and this included 'his friend Chiume'. He had heard that Banda was blaming the ex-ministers for the breakdown of the attempt at reconciliation the previous weekend. Jones's understanding was that the prime minister had attributed the failure to what the ex-ministers had said at the cocktail party on Saturday, 19 September.

Chipembere's second point was to protest about Banda's violent use of the young pioneers in Blantyre and Ntondwe the preceding Sunday and more recently at Zomba. Although, he said, they had been driven off with losses in Blantyre and Zomba, he protested that the police did nothing to restore order at Ntondwe. Jones disputed this, saying it was in fact the police who removed the roadblock illegally erected there – though he did not say that it took them a long time to do so, nor that the British high commissioner, who had passed through the roadblock in the course of the day, reported that the police had 'made no attempt to intervene'. Jones said he would convey Chipembere's protests to the prime minister's office.[161]

That evening Jones held vespers and then had a meeting with Youens. The situation was 'unsettled' and two companies of the Malawi Army were moved to the Fort Johnston and Namwera areas, it was claimed as 'part of normal training manoeuvres which had been planned for some weeks'.[162]

The following day, Wednesday, 30 September, saw 'all [African] government employees on strike in Zomba', where government offices eventually closed early, and most shops in the urban areas of the south were closed. In Zomba, Malawian civil servants – wearing white bands round their wrists to show they were not youth leaguers but, at least by implication, were pro-Chipembere – stayed at home to protect their families. They armed themselves with fence posts, clubs and sticks, with a view to marching on Banda's residence and burning it to the ground, or tearing it down 'piece by piece'. Large crowds assembled in the market

186 · *Revolt of the Ministers*

area to ward off pro-Banda gangs, which were thought to be on their way into the town. The two military companies that had been sent to Fort Johnston the previous day were hurriedly brought back to Zomba, thereby – though it was not said – weakening the protection that could be afforded to Chipembere at Fort Johnston.[163]

> The situation was tense and explosive, and the Army stood by in support of the Police, one company of troops being on immediate notice. During this difficult situation, not a single African Minister was in Zomba, and for all intents and purposes the elected African Government of this newly independent state appeared to have abdicated its responsibilities in the capital. The Governor-General, the Army Commander and the Police Commissioner and senior officials, all expatriates, were left in charge ... During the late afternoon the leaders of the civil servants in Zomba demanded to see a Minister. The only one who could be contacted in Blantyre refused, on a flimsy excuse, to show himself in the capital. Mr. Youens, the Permanent Secretary of the Prime Minister's Department, was sent to the African market to try and reassure the people that all would be well if they returned to work.[164]

Youens recalled these troubles and the part he played. He explained how 'Zomba was a dead town except for bands of people wandering round it with a piece of white cloth tied round their wrists'. He thought that at this stage Banda was momentarily uncertain: 'He had some doubts as to whether he was going to be able to hold the position in Zomba. And he departed to the central province where his home was and where ... he knew he could rely on very considerable support indeed.'

> On one particular day when the crunch came there was a large and angry crowd of civil servants in the [Zomba] market place ... We couldn't get any politicians to come and talk to them so in the end I did it, I went to the market place and talked to them ... They all expressed fear of what might happen to them by way of their safety when Banda returned, as he was reputed to be, to Zomba with his thugs from the central province – very tough bands of what he called 'Young Pioneers' who were, in fact, his sort of militia. They were totally dedicated to him personally. Well, since one was there in charge [in Banda's absence] one also had charge of the Army and one undertook that, in fact, one would inject the Army into the civil service lines and see that they and their people were protected from Banda's unofficial auxiliaries, and on that basis they came back to work ... It was an unpleasant episode. Of course, one really didn't know which way the situation would break. They were very angry people.[165]

Youens's suggestion that the civil servants should send a delegation to put their grievances to the government 'was not well received by the crowd' and there were demands that Chipembere should be called to address them.[166] Only an assurance that the army would protect their families induced the civil servants to return to work.

During the afternoon, Jones had a meeting with Youens and the British high commissioner. Cole was worried about 'the prominent executive role being played in the government of the country by British civil servants'. Although he accepted that what they were doing was praiseworthy in itself, he was concerned that in a situation such as the present 'an expatriate official should manifestly act on behalf of African Ministers, involving himself so directly in this internal political dispute'. He spoke of the need, as he saw it, 'for British involvement to be as unobtrusive as possible and for Africans to be openly associated with any major decisions or politics'.[167] He did not say what he would have done had he been in Jones's or Youens's place that afternoon. There had been previous occasions when senior government officers had addressed disturbed crowds of civil servants at times of strikes and violence, so it is unlikely that many Malawians would have thought this improper. It would have been irresponsible of Youens to stand aside and risk the army and police having to take forceful action. No ministers were available but none would have argued that he was not acting on their behalf – no doubt they were grateful to him. He was head of the civil service and was addressing civil servants. Banda had told Jones he was in charge of law and order and that if necessary the police should open fire and shoot to kill. His and Youens's response to the deeply difficult events fell well short of what the prime minister had empowered them to do.

The following morning the police and a company of the Malawi Rifles moved into the African residential area and were welcomed by the civil servants there who, being thus reassured, returned to work.[168] Thereafter things quietened down for a while.[169] The British high commissioner was clear that the provocation to violence in the townships of the south was caused by Banda's youth league and young pioneers, and he had no reason to doubt a report that the attacks were personally initiated by Kumtumanji. He diplomatically doubted if Banda was a party to this, but pointed out that the doctor 'studiously ignored what was happening, and never seemed likely to return from his northern tour to assume control'. He was disturbed, too, by accounts that Banda was refusing to accept police reports about 'the true origins of the unrest' – the action of the youth league – but preferred to accept 'the sycophantic explanation of his own advisers' that it was all due to the disloyalty of the Malawian civil servants.[170]

Chipembere later explained what happened in the period following the debate in parliament:

During the days that followed, attempts were made by various persons, black and white, including the Governor-General, to bring about reconciliation. But they were frustrated by Dr. Banda's insistence that certain ex-ministers ... should be excluded from any reconciliation talks and that we should stop making public speeches stating our side of the story while he toured the country denouncing us as traitors. We rejected these conditions. The result was that his supporters and ours, after listening to the conflicting versions of the causes of the split, began to clash and fight in [Zomba and Blantyre]. By now the Governor-General ... advised the army and the police ... to support the Prime Minister – not that the advice of the Governor-General was necessary in order for the British-controlled army and police to act in support of the Prime Minister. [The] ex-colonial British officers ... were inevitably going to back the man who stood for preservation and perpetuation of the European's privileged position. They carried with them the then politically insulated and uninformed African soldiers.

With the intervention of the army, the fate of the confrontation became a foregone conclusion. For the time being at any rate, we had lost the battle. In African politics, especially in the decade of the Sixties, any man who was supported by the army stayed in power or rose to power; he who was opposed by the army stayed out of power, if he was lucky! If he was not, he stayed elsewhere – in jail, or in exile, or in a cemetery.[171]

On the last day of September, as a reaction to the disturbances in the southern region, regulations were introduced that empowered Banda to restrict people to specified areas and require them regularly to report at local police stations. Immediately, Banda, in Kasungu, signed an order confining Chipembere within a four-mile radius of his house at Malindi. Chipembere was not at home when the army tried to serve the restriction order on him on 1 October. He had left the previous evening in someone else's car, leaving his own at his house, and had not said when he would return. People locally speculated that he was in hiding in Blantyre and would reappear at the weekend to defy the order.[172] In the event, the following day he sent them a message 'and accepted the order with a good grace'.[173] Pressmen visiting him formed the view that he was neither surprised nor perturbed by the restriction order, and they estimated that a thousand of his supporters were defending the approach to his home.[174] 'Although two police check-points on the road to Malindi made a note of all traffic, there was no restriction on visitors. He told journalists he was sure of ultimate victory in the sense that the people would realise the ex-ministers were right and Banda was wrong and would be pressed by them to change his ways.'

'We have Blantyre and Zomba on our side now, and what Blantyre and Zomba think today the rest of the country will think tomorrow.' He thought that if 'the present impasse continues, the point of no return may be reached. All that is lacking now is a clear and vigorous initiative – on the part of Dr. Banda'.[175]

Banda shortly gave his reason for restricting Chipembere. He spoke of the attacks he said Chipembere had ordered on Kumtumanji, Lubani and Chakuamba, and the violence in Zomba:

> Well, I wasn't going to allow that. So I rang ... the Governor-General, and the Commissioner of Police, from Lilongwe. Something had to be done because when I went to the north I left my powers of public security in the hands of the Governor-General. But there was nothing he could do. He couldn't do anything. The police were powerless because there was no power to restrain anyone as we stood, so the only thing we could do was to restrict him, and I alone could sign a document to restrict him. And I didn't hesitate to sign it ... I decided to have a showdown with Chipembere ... because I felt sure that, if I signed that document, it would show whether or not he had any supporters.[176]

When Banda signed the restriction order he said to his party officials and ministers, 'Boys, I am signing this, we can expect some little trouble, but we are going to deal with it.' He was somewhat surprised when there was no marked reaction to the restriction.[177] In a speech at Kasungu on 5 October, he declared that he would 'not allow any of the sacked or resigned ex-ministers to return to Zomba'. To the press this statement marked the final point of no return in the cabinet crisis and closed the door to reconciliation.[178]

To Banda it was important to confine Chipembere's movements and activities because of the significant damage that he – and he alone among the former ministers – was continuing to create to Banda's cause, particularly in the southern region. As Youens later recalled:

> The Ministers ... were all entirely unsuccessful in finding any people who would join to oppose Banda except Chipembere. Now, Chipembere did a certain amount of barnstorming in the southern province and he did, in fact, contrive to secure quite a lot of support to his cause. He was a fairly able politician in that he doctored his criticisms to the tastes of the people he was talking to. If he was talking to the civil servants in Zomba he always made great play upon the fact that the plums were still held for the Europeans, that not only had Banda not improved their salary conditions but was, in fact, talking about the need for economy and some sort of cutting down in the comparatively modest salaries which they enjoyed ... Zomba is the capital, it is the seat of Government ... it is

where the Government functioned from and where the bulk of the civil servants were, and Zomba went sour on Banda.[179]

The situation remained tense, and Jones continued to hold vespers daily. There was a persistent rumour in Zomba that civil servants were to be attacked again and their families molested. There was the additional story that on Banda's return to Zomba he would be accompanied by 'a massive force of League of Malawi Youth', who would beat up civil servants. A large crowd gathered in the main street of Zomba as a result of these rumours, but it was peacefully dispersed by the police mobile force.[180] Jones was concerned about these rumours and asked Kumtumanji, Muwalo, Chakuamba and Aleke Banda to meet him on 9 October.[181] They reassured him, and – having consulted the commissioner of police and the head of Special Branch – he wrote to the prime minister the next day:

> I know from the Ministers I met yesterday that there is not the slightest vestige of truth in these rumours but it is very difficult, as you know, to scotch them ... I wonder if it would be possible for you to say, when you make your speech in Kota Kota, that your policy is still peace and calm, and that no-one is going to be molested – neither Europeans, Indians, civil servants or anyone else.

Jones said he was sure the great bulk of African civil servants in Zomba, especially the more senior officers, were loyal to Banda. The issue at present was not their terms of service, following the Skinner report, but the rumours of intended violence. He was convinced that the best prospect of retaining a devoted and loyal service was to show them that he, Banda, had confidence in them and would protect them from violence. He believed the support of the ex-ministers was dwindling.[182] It is unlikely that Banda did appeal for calm and an end to violence, bearing in mind his record of reluctance and tardiness in responding to similar appeals by Jones over many years.

When Banda returned to the south on 14 October, looking fit and well, he seemed confident of his position everywhere in the country except Zomba.[183] He called on Jones three days later:

> [Banda] said he had pretty definite information that Chiume was plotting with the Frelimo people in Dar es Salaam, and that Chisiza and Chipembere and Chirwa were getting mixed up in it too. I suggested that it might be a good thing for the ex-Ministers to be given some employment if they would accept it ... I told him that when I had last seen Orton Chirwa some weeks ago he ... seemed definitely to be hinting that he would like a job. The Prime Minister's reaction to my suggestion was not

unfavourable and he agreed that I should summon Orton Chirwa to come and see me in Zomba to see if his views were still the same.[184]

The Governor-General lost no time in contacting Chirwa, who arrived in Zomba by plane in the afternoon of Monday, 19 October.[185] Jones said they had reached the point when it was no longer possible for any of the ex-ministers to return to the government, and Chirwa should face the fact that Banda had 'absolutely refused' to consider the return of any of them while they held to their 'all or nothing' attitude. For the foreseeable future they should accept that their political careers were 'in suspension'. Chirwa and his colleagues should recognize that Banda was constitutionally in power, he had a new cabinet that seemed completely loyal to him, and 'the country was very solidly behind him with the exception of a few pockets here and there'. He was stretching the term 'a few pockets here and there' to include extensive areas of the Fort Johnston, Liwonde and Zomba districts. With this 'preliminary talk' out of the way, Jones came directly to the point of his request that Chirwa come to see him:

> He would therefore be well advised to think in terms of serving Malawi in some non-political capacity, for example on the Bench. Clearly Orton had already given this some thought and said that he thought that not only he but Chisiza and Chipembere also might agree to retire from politics and serve Malawi in some other way. He would like to consult them both on the point. [He did not know that Chisiza had already left the country although it was well known to others.][186] As far as Chiume, Bwanausi and Chokani were concerned they had run away and he did not feel bound to consult them at all. The pact between the ex-Ministers had been two-fold: (a) not to return to the cabinet unless all came back, and (b) not to return to the cabinet unless the Prime Minister gave an assurance that he would be prepared to discuss the points at issue in cabinet. I then gave Orton a lecture on the position of a Prime Minister, who was not bound to accept the advice tendered to him and certainly was not a person who could be dictated to.

The pact to which Chirwa referred must have been entered into after the sackings and resignations, otherwise the words 'return' and 'all came back' would have no meaning. It must have been in addition to, or replacement of, the original 'marriage of convenience' agreement. By not feeling obliged to consult his colleagues, Chirwa was the first to split the ranks of solidarity. Running away did not break either part of the pact. Jones's 'lecture' reinforced the conclusion at which Chirwa must already have arrived: Banda would never agree to the partially collective approach – solidarity between Chirwa, Chipembere and Chisiza, but excluding the others – that he was proposing. He said he would none the less like to call on Banda, 'merely to pay his respects'. Seizing this late chance of re-establishing contact between the prime minister and one of his former ministers – contact he seems desperately to have desired – Jones immediately called in Youens, to whom the position was briefly explained and who then went straight away personally to convey Chirwa's request to the prime minister. As Youens recalled:

> Orton Chirwa was never really a wholehearted rebel, he was a great fence-sitter, he always liked to decide which side was going to win before he joined it, and he chose wrong. He thought it a fact that the dissident Ministers would emerge on top in this particular exercise but when he saw he was wrong he got in touch with the Governor[-General] and he said that he wanted to make his peace with the Prime Minister. Well, I was called up by Sir Glyn Jones and ... was asked to go and see the Prime Minister, and ask whether, in fact, he was prepared to talk to Orton Chirwa. I remember going to his house, it was fairly late at night, very dark, and explained the situation to him and he grinned at me, I remember, and said, 'Oh, yes, well, all right, bring Chirwa here and I will talk to him.' And he then rang his bell for his chief of bodyguard who appeared, and he said to him, 'Orton Chirwa is at Government House, Mr. Youens is going to fetch him and bring him here. See that the gate is open for them when they come through.' His house was always surrounded by a high wire fence and it also had searchlights all round it, it was lit all round. And he looked at me and grinned and oddly enough the penny didn't drop on that particular occasion because I went off to Government House and said, 'Yes. All right he'll see him. Let's go. He has told the guard to let us through.'[187]

On a number of occasions, when Banda was being disingenuous, he grinned at Youens, who normally understood what it was the doctor was thinking. What Youens did not know on this occasion was that after agreeing to see Chirwa, he had referred to him as a 'stooge' and told his entourage, 'You know what to do.'[188]

Youens left Government House in the government car and drove Chirwa towards Banda's house. When they arrived, 'by some odd feat of circumstance', which he could explain neither then nor later, he stopped the car further away from the gate than he usually did. Perhaps, subconsciously, the penny was beginning to drop and the significance of Banda's grin was becoming clear. Normally the gate was padlocked and when the guards saw him they would let him through. On this occasion, however, when he arrived, stopped the car and called to the gateman, nothing happened for a moment.

Then suddenly all the lights went out, the lights in the house and the lights round the perimeter of the fence, they were all switched off, and very suddenly the car was surrounded by I suppose about sixty of these guards and policemen, and all armed with heavy sticks and knives. I thought, oh, goodness gracious, and I told Orton, 'For God's sake lock your door!' Of course, the first thing they did was to try the door and try to get Orton out. They couldn't open the doors so they started beating the car, beating the windows and trying to overturn the car. [I feared, too, that they might set the car on fire.] So I decided this was sufficient by then, and purely by chance I had stopped further down the road than I normally do and there was a track leading off to the left which there wouldn't have been if I had stopped further up, so I just put the thing in gear and put my foot hard down and accelerated and we, I suppose, damaged several of them, but we got away. When I got back to Government House and told the Governor-General what had happened, he, of course, was very angry because Banda had, he felt, taken advantage of him in that he, the Governor-General, had been responsible for encouraging Chirwa to go and make his peace and he had seemed to acquiesce in the thing. So he rang Banda [Jones says Youens rang Banda] and Banda roared with laughter and he said, 'Oh, well, it just shows the strength of opposition to these people and the dedication of my own following.' [This] was odd ... I was a considerable friend of his, I mean he had always got on with me very well, and he had of course asked me to stay on with him [as Secretary to the Prime Minister and Cabinet]. But when he told me to bring Chirwa to that house he knew perfectly well what was going to happen and it didn't really worry him that a fellow who had had no particular part in this [affair should be seriously endangered].[189]

In Jones's account of this incident he added that when Youens reported the beating to Banda,

> the Prime Minister asked to speak to Orton. The conversation was in Chitonga and appeared to be friendly and Orton said afterwards that he had been greatly impressed by the Prime Minister's friendliness. He was 'over friendly' but, fearing that this might have a sinister meaning, [I] taxed him on the use of this phrase and clearly he meant 'very friendly indeed'. It was arranged that Orton should go and see the Prime Minister on the following morning at 9 a.m.[190]

It was extremely unusual for anyone to converse with Banda in Chitonga. Though he could not speak the language well, he would have understood what Chirwa was saying. Speaking in Chitonga, Chirwa's home language, must have been designed to prevent Jones and Youens understanding what was being said.[191]

Jones held vespers later that evening and decided to increase the guard at Government House. From his account of the event it would not have been necessary to increase the guard, but from Youens's account the reasons are clear. It is almost certain that Chirwa was to spend the night at Government House and they must seriously have thought an attack might be made on him during the night. They also decided that Youens should contact Banda early the next morning and say the Governor-General was anxious about Chirwa's safety and hoped Banda would agree to his being escorted to the prime minister's house by an adequate guard.[192]

Early the next morning, 20 October, Youens saw Banda, delivered Jones's message and was assured that a police escort was not necessary since he had warned everyone that Chirwa was not to be molested. Youens reported this assurance to Jones and added that he had seen no youth leaguers about.[193]

> At 9 a.m. Youens and Orton left in a Government House car with chauffeur Wilfred, without escort, Orton saying he felt most uneasy and apprehensive. Miss Kadzamira was at the gate to meet them. The leader of the body guard was on the verandah and was extremely polite. He deferentially searched them for weapons! They had a good meeting with the Prime Minister who, while being very frank, was cordial and said he would be very pleased to give Orton a non-political job. He should discuss the matter further with the Governor-General and give the latter a list of the sort of jobs he would like to have. There was some testiness when Orton described the part he had been playing in keeping Nkata Bay peaceful and pro-Banda, and also when Orton said he would like to go and discuss things with Chipembere.

The meeting ended on a friendly note, and the visitors took their leave of the prime minister. Youens, who was present during the discussion, recalled that during the meeting Banda 'said he was willing to forgive [Chirwa] for what he had done but he could not take him back into politics but he might find him a seat on [the judicial] bench'.[194]

Chirwa had a habit of whistling quietly to himself when he was slightly nervous. On this occasion his nervousness was rather more than slight and was no doubt accompanied by a feeling of relief that the interview had gone so well and was now over. Together, these feelings of nervousness and relief resulted in him gently whistling as he walked with Youens along the verandah of the prime minister's house on their way out. Then, suddenly,

> the Head of the bodyguard said 'How dare you behave so rudely at the Ngwazi's house?' At that moment two other guards advanced on Orton.

Youens held one off and said, 'Leave him alone, leave him alone.' Youens managed ['by dint of kicking and pulling'][195] to get Orton as far as the car but when about to get in one guard hit Orton and knocked him down: his head struck the car when he fell. He managed to get into the car and lock the door which was fortunate because the guard tried to open the door. Even so he got his hand through the small rear window. Miss Kadzamira was seen by Youens telling the guards to desist. The car returned to Government House without further incident. Orton had a cut inside his mouth, a swollen face and a profusely bleeding nose. His trouser was torn and he had an abrasion below the knee. He was shaken but said immediately that he had had a very friendly and satisfactory discussion with the Prime Minister. [Youens, an Oxford boxing blue, said of Chirwa that the guards 'really made a rather unpleasant mess of the poor chap'.][196]

The recollections of the Government House chauffeur, Wilfred Chipanda, remained clear more than thirty years later. Chirwa seemed anxious and frightened on his way to see Banda. They were met by Miss Kadzamira. Just before the meeting ended, Chipanda heard 'Dr Banda in a high pitched voice shouting "But where are your friends?"' As Youens tried to push Chirwa into the car he raised his hands to try and stop him being beaten further. Chirwa was 'beaten terribly', was badly hurt and his face was covered with blood. Only one member of the bodyguard, the head guard, did the beating, which took place on the steps outside the room in which the meeting had taken place. Miss Kadzamira told Chipanda to drive away quickly and not to stop. He drove fast through the gates and no one stopped him. Youens apologized to Chirwa for what happened. Chipanda was not surprised by the attack, since he knew Chirwa had opposed Banda and felt some trouble would occur. Had Youens not have been there, he believed much worse injuries would have been inflicted.[197]

Chirwa's reaction to all of this is puzzling. He knew that nearly all his former ministerial colleagues, except Chipembere, had considered it prudent to leave the country. A few weeks earlier he 'had narrowly escaped with his life from a hostile mob – near Zomba – when his Mercedes Benz motor car was burnt out'.[198] He narrowly escaped being badly beaten with heavy sticks and knives the evening previously, when he had gone to Banda's house. He was probably aware of the extra precautions that Jones felt were necessary to strengthen the guard at Government House that night. He must have sensed Jones's and Youens's anxiety over the visits to the prime minister. He was anxious and frightened. Yet he wanted to see Banda 'merely to pay his respects' and he described the meeting as 'friendly and satisfactory' despite the severe beating he received on his departure. Chipembere, Chisiza, Chokani and Bwanausi had shown greater wisdom in declining Banda's invitation a month earlier to call on him so that he could 'only shake hands with them'!

At the same time, Jones must have been most desperately anxious to re-establish some contact between Banda and at least one of his former ministers, otherwise it is unlikely that he would have run the grave, obvious and many would consider profoundly irresponsible, risks involved in encouraging and making it possible for Chirwa to see Banda while being aware of his unease and apprehension, at least just before the morning visit, of the physical attack the evening before and of Banda's belief that he was mixed up in Chiume's plotting with Frelimo. He knew, better than most others, of the outrages committed by the bodyguard and youth leaguers in the past and of the political beatings and murders of a distressingly large number of those who opposed Banda.

A little later in the day, Chirwa again saw Jones and – the ordeals he had been through the previous evening and that morning notwithstanding – said he would be grateful if the Governor-General could prevail upon Banda to appoint him a judge of the high court, which Jones agreed to try and do.[199] Chirwa had made up his mind on this without consulting any of the other ex-ministers. Jones was struck by the way 'he showed no bitterness at all about his unfortunate experience in the morning'. Maybe he was too frightened, dazed, bewildered – and too concerned with securing a judicial career – to be bitter.

It may be that Chirwa's calm reaction to the treatment he was receiving at the hands of Banda and his bodyguard resulted from his belief that he was indeed about to be reinstated, and since his other colleagues would no longer be in government, his own position would be the more distinguished. Certainly, others thought 'the first steps in a campaign to prepare public opinion for his eventual reinstatement' were being taken.[200] Although in retrospect such a campaign can be seen to have been unlikely to succeed, Chirwa may have viewed it as a distinct possibility at the time and have been prepared to suffer physical attacks and humiliation to secure rehabilitation. It is possible that Jones also saw things in this light.

The following evening, 21 October, Jones told Banda how shocked he was by the attack on Chirwa.[201] He also protested at the reports on the radio and in the press that Chirwa had 'come crawling back for forgiveness'. The grounds for this protest are unclear. It was typical of Banda to describe what happened as 'crawling back' and it was not stretching the words excessively to describe Chirwa's return to Banda's house, after the narrow escape the previous evening, as 'crawling back'. Youens's account of the interview makes it clear that forgiveness was in fact discussed and Banda was willing to forgive. So it may have been Banda's publishing the fact of holding the interview, or – less likely – the use of the belittling word 'crawling', that brought about Jones's protest. The Governor-General may also have been feeling uncomfortable about his own part in Chirwa being exposed to the doctor's wrath: however the visit was described, whether crawling back or not, it was done at Jones's instigation. Banda – repeating the sort of argument he had used on numerous occasions with Youens in the past, and which Youens believed to be disingenuous – said the assault showed the depth of feeling people had against Chirwa. Jones retorted that it also showed a lack of discipline in his guards, which gave him little confidence in their competence to protect the prime minister if things got tough. This retort suggests that Jones did not suspect that the guard may have been acting on the doctor's instructions, implied or explicit. With these words said, Jones told Banda that Chirwa would like to be appointed a judge of the high court. Banda – who had discussed this with Chirwa the previous evening – agreed, but said it could not be done through the judicial service commission because he would want to be able to get rid of him if he turned out to be unsatisfactory. He agreed to an acting appointment, but added that Chirwa should make 'a public declaration that he wished to resign from politics and disassociating himself from the other ministers'. Jones wrote to Chirwa in these terms the following day, 22 October:

> I hope you had a safe trip back to Nkata Bay and you are now feeling well. I saw the Prime Minister yesterday and he agreed that you should be appointed as a puisne judge provided that you first make a public declaration of your loyalty to him and of your political disassociation from the other ministers ... He told me that he himself would thereafter make a statement himself declaring that you are acceptable to the Malawi Government. The appointment would in the first place be an acting appointment which is usual in such cases.[202]

It was always of great importance to Banda that his followers should express their loyalty to him, and this, presumably, was why Jones added a declaration of loyalty to the provisos stipulated by Banda. He ended his letter by saying, 'The Prime Minister asked me to tell you that that he is very sorry that you had such an unpleasant experience at his house the other night.' It is strange that he said nothing about the significantly more unpleasant experience he had the following morning.

By this time, however, Chirwa had 'got the message and he left [Malawi] pretty quickly after [the meeting with Banda] and he had [in 1970] never been back again'.[203] His departure from Malawi was not easy: 'he had to hide himself in the engine room of the boat [in which he travelled] in order to escape from Fort Johnston to Nkata Bay on his way to Tanzania'.[204]

The other ex-ministers had fewer difficulties in fleeing the country. When Chisiza – whose driver had been badly beaten by party zealots - decided that he must leave Malawi, he made his way to the northern border with Tanzania. Here, in the first week of October,[205] he fortunately met the expatriate officer in charge of police for the northern region, Assistant Commissioner Frank Chevallier, whom he knew well and who allowed him to cross over the border. Chevallier later recalled:

> Because the principal *dramatis personae* were ministers from the northern region who were now assumed to be traitors, there was reason to believe their lives were in jeopardy. The first positive indication I had of this was about 8 p.m., when Yatuta Chisiza suddenly arrived at the rest house in an agitated state. He told me that he was leaving the country that night for Tanzania but would I please arrange to keep a covert eye on his family who would remain behind and whose lives would be at risk ... Before he left me that night at Karonga he told me, 'I shall be back one day to remedy the ills of this country and this will be sooner rather than later.' He was tired and dishevelled and was agitated about not having his pipe with him. At that time I was a pipe smoker and I had a spare pipe which I gave to him as a parting gift. He felt in his pockets and discovered that he had no tobacco either so I gave him my tin of 'Three Nuns' tobacco. He seemed very grateful. He then went over the border into Tanzania.[206]

Chevallier moved on to Fort Hill, also in the Karonga district, close to the border, and while there he and the African officer in charge of police at Fort Hill heard a crowd shouting: 'We've got one of them!' He recalled:

> Fort Hill township was normally a haven of peace. Imagine our consternation when we suddenly heard a commotion from the market place indicative of a riot. [The officer in charge] and I, plus about a dozen policemen, rushed there on foot to discover that a large crowd had surrounded a motor vehicle and were evidently bent on burning the car and killing the occupant who they said was a traitor. We quickly succeeded in breaking through the mob and rescuing the occupant whom we quickly identified as Kanyama [Chiume]. He was *very* shaken, to say the least. We got him back to [the] office very quickly and after giving him tea assured him he was safe while in the police station. I asked what his intentions were and he assured me that he wanted to go to Tanganyika. I contacted my headquarters by radio ... and about half an hour or so later I got authorisation for Kanyama to proceed. [Banda had been consulted and agreed.][207] I then gave him a strong escort to the border. He expressed his gratitude to us before leaving.[208]

Chevallier told Chiume to cross the border quickly and added that if he had any sense, he would never return. Chiume then crossed into Tanzania, as had Chisiza a little earlier.

From Tanzania, Chiume was quick to continue publicizing his criticism – and needling – of Banda. In an article in the government newspaper, for which he now worked, he wrote about an accumulating indictment against Banda of 'fraticide, corruption and venality as grim as the outstanding charges against Mr Tshombe' in the Congo.

> Banda seems hell bent at present to establish himself as the first African-born leader of an independent African state to choose deliberately to sell his country down the river to the Portuguese and South African imperialists ... The prospect of reconciliation between former Ministers and Dr Banda has now receded in spite of their initial overtures ... [Banda has reverted] to extreme forms of superstition, even to the use of witchcraft. [He] is so swayed by superstition that he now walks with a limp because of a human molar tooth he has been advised to keep under his toe to counter witchcraft being used against him.[209]

A few days later, Nyerere, who made it clear that Banda's foreign policy was 'in direct opposition' to that of Tanzania, said he would not countenance any of the refugees abusing his country's hospitality and campaigning against the Malawi government. Banda welcomed this last statement, but said it would be 'double faced' if it were not backed up by action to prevent the rebels continuing to attack him from Tanzania.[210] Although Nyerere's 'sympathy was with the ex-ministers', he agreed to a Ghanaian suggestion that he send a delegation to reassure Banda.[211]

The very evening that Jones wrote to Chirwa, 21 October, there were further serious incidents in the civil servants' residential area in Zomba, resulting in 'four people being shot; a man, a woman and a child were seriously injured'. Fearful for their safety and that of their families, the vast majority of African civil servants in Zomba stayed away from work the following day. They asked Youens and Roberts to go to the residential area to talk with them. When they arrived, there were about 100 civil servants gathered, but this number soon increased to between 400 and 500. Youens told them he had seen the prime minister that morning and Banda had authorized 'a Company of the Malawi Rifles to occupy the lines and protect the civil servants and their families night and day'. The company would arrive as soon as Youens and Roberts finished addressing them. Thereafter the civil servants should return to work, otherwise, Roberts pointed out, the prime minister and the government might doubt their 'loyalty and preparedness to work efficiently'. This, as Roberts reported with characteristically elegant understatement, 'occasioned a certain amount of interjection from the crowd'. There was a general feeling that the army was not a sufficient safeguard and what was wanted was Banda to order the immediate removal from Zomba of those who had caused the trouble: some of his bodyguard and the young pioneers from Lilongwe. They would return to work only if the army remained and the young pioneers were removed. Roberts pointed to the danger of this approach, which amounted to delivering an ultimatum to the prime minister to meet coercive demands. The crowd was orderly, peaceful and respectful. After Youens promised to tell Banda of their concerns and repeated that the army would remain as long as necessary to protect them, he and Roberts left. The following day the majority of civil servants returned to work.[212]

On 22 October Jones flew to Lusaka for Zambia's independence celebrations. In the early hours of the following day, sub-chief Timbiri from Chirwa's constituency in Nkata Bay was murdered in Zomba at the Manda Circle Hotel. He had come to the capital to see Banda about disputes among petty chiefs in his area, over whom Banda was considering making Timbiri the Native Authority. 'The appointment had political implications, and the police discovered what they believed to be conclusive evidence that Chirwa was involved in the direction for his killing.'[213] Chiume understood that Timbiri had been murdered, not by Chirwa, but in order to damage Chirwa's reputation in the Nkata Bay district and turn the people there against him.[214] Timbiri had arrived in Zomba on 22 October. Since Chirwa had left Zomba on either 20 or 21 October, it is virtually certain that he played no direct physical part in Timbiri's death, and most unlikely that he played any part in it. Indeed, some fourteen months later, three others were convicted of the murder and sentenced to death.[215]

While Jones was in Lusaka, on 26 October, he was visited by Chokani, who a few weeks earlier had fled from Malawi to Zambia. They had a long talk about affairs in Malawi and Jones recorded:

> Willie Chokani came to see me ... having travelled from Serenje where he was living with [his wife], Grace. He has been offered a job with Zambia ... He would like to come back in a non-political capacity – e.g. as a teacher. He asked me to see P[rime] M[inister] about this and then write to him ... I later wrote to Chokani and told him that the PM seemed agreeable to his returning to Malawi to work in some non-political capacity. I did not think the present time was suitable. I advised him to keep in touch with me and I would let him know when it would be wise for him to return.[216]

Chokani's own account has different emphases and in some respects conflicts with Jones's:

I recall travelling the two hundred miles from Ndola to Lusaka to meet Sir Glyn. It was at his request through the Zambian Government. Sir Glyn felt that I should return to Malawi. I politely declined the offer. There was no question of going to Malawi as both Orton Chirwa and Kanyama Chiume who 'delayed' in coming out, were man-handled and had motor car incidents. My own personal bodyguard in Malawi was chased like deer in the bluegums in Limbe and murdered in broad daylight.[217]

Jones must have been quite remarkably keen that at least some of the former ministers should return to Malawi at some stage in a non-political capacity, the way Chirwa had been brutally attacked when he took steps to remain in the country in such a capacity notwithstanding. The risks involved in Chokani returning to Malawi were obvious and appalling. It is difficult to understand how Jones could have contemplated suggesting a return. He had placed Chirwa in grave danger by encouraging the visit to Banda only a few days earlier and now – though subsequently changing his mind – was prepared to place Chokani in probably even greater jeopardy.

In Lusaka, Jones had an interview with Kaunda and gave him an account of what was happening in Malawi, which he was pleased to get. The Zambian president said that in accordance with United Nations principles he would give Chokani and Moxon – to whom Jones also spoke while he was there – and other refugees asylum, but they would not be permitted to organize an opposition in Zambia against Malawi. Kenyatta agreed with this view and had written to Banda about it.[218] Nyerere took the same line.[219]

Jones telephoned Zomba each morning and evening to keep in touch with what was happening there while he was away from 22 to 27 October. Banda did not attend the celebrations but remained in Malawi. While Jones was in Lusaka the Zambian Special Branch received reports that an attempt was to be made on Banda's life and a coup brought about. This information was given to Jones, and he immediately sought the advice of Leonard Bean, a senior former colleague in the secretariat, on what he should do and whether he should tell Kaunda. He also asked for a plane to stand by to return him to Malawi. Bean's advice was that the reports were as yet unconfirmed, he should not tell Kaunda – this was his big day and he should be left to enjoy it – and he should stay until the main celebrations were over. Jones accepted this advice, attended the main celebrations and returned to Malawi the next day.[220]

On his return to Zomba he saw Banda, whom he found safe and well, to tell him about the Zambia independence celebrations and convey to him the good wishes of many people he had met there.

At the end of the meeting I told him that the delegates to Lusaka from all over the world had approached me to express their deep concern at what was happening in Malawi. Malawi had been held up as a model of peace and calm during the past three years and now she seemed to be drifting into a state of violence in which people were taking the law into their own hands. I gave him very strong advice to the effect that he should control his Youth [League] and make a statement as soon as possible calling on all people to observe peace and calm. He agreed that the present pattern of violence was not good for Malawi but said that he must teach the rebels a lesson which they would never forget. He was going to make an example of the ring leaders. I pressed him again to make a statement urging his people to observe peace and calm and he finally said he would consider it.[221]

Violence and people taking the law into their own hands were not new in Malawi. Over the past three or four years there had been innumerable cases of politically motivated lawlessness, violence, assault, arson, intimidation and several of murder. Jones must have thought it advisable in his approach to Banda to make it sound as if it were something new – formerly a model of peace and calm but now drifting into violence and lawlessness – even though he, Banda and everyone else knew it to be far from the case. In the past Banda had made appeals to his people to be peaceful and law-abiding, never of his own initiative and always at Jones's imploring; they were usually delayed until further grave damage had been perpetrated, some thought they were not genuine and they were never effective for longer than a short time – as the periodic need to repeat them abundantly demonstrated. Moreover, the clear implication of what Banda said was that the current violence was designed to teach the ex-ministers a lesson they would never forget and to make an example of the ringleaders, whatever Jones's previous views were of Banda's innocence in the outbreaks of violence.

At the beginning of November, a number of politically prominent Europeans and their families left Malawi at short notice as a result of what the press dubbed 'deportation by intimidation'. Cameron was Chipembere's solicitor, and soon after being restricted, Chipembere sent him his passport and some private papers for safe keeping. He also asked him to represent him and challenge the restriction order in the courts. Although he was concerned about doing this, Cameron got the necessary papers together ready to take before the high court. In the meantime, he issued a statement on behalf of his client, saying that he was 'in Malawi, always has been in Malawi and will remain in Malawi'. This was to counter a report that Chipembere had escaped from restriction and was now in Tanzania. In fact he had escaped, but was in the mountains and forests near his home in the Fort Johnston district.

For his last few days in Malawi Cameron and his family lived, for their mutual safety, with Albert McAdam, a technical missionary of the Church of Scotland. McAdam was sheltering Africans who were afraid of attack by the youth league. Cameron and McAdam saw an MCP Land Rover draw up at the mission, and the men in the vehicle told them they should accompany them to the MCP headquarters. They were aware that this Land Rover had been used in the abduction and disappearance of a number of Malawians, and they were consequently profoundly apprehensive. In an effort to avoid having to go with the Land Rover, they took refuge in the mission workshop and moved to the far end. There was no door at this end of the workshop but, providentially, there was a telephone, and McAdam remembered the telephone number of a European police superintendent. Holding their attackers at bay, McAdam rang the superintendent, who must have got in touch with MCP headquarters, because shortly there was a return call and Muwalo told the leader of the Land Rover crew to leave Cameron and McAdam alone. As the gang left they shouted threateningly, 'We shall be back.' A lorry load of youths also parked outside Cameron's office and shouted party slogans and abusive threats at him. His children's nanny's house was attacked and its windows smashed. Cameron and McAdam remained convinced for the rest of their lives that they had only narrowly escaped being abducted and murdered.[222]

Moxon's request to be given a senior job in the army had been turned down some six months earlier, and he had refused to join Banda's cabinet. Now, the doctor told Jones he had documentary evidence that Moxon was in league with Chiume and would be prepared to take part in a military coup when the time seemed ripe. Banda promised to let Jones see the letter when they next met. It is unclear whether this happened.[223] With Cameron and McAdam, Moxon had seen the Governor-General on 28 September and spoken about their fears.[224] Banda was unable to give them an assurance that they would be safe in Malawi and the British high commissioner advised them to leave. Within a few days, Cameron, his wife and three children, McAdam, his wife and four children, and Moxon with his African wife and three children all left the country.

CHAPTER 8

Chipembere's Attempted *Coup d'État*: February 1965

WHEN Chipembere was served with a restriction order it was his third period of confinement and he had been free for less than two of the previous five and a half years. The years of freedom had been exciting and fulfilling for him: he was a government minister in a country moving fast towards independence after seventy years of colonialism. Now the excitement, fulfilment and freedom were behind him.

The area to which he was restricted has mountains close to the east and the lake close to the west, and he felt imprisoned in the narrow strip north and south of Malindi village. This feeling of being cut off is revealed in the request he sent to the principal of St Michael's teacher training college near his home, asking for reading material and complaining of his sense of isolation.[1] Some of his supporters urged that they should begin acts of violence as a protest against the restriction, but he rejected the proposal and sent out messages saying he disapproved of violence in any matter affecting himself. When the press visited him he 'spared no chance to criticise the restriction in the strongest possible terms'. Supporters by the lorry-load arrived from Blantyre, Chiradzulu, Zomba, Kasupe and Fort Johnston itself – the whole of the northern half of the southern region – 'coming to express their sympathy and solidarity and bringing [him] gifts and foodstuffs'. He realized that his remarks both to the press and to these crowds aggravated matters, but he confessed to being 'a prisoner [with] the usual bitterness of a man in confinement'.[2]

He was forbidden under the restriction order to hold meetings, but he attempted to get round this by inviting people to tea parties – much as he had earlier held the cocktail party in Blantyre and invited the press. One such invitation was to the students of St Michael's college, who were worried about accepting but eventually sent a message that their five student council members would attend.

A reply came back that this was an insult to Henry and the invitation was cancelled. Later that evening ... the windows of the office were smashed with axes, and we heard the sound of breaking glass throughout the College, together with angry shouts and the cries of terrified students. Eventually the noises died down and it was evident that the attackers had left. Many students had fled into the hills behind the College, some not to return for several weeks. We gathered ... together and awaited further developments. Eventually, a large group of men, armed with axes and spears, came up the drive to the front of the College [and told us] that Henry sent his apologies for the 'stupid behaviour' of his supporters and had now sent his bodyguard (we believed the same men who had attacked the College) to protect us. The evening ended with my wife showing slides of our voyage from Britain to both students and bodyguard in the College chapel![3]

Chipembere received frequent warnings that Banda had hired men to assassinate him, and although he brushed these aside for some time, their insistence impressed itself on him. His supporters in the police force sent him messages advising him to take detailed precautions, including having bodyguards, or to leave the country. When he heard of the shooting of a woman supporter, Mrs Bandawe, 'in cold blood by the Young Pioneers', he took the warnings seriously. Additionally, parliament was due shortly to debate Banda's reintroduced proposal to permit detention without trial. Although he had publicly assured Banda that he would happily stay in Malindi and 'not organise against the Ngwazi',[4] he now believed that, just as he had been the first to be restricted, he would be the first to be detained. Consequently, a day or so before the parliamentary debate – probably on 25 October – he broke the restriction order, left Malindi and 'went and hid [him]self with a party of seven in the mountains'. He felt he had no alternative but to do this. He had been in restriction less than a month. It was an unhappy departure, and as he left his wife he 'wept like a child ... it was so painful ... to have to part with home and all loved ones, one and a half years after return[ing] from prison'.[5]

Banda soon learned of Chipembere's disappearance and, expecting further trouble, he had the Malawian district commissioner of Fort Johnston, I. B. Itimu, replaced by an expatriate, John Bolt, on 27 October, not because Itimu's loyalty was doubted but because a European was less likely to be subjected to pressure by Chipembere's followers.[6] The following day he told parliament, 'Chipembere has run away ... I have ordered full search for him and I want him brought here, alive if possible, but if not alive then any other way ... He has been going to a singanga [witch doctor] ... and he is sleeping on the grave of someone because of *mankhwala* [medicine] ... he has been trying to protect himself [but it] won't help him.'⁷

Now that Chipembere's going into hiding was well known, Banda and Jones were anxious about the safety of his wife, Catherine, and their children, and they acted quickly. With the prime minister's approval, the Governor-General sought the assistance of Bolt, the Fisheries Officer at Fort Johnston, Bishop Donald Arden and his wife, Jane. The Ardens recalled:

> The Governor-General asked if Donald would ... go at once to Mponda's [on the west side of the Lake] to try and persuade the Archdeacon to go to Likoma Island. [He] had arranged for a large Fisheries boat to be on standby at Mponda's and on board would be the DC ... who would accompany the Chipemberes to Likoma ... At 4.00 am in the morning [we] drove to Mponda's. Archdeacon Chipembere ... listened quietly to the message Donald had brought. He then consulted his wife and together they accepted, with obvious sadness, that, for their own safety, and in order to reduce the possibility of public disturbance, they should go to Likoma.⁸

They then turned their attention to the best way of persuading Catherine to go with them. She was in hiding at Malindi and it was difficult to make contact with her. They agreed that the Bishop would sail with the Archdeacon and his wife on the Fisheries boat across the Lake to Malindi and Mrs Arden would drive around to Malindi and try to make contact with Catherine.

> On arrival at Malindi Mission station, Jane was told [to] drive some four miles north of Malindi to the village where Henry and Catherine Chipembere had a house, and make enquiries there. On arrival at the village Jane met some people who were looking after the house and said that she had a very urgent personal message for Catherine. She explained that she was the wife of the Bishop, that she knew Catherine well and that Catherine would know that she could trust her.

Mrs Arden was then asked to walk for about half a mile and to wait there. She sat at the back of a village house for a long time. The village people were polite but not over friendly, and separate groups of men and women sat under the trees keeping an eye on what was going on. Eventually Catherine arrived, looking tired and strained but glad to see Mrs Arden. It took time to explain that she brought a message from the Governor-General urging Catherine, for her own safety and that of her children, immediately to travel to Likoma Island with her father-in-law. Catherine asked many questions but eventually agreed to go.

Jane explained that Catherine would need to go down to the Lake shore at Malindi Mission as soon as possible in order to board the Fisheries boat. Catherine then walked off to go and collect her belongings and the children. Jane said she would return to the Mission and wait there for Catherine [but when she] arrived back at the car ... about fifty men blocked the road. The spokesman ... said very firmly that Jane would not be allowed to leave the village. 'How do we know that you have not set a trap so that Catherine and the children will be captured by the police?' So Jane sat and waited. [Eventually she, Catherine and the children drove to the Mission without incident.]

From the Mission it was possible to see the silhouette of the Fisheries boat as she rode at anchor about 200 yards from the shore ... On board were the Archdeacon and Mrs Chipembere, Donald and the District Commissioner. A small dinghy with an outboard motor was waiting on the shore to ferry Catherine and her children to the boat. It took several journies and Jane went with them ... After saying some prayers and Donald giving the Chipemberes God's blessing, [the Ardens] said goodbye, boarded the dinghy and returned to the shore and the Mission. From there they watched the lights of the Fisheries boat gradually disappear into the darkness.

Accompanying the Chipemberes to Likoma was a young British voluntary service volunteer, David Baptie. He was stationed temporarily at Malindi Mission while waiting to move on to Likoma towards the end of November 1964, travelling by the Lake steamer, *Ilala*. On Saturday 31 October, however, things suddenly changed, as he told his parents three days later:

> I didn't catch the steamer on [its usual departure on] Friday and was all set for another three weeks at Malindi, but on Saturday, however, things changed ... at about 11 am. Mrs Arden came charging unexpectedly into the house shouting 'Have you seen the launch?' She then explained to me that Dr Banda had ordered Archdeacon Chipembere, Catherine Chipembere and her children to go to Likoma Island ... At about 2 p.m. a Government Fisheries boat arrived and Bishop Arden, the Archdeacon and [the DC] came off the boat. I suggested that I might go on the boat to Likoma [rather than wait another three weeks until the Ilala sailed again] and it was decided that I should. So I hurriedly packed my things.
>
> I waited all afternoon as Catherine had to be persuaded to go, and at 6 p.m. [others and I] loaded the boat with medical supplies for the island. We finished ... by light of the boat's search light and at about 7.30 pm. my *katundu* (luggage) was loaded on. In the meantime the [DC] who had earlier set out for Fort Johnston, returned to tell us that the Africans had burnt a bridge down about three miles from Malindi. They had done this

to stop reinforcements coming in, or more likely for nuisance value. [It served the purpose, too, of preventing the Ardens' escape if the operation turned out to be a trick.][9]

By this time, however, the boat crew said they would not land near Catherine's house to fetch her, her children and luggage because it was already dark and they were afraid of being ambushed. It was decided that the boat would not sail until the morning. Later, at about 9.30 p.m., two of Catherine's guards assured the crew that they would be safe, and they left to pick up the Chipemberes.

> After loading, the crew decided to stay at anchor and to sleep the night. So after settling down to sleep ... we were suddenly awakened by the approach of a boat. The Chip[embere]s became frightened, so the crew took the boat to the other side of the Lake. Sleep again until 2.45 a.m. when the winds began to drag the anchor, so off we set to find a wind free bay. We finally got going at 5 a.m. We spent Sunday night on board and arrived at Likoma at 5 p.m. on Monday [2 November].

For several weeks Banda was uncertain where Chipembere was, and frequently indicated that he was in Tanzania. In fact he was in a training camp in the Namizimu forest reserve just north of Malindi. Chipembere called this camp 'Zambia', and for a while the security forces were misled when they were told that various people they were seeking had 'gone to Zambia'.[10] Despite having said he had ordered a full search for Chipembere and wanted him taken 'alive if possible, but if not alive then any other way', Banda did not, at this time, take determined steps to capture him. He was probably content to leave him in the bush because he knew that Chipembere's diabetes would sooner or later so debilitate him as to force his surrender, flight or capture.

In hiding, Chipembere became 'obsessed with the lot of the men in restriction and in detention' and he believed it should have been clear to Banda that he would sooner or later take action to secure their release. He was 'very sad about their suffering and [could] not rest until they [were] out.' At first he decided to mount a civil disobedience campaign and he called on the increasing number of supporters in hiding with him, to prepare for it. He was anxious to avoid violence and he stuck to this strategy until Banda announced his determination that the ex-ministers and their followers should 'rot in jail'. It was then that he 'despaired of the efficacy of non-violence and decided on rebellion'.[11]

His rebellion was launched on the night of 12 February 1965. During the evening, at about 9 p.m., a unit of some two hundred[12] of his followers, who had been living and training in the forests and mountains east of his home at Malindi, began to gather by the lake near St Michael's

Chipembere's Attempted Coup d'État · 209

College. They moved to the Malindi mission station, where they commandeered the mission seven-ton lorry and Land Rover and two high-calibre rifles. Then they drove to Fort Johnston township, being joined by others on the way, and crossed the river by ferry at about 10 p.m. They forced their way into the house of the senior Malawian policeman and took the armoury keys; released the prisoners from the gaol; attacked the police station; brutally killed the wife and child of the Malawian Special Branch officer, Inspector Changwa – in front of him and the rest of his family;[13] destroyed the telephone installations at both the police station and the post office; stole bags of maize from the district council store and guns and ammunition from the police station armoury; and burned down three of Chief Mponda's houses, a court clerk's house and the courthouse. They then left Fort Johnston in four lorries, travelling southwards.

The principal of St Michael's, Terry Stoneman, who, with his wife, Gill, was living there at the time, recalled:

> Francis Bell [lay engineer at Malindi Mission] was certain that Henry was planning a coup and had passed this information on to ... John Bolt. I believe he, in his turn, informed Zomba, but the Government were not convinced! ... On the night of 12 February I watched a considerable number of lorries with armed rebels pass along the road in front of the College and [later] heard a lot of gunfire in the surrounding villages ... The lorries were able to cross the Shire River by ferry at Fort Johnston – presumably with the cooperation of the ferrymen.[14]

Others at the college initially saw less than the principal. An American teacher, Roy Frasier, said later, 'Chip[embere]'s band gathered just a few hundred yards below our houses. It was late at night and we all slept through it.' He was puzzled as to how the attackers got across the ferry undetected because it could carry only a few dozen people and three vehicles at a time.[15] It is most likely that they were not undetected but that nothing was done to stop them or raise the alarm. Colleagues at St Michael's had been alerted by Bell from at least the beginning of February, and probably for a month or so longer, that 'trouble was brewing to the north of [the college]. It was a nightly point of discussion around our common dinner table. Someone would comment almost in a "tipping" sense, "When do you think they'll launch the coup?"'[16] Another American teacher, Bill Cleveland, recalled that when it was launched, news of it

> came as a message from the Mission to us to 'brace' ourselves as the coup had begun ... I do not know if Francis [Bell] offered any resistance over either the lorry or the rifles but in the circumstances he was hardly in a

position to do so. I believe he knew Henry Chipembere quite well and I
know from comments he made later that he thought highly of him. I also
do not know whether Chipembere himself was in the convoy which left
Malindi ... After some consultation with our [Principal] we delivered the
news to our roughly 90 students – all male, largely mature age students.
Some panicked immediately and literally disappeared. Others gathered
with myself and other staff members on the steps of the College feeling
that if we were to be attacked at least we could see them coming!

In fact it later transpired that they were never in any danger because
Chipembere had given specific orders that European civilians were not
to be touched. Since they did not know this at the time, they 'were very
frightened and very uncertain what would happen next'. Cleveland continued:

> We had heard a commotion coming from the direction of the mission
> earlier but had not made much of it as there were often commotions of
> one sort or another. In any case we sat and waited for events to unfold.
> [I] managed to sleep fitfully in my own cottage when it was clear that we
> were not in immediate danger ... I awoke to the sound of gunfire coming
> from the ... botttom of the college property and down the road several
> hundred metres. I was quite terrified and I retired to my walk-in wardrobe
> with my heart pounding in my ears. I must have stayed there for up to an
> hour when I began to hear the sounds of normal life outside my cottage.[17]

When the attackers reached Fort Johnston, several of the European
residents went to the river to try and escape by launch and there was no
attempt to stop them. It seemed to some of them on reflection 'that the
raid was well organised as there was not a lot of bloodshed, and looting
as the objective was arms and food'.

> George Harding, the head of the Public Works Department in the Fort
> was trying to start the engine of the launch when he suffered a coronary
> thrombosis. Loren Anderson, an American doctor was summomed from
> another boat but Mr. Harding was dead when he arrived ... I believe that
> Chipembere had people in all the key places – Radio Malawi, Government
> offices, Post Offices etc. – ready to take over if he succeeded in reaching
> Zomba ... The objective of the attackers at Mpondas village seemed to
> be to burn down the Chief's house, which they did ... After the raid a
> number of the rebels took three police Land Rovers and returned over
> the Fort Johnston ferry back to camp.[18]

The warden of St Thomas's student hostel in Fort Johnston, Rev. Ron
Tovey, recalled that he and the hundred boys who were living there just
across the road from the police station were awoken by the noise of

gunfire. They left the building by the back door and took refuge in the bush, returning in small groups after the firing had stopped. He tried to find Bolt and John Burdon, the European officer in charge of police, but found the boma and the police station deserted. Tovey

> went to the house of George Harding, who was in charge of the boats and later accompanied him and his wife to the river where some of the Europeans had gathered. It was while trying to start one of the boats that George collapsed and died. The boat eventually left for Palm Beach with many of the Europeans on board and I returned to the hostel.[19]

Tovey was accompanied by Bill Hayward, a Peace Corps Volunteer, who harboured about thirty of the students and the headmaster and his family in his house. By midnight 'the area was somewhat quiet but the Malindi side of the river was ablaze with huts set afire. Many of these were homes of Government employees.'[20] There was general agreement that a number of people locally took advantage of the fracas to 'join the fray', settle old scores and generally cause trouble.

Another Volunteer recorded his experiences in novel-form. He and a friend, Stewart, were having dinner in Fort Johnston when they heard gunfire from across the river.

> We both got to our feet immediately and Stewart said, 'It looks like it's begun.' We stuck our heads out of the door and at this point things were still quiet in the town, but we knew we might not be safe for long where we were. Ali [a house servant] ran in, 'There is trouble coming. Best go down to the river.' The road looked clear. We dashed across, taking a circuitous route via the hospital to reach the club. It was empty except for Mohammed who was getting ready to flee as well. 'The bwanas have just gone down to the river,' he said breathlessly ...
>
> Across the river, villages were in flame; gunfire was now constant; shouting was coming from all directions. We could make out the silhouettes of some of the Europeans as they tried to board one of the fisheries boats. We ran down to them as quickly as we could and several white arms reached down to hoist us into the boat. The engine had to be cranked to start, and I heard [George Harding] making endless tries to get the engine to turn over. Finally he said, 'This bloody thing is never going to start. We're going to be sitting ducks if we stay here! Let's go down and try one of the lifeboats.'
>
> We jumped out of the fishing boat and ran down towards a metal lifeboat whose bow rested on the sand. By now we could hear more shooting and shouting in the town itself. We moved quickly ... Stewart, Ali and the other men loaded the women into the lifeboat and then pushed it out into the water, pulling themselves aboard. There was only

one oar, but we were able to use it to reach the current that carried us into the tall reeds along the river's edge. Apparently others had gotten the same idea, for within ten minutes a second small boat drifted towards us. But something was wrong. Mrs [Harding] was wailing in a high pitched Greek dirge. Her anguish was understandable. Her husband ... while frantically trying to crank over the engine ... had keeled over lifeless ...

By now, the gunfire and shouting coming from the town was loud ... The commotion seemed to last a long time, but it must not have been as long as it seemed ... We stayed in the tall grass for at least three hours, shivering, being eaten by mosquitoes and trying to comfort Mrs [Harding] who was beyond consolation.[21] Villages continued to burn ... As daylight approached and the town remained quiet, we felt it safe to paddle back to the river's edge ... By evening the town was an armed camp with several battalions of K.A.R. camped on the D.C.'s compound, but all was quiet.[22]

On the night of the attack, Bolt, Pamela Jennings, a nurse friend of his who was staying with him on a fishing holiday, together with Burdon, left Fort Johnston early in the evening to dine at the Palm Beach hotel, about ten miles up the western shore of the lake. They returned shortly after 11.15 p.m. As they turned into the main street they were confronted by a crowd of about 200 people and could see that the telephone lines had been destroyed. Bolt quickly reversed his car and turned into the drive of Burdon's house. Someone told them they should get into the house and stay there. They went in, switching out the lights as they did so, and immediately walked out of the back door, back to the car and reversed at speed into the road. The two people at the gate were taken by surprise and although there were a few shots they drove quickly along the lake shore road to Monkey Bay where they knew the Malawi Railways' radio link, normally used to contact their ships on the lake, could be used to get in touch with Zomba. Given the seriousness of the attack, reporting it to police headquarters was clearly the correct priority. They then spent the remainder of the night at the club house at Monkey Bay. Given, too, the disarray at Fort Johnston and the uncertainty of how much, if any, support they could command there and the likelihood that most residents had either fled or joined in the fighting, this also was a sensible course to take.[23]

When Chipembere left Fort Johnston, he and his men drove southwards towards Zomba, where they hoped their ranks would be swelled by the many civil servants living there. They reached the Shire river at Liwonde, midway between Fort Johnston and Zomba, between 2 a.m. and 3 a.m. on Saturday morning, and found the ferry tied up on the far, Zomba, side of the river. Banda claimed that the security forces were already at Liwonde and had secured the ferry on the Zomba bank.[24] This was not the case: the ferry was secured by chance on that side of the river.[25] It was also claimed that the ferry had broken down and the rebels canoed across the river to try to speed things up.[26] This also was not the case, because the army – who had been alerted at 3 a.m. – arrived at about 4.30 to 5 a.m. and found the ferry in good working order and no sign of the rebels having been on the Zomba side, as opposed to the great deal of evidence on the Fort Johnston side.[27] Discovering that he could not cross the river by ferry, and not, it seems, having a contingency plan, Chipembere aborted his mission and began to retreat to Fort Johnston. Some of his men 'dispersed in the direction of Balaka which was a Chipembere stronghold'.[28] Chipembere escaped back to Malindi by disguising himself.[29]

When Burdon and Bolt telephoned the Commissioner of Police, Peter Long, in Zomba from Monkey Bay and alerted him of the trouble at Fort Johnston, he had just returned from a mess night at the Malawi Army officers' mess, attended by most of the army officers and a number of senior police officers. He immediately – at about 3 a.m. – told Paul Lewis, commander of the army, who had also been at the mess function and who initially thought a joke was being played on him. Lewis summoned his troops together at Zomba and sent the duty company to Liwonde to see what was going on.[30] Not knowing whether Chipembere had crossed the Shire, he warned them that the forested slope beyond Kasupe, down to the Shire plain, was a potential ambush area and they should take great care and appropriate deployment action there. Lewis and the other companies followed and caught up with them at Kasupe. When they got to Liwonde, the ferry was still on the Zomba side and the army was able to cross straight away. Their progress to Fort Johnston, however, was slow because they encountered several burned out vehicles and had to take precautionary steps in negotiating these road blocks and potential ambush sites. Chipembere must have realized, or guessed, by this time that the security forces were pursuing, or likely to pursue him, and he delayed them by roadblocks. Nevertheless, by noon the army was in hot pursuit and they caught up with one of the lorries on the Namwera escarpment. They opened fire and all save one of the occupants – who was captured – ran into the bush and escaped. They found Fort Johnston a scene of devastation with a great deal of destruction, other damage and vandalism evident.[31] It was the view of senior Special Branch officers that Chipembere and his men had been fortunate to find the ferry at Liwonde on the Zomba side of the river, 'as had they been able to continue, the Malawi Rifles would have been waiting for them [between Liwonde and Zomba, with their retreat cut off by the Shire river] and the whole thing extinguished in its infancy'.[32]

During the Saturday morning, the lorries carrying the rebels arrived back in Fort Johnston from Liwonde and stopped outside the boma while some of them went in. Tovey and some of the students stood on the verandah of the hostel to see what was happening, but they 'soon went inside when a rifle was pointed at' them.[33] Hayward had risen early and placed a white sheet on his house 'as a signal to whoever'. A single-engined, one-seater Portuguese fighter plane flew over and 'buzzed' him several times, with the pilot waving to him. The headmaster and his family and a number of other teachers were still at his house. A little later, 'a gang of not so young pioneers' came to the house looking for the headmaster. Hayward refused them entry: 'One of them pulled a gun on me. I told them to get the hell off my property – an old American custom!' Later that day the Malawi Rifles arrived.[34]

The next day, Sunday, the security forces followed Chipembere to his hiding places. He had two camps. One was not far from his house at Malindi, but towards the hills, and was deserted. The other, 'Zambia', was in the forest reserve, hidden in a valley, surrounded by mountain ranges and not visible from the air. It was occupied, but when the people there heard the security forces approaching they dispersed into the forest. Seven were captured and three shot dead. In the camp they found 'various bits of kit' and Chipembere's suitcase, which contained fairly comprehensive lists of the members of his army. The 300 names were organized in groups, each under the command of an officer such as Silombela and Ndomondo.[35] Shortly after the raid on Fort Johnston, Tovey had been asked to take a suitcase to a teacher at Mponda's, which he did, not knowing whose case it might be. Later that day, the police went to the hostel – where the majority of the students were pro-Chipembere – and asked to search the building because they had heard that Chipembere had left his suitcase there.[36]

In the course of the following week, fifty more of the rebels were captured and 'there then began the long, tedious business ... of cordon and search' as Chipembere and his men were hunted by the security forces.[37] 'Slowly but surely, the names on the list of rebels were scored out as they were arrested, some as a result of routine activity by the security forces and others as a result of information' passed to them.[38] 'One form of security force or another stayed around for nearly two years and it had a seriously depressing effect on village life. There was an air of suspicion everywhere and Special Branch police were constantly on the snoop for information.'[39]

Chipembere could have been in no doubt about the vigour with which this hunting down would be pursued. He had long been aware of how ruthless Banda was prepared to be. Many years later, he recounted of Banda, the man whom Devlin and Jones found 'charming':

I remember him telling us a story of how Stalin saved Russia during the war ... took over the running of the army himself and in the process lost millions of soldiers ... He was speaking admiringly of this when I said, 'But is it fair to do that, to sacrifice so many lives and so on?', and he got angry with me. And in his anger he said a lot of things which revealed his fundamental attitude, and he said – and I did not expect a man like him to say this – 'Don't worry about human life. You know, human life and being a human being is just being a cog in the machine. For the sake of the nation you must be prepared to get thousands, millions slaughtered. I hope at least this is not the attitude you are going to take when we take over the government.' We were in gaol at the time. And he said, 'You have to be prepared that some people have to die for the sake of the nation.' I said, 'After independence? I know we are dying now in the fight against the British but I hope this is the end of the problem of dying for the nation unless we have a war.' [He replied] 'No! The needs of the state. A situation can arise in which you can need to put your own people to death in their thousands.'[40]

It was not only Bell who believed that warning was given of the intention to stage a coup. Bill Jackson, an Irish missionary, learned via a driver who had returned to Zomba from Fort Johnston the evening just before the attack, that

> there would be an insurrection that very day in Zomba when ... government ministers [would be taken] and that included the Prime Minister. It would be a bloodless coup ... The fracas at Mangochi was the beginning of this coup, to draw troops and police from Zomba, eighty miles away ... nothing would happen before that night.[41]

Others in Fort Johnston were warned of impending trouble. Burdon told his successor that 'there was good information to the effect that a rebel army had been formed with the initial intention of attacking the town, but when he suggested that such an attack was imminent Zomba, it seems, thought otherwise and ... no precautionary measures were taken'.[42] Tovey was told later that the senior Malawian policeman had been forewarned and had left before the rebels arrived.[43] A European couple, the Johnstons, who managed a trading store in the township, were visited by Chipembere a day or two before the attack. Their premises and stock were untouched during the attack, which was surprising in view of the theft and looting from the government stores and the burning of African houses. Hayward, who met Chipembere during a visit to the store, was himself warned by one of his students that 'something' was about to happen but it would not involve him.[44] We have seen how a fellow Volunteer, on first hearing the gunfire, said, 'It looks like it's begun.'

A senior expatriate officer at police headquarters in Zomba recorded that 'The Zomba authorities, both police and military, knew beforehand of what would happen at Fort Johnston and the plans of the rebels.' The police training school, which he commanded, was placed on full alert before the assault on Fort Johnston.[45] Furthermore, the Governor-General shortly wrote in his private diary, when dealing with events in Fort Johnston, 'Question of why Zomba did not heed the warning', but he did not explain what he meant by this.[46] On the other hand, to the commander of the Malawi Army, a member of the Malawi intelligence committee, the attack came as a complete surprise. Also, 'Special Branch in Southern Division had no indication of the attack ... until it actually occurred.'[47] Banda, too, seems not to have had warning. About two weeks before the attack he wrote to Jones, on leave in Britain, to say 'There is no need for you to hurry back. Things are quiet and peaceful here' and it would be 'quite alright' if he returned in mid-February.[48]

Apart from limited warnings, or leaks, on the very eve of attack – which even then were not specific – there was a general rumour that Chipembere would make some sort of attempt to take over the government, and these would have been sufficient to place the security forces on alert from time to time. It was common knowledge in the Fort Johnston area that he was training an army in the forests east of Malindi and their general purpose must have been obvious.[49] For example, on 26 January 1965, in parliament, Banda criticized disloyal African civil servants in Zomba, spoke of the detention bill which was being introduced and said:

> These fools ... mustn't think and keep on talking about, 'You know Chipembere is coming' ... There are people in Chikwawa, Port Herald, Dedza, Lilongwe, Dowa, Salima, Nchisi. Some of these people even ten days from now, will be ... in detention ... Let Chipembere come and take them out ... let them wait for him in Lilongwe Prison Camp. I will keep them there and they will rot, they will rot.[50]

It may be that this statement hastened Chipembere's attempted coup, which indeed showed signs of being hastily and inadequately prepared. If he waited much longer, many more of his followers would be securely locked up in detention camps rather than simply be in restriction near their own homes where they could more readily join in the coup.

On the other hand, there are signs that a good deal of care was taken in planning the attack. Chipembere could not have mounted it much earlier for a number of reasons. First, he went into hiding only at the very end of October 1964 with only a handful of followers. It would take time to gather and train more. Second, Banda was away from Malawi between the end of November and the middle of December,

Chipembere's Attempted Coup d'État · 217

and while this might have been an opportune time to take over the government, Chipembere might still not have had enough time to gather and train sufficient men. Nor could he safely delay much longer. He may have calculated that it would be better to attack before the Governor-General returned from leave in the middle of February, knowing from experience the previous September that Jones was still playing an executive role in liaising with the prime minister, the police and the army, and in supporting Banda. As for the night of the attack, whether by chance or design, Chipembere selected a night when the senior army and police officers were enjoying a convivial mess night in Zomba, and when the local district commissioner and police commander were, as was probably their practice, dining several miles away from Fort Johnston and no doubt had their minds on matters social rather than professional.

There are other signs of care taken in planning the attack. Chipembere knew where he could quickly lay his hands on arms, ammunition and vehicles: the Malindi mission station and the Fort Johnston boma. Cutting the telephone lines at Fort Johnston was carefully planned to ensure that the security forces at Zomba were not immediately alerted. In the event, as Chipembere may have calculated, reliance on the Monkey Bay facility delayed their being alerted for some six hours. At first sight, the commotion, noise and burnings that occurred as the rebels approached Fort Johnston township appear to have been unwise, since they could have served to raise a general alarm in which the ferry could have been moved to the township side of the river, marooning the attackers on the Malindi side. Causing or allowing the rumpus, however, could have been deliberate for, whether by design or not, it certainly caused the European inhabitants of Fort Johnston, and probably even more the pro-government African inhabitants, to take fright, hide, and refrain from retaliating and from notifying officials outside Fort Johnston.

The débâcle at Liwonde ended Chipembere's chances of reaching Banda in Zomba. Failing to take the elementary precaution of ensuring that the ferry was on, or could readily be called over to, the northern bank of the Shire river, seems an extraordinary error. The Liwonde area was largely pro-Chipembere and it ought not to have been difficult to vouchsafe his passage at that vital point. In principle, he could have approached Zomba without crossing the river at Liwonde, first, by crossing back to the eastern side of the river at Fort Johnston, having seized the arms, ammunition and vehicles, and staying on that side; or, second, by travelling towards the Shire and crossing it by the Mpimbe rail bridge; or, third, by travelling via Balaka and crossing over the Matope road bridge. The first of these could have been accomplished by road, but only over very poor surfaces, made even worse during the rainy season, and over a longer distance. The second could not be crossed by vehicles and would have had to be approached on foot, either from the Matope road or the Liwonde road. The third could be done entirely by vehicles travelling on main roads, but would have taken at least twice as long and necessitated driving through Blantyre, where they would run a high risk of being detected and stopped long before they reached Zomba. The route Chipembere took was far and away the most sensible and the most likely to succeed, given that speed was an essential element of his plans. He needed to accomplish the whole operation during the hours of darkness, seizing the arms, ammunition and vehicles at Malindi and Fort Johnston after dark on Friday 12 February and reaching Banda in Zomba before daybreak on Saturday. Only travelling in vehicles over the Fort Johnston–Liwonde–Zomba road would enable him to do this. But the Liwonde ferry thwarted him.

A Marxist view attributes the failure of Chipembere and his 'liberation army' in their 'aim of liberating the peasants' to their lack of a 'political and ideological direction of the kind that could give a theoretical dimension to their struggle'.[51] The view is valid in that Chipembere felt that 'ideological orientation [presumably Communism] was ... the issue which could split any future government of Malawi', but it does not follow that a theoretical dimension would have helped him in the very practical matter of a *coup d'état*. Better planning might have.

Chipembere asserted that his plan was for a bloodless coup and, contrary to Banda's claim, he did not intend to assassinate the prime minister and his ministers. Rather the doctor was to be forced to abdicate and return to England or Ghana, together with those of his henchmen who did not accept the new regime. He admitted that some of his men were doubtful about the wisdom of such a gentle revolt, but he had asserted his authority and they agreed that there should be no killing and only a minimum of detentions – which would last only a few weeks. Throughout the conflict he claimed to be opposed to killing. At Fort Johnston, during his 12 February attack, when a policeman, the telephone operator on duty, prison warder, boma watchman, ferryman and other government servants fell into his hands, he let them go. He ordered that they and the other men on duty should not be molested. His intention was only that the communication lines should be impaired so that he could arrive in Zomba with his men 'unexpectedly and by surprise'. These were his orders to his men and to the best of his knowledge they were obeyed by them.

> But all sorts of people joined us at this stage and they didn't know my orders. Certainly some of the prisoners we released got possession of some of the rifles and guns we seized and disappeared with them. It is possible that they used these on Changwa's family; for Changwa had got himself thoroughly hated even by his own relatives.[52]

Chipembere may have felt confident of achieving a bloodless *coup d'état*. Stoneman believed he had 'people in all the key places – Radio Malawi, Government offices, Post Offices etc. – ready to take over if he succeeded in reaching Zomba'.⁵³ Furthermore, Chipembere claimed he was in touch with senior African officers and was sure of the support of a large part of the army and police, who had agreed to 'sit on their hands' if he actually reached Zomba.⁵⁴

> There were still many white oficers in both the army and the police, but there had been a rapid promotion of Africans. Chipembere came out of the hills to a very remote place, Lake Chirwa, and several senior police and army officers went to meet him. They told him that if he could get to Zomba they would take over.⁵⁵

So far as the 'rapid promotion of Africans' and the existence of 'several senior police and army officers' is concerned, there were in fact very few senior officers. Banda deliberately set a slow pace and was extremely sensitive to the security aspects of Africanising the army and the police. For example, when, in February 1966, he learned of the *coup d'état* in Ghana that ousted Nkrumah, he immediately ordered the army commander and the commissioner of police to submit plans to slow down the pace still further.⁵⁶ In February 1965, there were only eight Malawian commissioned officers in the army. Five of these were long-serving promoted sergeants-major and none of them was a Yao, the grouping upon which Chipembere largely depended. The army was based centrally at Zomba. Their freedom of movement outside the barracks without the knowledge of their superior officers was significantly restricted. They would have found it very difficult indeed for any one of them, let alone more, to be away from Zomba for the period necessary to get to and to return from a remote part of Lake Chirwa without their absence being noticed and checked on. Furthermore, it is extremely unlikely that any of them would have been inclined to commit treason and join Chipembere. The other three were recently promoted younger officers, only one of whom came from the southern region where Chipembere's support lay. A senior expatriate officer later felt that the younger Malawian officers, but not the former sergeants major, might have been prepared to join Chipembere.⁵⁷ The Malawian commissioned officers were too few to be able realistically to contemplate mutiny and organize the troops against the orders of the more numerous and senior European officers. The commanding officer had successfully resisted attempts to form companies on tribal lines and, as a consequence, every company was comprised of men from all parts of the country and none owed particular allegience to political leaders on grounds of coming from a particular area.⁵⁸

In the police the most senior officer was the bandmaster, with the rank of superintendent. There were two other superintendents and eight assistant superintendents. Two of these officers were in their fifties and the remainder – except the bandmaster, who was thirty-nine – were all in their forties. They were all long-serving officers. They, like most police officers during the period leading up to independence, had been the recipients of public abuse and criticism from Chipembere and his fellows. It is unlikely that any of them would be inclined to commit treason and join him. A senior and experienced Special Branch officer later wrote:

> I was unaware of any indication that army or police officers were in touch with Chipembere, and the story does not ring true. The army officers all appeared totally loyal to Paul Lewis, and the police officers I knew would have been most unlikely to have met Chipembere in the bush and been unable to talk to us about it.[59]

Indeed, the army and senior police officers were the very people who, save for the three younger army officers, had progressed through long and loyal service to the colonial government and, as a consequence, tended to be despised by Chipembere and his followers.[60]

On the other hand, there are indications – though not strong – that Chipembere may have been promised support, or at least a lack of resistance, from army and police officers. First, some four months earlier the British high commissioner had said, hypothetically: 'There could ... and I repeat the word "could" – be rumblings among the police and soldiers and elsewhere in the country.'[61] Second, it is probable that if Chipembere had in fact sought support from army, or more likely police, personnel, they may have said to him something to the effect that if he did get that far and looked like winning they would then join his cause but – though not saying so – they had no intention of committing themselves before then. Third, maybe police officers were used clandestinely, but with restricted official knowledge, to give an impression of support and to discover from Chipembere what his plans were, as with Chirwa in Tanzania several years later.[62] Fourth, there was a feeling among some – probably a few – expatriate army and police officers that 'if the rebels *had* marched on Zomba nothing would have been done to prevent Banda being deposed'.[63] Fifth, a European Special Branch officer later had a conversation in the bush with Chipembere, and when he asked how he was to explain this meeting to his followers Chipembere said he would tell them the officer was 'one of his supporters from Zomba'. Presumably, he expected his followers to believe he had support in the police, including expatriate officers. Since he was driving 'an obvious police Land Rover with a Force crest on the door' the officer thought this an extraordinary statement.[64] Finally, it may be that the willingness of Moxon, a former army officer living near Zomba, to take part in a *coup d'état* 'when the time seemed ripe' was connected to the understanding others had that army and police officers were prepared to join Chipembere if he reached Zomba.

Chipembere was well aware of the importance of having the army on one's side. Several years later, he wrote of the British officers commanding the Malawi Army:

> They carried with them the then politically insulated and uninformed African soldiers ... In African politics, especially in the decade of the Sixties, any man who was supported by the army stayed in power or rose to power; he who was opposed by the army stayed out of power, if he was lucky! If he was not, he stayed elsewhere – in jail, or in exile – or in a cemetery.[65]

Neither in this nor in any other of his direct accounts of the attempted coup did Chipembere even hint that he had tried to get the army or the police on his side. It is possible, though, that he told, or gave the impression to, those sympathetic to him that he was in touch with army and police officers, in order to strengthen his supporters' belief in the extent of his following and convince them that they were not acting alone and in isolation, and to persuade any doubters among them that he was bound to be successful in attempting to oust Banda.

Ten days after the attack on Fort Johnston, there was another attack, this time on Ntaja police station north-east of Liwonde, led by Medson Silombela. Whereas the police at Fort Johnston had not retaliated, at Ntaja they did, by opening fire on the attackers, who quickly fled. Silombela's unit shortly moved further south in Zomba district and attacked Chief Chikowi by firing at him through a window of his house, only three miles from the centre of Zomba. But, as Banda said, 'the Chief was a fighter, a warrior, a courageous Chief, yes, the old type of Chief we used to have in [the old] days'. Chikowi fought back and killed one of the attackers. The other five ran away.[66] The doctor appeared to forget that he had denounced and deposed Chikowi as a chief only a few years earlier and that he had been physically attacked as an opponent of the MCP.

There were also attacks in the middle of March in the far north of the country where, it was thought, Chisiza was behind a number of armed incursions by units, carrying automatic weapons, crossing over from Tanzania. They aimed at assassinating leading members of the MCP and then attacking the police stations at Chisenga and Chitipa.[67] By the previous December, Banda claimed, some of the rebel ministers had decided to send their followers to 'Communist countries to be trained in subversion and sabotage', 'shooting, bombing and petrol bombing'. They went to Cuba, Algeria, Peking China, and Morogoro in Tanzania. As he reported to parliament:

> By March 1965 some of these people had come back from their training centres ... and a group of them was sent to Chitipa ... The Young Pioneers and the Youth Leaguers [and] the whole village surrounded them and hacked them to death, with axes and hoes ... and their bodies were thrown into the Songwe River – meat for the crocodiles.[68]

Chisiza had accompanied the insurgents but fled when the villagers turned on them. The officer in charge of police in the northern region recalled this 'small incursion of rebels from across the Songwe River from Tanzania into the Chitipa area where our intelligence system was superb', and thought that Chisiza was reconnoitring the area for further attacks.[69]

Late in the morning of 9 March, the expatriate government agent – the new name for district commissioner – of Fort Johnston, Bolt, went to see the Governor-General, who had returned from leave three weeks earlier. The previous day, 8 March, Bolt had received at his office, through the ordinary post, a letter in an official OHMS envelope, correctly stamped for ordinary mail, bearing the Fort Johnston postal cancellation, and endorsed 'Personal and Urgent. The Government Agent, Fort Johnston'. The envelope contained another OHMS envelope, franked 'Hon. H. B. M. Chipembere, Member of Parliament', addressed 'Personal and Urgent. His Excellency the Governor-General (Sir Glyn Jones), Zomba'. The letter to Bolt, in Chipembere's handwriting, said:

> The ending of the present conflict in Malawi may well depend on the safe and expeditious delivery of this letter and there will be a grave moral (if not legal) responsibility on anyone who by design or by default causes it to be lost or destroyed. I therefore send it through you so that you can arrange its despatch by rider or by registered mail. This I do because I happen to know that some of my supporters have been destroying letters addressed to Dr. Banda.[70]

It is clear that the contents of the letter were intended for Banda.

The purpose of the letter, which Bolt handed to Jones in its envelope, was to give Chipembere's side of the story in the hope that the Governor-General would see he was 'not quite the villain' he had been called.[71] He was out of touch with his wife and parents and he did not know how they were faring. He supposed they were suffering a good deal, but felt they should not experience a life different from the families of the detainees who had been arrested as his supporters. It was fair that his own family should suffer if others had to suffer for him.

He exculpated himself from instigating the riots in Zomba the previous September. Banda had accused him of terrorizing his supporters in the capital and this was why he had restricted him. He thought this 'one of the unfairest accusations of the period' since, from the beginning of the crisis, he had spent only four hours in Zomba and they were at a cocktail party, which turned into a public meeting and gave him the opportunity to state in public his case and that of the other ex-ministers. This was two weeks before the riots, which he did not even know about until the following day. He claimed, as did also the police, he said, that his supporters reacted only because of the extreme provocation of the young pioneers. He was 'quite innocent' of the events in Zomba that day and consequently the restriction order was undeserved.

He did not, however, seek to escape responsibility for the attack on Fort Johnston: 'it is quite correct that the rebel force that attacked Fort Johnston and tried to march on Zomba was raised, trained and led by me'. If he got caught and was prosecuted he would admit it. The only thing he would deny was the murder of Mrs Changwa and her child, which was not by men in his army, but probably by the prisoners his men released, or by the villagers 'who rushed to join the fray when they heard of it'. His own men 'met all sorts of [civil] servants on duty, including two policemen but let them go unharmed'. He then explained why he had 'become a rebel':

> I had no option but to be a rebel. I had no real desire to rule the country. My desire is to see established in Malawi a Government that will make it possible for us, the ex-ministers and our supporters, to return to our homes and live in peace ... It is my determination that we should all regain our right to return to our homes from abroad, from detention, and from hiding in forests. It is this right that I am fighting for, and I will not give up until I am caught or killed. On grounds of principle I will NOT leave the country. This would be an act of desertion or betrayal of our supporters in jail. Dr. Banda says an invasion of the country is being prepared by Chiume. There may be substance to this but I do not believe in external invasions as long as there is room for an internal revolt or guerrilla warfare.

He was prepared to accept all the legal consequences of rebellion, including the death sentence, and repeated that he would not flee from the country although it would be easy to do so. Already his friends outside Malawi had twice sent men to escort him to safety in Tanzania, and he could leave at any time by canoe, dhow or on foot via Mozambique where he had friends and relatives. He did not say so, but Chiume made detailed plans for him, dressed in women's clothes, to escape to Dar es Salaam, but he had turned them down. There was also, Chiume claimed, a rescue operation planned in which a Zambia police Land

Rover was painted in Malawi police colours, ready to take Chipembere from Fort Johnston via Zambia en route for Dar es Salaam, but he declined to use it.[72] Chipembere recognized that his refusal to leave looked like 'vain and blind pride', but it was a pride he shared with Banda, who regarded it as humiliating to discuss reconciliation. He, too, in Chipembere's position, would refuse to leave the country or stop fighting.

> No man of principle ever betrays his followers, and in the whole of this conflict I feel I have exceptional responsibility for the suffering of the people in jail and in exile ... because most of them became our supporters because I had thrown in my lot with the ex-ministers. [Several] didn't know what the conflict was all about but that they felt they had to follow me wherever I went.

He found it impossible to desert these people who were suffering for having followed him, nor could he stop fighting for their release. Since he knew that Banda would not free them willingly – none had been released since the restrictions were first imposed – he had to fight for a government that would release them and let them and all others return to their homes. Banda was quite wrong in believing that his rebel army was breaking up, and he would shortly be in for a rude shock, because they were preparing their hideouts in a number of forests ready to launch a hit-and-run war that would continue until Banda either resigned or granted an amnesty. He had over 400 men in his army when last counted, but the influx had so overwhelmed his clerks that it was impossible to register them all. He had made arrangements for the war to continue even after his death or arrest.

He was saddened by the prospect of the economic damage that guerrilla war would bring about, 'but economic or other prosperity is meaningless while hundreds of citizens are in jail, in exile or in hiding in the forests'. These men were the breadwinners and supporters of many people and 'as long as their dependents starve and as long as they weep for their loved ones there is no prosperity or peace'. He loved Malawi and would hate to plunge it into economic chaos. If his planned guerrilla war started, it would do a great deal of harm. Young men loved loot. Anyone who promised them plunder and loot was sure to succeed in winning them over. Banda must have seen how his own young pioneers had completely looted large shops in a single night. The destruction of bridges, telephones and buildings would 'put the clock of development back by many years and capital would hardly come to or stay in a country in which this was taking place'.

Chipembere then came to the main point of his letter: the offer to call off his fight if Banda would declare 'some sort of amnesty'. If this were to happen, he would not only tell his supporters to cooperate with the government, but he would also do his best to persuade his colleagues in Tanzania to abandon 'whatever military preparations they may be making', if indeed they were making any, and return to live in Malawi peacefully. He himself would then be willing either to leave Malawi and work abroad or live on Likoma Island with his wife's family and 'keep away from pressmen and the lorryfuls of supporters that crowd[ed on him] when [he lived] in Fort Johnston and cause[d him] to make political statements which pressmen often distort, just to fan the fight'. He would not hesitate to bring the guerrilla war to an end if reasonable terms were offered, because he feared – though this was not his aim 'at present' – that lives might be lost in such a war. The only choice was between war and an amnesty:

> It is no good Dr. Banda talking of 'crushing' me and my men. I have read enough about hit and run methods to know that a guerrilla war is not easy to crush. Fifty armed men operating in three or four forests can do a lot of havoc before they are crushed and I'm a man who can raise thousands of men for this purpose in six districts of the Southern Region. Dr. Banda thinks I am extremely unpopular [and] that if I stepped on any part of the Central or Northern Region and even parts of the South I would be torn to pieces. That is correct. But, with due respect, it is true also of him. If he dared move into any part of the country that supports me, he would be torn to pieces ... Dr. Banda is surrounded by lots of bodyguards for every inch he moves. Why? ... I move a lot in the villages of Fort Johnston, Kasupe and Northern Zomba and I know he is extremely unpopular in these areas. I also have young men from other Southern districts with me[73] and I know what is being said by villagers in those areas ... If I did not have support I would be in jail or in my grave by now. But villagers themselves hide me, feed me and stand guard around the village to warn me about on-coming danger.

He asked Jones to mediate and seek an amnesty, not out of weakness or fear, but because he wished to avoid wrecking the country with civil war and because of his deep desire to secure the release of the men who were currently 'languishing in jail, exile and forest'. He hoped the Governor-General would be able to act quickly. The security forces had burned many houses and stores and caused large numbers of men, including many who were neutral, to flee into the bush. These refugees would, Chipembere was convinced, be forced to join him and they would exert still greater pressure on him for action to get 'food and blankets from Indian and European shops for themselves'.

Chipembere told Jones how a reply could be sent to him. He did not think the Governor-General would consider it appropriate to answer his letter, but if he did want to communicate with him, [a letter] can be dropped at any surviving store or canteen in the Malindi area, or at the house of any village headman there, with instructions to the receiver to announce to the village that he has my letter. A loudspeaker announcement by the police can also help. There are my agents in all these villages and the message would be sent to me by a chain of messengers. It would probably reach me after a week. I would then send one of my well-known companions to fetch the letter. If the police lay a trap there it will fail. My men are thoroughly drilled in these things.

As soon as Jones had read the letter from Chipembere he called together Youens, Roberts, Long, Lomax and Major Matthews, second in command of the Malawi Army – Lewis was still at Fort Johnston – and they met in the early afternoon to discuss it. They felt that it 'betokened a mood of desperation in the writer who had probably come pretty near to the end of his tether'.

[Jones] decided ... to send a copy of the letter by hand of Mr. Youens to the Prime Minister [as Chipembere said he could 'if necessary'] with the request that he should not make any public reference to it until he had discussed it with [Jones] and that he should meet [him] to discuss it at 9 a.m. on 10 March.

Youens delivered a typed copy of the letter to Banda at about 5 p.m. that day. The prime minister straight away said he was not interested and would rather not see Jones on the subject. For him the position was that 'he would either get Chipembere or Chipembere would get him'. He was not interested in an amnesty. He did, however, undertake not to divulge to anyone the contents of the letter unless Chipembere did something to force his hand. At 9 a.m. the following day, instead of going to see Jones, Banda telephoned him on the secret line from his office, thanked him for the copy of Chipembere's letter and said, 'I am not interested in the letter. I am not at all interested.'[74] Just as Banda had asked Jones not to intervene during the cabinet crisis itself, so now it was clear that he did not want even to see him on the question of an amnesty.

Banda had placed a price on Chipembere's head, and duplicated notices were distributed in the Fort Johnston district in English, Cinyanja and Ciyao offering £1,000[75] to anyone who provided information to the police or army leading directly to Chipembere's arrest. They also offered rewards in respect of Silombela, at £200, and eight others at £100 each. Ten pounds was offered for information leading to the recovery of any .303 rifle – presumably those stolen during the Fort Johnston attack. At the top of one of these notices, which Jones received at the time of Chipembere's 7 March 1965 letter, was an endorsement in Chipembere's

Chipembere's Attempted Coup d'État · 227

handwriting, with a rare touch of humour: 'Received and being returned with thanks. At present I am not willing to oblige. If proper terms are offered I will present myself.'[76]

Chipembere was anxious about the possibility of his letter not reaching the Governor-General safely, so he wrote again, this time to Lady Jones, on 16 March. Before his wife received this second letter, Jones wrote to him briefly and formally, on 17 March, acknowledging receipt of his letter and saying that, as he had suggested, he had passed a typed copy to the prime minister. Although he already knew, he did not tell Chipembere what the doctor's response was: an immediate and outright refusal to contemplate an amnesty.[77] It is likely that Chipembere believed Lady Jones might influence her husband to try and persuade Banda to agree to an amnesty, or that she might put the point to Cecilia Kadzamira in the hope of this being helpful. Chiume and others of his colleagues believed that Lady Jones had considerable influence over her husband's official actions.[78] In his letter to Lady Jones, Chipembere repeated the gist of his letter to her husband, explaining the conditions under which he would call off his opposition and either leave the country or go to Likoma to live, away 'from the crowds of supporters whose calls and pressures on [him had] tended to aggravate the situation in the past'. He tried to increase the pressure for an amnesty.

> In order to be quite explicit and unequivocal, but intending no blackmail, I have added that if these conditions are not accepted I will have no option but to continue my rebel activities and for this purpose I have organised two guerrilla squads which are now preparing their hideouts in certain forests with three or four more to be sent out soon. I take this stand in the name of principle and for the sake of my supporters who are suffering in jail or have had to flee from home. I feel more deeply concerned about them because probably 80% of them joined the ex-Ministers' side in this conflict because of their attachment to me, for although the clash was originally between Dr. Banda and my colleagues, many people remained neutral or pro-Kamuzu until they learned that I had joined the ex-Ministers. It was at this point that Dr. Banda lost the people that are now on our side, at least most of them. So most of the people who are suffering in this conflict are suffering in my name and for my sake. I therefore have an inescapable moral duty to fight for them. I dare not abandon them. My conscience and history will never forgive me if I desert them ... This is why when my colleagues now in Tanzania have twice sent a man and money to take me there I have refused and prefer to stand or perish on Malawi soil.[79]

At this time, late March 1965, Banda introduced, with retrospective effect to 1 January 1965, parliamentary bills to simplify, clarify and make more stringent the law of treason. So far as retrospectivity was concerned, he argued that the changes were not making unlawful an act then committed which was not at that date forbidden by law. The law of treason already existed and he was simply clarifying it. He also made the death sentence mandatory on conviction and empowered the minister of justice to determine what form the execution should take: 'whether it be by hanging or other methods'. He made it clear that he had the activities of Chipembere in mind, which compelled him to clarify the law of treason. 'In the light of what has happened at Fort Johnston we can't have a vague law in this country. We can't afford to have that.' He was determined to make the new provisions lawyer-proof and judge-proof.[80] At the same meeting of parliament he introduced a bill to amend the constitution so as to exclude criminal cases and political cases from appeal to the Privy Council: 'we must make sure that no restrictee, no detainee, can talk about appeal to the Privy Council'.[81] After unusually brief debate – in the sense of there being few speeches – motions to enact both alterations to the law were carried. Banda's remark about the form of judicial execution was ominous. Although he did not say then what other method he had in mind, a clue might be found in a remark a few months later when, in referring to judicial execution in Britain in the past he said, 'Yes. There was drawing and quartering, which is much worse than hanging an individual publicly.'[82]

On Saturday, 27 March the Governor-General left for a three-day tour of the Fort Johnston district. A European missionary told him that 95 per cent of the people in the district were for Chipembere.[83] He inspected a number of army units stationed in various villages and had three meetings with the district operations committee. He also held a number of meetings in villages, where he found the people 'sullen and unresponsive but not rude'. 'One man, ex KAR, said they were not happy. Soldiers were beating them, looting, burning houses. [Jones] said if he had evidence he should produce it to the officers who would take action.' Others told him of houses and cars being damaged. Presumably at a loss for other words, he told them the 'soldiers and police were doing their duty, [he] hoped they would have good crops and that there would be peace'. It is unlikely that either the villagers or the Governor-General found his visit reassuring or indeed of any value.

On the day of his arrival in Fort Johnston, Bolt handed Jones another letter. This also was from Chipembere, and, given that it was written on 25 March, it was almost certainly sent through the ordinary mail. He thanked Jones for acknowledging his earlier letter. It had nearly got lost or destroyed on the way, so he thought it would be better if future letters, whether from Jones or Banda, were handed in at the store belonging to Mtembo, 250 yards south of his house and about a quarter of a mile north of Malindi mission. He carefully explained that Mtembo was not one of his supporters but spent his time looking after his own business, and had been neutral until recently, when he had become a guide for the security forces in the Malindi area. He went on to say that

> [The security forces] are perpetrating unheard of brutalities. This may be on orders from Dr. Banda, since Malindi is my home, for their behaviour seems so different from that of security forces stationed elsewhere in Fort Johnston. Rape, burning of houses, shooting, beating of men, women and children, looting of homes, stores and gardens, indiscriminate arresting etc., are the order of the day. The result is ... a general flight of people into the mountains where they succumb to hunger and begin to descend on neighbouring gardens and property for loot. As time goes on they may be compelled to do worse things.

Unbeknown to Chipembere, while it was true that the security forces conducted a vigorous and bruising campaign in the area east of Fort Johnston to root out him and his units, it could have been worse. When the commander of the Malawi Army was instructed to carry out the campaign, he told his officers to take a drum corps with them and make plenty of noise to warn the inhabitants of their imminent arrival and give them a chance to escape.[84]

Of the 20,000 people in the Malindi area Chipembere claimed that only about a hundred men, mostly youths, were with him in the mountains before the attack on Fort Johnston, and probably only about another fifty joined in the rioting that 'took place spontaneously' that night. So the rest of the people in the Malindi area were 'quite innocent of politics and political enthusiasm or zeal of any kind'. They were therefore suffering without cause from the security forces' activities and the arrests. It was, however, the case that most reports gave a figure of two hundred rebel forces who attacked Fort Johnston in February. Also, the security forces seized a list of names of three hundred of his followers at that time. In either case, it appears that only part of the forces available to him – one-third to two-thirds – accompanied him in the attack. He continued his letter to Jones:

> It would ... help the chances of re-establishing peace immensely if the security forces in the Malindi area were removed. Many of those which were stationed in the Katuli, Makanjira and upper Jalasi areas have been removed. Since no further acts of violence have been committed since 13 February there is no need at all for the security forces in this district, and I do not intend to act as long as Dr. Banda's reaction to my offer remains unknown.

Chipembere added that he could not wait indefinitely for this reaction.

His camp was far away from supplies of food and his officers would shortly 'exert irresistible pressure for [his] authority to go to war again, if only to obtain their sustenance'. He indicated, though not explicitly, that after the failure of the attempted *coup d'état*, he had changed his strategy:

> We are not at present powerful enough to seize the Government by force, but we have an immense capacity for destruction, and can put back the clock of economic development many years. To quote an example of one of the proposals by my officers – one which I can afford to reveal because I have rejected it as too destructive – I have been under pressure to send a team to set the [ship] Ilala on fire with petrol bombs, etc. The frail and infant economy of this country can ill afford a guerrilla war which includes the destruction of vital sources of income and general wealth.

It was these considerations that compelled him to offer a settlement. No one, he said, should underestimate the strength of his support. Many men in several districts who pretended to be loyal to Banda were in fact supporting Chipembere 'secretly, morally and materially'. Without this support he would not have survived. He did not wish to place a specific time limit on his offer, for this would 'sound like an ultimatum and indeed [be] rude'. He still had a profound respect for Banda as a man with exceptional qualities and one with whom he had been 'mutually helpful', so he would not like to embarrass him too much with an ultimatum: 'I will wait for some weeks yet.'[85]

Banda had strongly stepped up his security forces' vigour in hunting down Chipembere and his men, and by early April 1965 he told parliament:

> A number of Chipembere's men have been captured and I am speaking ... of at least 400 known gangsters and suspects who have been captured [and are in custody in Zomba, Blantyre and Cholo]. Four of them have been shot dead. What remains of the gang is now split into groups of twos, threes and tens at the most, if that. Of the remaining gangsters, six to eight are supposed to be with Chipembere himself hiding somewhere in the Malindi area of Fort Johnston. Another number, probably about the same – six to eight or ten at the most – are with Silombela, a known gangster, a man who learned his gangstery in Southern Rhodesia and the Union of South Africa.[86]

If Chipembere was correct about the size of his army – four hundred – and if Banda was correct about the number captured – four hundred, which was rather less than the estimate of the head of Special Branch: 320 in detention and 180 in restriction[87] – Chipembere's forces must fast

Chipembere's Attempted Coup d'État · 231

have been becoming depleted. If this were so, the urgency to secure an amnesty would, for Chipembere, have been considerable and, correspondingly, for Banda, negligible. Indeed, from early in March, Banda believed that

> for the time being the danger of armed revolt on any appreciable scale was over. There was evidence to show that Chipembere's gang had largely dispersed and Chipembere himself was accompanied by a mere handful of followers. The reason why only little information was being given to the security forces by the local population was probably that the local population was quite unaware of Chipembere's movements and whereabouts.[88]

The security forces were, in fact, having great difficulty in finding Chipembere, as Banda shortly admitted with surprising frankness:

> Everything possible has been done by the security forces. They have hunted for him in the rain; they have walked miles; sometimes they have had to cross rivers, water up to their waists, and they have slept in the bush hunting for Chipembere … the area is very difficult, very mountainous, with no roads, very, very few, and even with traps for ordinary food purposes. [Chipembere] does not make his presence known to more than very, very, very few people, and these very, very few people are his very, very, very trusted people, the people that he knows cannot betray him and therefore they do not give information. [Also] he moves about, he never stays in one place more than a day, so that by the time the security forces get information and arrange to go and find him, he has moved and is elsewhere.[89]

About a week after Chipembere wrote his 25 March letter to Jones, he also wrote to the US ambassador, Sam Gilstrap, who received it through the ordinary mail. Late in the morning of 5 April, Gilstrap saw Jones 'on a matter of urgency' and showed him the letter, which 'was very long and its style was immature, almost schoolboyish'. It may have been showing increasing signs of the effects of Chipembere's inadequately treated diabetes and his desperation.[90]

> The gist of it was that Chipembere was confidently expecting an amnesty to be declared both for himself, the ex-Ministers and all the people who had taken part in the Fort Johnston disturbances. In this event he wished to leave Malawi and would like to go to America to study for an M.A. Degree in History at an American university. He would also like his wife and two of his children to follow him to America, and would like his wife to be given some post as a teacher in a Secondary School, for which he said she was qualified.

Chipembere added – perhaps with another touch of humour – that, 'for obvious reasons', he would not be asking the Malawi government for a grant. Instead he thought he would be able to borrow money so as to be no burden on the US government. He recognized that by going to the USA he 'would be earning the criticism of his fellow ex-ministers'.

Gilstrap told Jones he was in difficulties over the letter and had asked for guidance from his government in Washington. They said he should consult Jones and, if possible, get him to see if Banda would have any objections. Jones asked why Gilstrap could not himself approach Banda since he, Jones, had received letters from Chipembere and this placed him in some difficulty. The difficulty arose because he had not mentioned to Banda the second letter from Chipembere. Indeed he could hardly tell the doctor that Chipembere had written to seek a response to the first letter when Banda had already given Jones his reply. Gilstrap explained that the US government felt it important for him to try to keep clear of any political involvement in Malawi, and he added that 'there would be no difficulty whatsoever in finding Chipembere a place in a university and his wife and family could be looked after'. Gilstrap, presumably following the guidance from Washington, thought the best solution from all points of view would be for Chipembere to leave Malawi and go to a place like America for some years.

Jones said he would give the matter some thought and, the ambassador having left him temporarily, he asked Youens and Roberts to see him immediately. They discussed this most recent development and agreed there could be no harm in Jones mentioning the letter to Banda when he saw him, as previously arranged, later that day.

> I could say that Gilstrap had come to see me in a state of grave anxiety because he had received this letter from Chipembere which was quite unsolicited. He wished to keep himself quite clear from any political implication of this sort and had asked my advice as to what to do. I had undertaken to inform the Prime Minister of the letter and its contents. I could then note Dr. Banda's reactions and Gilstrap and I could have further discussions on the matter in the light of those reactions.

He was, it seems clear, unable to gauge what the doctor's reaction would be.

When Gilstrap rejoined Jones he entirely agreed with this proposed way of proceeding. Later that day, in the evening, when Banda came to see Jones, the Governor-General mentioned Chipembere's letter to Gilstrap. Banda's reaction was immediate. He required no advice or persuasion: 'he would not wish to block Chipembere's leaving the country for the purpose of acquiring further education, provided it was clearly understood that he should not use his time in America to plot against

Chipembere's Attempted Coup d'État · 233

this Government and to make speeches of criticism against the Prime Minister personally'. Banda saw political advantages in Chipembere's removal from the country. He would no longer be seen as a martyr and everyone would see that the solidarity of the former ministers was crumbling, a process that, he said, had started with Chirwa leaving for London to search for a job. It is true that the first evidence of crumbling, of breaking ranks as opposed to simply fleeing the country, was Chirwa's approach to him for a judicial post. Jones tried his best to persuade Banda that Gilstrap had received the letter entirely without solicitation, but 'he did not accept this with great enthusiasm' because, declining to give any details, he said the Russians were already saying the American embassy was in touch with the ex-ministers. Later that day, having consulted Youens and Roberts, Jones told Lewis, Long and Lomax about the letter to the ambassador. All of these 'we considered were reliable enough to be let into the secret'.[91]

When Gilstrap called on Jones the following morning, and was told of Banda's reaction, he 'expressed satisfaction at the outcome, limited though it was. At present he said he could give a categorical assurance that the American Government would not tolerate Chipembere's using the opportunity of studying in an American university for launching attacks on the Malawi Government or Dr Banda personally. He was very firm about this.'

> As to the next move to be made Gilstrap said he would leave that in my [Jones's] hands, and I promised to get in touch with him as soon as some plan had been devised. Gilstrap hoped that if Chipembere agreed to leave the country he could proceed to America via Zambia or Moçambique rather than via Dar es Salaam, where he would be exposed to the malign influence of Chiume and Red China.[92]

Within a few days of Gilstrap's meetings with Jones – between 6 and 9 April – a letter was sent to Chipembere telling him that Banda had agreed to his departure, including the two conditions attached to his permission, that Gilstrap had agreed to find him a place at an American university, that arrangements would be made for his wife to join him and that action would be taken on his supporters in gaol once he had left the country. The letter also gave him a choice of days – or invited him to select a choice of days – for his departure. It is extremely unlikely that any details of the evacuation arrangements were mentioned[93] – they may not yet have been worked out – and it would have been unnecessary and unwise to give them. Indeed, Chipembere himself referred to the 'vagueness of the safe conduct plan'.[94] The letter was sent by 'Gideon Banda', which was a pseudonym. Although Banda and Gilstrap knew there was to be an evacuation, the only people who knew of the arrangements in any detail were Jones, Youens, Roberts, Lomax, Long, Lewis and the person who actually implemented the evacuation. Of these the person most likely to be Gideon Banda was Roberts.

On 6 and 13 April, when he already knew of Chipembere's wish to leave the country and go to the USA, and when he had already privately said he would not stand in his way, Banda spoke publicly but guardedly, presumably to put pressure on Chipembere to leave, and to gain credit for having frightened him into doing so in the event of his leaving:

> [Chipembere] will be captured, unless of course he runs away. Yes, there is a possibility that he might run away ... Well, if he does, then there is nothing anyone can do, but as long as he hides there, either in someone's house or in a cave or in the reeds, the security forces will find him.[95]
>
> Very soon I will have a camp in Fort Johnston, at Katuli, to make sure my boys, my Youth League, will be there ... to make quite certain ... that Chipembere does not have a second chance, even to organise a few hundred men. My Youth League, my Young Pioneers will do their hunting practice in that area. No chance at all for Chipembere: no chance; and ... if Chipembere does not run away, and join his colleagues outside the country, he will be captured, and if he is captured ... well my Young Pioneers will be hunting there, and I cannot guarantee that they will capture him alive ... This is war! this is war! Not football; not tennis![96]

Chipembere replied to Gideon Banda's letter on 16 April by hand of 'one of the wanted men'[97] but since there were security forces on the shorter route, he had to take a longer route 'to the nearest post office'. This made Chipembere unsure of whether the letter would reach Gideon Banda in 'the estimated time'. Consequently he wrote another letter the following day, 17 April. It is clear from the precaution that he took, of sending a second letter a day later, that he was most anxious – possibly desperate – to leave Malawi. Chiume believed that Chipembere at this time was 'almost dying of diabetes'.[98] In the second letter he repeated the substance of the first:

> I accept [the letter's] proposals and have selected 26th April as the date of departure from Malindi with 28th April as the alternative. I have decided to arrange for one trustworthy and reliable man to know about these arrangements; he will get to know them on or about the 30th of April so that he can inform the world as to what happens if your plan turns out to be a trick to arrest me by taking advantage of my faith in the American Embassy and the Government it represents. I'm of course sending a message to this effect to my wife by hand via Mozambique so as to get her prepared for her journey.[99]

Clearly, Chipembere deliberately intended that news of his evacuation should not reach the 'trustworthy and reliable man' until after he was scheduled to leave Malawi. He could have sent the information when he received Gideon Banda's letter – a good two weeks before the event – but he did not do so, probably because he did not want to risk the information about the arrangements falling into other hands, or to risk the recipient acting precipitately or indiscreetly.

In his reply to Gideon Banda, Chipembere added that he had assumed from the tone of the prime minister's speeches that the peace offer had been turned down, and he consequently had resumed his rebel operations 'by sending out some squads of guerrillas into the field for operations against the Government'. When he received Gideon Banda's letter he immediately sent messages to these guerrillas to call them back, but it was not easy to reach them because they were trained to stay in the forests until the day of their operations. It was possible that there might be some attacks at about the time Gideon Banda received his letter and Chipembere was most anxious that these should not be interpreted as his turning down the evacuation proposals but were organized before he had received the letter containing them. Despite this, just before he left his rebel camp to be evacuated, he left written instructions to 'continue the fight' because he found it impossible to leave the forest without some such exhortation to his followers. These instructions were captured by the security forces. He recognized later that this was a set-back to the bona fides of his leaving Malawi peacefully, but claimed it was an order that he gave well knowing that the fight could not possibly go on without his leadership, 'inspiration, guidance, organization and planning'. There were indeed subsequent operations by Chipembere's rebel units which led, in his own words, to 'tragic events at Kalembo, in the Chimwala area, in Namwera, and at Makanjira [that] were the beginning of this intensified activity resulting from Government's silence to [his] peace offer'.[100]

Chipembere noted that Gideon Banda's letter did not contain an answer to his peace offer and particularly it did not refer to the amnesty that was a condition of it. Nevertheless, he accepted the assurance that action would be taken on his supporters in gaol once he had left the country – what that action might be was not stated, although it is clear that Chipembere thought it was their release. He agreed to leave in their interests and not his own, and he looked forward to receiving news of their release when he was 'in the other country'. The use of this expression 'the other country' reinforces the probability that while he knew of the US embassy involvement, he did not know to which country he was to be evacuated in the short term. He concluded his letter by saying that if the amnesty was not granted early enough, or if he was arrested by a trick, his men in the forest would continue rebel activities in his absence and 'violence then [would] be much worse'.[101] He said this despite the fact that it contradicted his assertion that the fight could not possibly continue without his leadership, 'inspiration, guidance, organization and planning'. But then, he had also emphatically vowed that on grounds of principle he would not leave the country because to do so would be 'an act of desertion or betrayal'.

CHAPTER 9

Chipembere's Evacuation: April 1965

CHIPEMBERE'S evacuation from Malawi to the USA via Rhodesia and Britain was arranged between Lomax, Lewis, Long, Jones, Youens and Roberts. The operation was masterminded by Lomax. The person executing the actual operation was a European Special Branch officer, Keith Denton – a pseudonym used for the operation – who recalled:[1]

> Government obviously considered it necessary to rid the country of Chipembere and his field operators, preferably by their extermination, but it became apparent their capture was unlikely so other means would have to be found. One afternoon [during the week 12–17 April 1965] I was informed by my colleagues of Southern Division HQ that Dougie Lomax wished to speak to me ... I went to his house and as I stopped he drove up behind me, got out of his car and said, 'We want you to get Chip out for us.' He informed me that it had been decided to dangle a carrot in front of Chipembere by offering him a place for further education in an American university, and if this was accepted he would thus be removed from the scene and the insurgency in Fort Johnston, without his leadership, would collapse. Dougie informed me that he had told Dr. Banda of his plans and ... that the time had come to be magnanimous. Dr. Banda ... had agreed.

Denton was told to attend a meeting at Government House on a day in the following week, 19–24 April. Jones took the chair at that meeting, which was attended by Denton, Long, Lewis, Lomax, Youens and Roberts. He continued:

> Dougie outlined the arrangements he had made via the US Ambassador to Malawi for a university place for Chipembere which the US Government had agreed to, for cooperation with the BSAP in Salisbury and for CIA assistance in London. He also stated that contact had been established

with Chipembere through, I believe, the Government Agent's office in Fort Johnston and he, Chipembere, had indicated that he was prepared to accept the offer. The Attorney-General [Roberts] produced a letter for Chipembere informing him of the proposals and stating that he would be picked up at a certain time and place the following Monday, and pointing out that should anything unpleasant happen to the individual [Denton] involved in this 'hazardous operation' then the Fort Johnston district would be subjected to unprecedented hardship. [Jones], who was not at all happy about the operation, gave me a short hand-written note for Chipembere ... giving him his word Chipembere could trust me and that everything I told him could be believed. Dougie later told me that if things went wrong I was to swallow this note.

Although the Governor-General chaired the meeting, it was Lomax who did most of the talking and everyone accepted his proposals: 'he was a great charmer and gave the impression it was a 'cast iron operation and likely to succeed'. Jones was much concerned about Denton's safety. While prepared to go along with the evacuation, he was conscious of the danger involved and worried about the possibility of Denton being harmed. He handed him a note towards the end of the meeting – 'on a scrap of paper no larger than a credit card' – written on the spot in his own handwriting. 'It was just a sentence or two giving his word that [Denton] could be trusted etc. And it bore his signature which he said Chipembere would recognise.' As Denton left at the end of the meeting, Jones called him aside and said, 'If things go wrong shoot your way out, and for God's sake be careful.' Such was his concern.[2]

Soon after this meeting, the letter Roberts had read out was sent to Chipembere by Gideon Banda, a pseudonym,[3] giving for the first time some details of how the evacuation was to be effected, but only the day, time and place for him to be picked up. Although the security forces had not been able to capture Chipembere, they were closing in on him and knew roughly where he was hiding.[4] Presumably the letter was handed in at Mtembo's store at Malindi, as Chipembere had most recently suggested, though on earlier occasions messages had been passed between an army officer and Chipembere by leaving them in a gourd at an agreed spot near a maize mill in the Malindi area and collecting them the following day, the security forces having stayed away from the area in the meantime.[5]

The following Monday, 26 April, the first of the two dates Chipembere had mentioned, Denton set off for Fort Johnston in a police Land Rover.[6] It was assumed by the police there that he was merely checking on the Special Branch staff in Fort Johnston district and there was nothing unusual in his being there. Gideon Banda's letter had said that the pick-

Chipembere's Evacuation · 239

up was to be about four miles east of Fort Johnston at 7.30 pm., outside a maize mill with a few scattered huts nearby. Denton would be there an hour earlier and if Chipembere did not appear before the appointed hour he would wait for a further hour.

All army and police patrols in the Fort Johnston area were withdrawn that Monday night and no reasons were given. Denton recalled:

> I left Fort Johnston police station ostensibly to return to Zomba just after 1800 hours and made my way to the pick up point where I turned the Land Rover around (to point for home!), left the side lights on and began to wait. Immediately after my arrival two young Africans came to me and asked, in English, why I was there, and I replied that I was from Zomba and was waiting for a friend. They disappeared back into the bush and a few minutes later a semi-circle of some 20 to 25 men appeared from the bush, most of them armed with shotguns, pangas and other weapons, and started to move towards me. When some twenty yards away they stopped, and from the centre of the group a man appeared who said, 'My name is Chipembere.' I immediately recognised him and shook his hand and explained that I was there to pick him up and take him to Zomba where a light aircraft would be waiting to fly us to Salisbury at first light. I took him to the front of the Land Rover and in the light of the side lights I produced two passports and two air tickets, both in false names, which I explained were to fly him and myself to London and, in his case, on to New York where he would be met and taken care of. He asked how did he know that he could trust me, and I pointed out that I was there in good faith, that I was trusting him at that moment, pointing to his escort, and that I was to give him [the Governor-General's] personal word that all I told him was true. (I declined to produce the note the Governor-General had given me; eating paper is not one of my party tricks!) Chipembere hesitated for just a few seconds and then said, 'I will come with you.' I asked him how he was going to explain his leaving to his friends and he said quite casually that he would tell them that I was one of his supporters from Zomba. I was driving an obvious police Land Rover with a Force crest on the door and thought this an extraordinary statement.
>
> He then said he would go and get his belongings and left us all together for a few minutes only before returning with a battered suitcase. I put him in a seat in the back of the Land Rover which had a blanket on it and told him to get down and cover himself with the blanket whenever I told him to. Needless to say I left the scene as quickly as possible, the pick up had lasted no more than 30 minutes so I was way ahead of the scheduled 1930 time.

Denton was armed, but left his pistol in the glove compartment of the

Land Rover when he went to speak with Chipembere: 'He was obviously less likely to feel threatened by talking to an unarmed individual and I did not move too far away from my vehicle in the hope that I could get at my weapon if things became uncomfortable.'

The league of Malawi youth, in their role of 'helping the police', had set up a number of roadblocks on the roads out of Fort Johnston. Had they intercepted the vehicle carrying Chipembere, the consequences for him and for Denton would have been disastrous. To avoid such a catastrophe, a second police Land Rover, driven by another Special Branch officer, Barry Malcolm, on his own, was waiting by the side of the road two or three miles from the pick-up point, just outside the Malawi Rifles base camp. The pick-up operation had been completed more quickly than expected and when Denton reached that point he had to flash his headlights twice to let Malcolm know it was him and to tell him, as previously arranged, to start off ahead of him. Malcolm then led Denton through the roadblocks, explaining to the youth leaguers that Denton's vehicle was immediately behind him and was to be let through. This worked well and most of the time Denton was sufficiently close to pull into the roadblocks just as Malcolm pulled away. They drove through each roadblock without incident, with Chipembere on the floor covered by the blanket.

Lewis also was near the army base camp during these proceedings as an additional precaution. He was in a Land Rover, unarmed, though his driver had a rifle. His vehicle was in fact noticed by the local police, who thought it 'odd' because it was 'in the area at a time and place which had no obvious connection with the ongoing operations'. It was dismissed 'as a ration or water run'.[7] Lewis stayed at Fort Johnston for the next six weeks because he did not know whether there would be a backlash once the local people and the youth league became aware that Chipembere was no longer in the area but had been removed.[8]

Denton and Chipembere arrived safely back in Zomba during the night and went straight to the air strip. Lomax, who was waiting for them, informed Jones that everything was going to plan, 'apparently much to the Governor-General's relief'. Denton handed his revolver and Jones's note back to Lomax at the airfield. Denton and Chipembere spent the remainder of the night in the Land Rover. Denton stayed awake, but Chipembere was 'half asleep most of the time'.

It is possible that a dummy pick-up had also been arranged. The Rev. Andrew Ross of the Church of Central Africa Presbyterian (CCAP), was asked by the US embassy to get a number of messages to Chipembere, which he did via a courier. One of these concerned Chipembere's evacuation: he should be at a 'canteen' in a village at a crossroads some ten miles or so east of Fort Johnston, on a given date, and wait there all day for someone to pick him up and get him to safety.⁹ Lewis believes there were two attempts, in one of which a senior army officer went by arrangement to a village store – a 'canteen' – several miles east of Fort Johnston, waited well into the night and then left because Chipembere did not show up, probably because, although he knew and trusted the officer, his followers did not and feared a trap.¹⁰ The actual pick-up was as Denton described it: much closer to Fort Johnston – where Chipembere would have felt more secure; at a maize mill rather than a 'canteen'; at a specific time for a limited period, not all day; the arrangements were made by letter directly from and to Gideon Banda and not by courier. If there were a dummy arrangement, then, either Chipembere knew it was a dummy, or the courier carrying Ross's message did not take it to Chipembere, for whatever reason. Knowing it was a dummy would explain why he did not turn up: he already knew of the 'official' arrangements and had selected the date himself, and as a wanted man with a price on his head, he would scarcely have hung around all day in an area frequently patrolled by the security forces. In any event, if there were a dummy, it was not designed to delude Chipembere – because it was unnecessary and there would have been no point in it – but others. The purpose of a dummy would have been to divert attention and speculation from the real operation – which it successfully did. It was later hinted to Ross by a US diplomat that his was an 'alternate line of communication' with Chipembere.

The civilian air wing of the British South Africa Police (BSAP) had provided an aircraft that had arrived the previous day, Monday.

> At first light the BSAP air wing pilot arrived and we [the pilot, Denton and Chipembere] got into the aircraft ready to take off. We taxied to the end of the airstrip when Chip decided he needed a pee. He got out and urinated in a bush and then rejoined the pilot and myself in the aircraft and we took off for Salisbury.

Chipembere recalled later that he was told before he left, by whom is not known, that as part of the peace and amnesty arrangements sixty-five detainees and restrictees were to be released the following morning. This 'filled [him] with joy'.¹¹

When they arrived at Salisbury airport the aircraft was taken directly into a hangar where a BSAP Special Branch officer was waiting for them. He took them by civilian car to his home, which was to be the safe house for the day and where Chipembere had a bath. He took Chipembere's measurements, went out and bought him a completely new set of clothes, all of which were much needed because he was still wearing the bush clothing in which he had been dressed when Denton met him.

During the day, Denton and the BSAP Special Branch officer tried to get from Chipembere information on where his supporters could be found in hiding in the Fort Johnston district, but 'he declined to disclose anything of value' and Denton was too tired to press him at length. In the course of their conversations during the evacuation, Denton asked Chipembere a number of times how in practice he was going to stop the fighting. Chipembere was adamant that there was no need for him to do so because the mere fact of his withdrawal would mean the collapse of the guerrilla movement: 'My men may carry on for two or three months in my absence but cannot continue beyond that.'

One of the lighter moments of the day occurred during the Tuesday afternoon. Chipembere was a very pale-skinned African with distinctive facial features well known to many. To prevent recognition at Salisbury airport or on the plane to Britain, Lomax had insisted that he should be 'made darker' and had provided Denton with some 'black up liquid' – Mrs Lomax was an enthusiastic member of the Zomba dramatic society. Chipembere stripped down to his underpants in the bathroom of the safe house and Denton applied the liquid. This was successful to start with but, subsequently, the longer they were on the plane the more the dye began to run and they reached London airport with the collar of Chipembere's immaculate new white shirt 'an unpleasant mess'.

On Tuesday night the BSAP officer drove Denton and Chipembere to Salisbury airport, where they waited in a private room until all the other passengers had boarded the South African Airways plane. They then boarded the aircraft themselves and occupied two reserved seats at the very rear.

> We arrived in London about noon the next day [Wednesday], remained on board until all other passengers had disembarked, and were then joined by a CIA officer and a senior immigration officer who took us directly to a TWA flight for New York which had been held up for Chipembere to join it. We watched it take off and [I] then flew back to Blantyre [where I] was met by Norah Lomax who drove me directly to Government House in Zomba where we had a final debrief, again with [the Governor-General] in the chair, together with the individuals who had been present at the meeting prior to the operation taking place.

At this final debriefing it was clear that Jones was much relieved the operation had been a success, mainly, Denton thought, because he, Denton, was still alive to tell the tale! Jones thanked him for what he had done and said that while he could not have his part recognized officially he was none the less grateful. When, two years later, Denton lunched with him in London, Jones said 'he still woke up with the hairs standing up on the back of his neck, thinking what might have happened [to Denton]'.

Denton had been selected for this evacuation operation, and had agreed to carry it out, first because he was a Special Branch officer, well acquainted with Chipembere's case and familiar with the Fort Johnston district, but second and equally, if not more important, he was about to leave the Nyasaland Police on transfer to another territory. If anything went amiss with the operation he could be got out of the country with little inconvenience or, if the story broke after Chipembere had left, he would be out of the country, his identity unknown and Banda's part in the affair, together with that of the Governor-General and the US ambassador, could more safely be denied. If challenged, the various parties involved could claim that Denton had acted on his own account without their knowledge, still less their support and agreement. Denton left the country two weeks after he had met Chipembere near Fort Johnston.

The number of people, outside those at the Governor-General's meeting, who knew in advance any of the details of the operation was small. It would not have been necessary for the Rhodesian authority sanctioning the BSAP part of the operation to know more than that Chipembere, with an escort, would need to be flown from Zomba to Salisbury on a certain day, be safely looked after there and be put on a flight to London. It would not have been necessary for Gilstrap, having arranged for Chipembere's entry to and accommodation in the USA, to know more than that he, with an escort, would arrive at Heathrow airport on a certain flight and would then be handed over to the US authorities to take him to America. Even this may not have been known to the ambassador, since it was likely to have been handled in Britain directly by a US intelligence officer and not in Malawi personally by Gilstrap. Denton knew of no US embassy involvement in the evacuation process in Malawi, but it is possible that Gilstrap learned some of the details slightly after the event, when he dined with him. The ambassador had left it to Jones to make the arrangements, and Jones had said that he would let Gilstrap know when a plan had been devised. He did not indicate that he would tell him what the plan was. Only five extremely senior people in the US State Department 'had any idea what was going on'.[12] It would not have been necessary at the time for Cole to know even about the provision of passports, though later he did know that a false passport had been provided for Chipembere, which was subsequently taken from him.[13] Denton explained that: 'Although the false passports used by Chipembere and myself were issued by the British High Commission, they were probably obtained on the old boy network as the passport issuing officers were ex-police officers temporarily attached to the British High Commission.' Although Cole may have been told that Chipembere was to be evacuated via London, he would not have needed to arrange immigration clearance there, since this was done within the security services: Denton recalled that 'On arrival at Heathrow, Chipembere and I were whisked off one plane and across the tarmac to the US aircraft completely free from any customs or immigration involvement and I left Heathrow with the American "friend" by a back door and did not see any passport or immigration authority.'[14] These people – the Rhodesian authority, Gilstrap and Cole – did not need to know more, and they probably did not know more, if indeed they knew that much. It was in their interests, and the interests of their governments, to be able to say they did not know.

A few days after he had been picked up near Fort Johnston, Youens told Banda that Chipembere had left Malawi.[15] On 20 May Jones told him the operation had been successful and Chipembere had arrived as planned in California. The doctor was 'very pleased' and said he would announce it the next evening on the radio and at a meeting at Fort Johnston itself. He was anxious to learn whether Jones had given the Americans his two conditions. Jones assured him that he had. A week later, Chipembere made a press statement to Reuters in the USA:

> I have come to America for health reasons. My physical condition had deteriorated to the point where I found it almost impossible to give the necessary guidance to my followers in our struggle to achieve a more democratic system of government for our country. I was unable to get proper medical care and diet when my physical wellbeing had reached its lowest ebb. Feeling that my services to my country were indispensable, my followers expressed deep concern about my health, and it was advisable that I seek medical assistance immediately. How soon I return home will depend on how my body responds to the medical treatment I am now receiving ... my doctors agree that it may be a long time before I regain my health completely.[16]

Banda was aware that Chipembere had sent for his wife and children – and his brother, who was captured in the process – to join him in America, and he took this as clear evidence that Chipembere had decided to settle there and never come back to Malawi. But just in case he did think of returning, Banda issued a warning in July 1965:

> Chipembere would be wasting his time. We would capture him and once we captured him I would see that he is hanged in public, and I am going to invite all the families of the men that he has killed to come and witness it. I mean just that. We will catch him and if we catch him alive, that's just what I am going to do, but on the other hand if he is caught dead, still I would invite the families of those that he has killed to come and crush his dead body.[17]

In his letters to Gideon Banda on 16 and 17 April, Chipembere said he had decided 'to arrange for one trustworthy and reliable man to know about these arrangements [for his evacuation] so that he can inform the world as to what happened' if the plan turned out to be a trick and his faith in the Americans turned out to be misplaced. He arranged that his letter should reach the person to whom he was to divulge information about 30 April. This person was Ross.

Ross, a longstanding friend of Chipembere, had visited and had numerous discussions with him when he was in detention at Kanjedza in the second half of 1960.[18] As CCAP minister in the Balaka area south of Fort Johnston he was able to stay in contact with Chipembere and receive a number of letters from him both before and after he had gone into hiding. Early in October 1964, soon after being restricted, but before going into hiding, Chipembere feared that the Malawi government would claim he was a Mozambiquan African and hand him over to the authorities in that country, where, he was convinced, he would be roughly and possibly fatally handled. Chipembere's father was born in Mozambique, though he was 'of Malawian stock'. He himself was born in the Nkota Kota district of Malawi. This question of his country of birth troubled him for a long period, not only because it might lead to his being handed over to the Portuguese, but also because it might affect his acceptability as a political leader in Malawi.[19] Ross undertook to travel to Malindi and collect Chipembere's British passport for safe keeping and to prove that he was not a Mozambiquan. With his wife and children, he drove through the roadblocks in Fort Johnston without being stopped, since he was well known in the area, had a picnic lunch, and was handed the passport. Mrs Ross carried the passport as they returned to Balaka, being fairly confident that the youth leaguers manning the roadblocks would not, at that time, intimately search a white woman.[20] Chipembere was wise to be concerned about his passport, because just before the September 1964 debate in parliament, Banda had considered seizing the rebel ministers' passports.[21]

At some stage, probably in November 1964, Ross visited a number of detainees in Dedza. He found them depressed and saying all was finished, Chipembere was dead and there was nothing they could do. With the British, if they locked you up you knew that one day they would let you out, but with Banda they would never be released. Ross comforted them by saying that all was not lost: Chipembere was alive and well. As Ross left the camp, the leader drew him aside and asked what the hell he thought he was doing speaking like that, since he may have been talking to a Special Branch informer. Ross realized he had been indiscreet and believed this was the way the Special Branch learned of his involvement with Chipembere. He was right: the Special Branch knew of it almost immediately.[22]

Once Chipembere had gone into hiding, Ross received letters from him by courier and replied to them by the same courier. Among these letters was one which asked him to 'relay to foreign governments his explanation of the cabinet crisis which was essentially that the Prime Minister exasperated the ex-ministers to an unbearable extent by repeatedly going over their heads to consult their European permanent secretaries'.[23] Ross was charged with putting over this account and rebutting Banda's allegations that the opposition was Communist-inspired. Chipembere was keen both then and later that his side of the story should be made widely known, and Ross's contacts with the overseas media would have helped him in this. He also contacted the American embassy and the British high commission. It is probable that this letter was written early in March 1965 at about the same time as he also wrote to Jones to give his side of the conflict.

Ross's early contacts with Gilstrap and Cole, on behalf of Chipembere, began soon after Chipembere went into hiding at the end of October. He later recalled:

> I dealt directly with the US Ambassador [and] I also dealt directly with the British High Commissioner with whom I established no rapport whatsoever ... I got much positive feedback, as well as money and medicine from the Americans. With the [British] I was keeping them well informed and asking them not to intervene if we were able to unseat Banda.[24]

This early contact with Gilstrap and Cole seems to have been designed to assess the extent to which they might be supportive of the ex-ministers if they reached a position where they could overthrow Banda: what their reaction would be to an attempted *coup d'état*. It would not be surprising if the Americans professed greater cooperation in this matter than the British who, convinced that Banda was better than any alternative leader and having backed him for the past five years, were unlikely to risk the investments they had made in him by having him toppled. The US embassy staff were helpful in providing Chipembere with soup and funds for his and his men's sustenance, medicine for his diabetes and money for his wife and family. Later contacts with the diplomats were in response to Chipembere's request that Ross tell foreign governments his side of the story of the dispute with Banda. Gilstrap's secretary knew that he could see the ambassador 'any time he wanted' and ensured he got an immediate interview.[25] Ross later said:

> I ended up being the go-between for Chipembere between him and the British High Commissioner and the United States Ambassador. At first I just had family messages [but then] Chipembere reckoned he could pull off a *coup d'état*, without any great bloodshed. [He] had already warned

the British and Americans of what he intended to do, and they now were embarrassed that an investigation might uncover their prior knowledge or complicity. They were happy to see him out of the country. He meanwhile contacted me saying it would be possible to start a civil war, by a tie up with the Mozambique rebels, but that he did not want to see Malawians massacre Malawians and wanted to try and get out. I relayed this message to the British and Americans. The British appeared not to want to do anything, though they did, but the Americans said they would get something set up. I ended up ... as a go-between to arrange the getaway ... The British and Americans did not want him caught, not for any particularly good reasons, but to cover up the fact that they had known that he was going to attempt a *coup d'état*.[26]

Chipembere's letters to the Governor-General make it clear that his wish to secure an amnesty and to leave the country was to avoid further hardship to his followers in detention rather than to avoid a civil war and Malawians massacring Malawians. He also told Jones that he did not believe in external attacks, which conflicts with the claim that he contemplated joining up with the Mozambican rebels. It is uncertain how easy he would have found attempts to link up with the Mozambique rebels.

At that time there were five different armed groups roaming the hills of the Namizumu Forest – the Police Mobile Force, the Malawi Army, the Malawi rebels, the Portuguese army and FRELIMO. For all this it was rare for one group to encounter another ... FRELIMO were well equipped and well trained and it was a concern that they might take sides with the Malawi rebels, but there was never any evidence of this, with both sides seemingly going their own separate ways.[27]

Establishing contact with the Mozambique fighters was not always easy, and they had their own war to fight without getting involved in Malawi affairs. Furthermore, Banda was affording some support to them by, for example, allowing FRELIMO to have an office in Limbe. To have joined forces with them would undoubtedly have brought the combined might of the Malawi and Portuguese armies against them, a prospect Chipembere could not take lightly. On the other hand, he would have been attracted by the possibility of benefiting from the good equipment, discipline, organization and experience of FRELIMO soldiers and he could have found ways of contacting them, even in Malawi itself. At one stage they had 'a large base camp blatantly set up in the forest well inside Malawi'.[28] Contact through such a camp could have been made. On balance it is unlikely that Chipembere seriously entertained the idea of starting a civil war by joining up with FRELIMO.

Gilstrap – and to a significantly lesser extent Cole because he regularly received information from the Governor-General who was briefed by Special Branch – would have been pleased with Ross acting as an apparently unrecruited source of intelligence and was so freely giving them information, limited as it was, about Chipembere, his thinking and intentions. Chipembere's warning of what he intended to do was almost certainly not a specific warning about the attack on Fort Johnston and the march towards Zomba, but a general warning, of which many were aware, that he intended to oust Banda.[29] In this case it is difficult to see why the ambassador and high commissioner should be embarrassed that an investigation might uncover their complicity or prior knowledge that Chipembere was going to attempt a *coup d'état*. Even if their prior knowledge was more specific, the existence of any complicity is unclear.

There were, no doubt, good reasons why Chipembere and the Americans should want to communicate through a third party in respect of funds and other help to his family and followers and in respect of letting the world know his side of the story of his dispute with Banda. In respect of arranging the get-away and entry to the USA and a university there, however, it was unneccessary, and a dangerous source of confusion and uncertainty, to communicate through a third party. First, Chipembere did not need anyone to tell the ambassador and the high commissioner about his wish to leave Malawi, since from at the latest early March he already had a channel of communication with the Governor-General, whom he asked to arrange with Banda an amnesty in exchange for calling off his guerrilla activities and being permitted to leave for the USA – and Ross knew this.[30] Second, Chipembere's letter to Gilstrap asking him to arrange a university place in the USA was delivered through the ordinary mail, and consequently there was no need for him to ask anyone else to approach Gilstrap on this point. Third, it was through the Governor-General and Banda's top expatriate officials that Chipembere was told the doctor agreed to his leaving Malawi and the Americans would look after him and his family in the USA. He did not need any other go-between. Fourth, since communications with Chipembere about the evacuation plan were being conducted by Gideon Banda, and since the US ambassador had left devising the plan to Jones and his colleagues, the Americans did not need to communicate with him about the plan either directly or through a go-between. In any case, Chipembere had already told the Governor-General, with considerable confidence and in detail, how to communicate with him, and this did not include using Ross. The Americans' undertaking to 'get something set up' probably meant, at the most, arranging for Chipembere to be accepted into the USA and securing a place for him at an American university.

In the last letter Ross received, sent just before the evacuation on 26

April and deliberately designed to reach him about 30 April, after he had left,

> Chipembere stated that he had agreed to go to America and detailed verbatim a plan under which he was to be picked up in the Malindi area and smuggled out of the country. The actual escape plan had been detailed in a letter to Chipembere allegedly written by someone who carried the authority of the Governor-General and of the American government. He feared a trap, however, and in this final letter to Ross had asked him to contact the American embassy to ascertain whether the offer was genuine. This Ross did by contacting the American ambassador, Mr. Gilstrap, who confirmed that it had official American backing. Ross stated that the only way he had of communicating with Chipembere was by sending messages back with the incoming courier but in this instance it was not possible to utilise the messenger since he could not delay him for the length of time needed for checking with the American embassy. The Americans, however, said that they would get word through. [They already knew he was in the USA.] Ross stated he had no idea how this was done and that whilst he knew of a system whereby mail could be sent to Chipembere through the post to a cover name and address in Fort Johnston he was also aware that Chipembere himself regarded this procedure as dangerous and insecure. For this reason he thought it unlikely that they would use this particular means of communication. He went on to explain that in this last letter Chipembere had given him instructions to 'raise hell with the international press and see that the Americans got it in the neck' should he learn of his murder or arrest.[31]

The words 'detailed verbatim a plan under which he was to be picked up in the Malindi area and smuggled out of the country' probably mean that Chipembere copied the actual words used in Gideon Banda's letter, and it was this letter Chipembere had in mind when he said 'the actual escape plan had been detailed in a letter ... allegedly written by someone who carried the authority of the Governor-General and of the American government', that is, Gideon Banda. The particulars he gave were confined to a place, a date and a time – they went no further and certainly not as far as the words 'detailed verbatim a plan' and 'the actual escape plan' imply. Indeed, Denton went to some trouble to explain that he was to be taken to America via Zomba, Salisbury and London. This would have been unnecessary if Chipembere already knew those details.

It is clear that in Chipembere's view, if it were a trick the American ambassador and his government – and not Jones, Banda or Malawi government officers – should be blamed. He probably took this view because he did not know who was to pick him up, but did know the Americans had agreed to his entry to the USA and to arranging a university place for him. It seems that he was not aware of any part played by the British high commission: in none of his letters to Gideon Banda, Jones or, later, British officials did he mention any such involvement.[32] He would have realized that international opinion was more likely to be won over by accusations of dirty tricks by the US government than by similar accusations against the Malawi government.

The number of people who knew any of the details of the evacuation plan was limited and those who knew them all, still fewer. We have already examined the extent to which the Rhodesian authorities, Gilstrap and Cole knew the details: it is unlikely that they knew more than the barest outline, if that. It is clear that Banda 'knew of and acquiesced in [Chipembere's] departure without knowing any of the details'.[33] Youens confirmed that Banda knew next to nothing about the evacuation, though he had agreed to it.[34]

Despite its successful implementation, Special Branch officers were anxious that no evidence outside their own records should exist that might lead to others learning how Chipembere escaped to the USA. They were concerned not about the method of escape, because the details had been confined to Gideon Banda's letter giving only the date, time and place of pick-up, but about Banda's acquiescence in it and the involvement of the Americans and the Governor-General. The Special Branch consequently were at great pains to get possession of any document that might reveal this acquiescence and involvement. They knew that Chipembere had intended to 'arrange for one trustworthy and reliable man' to know about the arrangements for his evacuation. They had little difficullty in discovering that this was Ross, for he had already alerted them of his being in contact with Chipembere by his indiscretions at Dedza, and the high commissioner, though probably not the ambassador, had almost certainly told them he was a contact. They were anxious, therefore, to get possession of any letters from Chipembere to Ross that mentioned the evacuation plan. This task was assigned to Malcolm.

Malcolm called on Ross on Thursday morning, 13 May 1965, and showed him, but did not let him read, a handwritten letter from Chipembere showing that he had arrived safely in the USA. He did this to demonstrate that there had been no trick and he asked Ross to hand over to him for burning all correspondence mentioning the evacuation plan. Ross agreed to do this, but explained that only one letter – the last – contained any reference to the plan. He promised, since the letter was currently in 'a safe place' and absolutely secure, to take it to Malcolm's house the next day. With this matter for the present out of the way, they continued talking in a general vein and Ross wondered what the reaction would be when it became known that Chipembere was in America. Malcolm replied that he thought Banda for one would be furious.

Chipembere's Evacuation · 251

At this Ross was visibly taken aback and, looking quite aghast,[35] asked if the Prime Minister was not already in the picture. [Malcolm] answered that [he] did not really know definitely one way or the other but personally was under the impression that the Prime Minister would never have given his approval of such action. At this Ross seemed quite agitated and commented that ... it had never for one moment occurred to him that the veil of secrecy surrounding the escape was such that even Dr. Banda himself did not know of it. He remarked that if the Prime Minister really did not know about it then he, Ross, was in an even more vulnerable position than he had hitherto thought and accordingly had reason to fear for the safety of himself and his family.[36]

In recognizing his vulnerability, Ross would have recalled the harrassment of his fellow Scots – Cameron, McAdam and their families – only a few months earlier and the way they had feared for their safety.

As soon as Malcolm left, Ross made arrangements to see the American ambassador and the British high commissioner. He called on them separately the following day, 14 May, and told them the Special Branch were 'on to' him and he was thinking of leaving the country. Gilstrap agreed that this was the only course open to him and advised him to get out as soon as possible. He also said he would be pleased to secure for Ross a full-time academic post in any American universitty of his choice, but Ross preferred to return to Scotland. Cole similarly advised him to leave as soon as possible and 'thanked him for the assistance he had rendered in the past'. It seems that they were anxious for him to leave, and that Gilstrap felt he was of no further use to him in Malawi, though he might well be in the USA.[37]

Ross's account to Malcolm of what then happened was that he went to see the Rev. Tom Colvin and the Rev. Jonathan Sangaya of the CCAP, told them he had been in contact with Chipembere and that the Special Branch were 'on his tail'. Colvin and Sangaya decided that, in order to keep the Church in the clear, they would have to send him back to Britain. They then made the earliest possible air bookings, which were wait-listings for 1 p.m. or confirmed bookings for 4.30 p.m. on 18 May from Chileka. They agreed that as soon as Ross was out of the country, either Sangaya would go to see Dr Banda or Colvin would go to see Aleke Banda and say they had sent him back to Britain because he had been found 'meddling in politics which was strictly against church policy'. They hoped that by these means the Church would emerge from the affair 'with credit rather than embarrassment'.[38] It is strange that Ross did not feel that by telling a senior Special Branch officer of this ruse, Banda would learn of it and its value would thereby be destroyed.[39]

Special Branch knew almost immediately and in detail of the steps being taken for Ross to leave Malawi in a hurry. They were now concerned that he might be intending to leave without handing over the last letter from Chipembere, as he had promised. In fact, however, Ross rang Malcolm early on 18 May and told him that he could not deliver the letter to his house in Zomba that morning as they had agreed, because he was in Blantyre. When asked, he said he had with him the letter in which Malcolm was interested. He did not mention that he was intending to leave the country later that day. They agreed that Malcolm should travel to Blantyre straight away and meet later that morning outside the CCAP church. This they did.[40]

At Blantyre Ross handed Malcolm a three-and-a-half-page letter in Chipembere's handwriting, from which the bottom half of the fourth page had been removed. He explained that he had destroyed the last half-page as soon as he received the letter, and the missing piece simply said, 'Look at this. I intend to accept but fear a trap. Check with the Americans and see if the offer is genuine.' Malcolm was puzzled that the letter and the account of the contents of the missing half-page made no reference, as he understood Ross to have said that it did, to going to the international press and ensuring that the Americans got it in the neck if the offer of escape turned out to be a trap. Ross maintained that the only instructions he had received from Chipembere were those contained in the missing piece, that is, to check with the Americans that the offer was genuine and not a trap. There was further confusion when Malcolm claimed that Ross had agreed to hand over not only the instructions to check with the Americans the genuineness of the plan but also Chipembere's copy of Gideon Banda's letter. Ross said that he had misunderstood Malcolm. When asked if he had any other letters from Chipembere, he said he had only those written before the escape plan and he had no intention of handing these over. The last letter Ross received would not have fallen into this category and it probably included, on the last half-page, in addition to the request that he check the genuineness of the plan with the Americans, the letter – from Gideon Banda – making the pick-up arrangements and what Ross should do if the plan turned out to be a trick.

Ross told Malcolm he had destroyed not only the last half-page of the letter but also the envelope, which was endorsed with a note to Mrs Ross in her codename, saying that if her husband was not there she should act on the letter. This disturbed Malcolm, because he now wondered how many others knew of the correspondence and the evacuation arrangements. Ross explained that his wife was 'fully in the picture', was completely secure and would tell no one. He himself had told no one else. After a little further conversation Ross said he intended to leave Malawi that afternoon and he seemed 'rather taken aback' when Malcolm said he already knew. Malcolm then 'bade Ross farewell, [wished him] the best of luck' and took his leave of him.

Senior Special Branch officers, still worried about the possible existence and potential danger of a letter mentioning the evacuation and revealing those implicated in it, instructed Malcolm to go to Chileka and ask Ross for the letters which he still had. He was authorized to search him and his baggage and if necessary to use the threat that unless he delivered up the papers Malcolm would prevent him from boarding the plane. It was made clear, however, that under no circumstances was he to stop Ross from leaving and if his bluff were called Malcolm was to let him go.

Malcolm went to Chileka for the 1 p.m. plane departure, but Ross was not there. He went again shortly after 3 p.m., this time taking with him assistant superintendent C. Munro and Mrs M. Scullion, a former Special Branch stenographer and the wife of another police officer, both of whom were to help with any search of Ross, his wife and their baggage. When Malcolm asked Ross for the letters he seemed embarrassed and said he did not have them because they were in a sealed envelope with the American ambassador. These must have been the letters that Ross had said he had no intention of giving up. Since he now realized that the letters were 'all but unobtainable', Malcolm asked for a letter authorizing him to collect the documents from the ambassador. In this way, even if he did not receive the documents, the letter from Ross would be evidence that such letters existed and the Americans had knowledge of them. Ross agreed and wrote the letter to Gilstrap for which he had been asked, saying: 'The Governor-General insists that I hand these [letters] over else I cannot leave the country. I have undertaken on my honour that all these papers be handed over and they have accepted this assurance in good faith and are letting me proceed.' He assured Malcolm that the Americans would be honour bound to respect his wishes in handing over the documents because they were his property to be disposed of as he wished. He added that the Americans had already received a tip-off that the Special Branch might try to prevent him leaving the country and consequently were sending a representative, Wayne Conner, to Chileka 'to facilitate his exit'. It is unlikely that the US embassy staff would put themselves in a position of openly helping a non-US citizen being delayed by police officers of the Malawi government. More likely, they were apprehensive that Ross would make their part in the evacuation known to others who did not already know. Ross suggested that when Conner arrived the three of them should discuss arrangements for Malcolm to recover the papers. Malcolm recorded:

> While this conversation was taking place Wayne Conner arrived and he

was obviously agitated at finding Ross closeted with me in the VIP lounge where he was unable to ascertain what was taking place, what disclosures he was making and what undertakings he was giving. He immediately intercepted Ross [as he went to join his friends gathered to see him off] and had a long, earnest, conversation with him on the stairway. Conner looked distinctly uncomfortable at what Ross was telling him and kept giving me thunderous looks.

After a few minutes, Ross returned to Malcolm and told him Conner had undertaken to see that Malcolm got the papers. Malcolm then insisted that Conner be called over and the undertaking be repeated in his presence. Despite Ross's initial reluctance, on the grounds that this would make Conner 'rather irate', he reluctantly agreed. In Conner's presence Malcolm threatened not to allow Ross to leave unless Conner gave an undertaking that the papers would be handed over to him. Conner gave this undertaking, but said he did not know whether the papers were at the embassy or at the ambassador's house. Malcolm said his instructions were that he should not return without the letters and for this reason he was anxious to collect them that evening. Conner, in Malcolm's opinion, was playing for time, but when he threatened to prevent Ross boarding the aircraft Conner said that as soon as the plane took off he would go straight to the ambassador's residence and relay the message to him. Conner expected to arrive at the embassy at about 5 p.m. and suggested that Malcolm should call about half an hour later. This seemed all that Malcolm could do, so he 'shook hands with them and expressed relief that the whole business had been satisfactorily concluded'. Neither Ross nor his wife had been searched.

This matter of the packet of letters and the actions of Ross and Conner at Chileka is interesting. It is clear that Conner was keen the Rosses should leave the country as quickly as possible. Ross said Conner went to the airport 'to facilitate his departure'. The embassy would have wanted the person most able to reveal the Americans' financial and other help to Chipembere, his family and followers, out of the country as soon as possible. The distinct possibility that if Ross were detained in Malawi and questioned by the Special Branch, he might reveal this help, would have alarmed Gilstrap and his colleagues profoundly, since it would undoubtedly have brought about a major diplomatic rift between his country and the Banda government. It was this, the revelation of the US embassy's contact with, and practical help given to, Chipembere, and not of the negligible part they played in his evacuation, that deeply troubled the Americans.

Ross's later account was:

We went out to the airport, and ... the two security officers turned up and took me aside. They told me I was daft to think that I could leave without them knowing [he had in fact already told them he was leaving] and without giving them names [of others involved with Chipembere]. At that point a friend who had apparently arrived to see me off intervened. He was ... the key CIA man for the area. When he came across to see me the two police officers showed him their ID and told him to [clear] off. I said, 'Well, don't, for they are not letting me go.' My friend turned to one and said, 'You know what I know about you, and they go on the plane or you're dead.' He blanched under his tan, and the two then simply left. I gathered later ... that it had been he who drove the car for Chip[embere]. That's why he was so keen to clear everything up.[41]

As we have seen, it was not Malcolm, as Ross and probably Conner believed, who had driven Chipembere, though he had travelled ahead of Denton after the pick-up. Also, it is clear from contemporary Special Branch papers that Malcolm's purpose was not, as Ross believed, to learn the names of Chipembere's accomplices – they already knew a large number of them – but that his sole objective was to get hold of any letters containing references to the evacuation plan.

The plane, with the Ross family, took off, Conner returned to Blantyre and shortly Malcolm followed him. When Sangaya later visited Ross in Scotland, he told him that 'as the plane was a dot on the horizon, police cars had arrived with sirens blaring'.[42] If this was so, the police were not after Ross, because it had been made clear to Malcolm that he was not to prevent his departure. When Malcolm arrived at the ambassador's house Gilstrap feigned anger and surprise and asked what Malcolm was doing coming to see him without telephoning him first, but since he was there what was his business? When Malcolm produced Ross's letter, Gilstrap 'forced a laugh' and said:

> 'Well, I guess you've been outsmarted.' He handed the letter across to Colby [an embassy colleague] who, having studied it, said 'Doug (Lomax) asked some ten days ago if there were any other letters and we told him there were not.'
>
> [Malcolm] then asked the ambassador whether in fact he had any letters from Ross, whereupon he said that he did not and that [Malcolm] had been tricked. He went on to say that he knew of one letter only and that was the one which had led to the escape plan which of course he had produced already. [Malcolm took Ross's letter back and said he] had clearly been taken in, adding that [he] had been foolish to allow [himself] to be deceived ... All three [Gilstrap, Colby and Conner] winced, and, on heaping further apologies on Mr. Gilstrap for disturbing him, [Malcolm] made good [his] exit with Ross's letter secure in [his] pocket.

Ross later wrote of his departure from Malawi that he had destoyed all the letters and papers Chipembere had sent him, except one – 'a scrap of paper' – which he had kept for sentimental reasons. It was 'personal, but also included a reminder to get out of the country and tell his story if the escape plan turned out to be a trap'.[43] His wife had been sitting with it in her hand on the other side of the airport lounge, 'wondering what to do with it, if the police came to pick her up'.[44] This 'scrap of paper' could have been the lower half of the fourth page of the last letter Chipembere wrote to Ross – and which he told Malcolm he had destroyed.

In speaking of knowing 'of one letter only and that was the one which had led to the escape plan which of course he had produced already', Gilstrap was almost certainly referring to the letter he had received from Chipembere asking for help in finding a place at an American university and for permission for him and his family to live in the USA. It appears that he was not involved in any other correspondence with Chipembere.

Ross had in fact left a bundle of letters with Gilstrap. He told Malcolm about them in order to induce him to allow him and his family to leave on the plane. Later he asked the US embassy to send the letters to him and was told they had no knowledge of them. He has never received them.[45] The Americans, and not only the Malawi Special Banch, were keen that no letters about the evacuation should remain in Ross's possession, and consequently they had agreed to look after the package of letters for safe keeping and forwarding to him later. Conner's looking 'distinctly uncomfortable at what Ross was telling him' at Chileka was no doubt the result of Ross revealing that he had told Malcolm the letters were with the ambasssador. Malcolm had been deceived, but not by Ross.

It would have been very important indeed to Ross that he and his family should get away from Malawi as quickly as possible and without being searched. He had already indicated that he was fearful for his safety, since Banda might not know or have approved of the evacuation, and he knew the treatment Cameron and McAdam had received – and, far worse, that which they had narrowly missed. He would have been deeply concerned that Malcolm's purpose in being at Chileka might be to prevent his departure. To avoid this and to avoid searches which would lead to the discovery of the 'scrap of paper' mentioning the evacuation, he agreed to Malcolm being given the bundle of letters that he had not intended earlier to hand over.

During their various conversations, Ross made a number of interesting points to Malcolm, which throw further light on the political atmosphere in Malawi at that time.[46] He considered Chiume to be 'an unscrupulous, calculating chancer who did not actually side with the ex-ministers in the pre-crisis tension until very late and indeed at one point showed signs of siding with Banda'.[47] Chiume did indeed not side with his colleagues until late in the day, but he did join them from the time of the minister's first meeeting after the Chileka speech, and thereafter he showed no signs of siding with Banda. Ross saw the present developments in Malawi as the triumph of the non-graduates over the graduates in the MCP and government, and he was especially critical of Chakuamba, Kumtumanji and Chidzanja. He went further in the case of one leading MCP official for, through the medium of the Presbyterian equivalent of the Catholic confessional, he had learned that a murder squad had been operating in the Blantyre and Limbe area under his direction and had placed a vehicle at its disposal. It was alleged that this same person had overstepped the mark in his terrorist activities and had so persecuted a secondary school headmaster in Blantyre that he fled to Zambia. The Church protested to Banda, who sent two parliamentary secretaries to Zambia to persuade the man to return to Malawi.

Ross spoke at length about Chipembere, whom he greatly admired, seeing him as a peculiar combination of fanaticism and devoid of intrigue, cunning and devious thinking: he was 'altogether much too plain spoken, forthright and genuine for his own good'. Were it not for his known support of Chipembere his own position as a clergyman in the Balaka area would have been untenable because 95 per cent of the people there were pro-Chipembere. There had been little violence in the Balaka area because Banda's supporters recognized they were in a minority and had not therefore taken any violent action against their political opponents. If they did take violent action they would 'be for the chop'.[48]

By the time Ross had these conversations with Malcolm, Chipembere was already safely in the USA. The transition from the life of a cabinet minister in a newly independent African state, via life as a hunted guerrilla leader, to life as a graduate student in a large American university, could not have been easy for him. The difficulties of adapting to this new and different environment remained with him throughout his years in America:

> Chip[embere] never fully adapted to the 'fast life' – his descriptive term for life in Los Angeles. He was thrown by the freeway system, by the social life, and most importantly by the financial cost of supporting himself and his family in the United States. He was always broke. During most of the ... years he spent in Los Angeles, he lived with his wife and seven children in a two-bedroom apartment with one bathroom. Being terrified by the freeways meant that ... he had to commute by bus to his job at Cal[ifornia] State [University] Los Angeles, a round trip which took him a total of five precious hours every day.[49]

He stayed in touch with a large number of people, and during his first year in Los Angeles 'he received literally hundreds of letters from his followers and supporters and admirers around the world, urging him to return to Africa'. His correspondence was voluminous and he wrote all his letters by hand.[50]

Following Chipembere's evacuation, the security forces did not lessen their attempts to arrest his followers who had joined him in the bush. Some of the methods were notably unconventional. It seems that at least one village, Taliwa, north of Chipembere's home, was wiped out The women and children were ordered to assemble on the football field and to take with them as many of their possessions as they could. The village was then destroyed, on orders from Zomba, starting with the church, then the school, then all the houses.[51] Young American and British volunteers sat at night on the verandah of their house at Malindi and 'watched the grass roofs of supposed rebel supporting households go up in flames'. Part of this was probably retribution for some of the government supporters' homes that had been burned down by the rebels as they made their way to Fort Johnston on the night of the coup attempt.[52]

The misery of the people in Chipembere's home area was added to by the activities of those fighting in Mozambique. It was alleged that early in 1966 Portuguese security forces 'bombed a peaceful village in the Mponda area; seven Malawians were killed'. Because of an agreement with Portugal that their security forces could use the area near Fort Johnston for manoeuvres, the Malawi government had little choice but 'to ignore the public outcry'.[53] Towards the end of 1966, 'the most serious incursion to date' by Portuguese troops into Malawi took place at Makanjira, in which a number of Malawians were killed, including a child, several others were wounded and many were missing. Although the Malawi government made an official protest to the Mozambique authorities, no additional security forces were sent to the area to prevent further similar action.[54] The officer in charge of police in Fort Johnston recalled:

> Incursions into Malawi by the Portuguese became common all along the border from the lakeshore north of Makanjila south to Namwera. It was responsible for a lot of deaths; in particular the Portuguese killed many undoubtedly innocent people in villages which no doubt had been 'fingered' as having given succour to FRELIMO fighters. One morning, I well recall, the Portuguese raided a village just north of Makanjila killing some twelve villagers, and abducting a further twenty other males. If only to identify the unit responsible and to obtain the release of those abducted – and in the absence of any other bright ideas – I followed the

raiding party up to the border, a mere track in the bush, and crossed it briefly into Mozambique. Within a hundred yards or so I encountered a heavily armed FRELIMO group of about company strength whose commander told me they had engaged the Portuguese a mile or so distant and that in the exchange of fire the Malawi captives had escaped. Despite the use of heavy machine guns, rockets and the inevitable AKs, there were no casualties and the contact was broken off by both sides, he told me, because it was lunch time!! He was correct about the Malawians: they all returned to their village during the afternoon.[55]

Others recorded that 'a reign of terror was created throughout the country in which many lost their lives, many were beaten and many fled into exile'. They were assured at the time by many informants, including those deeply involved, that 'Muwalo was the executive head of this whole campaign'.[56] In many cases, long periods of incarceration followed. Machipisa Munthali – 'Chiume's chief gangster' – for example, was charged with illegal possession of arms and was

> imprisoned in 1965 ... and only released in July 1992 ... After his arrest his feet were burnt and he was made to walk on broken glass. [When] denied a lawyer, he pleaded guilty [because] he was threatened with death if he did not do so. After serving an eleven years sentence [he] remained in detention under presidential order, most of the time in solitary confinement in Mikuyu Prison in a cell measuring one metre by two metres.[57]

During Banda's absence in London and Germany late in May 1965 the security forces captured 'all the so-called generals of the so-called Chipembere's army': Arthur Chipembere – Henry's brother – Matola, Mtiesa and George Chimondo. They used a variety of ruses to effect the captures. In the case of Arthur Chipembere and some half-dozen others with him,

> They had been led to believe that arrangements had been made by fellow dissidents that a boat was being sent to transport them to Tanzania and that on a certain night it would be moored off Malindi. Sure enough it was there ... and with Arthur and his friends taken on board and locked in the hold, it made rapid progress to the jetty at Fort Johnston where when the hatch was removed they found themselves looking down the wrong end of a light machine gun. Although they were armed with at least one .303 rifle stolen from the Police Station they were in no position to resist.[58]

Even this serious event had its lighter side. Just after Arthur Chipembere and his colleagues were arrested the government biologist, who was nearby, excitedly shouted that he had 'found another'. The officer in charge of police assumed that another rebel had been apprehended, but in fact the biologist, 'a total boffin', had just discovered a second example of a rare water snail that had been named after him.[59]

With these arrests, the 'only man of importance left in Chipembere's gang' was Medson Silombela, who had killed a member of the youth league and others at Katuli on 23 May.[60] At some stage shortly after he left Malawi, Chipembere issued instructions to his lieutenants in the bush that they were to stop their terrorist activities. Most of them obeyed, but Silombela refused and carried on.[61] Banda was confident that he would shortly be arrested.[62] When Jones wrote to him during his absence at this time he said, 'Things here seem to be quiet and I trust they will remain so while you are away.'[63] The people of Fort Johnston would have shared his hope, though not his assessment of the situation in their district. A little later, Chipembere himself wrote:

> A few weeks after my departure my own only remaining house was demolished by the security forces ... On 27 August, Banarba Ndangwe, my former driver and, until the crisis, my general factotum, was shot dead by the security forces at Malindi ... My brother, my nephew, my cousin and several other men who came into the fight solely because of their association with me were arrested a few weeks after my departure. My distant cousin, Miss Page Bango, was beaten to unconsciousness at Malindi by Young Pioneers ... Some of my friends who had been released were rearrested ... These are only some of the things that have happened. There are many more.[64]

In July there were further worrying incidents of rebel activity in the north of the country, which continued those occurring in March. Banda believed that when Chiume failed to organize the Malawians resident in Tanzania he turned to the Malawians who had fled from their home country after the cabinet crisis. Banda claimed that initially he intended to form an army to invade Malawi, but having sought the advice of friends in Tanzania he decided to send his followers for training, not so much in invasion techniques as in infiltration and assassination methods. His aim was to assassinate Banda, his ministers, members of parliament and members of the central executive of the MCP, and to enter villages in groups of five, terrorize the inhabitants and persuade them to change their allegience from Banda to himself.[65]

Banda believed, for example, that the rebels intended to assassinate him on his way to the independence day anniversary celebrations at the Blantyre stadium on 6 July, but the security arrangements were too tight for them to get close enough. At Rumpi on 17 July they attacked and tried to kill the local member of parliament and his colleagues. On 29 July they attacked the member of parliament at Nkata Bay, and early in

September another member at Chitipa. A little later a gang fired an anti-tank rocket at the house of the member of parliament for Karonga North, reducing it to a shell. The member only narrowly avoided being killed, but his girlfriend, who was with him at the time, was killed. To fortify the people of the north, Banda sent his young pioneers to reinforce the police there and to encourage the people not to submit to rebel intimidation. He instructed all chiefs and village headmen, under threat of dismissal, that if they saw strangers in their areas they were to arrest them, and if they resisted they should be killed: 'This is war! This is war!'[66] Sending the young pioneers to Karonga was a reaction to his being 'very disappointed ... that after the attempt to assassinate [the Karonga North member of parliament] the security forces made no move to try and follow the perpetrators until 24 hours had elapsed. He wished to see closer cooperation between the security forces and the young pioneers.'[67] Some pioneers were already informally being used to help the police, and a little later selected members were formally recruited into the PMF. The rebel group was eventually traced to a forest camp north of Nkata Bay. One of them was captured but the rest escaped back to Tanzania.[68] Shortly, as a result of this capture, Banda published extensive lists of Chiume's followers in Tanzania, divided into the places where they were in camps and places where they had been trained.[69]

Silombela in the south, however, was still free, though many of his followers had been captured or had surrendered. He had killed Chief Mlomba and others in Zomba district, and Banda now believed his motives were not political but merely criminal: he offered his men 'not a political future, but immediate loot in the way of money and goods that they got from those that they killed'. These views were shared by Roberts, Lewis and a number of senior police officers.[70]

> He carried a standard military FN 7.62 rifle which, it was later discovered, went missing from the Zambian army. His *modus operandi* was to go into a village, round up the occupants and raid any reasonably convenient but isolated store, mainly Indian owned, and strip it bare of contents [so that] nothing, but nothing, was left in them ... he couldn't resist using the rifle and inevitably it was the watchman who got shot.[71]

Banda was becoming impatient, and he discussed security force training tactics with the heads of the army and the police. He felt that they were 'operating in too traditional a fashion' and were not therefore getting the best out of their efforts in tracking down Silombela and other wanted men. He felt 'the tactics should be be altered to guerrilla and jungle techniques' and he wished to see closer cooperation between the security forces and the young pioneers.[72]

Frequently using 'guerrilla and jungle techiques', by early November

1965 the police, army and young pioneers had caught Silombela, and he was on trial. His capture led to the arrest of others, including Machipisa Munthali, and the surrender by still others who had been working with him. As a consequence, the districts of Fort Johnston and Kasupe returned to a much more peaceful condition.[73] A senior expatriate army officer spoke of the capture of one of the rebel leaders – a former soldier – whom he subsequently, though mistakenly, thought was Silombela:

> A patrol caught Silombela asleep and brought him in. In a Fort Johnston police cell I went in and he stood to attention and said, 'Good morning, Sir.' I apologised to him and said my orders that he be shot [rather than captured] had been disobeyed. He said, 'Don't worry, Sir, I can take it.' We shook hands. Villagers were brought in from all around. I had to hand over command to [a Malawian officer] so that there would be no European witnesses. They hung him from a mango tree at Fort Johnston, outside the police station where I made the soldiers play retreat and take down the Malawi flag.[74]

Lewis recalled the arrest of another rebel leader, also thought at the time to be Silombela, who was found hiding on Ntonya hill near the Blantrye road about three miles south of Zomba: 'When he was captured, Charles Lucas, who brought him in was so excited that he accidentally let off a round from his rifle, which only narrowly missed my head.'[75] Lucas also recalled the occasion and added that the round went through the brim of the bush hat worn by his commanding officer, who turned to him and said, 'Lucas, your rifle drill needs brushing up!'

A Special Branch officer in Fort Johnson was given information as to where Silombela could be found. When he went to the address given, with a police and army party, no one was there. The Special Branch officer saw his informant again and was given a new address near Lake Malombe, south of Fort Johnson. This time he sent his Malawian colleague, detective inspector G. Mvahiwa, to find Silombela. Mvahiwa was accompanied by an escort of soldiers and a police dog party. They found Silombela at the house and after a struggle he was arrested. Mvahiwa was badly bitten by one of the dogs in the process. He was shortly decorated for his part in the arrest.[76]

On 10 November, Banda introduced into parliament a short bill to alter the penal code so as to permit judicial execution to be carried out in public. He was explicit that he wanted this provision so as publicly to hang Chipembere's terrorists. He was aware that this would incur grave external criticism, but he pointed to precedents in many other countries at different times, including Britain.

> We cannot listen to what outsiders, who do not know the circumstances

under which we live, say. Our people in the villages ... will not know that we have really punished these gangsters the way they should be punished if they don't see them themselves. In order to make sure that no one among our people is left in doubt as to whether or not the Government is doing its duty to punish those who have committed hideous crimes, the thing must be done publicly. Where everyone can see.[77]

Jones came in for huge criticism, indeed abuse, for assenting to the bill, but the British government defended him by saying he was constitutionally obliged to act on the advice of the Queen's Malawi ministers and that 'any personal reflection on the Governor-General [was] unfair and entirely unjustified'. Others, however, thought this was a mockery and that he 'should have resigned rather than assent to such a savage and monstrous demand'.[78]

Silombela was tried before Judge Cram, was convicted and sentenced to death. Before being sentenced, Silombela said he wanted to make it clear that there had been no instructions from Chipembere that his supporters, including himself, should kill anybody.[79] Banda had already announced his decision that the execution should be in public. This, not unnaturally and as he expected, caused an international outcry and allegations of barbarism.[80] A sum of money was made available in Scotland, with which Silombela was told he could attempt to bribe his prison guards to allow his escape, but he declined the offer.[81] Many pleas were made that Banda should change his mind, including a petition to the Queen by several hundred people in Zambia;[82] personal pleas by Macleod; by Nkrumah, president of Ghana and a longstanding friend of Banda; and by Jo Grimond, leader of the Liberal Party in Britain.[83] British ministers recognized that Banda was 'not the man to be deflected from a purpose to which he has committed himself – and which the vast majority of his people appear to support – by disapproval from outside'. Cole pointed out that 'any example of African barbarism at this stage would add grist to the Rhodesian mill' – that country having recently unilaterally declared its independence.[84] Nkrumah wrote to the doctor on 10 January 1966, opening his letter by saying that he understood Silombela had been found guilty of subversion against Banda's person and government, as a result of which he was to be hanged in public. He made a 'special appeal' to Banda to commute the sentence 'on purely humanitarian grounds'.[85] This was followed by a visit from the Ghanaian high commissioner to Malawi carrying a personal message from Nkrumah, again pleading for clemency.[86] When the high commissioner handed the message to Banda,

> He read through, held his chin up and said that he could not reconsider his original decision ... The inhabitants of Fort Johnston district are

predominantly Muslims and their belief in absurdities is profound. During the uprising in Malawi Mr Chipembere ... had, through his agents managed to propagate the idea that he and his army commanders had medicine that made them invisible. Most of the people in the area, still retaining the primeval simplicity ... continue to believe the story. I want to give them a practical demonstration that Chipembere and his henchmen are not superhuman beings. The relatives of the people Silombela killed would feel amply rewarded and relieved to see the tyrant hanged.

The high commissioner's pleas were rejected and he found the insistence on hanging Silombela in public 'disquieting'. He understood the scaffold – which was a mobile gibbet on wheels – was already being made in one of the young pioneer training camps. He concluded his report to Nkrumah with the words, 'This will be a horrible execution.'

Banda shortly wrote to Nkrumah to put him right on the facts and to explain the grounds for his decision:

No doubt this is what the newspapers have made the world believe, namely, that Silombela is to be hanged for subversive activities against my person and the Government. This is not at all true, Kwame. Silombela has been found guilty of murder. He admits having killed eight people. But it is known that the gang, of which he was a leader, murdered at least twelve to fifteen people. He was tried on a charge and found guilty of murdering John Ali Mbawa, a branch chairman of the Malawi Congress Party in Kasupe district. It was for [this] that he was sentenced to death and not for subversive activities against my person and the Government.

The decision to hang Silombela publicly, arises from circumstances under which he committed murder ... Silombela was the first hand man to Chipembere who led the open armed rebellion against the Government last year ... Chipembere took advantage of the ignorance and superstition of the people and spread the story that the security forces could not arrest or kill him, because ... he had medicine which made him [and] all his followers invisible to the police and the army and their bodies impenetrable to bullets.

When Chipembere left, Silombela carried on this propaganda in order to recruit more men into his gang. A number of people joined his gang from both superstition and fear. It is therefore necessary to hang Silombela in public in order to destroy this legend of invisibility and impenetrability.

Believe me, Kwame, no one likes this kind of thing. But in matters of this kind, it is not what one wants but what is necessary in the interest of law and order and security and safety of the ordinary men and women in the villages.[87]

A fortnight later Banda ordered that the Malawi diplomatic mission in Accra and the Ghanaian mission in Zomba be withdrawn.[88]

Banda also wrote to Grimond, making the same points about public execution as he had made to Nkrumah, emphasizing that 'under the circumstances of this country now, it is a dire necessity' – 'No one likes this. Certainly I do not.'[89]

Though the Governor-General personally thought Banda was right to order the public execution – 'Privately this procedure was entirely in accordance with my private wishes' –[90] he twice asked him to reconsider his decision. Refusing, the doctor gave his reasons:

> It was essential that as many people as wanted should actually see a dangerous criminal such as Silombela die. There must be no lingering belief that a man executed in the secrecy of the prison continues to be at large. The relatives of the people murdered by Silombela would wish to have the satisfaction of seeing him swing. The deterrent effect on other potential murderers and traitors: this was a very important consideration in a country such as Malawi which had not had the hundreds of years of civilisation of a country like Britain.[91]

Such was the outcry against the proposal to hang Silombela in public and such was Banda's determination to do so, the effect it would have on his reputation notwithstanding, that his official advisers sought ways of satisfying – or at least securing the acquiescence of – both Banda and those seeking to persuade him to reverse his decision. In the event, Roberts suggested that Silombela should be hanged within the prison walls and before an invited audience of villagers and those whose relatives had been murdered.[92] Banda did not accept this suggestion straight away, but as Roberts persevered he gradually 'became more receptive ... to the dangers of adverse reactions abroad'. Roberts made a major advance when he pointed out that a genuinely public execution would involve several days' work in public in erecting the scaffold, which would inevitably reveal to the press when and where the execution was to take place. When he repeated this point at a further meeting, Chidzanja and Kumtumanji, who were present, 'overplayed their hands by arguing that no preparatory work was required since it was only necessary to "string Silombela up from a tree". This was altogether too much for Banda and he ruled that the execution was to be properly conducted within prison precincts with [a] limited number of invited guests.'[93] Cole, who knew of the discussions with Banda, saw Roberts's actions as 'courageous and effective'.

Silombela was hanged a week later, on 1 February 1966, at Zomba prison at 7 a.m. The execution was witnessed by between four hundred and four hundred and fifty people, who had been told to gather at Zomba airfield to hear a speech to be made by Banda. They were instead each issued with a special pass and then all were taken in army lorries to the prison. Kumtumanji and probably Chidzanja were also present at the hanging. Banda, in deference to British views on the hanging, had given clear instructions that no British police officers were to be on duty in the prison, though some of the prison officers were British. There was a platoon of the PMF on duty outside the prison and the army had a company on stand-by in their barracks about a quarter of a mile away.

> Silombela was escorted to the scaffold by two African warders and an African Padre. The execution was carried out by Mr Catchpole, an expatriate citizen of Zambia, but it was so arranged that he was hidden from the view of the witnesses and only his African assistant was seen ... The actual execution was not witnessed, as Silombela's body dropped out of sight behind the scaffold. To prevent any subsequent disinterment, or demonstrations, the body [was] buried in one of three unmarked graves in the felons cemetery within the prison perimeter ... After the execution the witnesses dispersed to their villages without any form of demonstration.[94]

During this period, the months following Chipembere's evacuation, some half a dozen or so 'friends close to Malawi'[95] sent him every week news and newspaper cuttings of what was going on in the Fort Johnston district. The news disturbed him deeply. By late October – about the time Silombela was captured – his anxiety was profound, and he wrote to Gideon Banda about it and the undertaking of an amnesty, which had been the basis of his agreeing to leave the country. He received no satisfaction from Gideon Banda, and as his anxiety reached near desperation, mingled with remorse for his responsibility, as he saw it, for the plight of his relations and followers, he wrote to Jones.[96] He hoped the contents of the letter would be communicated to Banda, but he thought it 'fitting and proper' that he should address it to the Governor-General because it was to him that he had addressed his original peace offer. In fact, of course, he knew that Banda would give the letter short shrift and that there was no one else in a position of authority to whom to turn, save Jones, in the hope, forlorn as it undoubtedly was, that he could influence Banda.

His letter was more formal than his earlier letters and its purpose was 'to find out what ha[d] in fact been done about [his] supporters in restriction, detention and prison'. Jones would recall that it was on the basis of the promise that something would be done about an amnesty that he had decided to stop fighting and leave Malawi. He referred to 'the promptitude with which he accepted the Government's safe conduct plan despite its vagueness'. If the amnesty suggestion had been rejected out of hand he would never have left the country, but would have intensified his guerrilla activities, as in fact he had done in mid-April when he thought the peace offer had been rejected, because there was no reply from the government, and before the evacuation proposal was put to him. He had placed faith in both Banda and Jones.

Chipembere referred to the guerrilla attacks during April – which followed his departure and which he was too late to stop – and said they were events of which he was not proud. Their memory made him sad. He referred, too, to the arrests of the men he had left in the forest and the collapse of the guerrilla movement, and said that he was not surprised – indeed he had forecast that there would be a collapse after his leadership was withdrawn. The only thing that did surprise him was the absence of the promised action on his gaoled friends, for he had expected Banda to release them – as people who had been misled by Chipembere – on one of the national days of celebration, warning them to behave themselves in future and calling on those still in the forest to return to their homes and live peacefully.[97] Instead, there had been brutal action by the security forces, especially in the Malindi area, and he was now beginning to believe that the intention to pardon his followers in accordance with the agreement reached with him had disappeared or had never existed. If government's obligations were not fulfilled, he would be forced to conclude that the 'paper acceptance' of his plan was 'merely a way of getting rid of a strong opponent in order to destroy his men easily'.

There were two parts to the deal that Chipembere had sought: an amnesty in exchange for his withdrawing hostilities, and agreement that he could leave the country. As to the first – delivered via Jones – no one told him that Banda had immediately and unequivocally dismissed it out of hand. All he really knew was that Banda had readily agreed to the second part, which was delivered via Gilstrap – going to the USA – and he had assumed that the first part also was agreed. Banda had treated the two as quite separate matters. Chipembere, as a result, believed he had been double-crossed.

Chipembere continued his letter to Jones by saying that if the government defaulted on what he saw as its agreement, the whole operation would be a betrayal by him of his followers.

> I will have betrayed them, not by design but unwittingly by a trick of the Government. I do not accept this. I am not willing to go down in history as a man who betrayed his followers, and so I will use every means at my disposal to press for action by the Government. I am not being ambitious. I only ask for what is due to me by a solemn undertaking. I now gather that some of the men I had expected to be released by an act of humanity in accordance with this solemn undertaking are going to face trial [and therefore] I offer that my name can be used for obtaining lenient sentences for my men facing trial. I suggest that during the trial of each man the

prosecution should declare to the judge or magistrate that since these men were mostly ignorant men or men of very low education who had been 'incited' or 'misled' by a man of much higher education and sophistication, the state does not demand severe penalties for them. Although I do not accept that I misled anyone, I wish to offer this destruction of my own reputation if only it can make easy the Government's task in giving them some measure of amnesty ... The Prime Minister has power to prevent prosecution of offenders and has used it extensively both when we were with him in the Government and on 'pro-Government' offenders since the crisis. But since he appears to be reluctant to use this power on the men I was made to hope would be set free, I make this courageous offer to the prosecutors in all trials of my men.

He went on to say that the arrest of most of his men after he had left the country, people like George Ndomondo, Chipembere's brother and nephew, Mtiesa and others, was made possible only by his absence and because he had left them without a leader. It could 'in fact be said that [his] peace offer and [his] faithful acceptance of Government's reply [was] the cause of their arrest'. The government would sink to 'unthinkable depths' if it took advantage of his goodwill and faith to imprison these people for long periods. He would be glad to arrange a scholarship for Ndomondo so that he could leave Malawi at the end of his prison sentence, as he had been planning for his brother and nephew at the time of his departure. Indeed, that was why his brother was travelling towards Tanzania when he was arrested. His confidence in being able to arrange a scholarship for Ndomondo, and his having been in the process of doing so for his brother and nephew, may be indicative of the extent to which he believed the American government was prepared to assist him. Gilstrap had quickly agreed to finding him a place in an American university and had made a similar offer, on the staff, to Ross. It has been claimed that Chipembere was supported by the CIA and became a CIA pensioner.[98]

At the close of his letter, he wrote that if either side adopted an uncompromising attitude, 'hundreds of innocent men, women and children [would] die painful and altogther meaningless deaths'.

On both sides men are committed. On both sides men have received military training, and military training tends to make young men want to try their skill. For my part, I have, for the time being at any rate, abandoned politics and chosen my new career. From the purely personal point of view I have nothing to lose by boycotting Malawi affairs; but out of love for that dear motherland I would like to say that I am ready to consider any proposals for permanent restoration of peace. This is a delicate offer, but I make it hoping it will not fall on deaf ears. No one will win an absolute and total victory in the present strife. Any victory will at best be pyrrhic and at worst one achieved after meaningless losses of lives, resources and reputation.

This letter from Chipembere to Jones was one of a number of threads that began to come together at this time, late October, early November 1965: a decision by the Anglican Church to post Archdeacon Chipembere, Henry's father, to Tanzania; Catherine Chipembere's escape from Likoma; fears by Arden that the Church might be thought to be implicated in Chipembere making anti-Banda speeches in the USA; and threats by the US government to disclose publicly the involvement of Banda and Jones in Chipembere's evacuation from Malawi to the USA.

The possibility of the archdeacon leaving Likoma Island had been considered for several months. In the middle of April, Arden had written to Jones to say that because of inflammatory speeches by visitors to the island, the archdeacon no longer felt that he, his wife and his daughter-in-law, Catherine, were safe.[99] On 5 November, Banda spoke to Jones of the Church's intention to move him from Likoma Island to 'a remote station in the Mwera district of Tanzania'. He initially said he should make his own way there without govenment help, but three days later, he said he would be prepared for the government to transport him and his family with an escort of young pioneers from Likoma to Mbamba Bay in Tanzania. Before agreeing to this, however, he would require him to undertake never again to return to Malawi.[100] Arden wrote to the archdeacon, telling him of Banda's offer to provide transport to Mbamba Bay and of his agreement to him leaving Malawi, but to do so for ever. The archdeacon was profoundly distressed:

> I am ... full of tears of shame for all that is happening in this country. I cannot escape from the consequences of this situation. [I do not want to leave Malawi for good because my three daughters are married to people in this country] but if the Prime Minister [says] I cannot return back to this country then I shall bow my head with tears under the Prime Minister's feet and obey his orders.[101]

Shortly, Banda said that in view of possible suspicion of collusion in Chipembere's escape to the USA, he did not now wish to appear to be having anything to do with any of the Chipembere family leaving the country. If the archdeacon could make his own way, he would let him go. Banda would have nothing to do with it.[102] The archdeacon and his family may in this way have been fortunate, because they would have been at the mercy of their young pioneer escort, who may not have treated them gently. Banda would have been aware of this possibility and it may well have been the cause of his second change of mind.

At the end of November, Catherine and her children were smuggled aboard the *Ilala* at midnight – the boat had delayed sailing so that this could be done – since the mission authorities were afraid that the young pioneers would prevent her leaving. The *Ilala* went to Nkata Bay, where it was indeed searched by the young pioneers. Catherine, however, was well concealed, and the boat travelled on to Mbamba Bay in Mozambique. From there, she and the children were taken by car to Dar es Salaam. Shortly, she was taken to the USA.[103] The archdeacon, assisted by the Church, left Likoma towards the end of December intending to go to Zambia, but at the last moment he changed his mind. Once on the mainland, he was picked up by a European police officer, who took him to the Tanzanian border and with whom he spent his last night in Malawi, sharing a room in Chitipa rest house. The police officer recalled:

> I am sure it was difficult for him but we had a reasonably pleasant evening; he was friendly and we shared what food we had and we avoided talking politics. It was an incident-free trip despite some aggro by Young Pioneers who had a semi-permanent road block near the border; they clearly knew who my passenger was and were keen to make some mischief but I was able to persuade them otherwise, aided, I'm sure, by the fact that I was armed.[104]

The archdeacon left Malawi on 30 December 1965 and travelled via Mbeya to Dar es Salaam. He and three others on Likoma Island had been interrogated by Special Branch. The other three had been detained, but the archdeacon had been released. Special Branch would have liked to keep him as a 'hostage', but they did not want to deploy this argument with Banda in case he ordered that he too be placed in detention.[105]

During November, Arden learned that Henry Chipembere had been addressing audiences in the USA. It was alleged that the speeches were arranged under the auspices of Canon Young, who had visited Nyasaland early in 1964 and had become friendly with a number of members of the cabinet. Arden was concerned that the inference was being drawn that he was privy to the public addresses – because Young was formerly his commissary in the USA – and that funds collected in the name of the diocese were being diverted elsewhere in the USA. Arden wrote to seek Jones's advice as to what he should do to clear the air.[106] At their meeting on 24 November Jones and Banda discussed Arden's letter. Banda was relaxed about Young, especially after Jones told him that he had 'been kicked out of the episcopalian organisation although not defrocked. [He was] a bit batty.'

Chipembere's speeches were less of a worry to Banda than they were to the American authorities. The concerns were not so much about the speeches in themselves as the danger that they would bring about a disclosure of the way in which the American embassy was involved in Chipembere's evacuation, and particularly their contact with, and the practical help they had afforded, him before his departure. This was still a matter that worried them and that they had hoped would disappear once Ross had left Malawi. It appears that the Malawi ambassador to the USA, Vincent Gondwe, had not been told anything about the mechanics of how Chipembere got to the USA until someone in the State Department told him that the US government had been involved. Gondwe, who had been at school with Chipembere, seems to have harboured a grudge against him and Chiume after they had succeeded, and he had failed, to secure selection to the legislature in 1956.[107]

Banda had not given his ministers any information about how Chipembere got to the USA, but

> partly through indiscreet talk on the part of a State Department official some of the Malawi ministers got to know of the American part in the exercise and they initiated an anti-American campaign in which Dr Banda, in spite of being privy to the broad outline of the scheme, felt it necessary to acquiesce. He even took part to some extent in the hue and cry.[108]

On 8 November 1965, Gondwe was called to see the deputy director of the Africa division in the State Department, who told him that in discussion with Banda the American ambassador had been told that Gondwe insisted his informer was someone in the State Department and Banda agreed that Gondwe should be questioned again on this point. He told them he would not divulge the name of the person concerned, just as he had not revealed it to his own government. The deputy director suggested that the person could not be 'connected with the Chipembere story' because only five top people in the department 'had any idea what was going on'. Gondwe pointed out that he had already been told 'in an earlier encounter' that if Chipembere dabbled in politics he would be breaking an undertaking given to the US government not to do so. This showed at least some involvement of that government. He added that Banda had received information about Chipembere's speeches from people within the USA, and when he was asked the names of the people arranging the events at which the speeches were made he told them: Canon Young and Jay Jacobson, a lawyer who had worked in Malawi.

It appears, too, that either Banda indicated that he would demand Chipembere's return to Malawi, or that the Americans feared he would, on the grounds that the undertaking not to engage in activity hostile to Malawi had been broken. Since the Americans were not prepared to return Chipembere, and in order to counter a possibile demand for this, they threatened to reveal Banda's and Jones's involvement in the escape. In writing to Banda, Gondwe said:

The Americans seem genuinely concerned about present developments and are anxious to stabilise relationships with us. They are not prepared to let go of Chipembere and will try, and tried it on us, persuasion, brow beating, and any other methods including possibly monetary bribes to balance their interests and relations with us and Chipembere. Chipembere's coming [here] becomes more and more fishy. The allusion to collusion with the Government of Malawi and the Governor-General or his office is rather ominous. I do not like the threatening tone in which the US talks of publishing confidential information to cause embarrassment. We should attempt to get to the bottom of the story surrounding Chipembere's coming even as we find out the activities for the present and plans for the future. Having done this, we should make a decision as to how far we intend reaching and shoot for the target boldly.[109]

It is clear that Banda was already concerned about US relations with Malawi, probably because of Chipembere's speeches, contrary to Gilstrap's undertaking to prevent them. Early in October he suggested that the Americans might be grooming Chipembere as his successor, just as Red China was grooming Chiume. For whatever reason, Gilstrap was 'discreetly withdrawn' from his post as US ambassador to Malawi during October 1965.[110] The *Malawi News* thundered: 'Malawi will not tolerate the Reds and the Yankees in interference in our affairs.'[111]

Banda showed Jones the letter from Gondwe. He said he had nothing to hide and the Americans could publish what they liked. Nevertheless, Jones 'went through everything with him', whether to ensure that he, Jones, recalled the circumstances correctly, or whether to refresh the prime minister's memory, or whether otherwise to rehearse a joint account of what happened, is unclear. Confining themselves to how entry to the USA and to a university there was secured – matters in which the US authorities were intimately involved – and ignoring the mechanics of how he was evacuated from Malawi – matters in which the Americans were not involved and of which they had little, if any, knowledge – they agreed that the approach was from Chipembere to Gilstrap to Jones to Banda. In view of Chipembere's illness, his desire to study and his determination to get out of politics, Banda decided that he would not block his way to America, provided the Americans agreed to two conditions: they would ensure that Chipembere engaged in no hostile activity against Malawi and made no criticism of Banda. 'That's all he knows and [he] is not afraid of that coming out.'[112]

The Americans did not attempt to publish any of the details of how Chipembere got to the USA, but there was a further worry some six months later when Banda learned that he might move from America to London. It is possible that the Americans, concerned about their relations with Banda, put pressure on Chipembere to leave the USA. When the Governor-General spoke with Banda about this, early in June 1966, the doctor said that 'if Chipembere moved from America to London he might feel justified to ask for his extradition since it could be proved that he led an armed rebellion in February, 1965'.[113]

Instead of going to Britain, however, Chipembere went with his wife and family to Tanzania, arriving on 29 August 1966. He did this because of his 'sense of obligation to his followers' there.[114]

CHAPTER 10

The Fate of the Ministers

AT the time Malawi became a republic, on 6 July 1966, the former ministers were all in exile: Chirwa, Chiume and Chisiza in Tanzania, Chokani and Bwanausi in Zambia, and Chipembere in the USA, though he was about to move to Tanzania. In the months leading up to republic day there were frequent reports that the exiles would make some sort of incursion into Malawi or create some sort of disturbances during or immediately after the celebrations. The government's reaction to these reports was 'fairly relaxed', mainly because:

> The morale of [the] dissidents is extremely low and with some of them taking jobs in Tanzania and Zambia their numbers have decreased; their leadership, apart from Chisiza, has largely disintegrated; their support from Tanzania has greatly declined with [the] absence abroad of Kambona and Nyerere's moves towards rapprochement with Banda; [the] present location of most militant dissidents is known and ... they are nowhere near Malawi.

Nevertheless, the government was not complacent. Chisiza had visited China earlier in the year, he might have Chinese arms and money available to mount an attack, and he had spoken of an 'assassination group'. 'It would need very few men to create [a] serious disturbance and there are some rabid hard-core terrorists among the exiles.' Though Banda did not think an early return was likely, Chipembere's arrival in Tanzania could 'give new heart' to the dissidents. Consequently, Banda took a number of precautions ready for any trouble. A company of the army was on call throughout the whole of the celebrations. The PMF was held in readiness in the northern and central regions. The police, young pioneers and Special Branch were 'on watch for suspicious movements throughout the period of the celebrations.' And steps were taken by the British high commission to have an aircraft on call at Chileka airport, presumably for evacuation purposes.[1]

In the event, there was no trouble, and shortly Banda reassured the public that although a number of supporters who had left Malawi with the former ministers had been given military training in Tanzania, China, Algeria and Russia, they had not achieved any success. There had been no violence in Malawi for over a year. The refugees still in Tanzania were no longer being supplied with money. Many were unhappy and wanted to return to Malawi, but were afraid to do so. Banda felt sufficiently secure to announce that 'Any of them now resident in Tanzania or Zambia were invited to return if they were truly repentant, [and their relatives] should write to them to encourage their return.'[2] He had already released three hundred detainees at the time of the republic celebrations, including a number from the Fort Johnston area, and they had 'proved helpful to the Malawi authorities'. Most of them had settled back in their villages without trouble. He intended to release another two hundred in time for Christmas, and they should be treated with sympathy and not dealt with harshly. If they were not 'truly repentant they would be sent back to detention camps for ever'.[3]

Cole reported that while the country was, 'to all appearances, peaceful and stable', he was not deluded.[4] There was no current internal threat to Banda's supremacy, but the rebels outside Malawi were still determined to remove him. 'Though they have their problems they would need only one well aimed bullet to achieve their objective.'

> There are also [other] grounds for concern – his power is a man of great arrogance, intolerant of criticism and opposition. His power is supported by a dictatorially inclined constitution and party machine. Educated Africans are treated with suspicion, 700 people are in detention, the threat of oppression and intimidation never seems far round the corner, stability is being purchased at the price of incipient dictatorship.[5]

Even so, Cole saw distinct advantages to Britain and Malawi in Banda staying in power: 'his determination to maintain stability, his abhorrence of corruption, his rejection of idealistic ideology, his underlying friendliness to the West and his fund of common sense and realism'.[6]

Although Bwanausi and Chokani seemed content to continue to live in Zambia, and Chiume to stay in Tanzania, the other three – Chirwa, Chisiza and Chipembere – wished, for varying reasons, to return to Malawi. Banda's intelligence officers continued to keep a close eye on all their activities.[7]

Bwanausi – who spent some time in Tanzania – became a schoolteacher in Zambia where fellow exiles looked upon him as their leader. He spent the early part of his time 'preparing himself for the resumption of his duties as Malawi's economic planner' – a role he had taken up after Dunduzu Chisiza's death – if the ex-ministers returned to power.[8] He died in a car crash with two colleagues in Zambia on 30 November

1968 and the accident was blamed on Malawi government agents.⁹ 'After his death ... Banda was reportedly "very pleased" and publicly stated that his opponents would "die one by one".'¹⁰

Chokani also became a schoolteacher in Zambia, where he was a 'great source of morale and hope' to other exiles.¹¹ He returned to Malawi after Banda was defeated in the 1994 general elections, and became his country's ambassador to the USA.

Chiume, having sought refuge in Tanzania – where he had spent a good deal of his life before entering politics in Malawi – stayed there until he returned to his home country after Banda's defeat in 1994. While in Tanzania he worked as a member of staff of *The Nationalist* newspaper and wrote his autobiography. He founded a political party in opposition to Banda, the Congress for the Second Republic (CSR), and recalled:

> Privately we kept the OAU and United Nations informed of what was happening in Malawi particularly as regards the violation of human rights. We monitored almost all activities of Banda and used whites ... to slip into Malawi propaganda material against him. In addition we used the local as well as international newspapers and magazines to fight against and expose Banda.¹²

Chiume gave an account of how his colleagues were faring in Tanzania at this time. The Tanzania government was paying them £200 a month and finding work for them.

> Chisiza, however, was a problem because, as a foreigner, he could not be given a job in the police force in which he had served during colonial times. In addition, he drank very heavily indeed and was a great embarrassment to the other ex-ministers there. To avoid the continuation of this embarrassment we sent him off to China. After his return he was virtually working on his own.¹³

In February 1966, in a nation-wide broadcast, Banda claimed that Chiume was planning to send armed infiltrators to Malawi along the Zambia–Malawi border in the north and the Mozambique border in the south. He added, 'This is not the time to be complacent. The Army, Police, Young Pioneers, ordinary villagers must be alert and on their guard constantly.'¹⁴ This infiltration did not take place, whether because Banda was misinformed or because the infiltrators changed their minds is not clear.

About the middle of June 1967, Chirwa travelled from Dar es Salaam to London to see his wife, Vera, who was studying law. She had been living on charity since 1965. Chirwa's return fare from Tanzania was paid for by Lomax, who also gave Jones £50 to give to Vera to help with her rent.¹⁵ Chiume, who did not learn of Lomax's payment until many years later, had also collected and handed money to Chirwa for his return air fare to London.[16] Jones, now retired, saw both Chirwas, and then wrote to Banda, still trying to effect a reconciliation, what most people would have seen as the manifest impossibility of success and the grave dangers in it notwithstanding:

> I found that [Vera's] demeanour was calm and peaceful and she assured me that she is having no communications with the rebels. In fact, she expressed what I believe to be her genuine horror at the tone of some of the rebel circulars which have been sent to her ... She told me that she considered that you are doing fine work for Malawi and that no other person could lead the nation at the present time.
>
> I have also seen her husband, who ... also appeared to be of a peaceful disposition and expressed his admiration for you and his desire to help Malawi under your leadership as soon as an opportunity occurred. He ... would like to get out of Tanzania if a suitable job could be found for him elsewhere. He realises that it would not be possible for him to return to Malawi at present but he is hoping that he and his family will be able to return in the not too distant future. If some post could be found for him in an organisation such as the UN on the recommendation of Malawi, this would be ideal for him in the transition period.
>
> He gave me some interesting information about ... Chisiza [who] is unemployed and is rapidly degenerating. He has no communication with the other rebels and seems now to accept that you are the only possible leader for Malawi.

He believed that if one or two of the rebel ministers could be seen to accept Banda's authority once more and to be working under him 'for the good of Malawi', the effect on the people of Malawi and the outside world would be most favourable and would tend to show other ex-ministers that their cause was hopeless.[17]

On one of his visits to Dar es Salaam, Lewis was approached by an African who asked, 'Do I have the honour to be addressing Brigadier Lewis?' The questioner was Chirwa, who went on to ask if Lewis would ask Banda if he, Chirwa, could return to Malawi. Lewis 'told him not to be a bloody fool'.[18] This bluntly expressed and undoubtedly sound advice was directed not at the unlikelihood of Banda agreeing, but at the imprudence of attempting to return – as he should have learned from the repeated beatings he was given just before leaving Malawi and as he was to learn to his even graver cost a few years later.

In February 1968, Chirwa, who was employed in the lands office in Dar es Salaam, was reported to be 'drinking himself to death', and Vera Chirwa was working in the attorney-general's department in Morogoro, Tanzania.[19] Chiume later said:

When the ex-ministers were in Tanzania, the others ... put Chirwa forward as the leader of a new political party [the Malawi Freedom Movement: MAFREMO] set up in opposition to the MCP. Chirwa, who was drinking heavily ... took the position seriously and was not suspicious when eight Malawi police officers came to see him [purporting to be delegates from secret cells of MAFREMO in Malawi] and pledged their support if he returned to Malawi to take over the government. They said Malawi was ready for him to return and take over. They arranged a preliminary tour of Malawi by one of Chirwa's relatives [the secretary-general of MAFREMO, Mackenzie Chirwa] on his behalf. He visited and held meetings at Mwanza, Blantyre, Zomba, Lilongwe, Mzuzu and Nkhata Bay, and reported favourably [indeed, enthusiastically, to Chirwa] on the climate of opinion in Malawi. This encouraged Chirwa to return, in 1981. [My feeling was that in his lust for power, Orton's coefficiency of suggestibility had become dangerously high. I tried to tell him and warn him of the dangers but this frequently earned me public abuse and particularly when he was boozed up.] Chirwa and his wife [who now had a law teaching post in the University of Zambia, together with their son, Fumbani] flew to Zambia [and drove towards the border at Chipata in order] to enter Malawi. Here they were abducted and arrested by the Malawi police.[20]

They were taken to Malawi, placed in detention and held separately at Zomba central prison, manacled to iron bars for long periods. Fumbani was detained incommunicado without charge until February 1984, but his parents were tried on charges of treason before the Southern Regional Traditional Court in May 1983. They were not permitted to call witnesses in their defence, were convicted and sentenced to death.[21]

Their sentence occasioned an international outcry and there were pleas for clemency from many sources. Banda was not the sort of man to pay a great deal of attention to the pleas made, and in any event, though he did not announce it, he had already decided at an early stage to commute their sentences to life imprisonment. This he did in 1984.[22] Although they were both held in Zomba prison, the Chirwas did not see each other from the time of their appeal until September 1992, when a delegation of British lawyers visited them. Chirwa, 'nearly deaf and almost blind from untreated cataracts', died in prison – where he had been frequently placed in leg irons – in October 1992. 'Thousands of supporters attended [his] funeral in his home area of Nkhata Bay, but Vera Chirwa was not allowed out of prison to attend her husband's burial.' By this time she was 'the longest serving African prisoner of conscience known to Amnesty International'. She was released from gaol three months later.[23]

Jones's June 1967 impression, that Chisiza accepted that Banda was the only possible leader for Malawi, was a grave miscalculation – or misrepresentation – as Chirwa must have known when he gave Jones that impression. After training in China, Chisiza returned to Tanzania and operated independently of the other former ministers. During the first half of July, he left Dar es Salaam and went to the Pangale refugee and training camp in south-west Tanzania.[24] Here he told the men that he was going to invade Malawi to assassinate the president, ministers and other leading members of the MCP. Once they knew of this intention, only seventeen agreed to join him, though he had hoped for more. Banda knew the names of at least four of them. At Pangale there was a split between those following Chisiza, known as the Saigon group, and those following Chipembere, known as the Washington group.[25]

Chisiza and his seventeen volunteers left Pangale at different times and in small groups so as not to attract attention. They arranged to meet at Abercorn, most of them travelling across Lake Tanganyika by boat, though Chisiza and one or two others went by road from Dar es Salaam. They then travelled separately in cars to Lusaka. For two weeks they lived, by arrangement with George Nyandoro and James Chikarema, the Rhodesian ZAPU leaders, in a large house in a camp between Lusaka and Broken Hill. Chisiza had been in touch with Nyandoro and Chikarema for at least the past ten years. Nyandoro had been at the January 1959 'murder plot' meeting of the NAC.[26] The camp contained 'all sorts of arms and ammunition, rifles, sub-machine guns, machine guns, rockets, bazookas, hand grenades and many other instruments of destruction', all from Communist countries. During this time Chisiza lived in Lusaka and travelled daily to the camp to decide the details of their mission, what kind and quantity of arms and ammunition they would carry, what type of uniforms they would wear, how much money they would need and how they would get it, the point at which they would enter Malawi and whom they would contact. He received money from the Chinese ambassador and the ANC of South Africa. It may be, too, that Americans – individuals if not officials – also provided support. Chiume later claimed that two Peace Corps women with whom Chisiza had been close when in Malawi were implicated in his attempted *coup d'état*. They travelled to East Africa to stay with him and were responsible for acquiring the Malawi police uniforms Chisiza and his group wore to invade Malawi. It has been implied that, rather than helping Chisiza, they may have been working on Banda's side to entrap him.[27]

The unit – 'disciplined rebels' posing as Frelimo soldiers – left Lusaka by lorry between 15 and 17 September at night and crossed the Luangwa river surrounded by petrol drums and concealed under a tarpaulin. From Fort Jameson they walked via Mwami mission and along the Malawi-

Mozambique border, sticking carefully to the Mozambique side, until they reached the Mwanza area on 30 September. Coincidentally, the route taken by the infiltrators bore a close resemblance to the one Banda had said Chiume was planning eighteen months earlier, later taken by Mackenzie Chirwa. Three days after the insurgents reached the Mwanza area, assistant superintendent John Singo, the officer in charge of police at Mwanza, learned that armed and uniformed people had been seen in the border area.

> He immediately organised a police patrol which he led to the area ... Guided by villagers, [he] was following the tracks of the intruders when he heard a police whistle [blown by] his station Special Branch officer [detective sub-inspector Isaac Chiweta whom he found] surrounded by a group of heavily armed men who [held him at gun point and] then discussed whether to kill the two policemen. Although recognising [from their accents] the intruders as Malawians from the Northern Region [Singo] pretended to believe them to be a Frelimo unit, and offered imaginary information concerning Portuguese dispositions. He was allowed to go free, and once clear of the immediate vicinity, sent radio messages to his headquarters which enabled the security forces to be deployed against the rebel infiltrators.[28]

Banda now knew the names of more of the men in the unit and the detailed route they had taken to enter the Mwanza district. He immediately informed parliament, which was sitting at the time:

> They are supposed to have entered this area ... passing as Frelimo. They are dressed in our PMF uniforms ... They are heavily armed with machine guns, automatic pistols and possibly a bazooka ... I only wish that Yatuta Chisiza and Chipembere were among them now so we could deal with them. I have given orders that the relatives of all these people be arrested now [and their houses burned] so that there can be no possible chance of their being hidden safely by their relatives ... Everyone, all the families and relatives of those people now in Zambia and Tanganyika must be detained.[29]

He instructed the people of Mwanza, Neno, Ncheu, Dedza, Lilongwe and Mchinji to be on the look-out in case the infiltrators turned back in their direction. He attributed this infiltration to Chipembere and Chisiza having failed to rouse their people in Tanzania and Zambia to invade Malawi, and as a result they were being criticized by those who were providing them with money and equipment for taking it and not 'producing the goods'. Banda understood that Chipembere was not keen on invasion as a means of taking power and was now biding his time until the doctor died so that he could take over as president. Some two and a half years earlier Chipembere had indeed claimed that he did not believe in external invasion so long as there was room for internal revolt or guerrilla warfare. Banda, exploiting the rebel Washington–Saigon group split, continued by saying that Chisiza wanted 'to pose as a real hero, the real leader between the two of them' and that was why he had taken action to invade Malawi.

> They are already paralysed. They are definitely trying to get away back to Zambia but they will be lucky if they can slip through ... traps are laid for them everywhere. They won't succeed ... The army is ready, the police are ready, Young Pioneers are ready and above all, the ordinary men and women in the villages are ready. *Nkhwangwa, Mpeni, Mkondo* [Axe, Knife, War.][30]

On 6 October Corporal Frederick Kanduma of the Malawi Rifles was on patrol in the Mwanza area when he learned that armed rebels were hiding in a nearby village.

> He decided to investigate and directed his men to surround the particular house, thus cutting off the possibility of escape. [Although it was night time and dark, he] entered the house and called upon the enemy to surrender. At that time he had no idea of the strength and intentions of the rebels, nor of how heavily armed they might be. Having effectively surprised the enemy, he disarmed them and took them prisoners. These were the first prisoners captured, and they provided much useful information which assisted the remainder of the operation.[31]

The following day, Saturday, 7 October, the security forces captured three more insurgents, from whom they learned that the unit – all of whose seventeen members they named – was being lead by Chisiza himself. The capture was a lucky break for the army: 'The sergeant major who caught the first man was in the wrong place and going in the wrong direction when he came across him, lost and not knowing where he was going.' The captured man said Chisiza had simply told him he was going back to Malawi, and when he asked if he wanted to go with him, he agreed.[32] On the Sunday, four others were captured, the next day one more and on Tuesday another.

On Wednesday, 11 October, Company Sergeant-Major Manfred Ndache investigated a report from local villagers and he and his section tracked Chisiza to his 'lair', arriving mid-afternoon.

> This lair was in ... the dry bed of the River Lisungwe [near Mpatamanga bridge]. It was this camp that was used as the headquarters of the whole gang. When Chisiza saw [the] soldiers approaching, he and his gangsters opened fire. Naturally, [the] soldiers returned Chisiza's fire and so a fierce

battle developed ... For two and a half hours the battle between Chisiza's gang and [the] soldiers raged.[33]

The section came under fire from automatic weapons in concealed positions. CSM Ndache ... deployed his men to surround the enemy and he himself moved alone until within twenty yards of the rebels. When the leader of the group, Chisiza, rose to throw a grenade, CSM Ndache shot him dead. This so disheartened the remaining rebels that they fled, losing one other killed [C. J. L. Mwahimba] during their retreat [under cover of darkness].[34]

For these actions, Ndache was awarded the Republic of Malawi Medal, Kanduma was given a Presidential Citation, Singo was created a Member, and Chiweta was awarded the Medal, of the Order of the Lion of Malawi. The Republic of Malawi Medal and Presidential Citation were established only a few days before these first awards were made.[35]

Lewis privately hoped Chisiza could be allowed to escape rather than be shot, but this was not possible. He also wanted Chisiza buried quietly, but Banda insisted on the body being publicly displayed.[36] The corpse – 'emaciated, indicative of the hardships he had endured' – was examined by, among others, Chevallier. He was now in charge of the southern division and he was much affected by discovering that Chisiza still had in his pockets, when he was shot, the pipe and 'Three Nuns' tobacco tin – now containing crushed dried banana leaves in place of tobacco – which he had given him exactly three years earlier.[37] Chisiza was also carrying with him a plastic bag containing a dark green military uniform, which he proposed to wear when he took the salute at the ceremonial march past after he had taken over the government. In his pocket, too, he was carrying a well-used and much annotated copy of *The Thoughts of Chairman Mao*.[38] The insurgents who were arrested 'were tried, publicly, for treason and were hanged' early in 1969.[39]

Exiles in Tanzania were horrified by Banda's orders following Chisiza's death, which they dubbed a murder at the hands of the security forces 'operating under the direct guidance and supervision of foreign mercenary officers [Lewis and Long] who are both British'.

> Banda has made all mourning of Chisiza's death illegal and punishable by shooting or imprisonment ... Relations of Chisiza were warned not to mourn the death or observe any of the rituals required by Malawi custom. Chisiza's mother, Khumbata, a widow approaching the age of 90 was summoned to the State House ... firstly to be shown the dead body of her son and to 'learn a lesson that the Ngwazi is not a man to be played with' and secondly to be told that if she dares to mourn the death of her son she too will be shot dead.[40]

The part Zambia played in facilitating Chisiza's incursion and in being a refuge for Malawian dissidents, not unnaturally caused friction between the two governments. On 15 November the Zambian president wrote to Banda to express regret about the strained relations. In his reply, Banda, too, regretted the deterioration, but pointed out that his country was vilified by the Zambian media, mostly owned by the government, because Malawi did not toe the OAU and UN lines in southern Africa politics.[41] He 'bitterly resented' the attacks made on him by Kaunda's leading colleagues, and continued:

> whether you personally and your Government know it or not, the truth is that those ex-Ministers ... have been from the time they entered Zambia, actively engaged in subversive activities against the Government of this country. Not only have they been holding subversive meetings at night, but also they have been constantly sending subversive circulars into Malawi from Zambia ... . The authors have been and are, Chiume, Chipembere, Chirwa and, until recently, Chisiza. But Bwanausi, Chokani [and others] in Zambia distribute them in Zambia and send some to Malawi.

He gave 'a full account of what happened and the background to the whole business', including the rebels' accommodation and training in Zambia. This very detailed report was compiled from what the captured men individually told Special Branch officers, who then cross-checked each with the others. The doctor was taking the opportunity to demonstrate how competent his own Special Branch was and to warn Kaunda that little could happen in Zambia that affected Malawi without him knowing a great deal about it. He was also putting Kaunda in a position where he would have either to admit he did not know what was going on in his own country – and could not therefore trust the competence or loyalty of his own Special Branch – or admit that he did know – and was facilitating grave anti-Malawi activities, including an attempt to assassinate Banda and overthrow his government. The doctor rounded off his letter by repeating what he had said in 1966 when he received reports that Chipembere was intending to invade Malawi from Tanzania: that if any country allowed itself to be used as a base to invade Malawi, he would, in chasing the invaders from Malawi, 'in turn, invade that country, to make sure that the invasion is not repeated'. This was dangerous talk in which Banda raised the stakes – extending the doctrine of hot pursuit to include retaliatory invasion – to a level Kaunda could not ignore.

Banda was prepared for a reconciliation, but he was not going to let Kaunda get away without clearly and forcefully speaking his mind. His letter seems to have been effective, because he and Kaunda settled their differences about a month later in a private and secret meeting, which resulted in much improved relations. The effect, though it was not articulated, was to show the dissident exiles that Zambia was no longer a safe refuge for them and especially was not a safe place from which to try and topple Banda – as Chisiza had recently learned and as Chirwa was later to learn.

Banda was disappointed Chipembere had not accompanied Chisiza, so that he could dispose of him as he had Chisiza.[42] After he had been in America a year, US government officials, concerned about their relationships with Malawi, were keen he should no longer remain in their country. The British government thought that while the Americans had originally looked upon him as a successor to Banda, they now saw him as an 'embarrassment'. They appreciated that it was only sensible for the Americans to want to get rid of him, because as a long-term investment he now had little value and in the short term he had 'proved a serious liability'. The Governor-General spoke with Banda about this early in June 1966. The doctor's response was that 'if Chipembere moved from America to London he might feel justified to ask for his extradition since it could be proved that he led an armed rebellion in February, 1965'.[43]

The possibilities open to Chipembere were to seek to remain in the USA, to go to Britain, to seek asylum in Zambia or Tanzania, or to return to Malawi. He considered each of these.

The American ambassador in Malawi was clear that he and his government wanted 'to see Chipembere out of the United States', and he told Banda it was not possible for Chipembere to remain there. For a while this ruled out his remaining in the USA as a solution to his problem.[44]

In June 1966, Chipembere applied to the Zambian government for permission to reside in their country. The reply was that he would be given sanctuary, but would have to reside in Barotseland, far from the towns, and would not be permitted to take part in any subversive activities.[45] He rejected the offer of a teaching post under these conditions. Banda doubted whether Kaunda would in fact have Chipembere in Zambia: he may have had some leverage on Kaunda because oil for Zambia was being transported through Malawi during the early part of Rhodesia's unilateral declaration of independence. Zambia as a solution to the problem of having to leave the USA was also now ruled out.

He next applied to enter Britain to research for a book or a doctorate at Oxford. Until then he had been supported by the All Africa Institute of Boston, but they could not continue this help outside the USA. Instead, to his 'own money in the bank' would be added the help of 'a group of private friends'.[46] This application placed the British government in a dilemma because of Banda's 'calm but very firm' stance:

> If Chipembere's presence in Britain became at all conspicuous and especially if he indulged in political activities there would be nothing he could

do to stop his Ministers and his party from becoming bitterly hostile to Britain. He reminded [Cole] of the hostility which had been directed towards Americans on [the] same issue. He said this had been felt right down to village level and he personally had been concerned for [the] safety of [the] peace corps. All this would be transferred to Britain with [the] gravest effects [and] deep animosity would be felt towards [Cole] personally.[47]

The hostility towards Americans was a reference to his ministers having learned of the US involvement in Chipembere's evacuation.[48] Banda told the ambassador that the USA should keep Chipembere, but when told this could not be done he retorted, 'You are out of this. This is between the United Kingdom and me.'[49]

Banda told Cole that if Britain did accept Chipembere 'it must certainly be on the condition that he indulged in no political activities', and in any case he would immediately ask for, indeed fight for, his extradition to Malawi to stand trial. Cole consequently advised the Commonwealth Office to exclude Chipembere, if this were possible, on the grounds that 'if we cannot find means of keeping Chipembere out of Britain ... we shall be confronted with danger of grave deterioration in relations between Britain and Malawi'. The Commonwealth Office agreed that relations would seriously deteriorate, but thought Britain should treat Chipembere's application entirely on its legal merits. To try and exclude him on medical grounds would 'mean deliberately bending the rules', and they were sure the home secretary would refuse extradition on what they saw as a 'purely political charge'.[50] Bottomley, the secretary of state, was advised by his officials to reply that Britain intended to maintain its liberal tradition and did not propose 'to follow the extremism of African countries who declare persons prohibited immigrants on flimsy grounds'. More cynically, they added, 'Chipembere might be out today, or others like him, but could be tomorrow's leaders'.[51] That Britain should see Chipembere's violent actions at Fort Johnston and his attempts to overthrow the constitutional government by force of arms as a 'purely political' matter and 'flimsy grounds' for seeking to have him prosecuted was remarkable.

However, parallel with their principled stand, the British government took a pragmatic approach, prepared to do almost anything to keep Chipembere out of Britain. They instructed Cole to try to persuade the Americans to keep him, though they had little confidence he would succeed. A Commonwealth Office official spoke with his counterpart in the US embassy in London and frankly told him that the British government would be angry if the Americans forced Chipembere out of the USA. For a while this seemed successful because, shortly, the embassy confirmed that he had been accepted to Harvard. They professed to be pleased about this prospect, claiming, but not being believed, that it was what they always preferred but had been unable to head him off going to Oxford. British officials' delight – 'we can all be pleased with the satisfactory, and we hope long term, result'[52] – was short-lived, as the Harvard prospect quickly fell through.

The British government's next priority was to do all they could to keep Chipembere out of Britain, but they realized they could not succeed if he found enough money to maintain himself, possibly with the help of friends or of the US government hoping to get him off their hands. Their intention was to try and frighten Chipembere 'by making his flesh creep' at the prospect of being extradited to face a charge of being an accessory to murder. They were hopeful that if this step succeeded it would probably 'drive him to Tanganyika'. They thought it would still be a bad outcome, but not as bad as having him in Britain. In the meantime they proposed 'to explore the possibility of fixing him up with a course at Dublin which might suit him better than Dar es Salaam and avoid embarrassment to us'.[53]

Chipembere persisted with his application to enter Britain. Jacobson – 'Chipembere's chief spokesman in America' – asked to see the minister of state, but she was too busy to grant the request.[54] On 23 June, Chipembere wrote to Bottomley, commonwealth relations secretary, to explain that he had now come to the end of his period of study and medical treatment in the USA and wanted to leave that country to live near members of his family, some of whom were in Malawi and others in Zambia and Tanzania:

> But I am satisfied that if I return to any place near Malawi I will inevitably be involved in further activities against Dr Banda's regime. Contrary to what the newspapers say ... I have no intention of continuing the armed struggle against Dr Banda ... If I wanted to continue the armed fight I would have no difficulty at all in returning to one of the countries near Malawi and to operate from there. But my one year of silent reflection has satisfied me that this is not the correct course in the interests of the country. So I have decided that I must not go to Africa and must instead come to stay in England. In order to keep myself profitably occupied and to protect my mind from negative and non-constructive thinking, I would like to do some study.[55]

He went on to explain, however, that he would not go to Britain unless he had the British government's promise that he would not be extradited to Malawi if Banda demanded it. He did not think the doctor would do this, because his lawyers would publicly reveal Banda's acquiescence in his evacuation. He was not taking any chances, however, and sought a promise from the British cabinet that if he did go to Britain he would not be extradited. Bottomley – in accordance with the decision to make Chipembere's flesh creep and not to do anything to enable him to go to Britain – firmly declined to give this promise: 'it would not be right for the government to commit itself to any particular course of action or decision on the basis of hypothetical circumstances'.[56]

Banda's attitude to Chipembere going to Britain did not soften, indeed it hardened, and Cole discussed with the American ambassador – who thought Banda was enjoying 'having Britain on the hook' – why this should be so. They thought Banda's reference to Chipembere leaving the USA in a recent speech may have been designed to test public reaction, and the reaction from party leaders had been strong. In Cole's view, 'many of his Ministers and senior supporters [were] literally terrified by the thought of Chipembere's return to Malawi and would become greatly excited by his renewed appearance and activity anywhere, and perhaps particularly in Britain'. He thought that while Banda was not afraid of Chipembere, he did see him as 'the one potentially serious contender for power'.[57]

Cole was sufficiently concerned about the possibility of deteriorating relations between Britain and Malawi that he called on Banda once more and repeated that, in view of his anxieties, Britain had examined the matter again but had concluded that they had no option under the law to alter their position.

> If, therefore, Chipembere applied to enter Britain and satisfied necessary conditions there was nothing we could do to exclude him. Banda did not directly deny this but began to fidget in his chair and ... remained distinctly sceptical ... Banda then said that if Chipembere were admitted to Britain, it was imperative that he should not be allowed to indulge in political activity. I explained our difficulties about control. Banda became even more restless and appeared to take note of rather than to accept what I was saying. [He] personally understood our motives but he could give no guarantee that his 'people' would. They 'hated' Chipembere and would regard us as giving refuge to him.[58]

The approach to Bottomley having failed, Chipembere wrote to the Governor-General early in July. It was a 'most unpleasant' letter, threatening that if his extradition were sought, he would immediately subpoena as witnesses all those expatriates from the Governor-General downwards who knew anything about his evacuation to the USA. He presumably did not know how few these were and overlooked the fact that he did not know the identity of some of the more important of them – at least two were known to him only by their pseudonyms. He then said that he needed money for his education in Britain, and although he could easily obtain this by writing for the press, he 'thought it would cause less trouble all round if he obtained it from Government sources'. On Roberts's advice Jones did not to reply to the letter. Roberts hoped that Banda had dropped the idea of extradition, but if he revived it he would warn him of Chipembere's threat publicly to expose Banda's involvement. The Malawi government had no intention of helping Chipembere financially, and he warned Cole that 'if the British government admitted him and did not help him financially they might have much trouble on [their] hands'. Cole thought it unlikely that Britain would submit to this kind of blackmail.[59] It appears that the funds Chipembere claimed were in his bank and expected from friends in the USA were not forthcoming, and he was now verging on desperation about how he would support himself if he were admitted to Britain.

With America, Zambia and Britain – all of which were at the very least reluctant to accept him – now removed from his list of immediate safe havens, Chipembere turned to Tanzania, which was significantly less reluctant, though there is no indication that they were anxious to receive him. He arrived in Dar es Salaam with his wife and family on 29 August 1966 and said he did so because of his 'sense of obligation to his followers' there.[60]

At the time he was preparing to leave the USA, Chipembere formed the Panafrican Democratic Party of Malawi (PDP) 'to lead and strengthen the fight against the unjust and corrupt Government of Hastings Banda'. This is contrary to what the American ambassador had recently told Cole: that Chipembere had informed 'friend and foe' that he was withdrawing from Malawi politics.[61] Shortly after he arrived in Tanzania, he set up the PDP provisional central committee. The committee sent circulars to many Malawians, announcing the formation of 'branches, study groups and study cells' whose meetings were to be 'strictly secret'.[62]

Banda attempted to counter the effect of these circulars by ordering that they be handed in to the police immediately anyone received them. Failure to do this would result in prison sentences. He also 'banned all mention of the name Chipembere'.[63] He claimed that Chipembere was staying in Dar es Salaam at a minister's house, where he worked, usually at night, plotting to continue his campaign against the doctor and his government by sending circular letters, over the name of Gloria Phiri, the assistant secretary-general of the Panafrican Democratic Party, operating underground in the central region of Malawi.[64] It was in one such circular that the PDP railed against Banda's behaviour after Chisiza's death. The doctor claimed that Chipembere had no such organization in Lilongwe and that Gloria Phiri was 'a fictitious individual'.

What has happened is this, that ... when Chipembere [came to Dar es

The Fate of the Ministers · 289

Salaam] he said, give me only four months, I will organise people. They will go to Malawi, and after four months the whole of Malawi will be in a mess because of my agents that I have sent, 10–15 men who have been in Tanganyika for so many years, who will not be suspected, and these people will organise freedom for the people that have sent the letter. Then in four months time there will be riots all over Malawi.[65]

About the middle of March Banda held a press conference at which he produced a woman called Gloria Phiri, but explained that she simply had the same name as that made up by Chipembere. By this time, he said, Chipembere's efforts to organize people in Tanzania had failed and he had now shifted the centre of his operations to Lusaka, trying to organize the people there, though he stayed in Dar es Salaam.[66]

Chipembere spent his early months back in Africa 'travelling all over East and Central Africa to study the problems facing his fellow-Malawians in exile and to offer them assistance.'[67] But his return to Africa was not a success, as he soon realized. Nyerere was attempting a rapprochement with Banda, and the effect of this may have been to make Chipembere less welcome in Tanzania. Maybe, also, the change from living in the USA was too great to be comfortable, or perhaps his financial circumstances were too constrained. Most likely, he found that he was simply one of a number of exiles, many of whom wished to return to Malawi; that not all of them were inclined to accept his leadership – we have seen how there were two groups, one following Chisiza and the other Chipembere, while Chirwa, who also wanted to leave Tanzania, was a law unto himself; that even in Dar es Salaam he was not beyond Banda's grasp; and that continuing Malawi political activity in Tanzania was a forlorn and probably pointless prospect. Before Chipembere had left the USA, Surtee, the Speaker of the Malawi parliament and a man usually well informed about MCP feelings, said he would much prefer Chipembere to go to Tanzania rather than London: 'Chipembere was a man who had always made big promises. If he went to Tanzania he might temporarily raise rebel morale but he would soon find that he could accomplish nothing and would be cut down to size.'[68] It may well be that Chipembere was finding Surtee's assessment correct.

For whatever reason, after only three months in the country, Chipembere began to add Tanzania to the America, Zambia and Britain list of closed doors. Only one prospect remained: Malawi itself. To prefer returning to Malawi rather than remaining where he was suggests that he was quite desperate about staying in Tanzania. He first approached the Canadian high commissioner and said he wished to return to Malawi. 'Chipembere spoke of the arms and advice being pressed upon the Malawi exiles and virtually threatened that if Dr Banda would not have him back amicably, he would start a military campaign to take over Malawi.' Next, when the Canadian high commissioner pointed out that his country did not have a resident representative in Malawi, Chipembere asked the British high commissioner in Dar es Salaam if he would see if the high commissioner in Zomba 'might be authorised to enquire of Dr Banda whether he would be willing to permit Chipembere and others to return to Malawi and cooperate with the Government'.

> Chipembere said that he had no mandate from other former ministers, who were not aware he was making this approach, but that he believed he enjoyed sufficient authority among the exiles to be able to expect support. He would expect most of the exiles in Tanzania to return to Malawi if they could safely do so. Chirwa was almost certainly the exception.

He repeated the threat of a military campaign. The British high commissioner said he was willing to ask if British official channels could be used for this 'peace feeler' but he could not possibly act as a channel for threats or an ultimatum.[69]

The British government quickly rejected Chipembere's request. They thought it would be unwise to mediate between him and Banda. The doctor was so set against Chipembere that he would accept 'nothing short of abject surrender', and Chipembere's reference to military action did not 'appear conducive to framing any approach conciliatory enough to do other than enrage Banda'. Indeed they felt that Banda's wrath would also be directed against Britain. They wondered if they should tell Banda about the approach, but decided against it, fearing he might be unable to resist the temptation to refer to it publicly.[70]

A little later, early in February 1967, Chipembere asked Judith, Lady Listowel, who was visiting Dar es Salaam, to see him.[71] He telephoned her while she was having a drink with the Australian high commissioner one evening and asked her to go round to the nearby house where he was staying. This she did almost immediately, and Chipembere, revealing the truly desperate nature of the position in which he found himself, told her:

> I am finished and useless. I can accomplish nothing, am unemployed, receiving a small pittance from the Tanzanian Government. I am not allowed to undertake any political activity, nor to see anyone, that is why your visit to me has to be clandestine. We mishandled the situation in 1964; Yatuta Chisiza and not Chiume was the determined ring leader and made all six of us make a pact that we should all either stay in Government or leave it together. I now bitterly regret the decision. There is only one man I can trust to help me and that is Sir Glyn Jones. Please tell

him to help me. I do not wish to crawl back to Dr. Banda but I am desperate.

On 18 February 1967, Jones arrived in Malawi on his way to Lesotho and was told by Lomax that Chipembere was trying to get in touch with him, that Lady Listowel was the go-between, and that she had seen Chipembere recently and was keen to meet Jones urgently. The following day, when Banda met Jones, he said he was aware that Lady Listowel wanted to see Jones and convey a message from Chipembere. He agreed that Jones should meet her and find out what she had to say. The next day, 20 February, Jones had lunch with Roberts, who was also entertaining Lady Listowel. After lunch she and Jones had a private meeting in which she told him of her meeting with Chipembere and of his request. Jones discussed with Lomax what she had said and then he went to see Banda again.

> Dr. Banda said that he would be glad if I would try and meet Chipembere and probably the best place for the meeting would be Nairobi. He said he would be prepared to consider forgiving Chipembere if the following conditions were observed by him: a) He must write a statement in his own hand and sign it. b) The statement must show that he is finished as a political opponent of Malawi. c) It must state his regret at his former rebellious activities and that he must recant. d) It must state that he supports the President of Malawi and the policy of the Malawi Congress Party. e) That he will never again intrigue against the President and Government of Malawi.

Later, Roberts and Lomax met with Jones and agreed that he should visit Nairobi, after he had finished his business in Lesotho. Lomax would make the arrangements to get Chipembere there. After the meeting, Jones would return to Malawi to report to Banda what had transpired. He then went off to Lesotho and made arrangements to fly on to Nairobi. While he was staying in Johannesburg overnight on 9 March, however, Roberts rang him to say that they had been unable to contact Chipembere and he consequently asked if Jones would go to Malawi instead of Kenya.

Jones arrived in Zomba on 10 March, and the following day Lomax received a message from Chipembere saying he did not wish to meet anyone from Malawi and would not go to Nairobi. Lomax suspected this was Chipembere's answer to a message he had sent asking him to meet him, Lomax, in Nairobi, which had been sent before it had been arranged for Jones to meet him there. Lomax felt that Chipembere had not received the subsequent letter about Jones's visit. When they saw Banda he seemed disappointed and felt they had made a tactical error in sending a message through Lomax because this would make him unduly suspicious. Privately, Jones did not agree, because he had had other dealings with Chipembere through 'the Lomax channel'. They decided to make no further approach to Chipembere but wait and see if he sent another message – he did not.

It is virtually certain that had Chipembere returned, or otherwise placed himself within the doctor's reach – even giving the assurances Banda sought – he would have been arrested, tried and hanged in public. The countess's efforts on his behalf would have done him no favour: quite the contrary. It appears, however, that her talkativeness frightened Chipembere off, and in that respect she rendered him a considerable service, albeit inadvertently. It is surprising that Jones, who must have known that arrest, trial and public execution would almost certainly be the outcome, was still prepared to facilitate Chipembere's return. He was, of course, extremely keen that some reconciliation should take place between Banda and at least some of his former ministers in order to counter the criticism that his governorship had failed to produce a coherent political leadership team that could survive more than a week or so of independence.

A close American friend, Gerry Bender, said of Chipembere's stay in East Africa:

> He lived in Tanzania for three years, primarily teaching school at Kivukoni College. He worked closely with other exile leaders and among the Malawian refugees. He particularly hoped to channel the latter's energies and frustrations away from dreams of returning with arms to Malawi – which he knew would be futile – into preparing themselves to take over the government some day. He also tried fervently to keep the exiles from directing their energies against each other.[72]

Given the existence of rival groups – Washington, Saigon and others – and of rival parties – Chipembere's PDP, Chirwa's MAFREMO, Chiume's CSR and others – Chipembere's fervent attempts to prevent his fellows' energies being directed against each other do not seem to have been blessed with conspicuous success. Also, his hope to divert his fellow refugees from an armed return to Malawi conflicts with his threats to the Canadian and British high commissioners in Dar es Salaam that if Banda would not accept his return peacefully, he would start a military campaign. Perhaps this was an example of Surtee's contention that 'Chipembere was a man who had always made big promises' – and threats.

Chipembere knew, when he went to Tanzania, that he was incurring the risk of assassination 'because Banda had sworn to have him killed'. Bender claimed that the threat was a real one and three attempts were made on his life while he was in Tanzania. Edwardo Mondlane, leader of the Mozambique nationalists, also in exile in Tanzania, warned him, 'if they ever get me, you must leave here because they will get you too'. Consequently, shortly after Mondlane was assassinated in 1969 by a bomb at his house – either by the Portuguese secret police or by fellow nationalists – Chipembere wrote to ask if the University of California at Los Angeles would have him back after the interruption to his studies. 'There was no question about that at [the university] because all the faculty had been very impressed with his performance as a student and with him as a human being.' It was also the case that Chipembere was not well in Tanzania. His diabetes became worse and on at least one occasion Chiume had to arrange to rush him to hospital in a taxi.[73]

Just before he left for the USA in June 1969 – probably with Banda's agreement[74] – Chipembere was interviewed by David Martin, a journalist. He found that Chipembere was downcast and had lost a good deal of weight. He hoped to leave Tanzania and go to America to teach, but the Americans – officials, presumably, rather than academics – were 'somewhat less than enthusiastic' about it and were requiring him to give certain guarantees, probably of good behaviour. Martin added that Chiume was still the militant one and was trying to maintain the enthusiasm of the rebels, although he was beginning to realize that the cause was lost.[75]

Having returned to Calfornia, Chipembere registered for a doctoral programme, with his thesis subject essentially being his own life story. To support himself and his family he also undertook some teaching. It was hard work:

> Once back at Los Angeles he was determined to finish his Ph.D., despite the fact that it required him fitting it in between five-hour bus trips, teaching three and four classes a quarter ... attending classes at UCLA then later writing his thesis, and trying to be a good father to seven growing children.[76]

A year or so after Chipembere's return to Los Angeles, Earl Phillips, head of the history department at California State University, Los Angeles, persuaded his university that getting Chipembere on their staff would be a significant coup, since he was 'a major African political figure who could one day become President of Malawi'. The normal national advertising of the post was dispensed with and Chipembere was appointed lecturer in history. At the time he 'was penniless and in dire straits'. He was grateful for the appointment and turned out to be 'an exceptionally conscientious and efficient lecturer, preparing himself thoroughly and – the only person known to [Phillips] to do so – rewriting his lectures each time he delivered them. He was a very good teacher and his assessment ratings by his students were high.'[77] Another colleague added: 'if you talk to any of his students they will confirm that he really was very successful'.[78]

He did not feel entirely safe, even in California. He was habitually driven by other people because he would not drive a car himself. Although this was attributed to his lack of familiarity with traffic conditions in America, it is more likely that his fear of accidents arose from the fate of former Malawian colleagues who had died in car crashes, not all of which appeared accidental.

On 1 February 1971, Chipembere – now aged forty-one – spoke at a California Institute of Technology seminar.[79] His presentation, six years after leaving Malawi, is important for a number of reasons. His health was now much better than it had been for several years, he felt comparatively safe in California and these, together with having time to ponder the past in peaceful surroundings, enabled him to reflect on the cabinet crisis, on his and his colleagues' disagreements with Banda, and on Banda himself. He was one of a limited number of people who could speak on these matters from personal experience. He spoke mainly about Malawi's external relations, one of the major bones of contention in 1964. He examined the uniqueness of Banda's foreign policies, the reasons for them and why, in his view, they were not valid. He gave Banda's views and his own comments on them. He believed that Banda pushed his policies further than was necessary to overcome the inherent difficulties of the country's geographical position. He adopted a restrained and balanced approach to the difficulties Banda encountered. He welcomed the opportunity to 'put across [his] point of view in the Malawi controversy'. This was important to him and a matter that bothered him for the rest of his life. He had been keen that Jones should be told his side of the story, and that Ross should make his case known to the international media. Most importantly, one might see in what he said at this seminar an attempt to make clear what his own policies would be were he to take over one day.

He started his talk by showing how unusual, and often unique – differing fundamentally from the policies of other black African countries – Malawi was in respect of its foreign policies. He gave as examples the country's diplomatic relations, especially with South Africa, Portugal and Rhodesia. Banda declared that he did not intend to implement OAU and UN resolutions because they did not take reality into account. For some time after independence the standing instruction to Malawi's representatives at the UN was that unless they received explicit contrary instructions they should speak and vote the same way as the British delegate. He consistently took a pro-Western line, often being 'more western than the west'. It was the case that Banda himself had said that although 'by culture, race, origin and background I am an African ... by education I belong to the West. I admire the Europeans in the West.'[80] The army and police had the same heads as in colonial times. 'His closest adviser is Bryan Roberts, a British lawyer who ... is now almost the vice-president of the country: very powerful indeed.' British officials were still in post in large numbers and were the most powerful officials.

Chipembere then went on to give the reasons normally advanced to explain this state of affairs.[81] First, 'Malawi, being near to South Africa, has to be careful about its relations with that country. Certainly it must avoid getting into any hostile relationship.' The argument was that South Africa was strong militarily, and Malawi could not afford to antagonize its powerful neighbour. In any attack by South Africa on black African states Malawi was likely to be one of the first victims and would come off badly. Second, the country was landlocked, needed access to the sea via Portuguese territory, and consequently had to stay on good terms with the Portuguese. Third, Malawi's poverty compelled many people to work in South Africa and Rhodesia; their repatriation, unemployed, would cause political instability in the country.[82] It followed that Malawi had to maintain good relations with South Africa and Rhodesia. Fourth, Banda's policies sprung out of his realism and awareness of the country's lack of money. This induced him to tap any source of funds – even to go to the devil, as he put it – to develop the country and raise the standard of living, and not bring political considerations into the matter. Chipembere was putting Banda's policy stance fairly.

The realism alleged, and the ignoring of politics in seeking aid did not, in Chipembere's view, stand up to examination, since Banda consistently rejected Communist aid because he did not accept the political philosophy of the Eastern Bloc. Chipembere rejected as invalid the view that South Africa was too strong, because one needed to take a stand against oppressive regimes. The South African government had not so far demanded a political alliance for the flow to continue and it was recognized by them to be to their advantage – immigrant labour was cheaper, more compliant and skilled, and it undermined the indigenous Africans. He believed it was not necessary for Malawi to become a political ally or puppet of South Africa for Malawians to continue to emigrate for employment. Certainly, there was no need to establish diplomatic relations and to become such a great friend of South Africa, and appear an enemy of the rest of black Africa. He pointed out that Zambia traded with South Africa but took a stand against its policies. All he and his colleagues had asked Banda to do was to take a similar stand while continuing to trade, and avoid antagonizing South Africa on other matters, since their position was a difficult one. The OAU recognized this, but Banda 'went beyond what was really necessary'.

Concerning Malawi's landlocked location, he said, 'this is a delicate position which we also recognise, but again it is a matter of degree. Our recognition does not go so far as to say because we are landlocked therefore we must enslave ourselves [and] become a kind of political prisoner of the Portuguese.' Provided Malawi refrained from antagonizing the Portuguese in other respects, it could continue to pass traffic through the country to the sea without becoming an ally of the Portuguese and becoming a 'kind of leper, ostracised by the rest of Africa'.

He then looked for the reasons why Banda went further than he need have gone – a point he repeatedly made. There were fundamental traits in the doctor, and factors in his background, that accounted for this.

> Firstly, Dr. Banda is a very keen reader and a very great admirer of the mediaeval and late mediaeval kings and rulers and dictators of Europe ... People who were dictators, people who succeeded in building their nations at the expense of their neighbours, people who acquired territory and power by using various masterstrokes of diplomacy, some of them foul, others fair ... he speaks not only in great admiration of them but also reads about them extensively. One can see in some of his deeds he modelled himself on these people. This explains his attitude towards the Portuguese in the east. It is true ... that we need a passage to the ocean, but Dr. Banda feels that Malawi is too small ... He had told us many times [in Gwelo] that Malawi is too small. Small countries ... suffer a lot of disadvantages, the bullying, they are pushed around and so on. In early 1963 he called me and a friend of mine [and said] 'I pledge myself to work to strive to ensure that Malawi shall not only expand in size but that she shall have a window to the sea as Peter the Great did for Russia'.

In respect of this last point, in 1963 Banda asked Chiume and Chipembere to accompany him to Mozambique, where he was invited to a dinner where Banda was to be offered the northern part of Mozambique, including the port of Nacala, on condition that he prevent Frelimo incursions into Mozambique. Chipembere and Chiume refused to go, on pan-African grounds, and Banda took Aleke Banda and another MCP official instead.[83] It was probably at this meeting that 'the territorial exchange agreement [was] signed between Malawi and Portugal [which gave] the right of access to the Indian Ocean in exchange for the right to use Malawi territory for military manoeuvres'.[84]

Chipembere next dealt with what he saw as another of Banda's traits: his 'great pride and sensitiveness'. Banda was a proud man and one had to be careful how one handled him. He and the other former ministers thought that one of Banda's basic reasons for turning away from black Africa towards South Africa was a feeling that Africa had not accorded him the 'respect, prestige and hero-worship' that he had expected and thought was due to him. Chipembere illustrated his point by reference

The Fate of the Ministers · 297

to the All Africa Peoples conference in Accra in December 1958, less than six months after Banda's return to Nyasaland.

> He didn't perform very well in his speech [and] he came back very bitter, very bitter, and ... in the years that followed one can see signs that he was looking to the south because Africa did not offer him enough prestige, glory and so on. He had come on the pan-African scene with a lot of acclaim because of his martyrdom, his suffering and the great publicity he had received throughout the world and he had expected that sort of acclaim to endure. But then it wasn't justified by his performances at Pan-African conferences where there were more professional politicians.

Cole had earlier attributed Banda's attitudes, especially his foreign policies, to 'his own personality, his excessive "realism", his conservatism, his arrogant delight in being "odd man out", and his relative lack of any profound emotional feeling on the racial problem'. It is unlikely that Chipembere would have disagreed with this assessment.[85]

Chipembere's address to this February 1971 seminar is revealing. He was careful to be fair to Banda, sympathizing with his difficulties, though not accepting his solutions, and trying to explain what it was about Banda and his background that made him the sort of man he was. In this way, presumably, he was attempting not to alienate those in Malawi who supported the doctor. It was a thoughtful presentation in which he indicated how, should the time come, he would approach governing Malawi. Banda was already a septuagenarian and Chipembere was content to bide his time, studying and teaching at an American university until the presidency became vacant and he was in a position to return home and actively resume a political career.

He never lessened his concern for the people of Malawi, especially those who suffered because of being his followers. Nearly three years after his seminar, he wrote to Jones in England, saying that a few weeks earlier the Malawi Traditional Court had sentenced to death twenty-six people who had been convicted of murdering Mrs Changwa during the February 1965 attack on Fort Johnston.[86] The sentences of some of these had been commuted, but eight were to be hanged. He did not wish to go into the merits of the case, but continued:

> It is enough to say that the uncertainties of the act are such that to this day I too do not know who killed Mrs Changwa. Any killing was contrary to my instructions and ... I still believe that some people with old scores to settle took advantage of the confusion and committed the act.

The point Chipembere wanted to make was that practically all the twenty-six men had been in detention for eight years or more, and it was inhuman to order the execution of any of them 'after such a long ordeal'.

He thought that the secrecy in which the trial had been shrouded, especially 'the clamping down on any press leakages to the outside world, indicated that there was some recognition of the damage which could be done to Banda's name'. Since the Fort Johnston district was now peaceful and stable, retribution was unneccessary. The executions would 'revive old grudges and recriminations and cause a revival of fighting and killing'. He thought Banda was taking great risks and would destroy the effects of his own success. 'It could signal the return of turmoil in the country.' He asked Jones to use his influence on Banda to try to have the decision to execute the convicted men reversed. It is unlikely that Jones did so, or that he would have been successful had he tried.

Chipembere died in the USA at 7.30 p.m. on 24 September 1975.[87] Bender, in paying tribute to him, wrote:

> He had lost a long battle with diabetes and cirrhosis of the liver – the latter disease a bitter irony for this puritanical man who never drank.[88] He left his wife, seven children, a brother in the States, five sisters in East Africa, a brother in a Malawian prison who lay paralysed on one side of his body and unable to speak after ten years of torture, parents in Dar es Salaam who were solely dependent on Chip's aid, and thousands of followers in Tanzania.[89]

Bender added that Chipembere was a fighter to the very end. Only a few hours after coming out of a week-long coma, 'attached to five machines and barely able to talk', he insisted that he was coming out of hospital the following day and that Bender's car should be ready for him. When his friends remonstrated, he compromised by saying that he would delay his leaving until the evening rather than the morning of the next day. Three days later he died.[90]

Chiume – whose survival through all the ups and downs of his career owed much to his being keenly and eternally suspicious – thought there might be a sinister explanation of Chipembere's death:

> When Chipembere was in Los Angeles, the Malawi government sent over 19 Young Pioneers for education. Chipembere, who was both a member of staff and a student there, befriended them. It is possible that one or more of these Young Pioneers brought about Chipembere's death by poisoning him and sending him into the long coma after which he soon died – at the age of 45, the minimum age under the Malawi constitution at which a person may become president of the republic.[91]

With the death of Chipembere – always the most significant danger to Banda – the last realistic threat to the doctor from his former ministers disappeared.

CHAPTER 11

The Ministers' Revolt and Its Legacy

THE ministers' revolt in 1964 brought into the open two closely linked aspects of political life in Malawi that had existed for some time but had been largely hidden from the public gaze: opposition to Banda, and the extent of his strongly authoritarian make-up. They were substantially concealed until shortly after independence because neither the doctor nor his ministers wished to expose rifts and defects that would jeopardize the achievement of rapid constitutional advance to self-government, secession and independence. In deciding when to take the final step of granting independence to its colonies, the British government looked for two principal factors.

First, they wished to be reasonably sure that the colony was sufficiently stable financially and economically to stand a fair chance of surviving on its own without too long a period of support from Britain. This was a major consideration in Britain's wish that Nyasaland should remain in a federation that would give that stability. When this became politically impossible, Britain was prepared to supply the necessary finance, provided it was on a diminishing scale and was subject to strict economies in Nyasaland government expenditure.

The British insistence on economies, which Banda personally accepted and did his best to implement, provided some of the main bones of contention between him and his ministers. Internally, these included effecting economies in the African civil service, and introducing hospital charges. They also included filling top public service posts with expatriate officials rather than Malawians, whom Banda did not trust to be sufficiently incorruptible as not to deter inward investment. They included, too, the wide range of his own portfolios to give confidence to investors that the key ministries were being properly controlled. Externally, they included the accommodation with Portugal through whose Mozambique territory the continued passage of Malawi's external trade was essential, and the accommodation with South Africa and Southern Rhodesia, where the earnings and savings of migrant workers contributed to Malawi's own economy. Having first sought, and secured, the political kingdom, Banda acknowledged that his government could not afford to continue to ignore its economy. Here, to a large extent, especially after Dunduzu Chisiza's death, Banda was alone, unable to rely on his lieutenants to accept – and to help him impress upon the people – the economic realities of their situation. Indeed, as Roberts pointed out, Banda alone among Congress leaders, publicly warned of the difficulties ahead rather than making extravagant and ill-considered promises.[1]

Second, Britain was reluctant to grant independence until a national leader had emerged with sufficient following to enable the country to start its life as a sovereign state with a fair degree of political stability. There was little difficulty over Nyasaland meeting this particular requirement – not that Banda emerged so much as exploded on to the political scene. In the case of this factor, Banda could readily rely on his lieutenants to help him. It was they who brought him back to Nyasaland, deliberately built him up as a messiah and granted him sweeping autocratic powers to control Congress. They, too, tolerated and in some cases stimulated the violence and intimidation that expunged opposition parties and ensured massive support for him at the polls in 1961 and a total absence of contest for parliamentary seats in 1964. Save for a limited exception led by Dunduzu Chisiza in 1962, they did not seek to demonstrate anything other than complete unity behind Banda. The practical possibility of a pre-independence challenge to dent his absolute supremacy, remote as it might have been, was removed after Chisiza's death and during Chipembere's incarceration, though Chiume, Bwanausi and Chipembere seriously contemplated it a few months before independence. Banda's strategy of divide and rule, through tolerating, fostering and encouraging friction between his ministers, significantly lessened the possibility that any of them would challenge him – and thereby expose themselves to their colleagues' intrigue and to Banda's wrath – let alone all join in a united front against him. It may have been to avoid still further the possibility of a pre-independence challenge – or any hint of one – that Banda so adamantly refused to have a constitutional conference, at which some of his lieutenants would be delegates, to agree on independence.

Banda also derived much support from the Governor, Jones, in becoming the undisputed and unchallenged leader of the Nyasaland Africans. The origin of this support was Macleod's acceptance of the doctor as their leader, and the sole person with whom he would deal, long before that leadership was tested in an election. To this acceptance was linked Macleod's appointment of Jones as Chief Secretary and then Governor. Jones was a great admirer of Macleod, believing him to be a future prime minister of Great Britain, and could be relied upon to follow the Colonial Secretary's lead, virtually without question. He was convinced that Banda was not simply far and away the best, but indeed the only, person able to bring about that to which he was devoted: the well-being and best interests of the African population. No other Malawian came anywhere near being able to do this. Everything, in his view, depended upon having Banda in supreme authority, and he did all he could to strengthen and maintain him in that position, his undoubted awareness of the doctor's strongly dictatorial attitudes, and of the politically motivated atrocities, violence and lawlessness which occurred under his leadership notwithstanding.

Once Banda had successfully deployed the Gwelo card to secure the release of the hard-core detainees, he could – and did successfully – use it whenever there was the possibility that Jones might not automatically accede, or recommend that Britain accede, to his wishes. This state of affairs was established within a few days of Jones becoming Acting Governor in August 1960, and was firmly in position by the time he became Governor in April 1961. There was a short period between December 1963, when Federation was abolished and independence agreed, and July 1964, when the country became independent, during which no one would have believed Banda was serious if he had threatened to return to gaol. During this period he replaced the Gwelo card with the threat of unilaterally declaring independence.[2]

Thus, at the time of independence, the ministers found themselves handicapped by both factors on which the British government insisted. They had, by ignoring or distorting the financial and economic realities, raised public expectations to a high and unfulfillable level. The people now looked to them to make a quick delivery on their promises. Their only hope of doing this and avoiding strong criticism from the masses was to persuade Banda to change his mind on the Skinner report, the hospital charges, the slow rate of Africanization and Malawi's relations with white regimes in southern Africa. They wished to avoid facing the people on these issues because only one of them, Chipembere – whose oratorical powers of rousing his audiences and winning them over to his view were unsurpassed – had a major power base in the country, while the others could less well afford to risk alienating their constituents.

They were in an even greater dilemma over the second factor, Banda's position of supreme authority and power as head of the party and of government, for it was they who had deliberately, diligently and maybe indelibly, put him there, strongly aided by Jones, now the Governor-General. It is possible that when they invited him to return to Nyasaland in 1958, they intended from the outset that he should be the unchallenged leader only until he had achieved secession and independence, and that thereafter he should play a simply symbolic role while they ran the government and exercised the real power. Banda's age – twice most of theirs in 1958 – had two advantages for them. It brought maturity to the leadership in the struggle for secession and independence and it opened up the possibility that he would not wish to hold on to power thereafter or could easily be persuaded to relinquish it. None of the principal lieutenants was the sort of man voluntarily to forgo real power permanently.

Why did the ministers revolt when they did? It is clear that they did not do so earlier because of the need publicly to preserve party unity until independence was achieved and because the factions at the top of the party rendered individuals within each faction vulnerable. The ministers lessened this potential by waiting until all the lieutenants were members of the cabinet, including the former parliamentary secretaries, Chirwa, Chisiza and Tembo. Had some of these not been in the cabinet, and thereby not in a position formally to challenge the prime minister, the chances of his being able to drive a wedge between, for example, the cabinet ministers and those keen to become cabinet ministers – which is precisely what he did in September 1964 – would have been significantly greater.

The ministers delayed just long enough for them all to recognize that only by uniting could they hope to provide a front against which Banda's autocratic attitudes and his divide-and-rule strategy would not prevail. When the doctor dropped Msonthi from the cabinet immediately after independence, his colleagues believed he was being used as a guinea pig to test their reaction with a view to further dismissals. The detention bill provided the imperative stimulus for unity. Coincidentally, it disposed of the remaining minister, Cameron, who had told Banda two years earlier that he could not automatically rely on his support beyond independence but who recently had told him that he would faithfully serve him as long as he desired in any position that he directed. The bill immediately threatened *all* the ministers. If they delayed taking action any longer, they might themselves fall foul of its provisions. They needed to make a stand, too, before Malawi became a republic and Banda its executive president, with wide Nkrumah-style powers. At the time of independence, Banda intended waiting only a few months before declaring a republic. The prospect was not a distant one. It was imminent.

To secure unity the ministers needed Chiume on their side, despite – and possibly because of – the fact that, at least in the past, they believed him to be Banda's favourite. He, most of all, saw the unity, brought about by the twin threats of the detention bill and the republican proposals, as a marriage of convenience. He stood as great a chance of falling foul of their provisions as any of his colleagues. While he continued in a separate camp, with or without others, the divide-and-rule potential remained. In the case of Chipembere, in spite of the fact that his colleagues at one stage may have been prepared to form a government and leave him out of it, it is unlikely that they deliberately timed their strike to take effect before he returned from Canada so as to leave him out on a limb. He was not the sort of man to take kindly to being left stranded. Indeed, when the going got tough they – or at least Chiume – sought his urgent return to join them. Even when Jones tried to secure a reconciliation meeting, the ministers said they would see Banda only if Chipembere were with them.

The seeds of revolt had been germinating over a long period. Even in June 1958, a month before Banda's return, when Congress delegates visited him in London, they reported that he 'was extremely arrogant, given to impatience and flying off the handle, domineering and would cause trouble'.[3] Chiume was dissatisfied virtually from the time of Banda's return to Nyasaland in July 1958, despite his high standing in the doctor's esteem at that time. By December 1960 he, Chipembere and Bwanausi were sufficiently distrustful of the doctor's attendance at the federal review conference as to tour the country, making speeches whose intemperate nature landed Chipembere, as they almost landed Chiume, in gaol. Their intention was to prepare the people, should this become necessary, for a showdown. There had been criticism of Banda in Karonga district for some time and now there seemed to be a more widespread feeling that, since he had not achieved secession, a more militant leader should be found. A month later, in January 1961, Chiume and Bwanausi felt that Chirwa, at Banda's behest, was deliberately making a poor job of defending Chipembere. In April 1962, Cameron told Jones that Banda's reluctance to press the British government for secession was unpopular with his immediate advisers and was 'causing rumblings among the more extreme of Malawi's rank and file'. The doctor was 'passing through an extremely difficult time' and was 'lonely and vulnerable'.[4] Though the mini-revolt led by Dunduzu Chisiza in July 1962 was against Chiume – and an attempt by Chisiza to take over the informal deputy leadership – it was also an indirect criticism of Banda for not being prepared to do anything about Chiume. In Chisiza's case, he repeatedly emphasized his loyalty to Banda upon whom, he insisted, the country's progress and welfare depended. On the other hand, his was a time-limited undertaking of loyalty, because he told Chibambo he intended to form a new political party after independence.[5] Additionally, he warned Banda that he would not automatically support him after independence, though this may have been confined to withdrawing automatic support if Chiume were still allowed to harm the work of others. Again, one might see in his 4 August 1962 letter to Jones evidence that it was a time-limited loyalty: 'members of the MCP that I know are as loyal to [Banda] as they were on 3 March 1959. They will continue to be so until independence is won.'⁶ These words probably meant that they would not falter so long as Nyasaland was a colony, rather than that the loyalty would cease at independence. Within a short time of his release from prison in January 1963 – as with his release from detention two years earlier – Chipembere took an independent approach to political activism, and demonstrated that Banda either could not, or would not, control him. About the middle of 1963, too, Chipembere and Chiume declined to accompany Banda to Mozambique and made it clear that on pan-African grounds they disapproved of his visit.⁷ Banda believed that while he was away in October 1963, Chiume attempted to take over the leadership of the paramilitary young pioneers. In December 1963 there were signs of a split between Cameron and Banda over the question of a racially based franchise in the proposed independence constitution.⁸ In February 1964, Cameron inadvertently also put himself at odds with Banda over negotiations with the Nyasaland Railways board. The doctor felt that Cameron had gone 'much beyond his brief' and concluded, 'I have now lost faith in Cameron's judgement and discretion though I still respect his integrity.'⁹ In May 1964 Chiume, Chipembere and Bwanausi considered setting up a new political party and opposing Banda at the pre-independence elections. At the independence day garden party in Zomba, ministers moved from group to group, seething with anger and taking few steps to conceal their dissatisfaction with Banda's dictatorial behaviour.

At the time, few outside observers noticed, still less remarked on, even in private, the suppressed signs of ministerial dissent. Indeed, shrewd and experienced observers like Sanger went into print to emphasize that Malawi's 'calm water' seemed to 'stretch ahead out of sight'. Even from within the cabinet, Cameron publicized Malawi's unparalleled unity under Banda, and Phillips wrote that 'under the leadership of the Prime Minister ... the unity of the country is beyond challenge'. It is clear in retrospect, however, that despite the apparent calm water, a storm, potentially of ship-wrecking proportions, could not be far distant. This must have been clear to Banda for some time. He had ample warning of an impending storm of some sort or other. The period of pre-independence restraint, promised him by three of his ministers in 1962, had run out. It is true that of the three, two were no longer in a position to withdraw support – Chisiza was dead and Mkandawire no longer a minister – and the third, Cameron, had recently expressed his personal loyalty. Nevertheless, while no minister other than these three had indicated that they might not invariably support Banda after independence, he may well have suspected that others were like-minded. It is virtually certain that Chibambo, ever his loyal supporter, had told him of Chisiza's intention to form a new party after independence, and although Chisiza was now dead, the doctor would have doubted whether he had intended to act by himself and not in concert with others. For eighteen months before independence, Banda had seen the intelligence digests, which included reports on his colleagues, and he had his own party and personal sources of intelligence. He may long have suspected that his lieutenants' intention in inviting him back to Nyasaland in 1958 was simply to use him to secure secession and independence and thereafter merely to be a figurehead. It would not have escaped his notice that, in his report on the 1959 disturbances, Devlin said that, in calling the doctor back to his homeland, Chipembere was looking for a man with 'a spirit of co-operation', presumably cooperation with the lieutenants.[10] By mid-1962 there was a fairly widespread feeling among expatriate civil servants that after independence Banda, for political or health reasons, might not last long, 'in which event they fear that his place would be taken by either Chipembere or Chiume who are both regarded as being fanatically anti-European'.[11] The view that the doctor – already only a few years short of being a septuagenarian – might not last long after independence was very probably shared by some leading Africans, and some, rather than fearing, hoped this would be the case.

Banda would have been vigilant for signs of trouble. Yet he did nothing to avoid his ministers' discontent spilling over. Indeed, there are indications that he was keen to let the simmering anger and dissatisfaction come to the boil. His speeches in Cairo and particularly at Chileka were, whatever their other intentions, openly defiant of his ministers and in effect were an invitation to them to challenge him. Dropping Msonthi from the cabinet immediately after the independence day celebrations had the effect, as he almost certainly intended, of desperately worrying the other ministers. Elevating three party stalwarts to ministerial rank on 21 July, without discussing it with his cabinet colleagues, was bound to annoy them. Bringing the detention issue to the cabinet on 29 July, with little warning, could be seen as deliberately provocative and designed to bring any continuing criticisms to the surface and to expose more fully the extent of the opposition facing him. Banda's agreement, for the present, not to move forward with the detention proposal, emboldened his colleagues and made them more likely to take their dissatisfaction further. Giving his ministers the impression at the 10 August meeting that he might mend his ways, and allowing four of them to go away on visits to other countries, may have been designed to lull them while he decided on his next steps in bringing matters to a head. It is unlikely that he really intended to change either the scope of his responsibilities or his public demeaning of his colleagues, which were their complaints at that time. His derogatory remarks at Chileka, which were not being uttered for the first time, were not impromptu and accidental: he told Youens he knew what he was doing and seemed surprised that Youens had not straight away realized what he was up to. At this stage, it was reform, rather than resignation, the ministers sought. If he would reform sufficiently in practice to pass power over to them and become simply a figurehead – to be 'Nyererized' and become a puppet as he saw it – there would be no need to force his resignation. Indeed, with his standing both internally and externally, he could be useful to them just as a titular head of government. If they had hoped he would mend his ways during their absence, they were disappointed. Consequently they significantly increased the pressure – and widened the scope of their complaints – at the 26 August cabinet meeting, soon after Chiume, Chisiza and Bwanausi returned from their tour, during which they had been able to discuss their dissatisfaction over Banda and how to deal with him.

In the meantime it is probable that at the 29 July cabinet meeting when Cameron resigned, Banda had sensed the unity and the intention of imminent confrontation, even though the ministers held back at that stage – and Chiume rather more than the others. Then the meeting on 10 August had served to confirm beyond doubt that they were united and bent on challenging him on at least his public belittling of them and his personal retention of several ministries. Consequently, although he may have decided some time previously to bring matters to a head after independence, he now decided to do so speedily while, in the euphoria of independence, he was riding even more high in the public esteem than in the past; while Chipembere was out of the country; while the ministers' unity was still new, untested and possibly fragile; and while the senior ranks of the army and the police were still expatriates upon whose loyalty he could rely. Bringing matters to a head would reveal the full nature and strength of the opposition and enable him to decide how to deal with it. The calm with which he faced the unprecedented personal criticism in the 26 August cabinet meeting was more likely to have been calculated and part of a deliberately moderate reaction than simply his being stunned: one would have expected him, unrehearsed, to fly into a rage. The meeting went on far too long for his moderation to be attributable to his being flabbergasted by his ministers' temerity and audacity: the shock would soon have worn off. There are signs in the cabinet minutes that he went out of his way to make brief points that drew still further criticism from the ministers, as if he were deliberately providing openings for them fully to reveal their hand and go beyond a point from which they could retreat. By this time it is likely that Banda, having assessed the nature and extent of the opposition, had decided on a trial of strength in which he was confident of triumphing and as a result of which he could more readily dispose of the real trouble-makers, whoever they turned out to be.

The 26 August cabinet meeting was not a turning point but simply a further – though large – step in the deteriorating relationships between Banda and his ministers. It was then that the matter of his resigning emerged. The ministers were clear they did not want him to resign. At best this meant that they still believed he would reform his ways, and at worst that they individually had insufficient confidence in any other of their number to take his place. The resignation issue was very short-lived. Banda mentioned the possibility just before 4.30 p.m. when the meeting ended.[12] He sought Jones's opinion early the following evening shortly after 6.15 p.m., and a little later that evening, told his ministers he would not resign. So far as he was concerned, that was an end to it. The evidence is strong that he simply pretended he might resign and that he never genuinely intended or even contemplated doing so, except – and this was later – momentarily before instantaneously being re-appointed. Though by no means in a playful mood, he was playing hard to get, and teasing his ministers by flirting with the idea of resignation and by the bizarre threat to send Chirwa or Chiume to the Governor-General to be made prime minister.

The significant turning point occurred two or three days later, over the following weekend, when the production of the Kuchawe manifesto and the rumours that he had capitulated combined to rile the prime minister mightily. To these were added the anonymous letters of support, the visitors pleading with him not to resign and the reassuring encouragement of the party stalwarts. Shortly, too, Banda considered that he had the additional support of the chiefs and of the people of the Port Herald, Mlanje and Zomba districts. If any one of these was the most important factor in bringing about the turning point, it was the *scandalum magnatum*, the manifesto. Jones consistently and obsessively considered it so, and Banda said it was when he received it that he determined not to give in to his ministers' demands. It was Chirwa's particular misfortune that he was the carrier of the document.

It was probably at this point, too, that Banda decided to handle things himself. Already, he had pointedly not discussed with Jones the explosive detention proposal before placing it on the cabinet agenda; he had not told him about the 10 August meeting; and he had declined to see him after the 26 August cabinet meeting even though asked – just as he did after the first day's debate on the motion of confidence. After his meeting with them on 27 August, he made no arrangements for a further meeting with the ministers – though he did meet them briefly on 2 September – and he made it clear he did not want Jones to intervene. It was obvious to Banda from his meeting with him on 27 August that the Governor-General shared the dissident ministers' criticisms – just as he had done in the Chisiza–Chiume dispute in 1962. Jones was trying to hold the scales evenly between Banda and his ministers. This was a change that would not have escaped Banda's notice. Over the preceding three years, Jones had surprisingly little direct and individual contact with ministers other than Banda, even when he presided over executive council.[13] Up to this point, he had unreservedly supported the doctor's views, whereas now, without withdrawing that support, he was sharing it with the ministers. Banda continued to meet with Jones, usually quite briefly – often for only five or ten minutes – but much of what followed between them may be seen on Banda's part as polite playacting. The important steps thereafter were all taken on Banda's initiative and in most cases without prior discussion with Jones: the repeated changes in the date of the next meeting of parliament; the discussions with colleagues outside the cabinet; the telegram calling Chibambo back from Britain; the intriguing proposal that he should momentarily resign and instantaneously be re-appointed; the plan that Jones should determine the doctor's support among members of parliament; the speed with which this should be done; the idea, which it is true occurred also to Jones, that Banda should call the members to Zomba for an informal meeting; the alteration of the date of that meeting; the decision that Banda himself should not address it; the individual private meetings with members; the proposal that the following day there should be a formal meeting of parliament; having a motion of confidence; dismissing three of the ministers; the timing of those dismissals; and the letter asking Chipembere to stay in the government.

The turning point became a point of no return on 2 September, when Banda told the ministers he would not be 'Nyererized', and walked out on them, and they in their turn concluded that, given the failure to persuade him to reform and the way he had rebuffed them, he should be ousted. The accompanying decision to have Chirwa as prime minister and to leave Chipembere out of the cabinet was ill considered and probably not taken with full seriousness, for Chirwa became despondent rather than elated, was soon made to realize that the constitution did not provide for this sort of take-over, and accepted that a stalemate had been reached. It is extremely unlikely that his colleagues really intended that Chirwa should become their leader. They were content to let him be their spokesman in their dealings with Jones – just as he was selected to deliver the Kuchawe manifesto to Banda – and thereby let him take the blast if things went wrong, but as compared to Chipembere, Chiume and Chisiza, he was a lightweight. His political loyalty had been in doubt after 1953. The colonial government had been uncertain of the need to detain him in March 1959, and his period in detention was the shortest of any of the lieutenants. Chiume had gravely resented his founding of the MCP and had long been convinced of his ambition to become the country's first prime minister. British ministers and officials had concluded in 1959 that he was 'certainly not a political leader'. Banda had been in some doubt as to whether he should be made a parliamentary secretary in 1961. He had been the one African member of the government who had not been involved in Chisiza's bid to oust Chiume in 1962. His personal following in the country, especially when compared with of that Chipembere, was limited. His experience of running a ministry was less than that of any of his colleagues, other than Tembo and Chisiza. He may have been considered somewhat more Western and less African in outlook than many of his colleagues: while the Chisiza brothers and Chiume had been happy to appear in public in a grass skirt or an Nkrumah-style toga, Chirwa had preferred to appear in academic dress; and he revelled in the language and ritual of the legal profession.[14] His fellow ministers may also have doubted his resolve – other than in a personal sense – in the face of acute pressure, as his later breaking of ranks and repeated attempts to make peace with Banda showed.

From this point, 2 September, onwards Banda moved relentlessly towards the *coup de grâce*. He was now determined to hit the ministers hard. He had already restored Msonthi to the cabinet and had conferred ministerial status on the three regional chairmen of the party. He continued to gather support from the party stalwarts and to increase his support in the districts – though probably not in Fort Johnston and in the north. He summoned Chibambo back from Britain. He considered prosecuting the rebels for sedition, and seizing their passports. He refused when Chokani, Chisiza and Msonthi asked to see him. He summarily dismissed Chiume, Chirwa and Bwanausi and without hesitation accepted the resignation of Chisiza, Chokani and Msonthi. Equally readily, he accepted Msonthi's withdrawal of his resignation. Finally, he secured the overwhelming support of members of parliament at the informal meeting, and he eliminated any possible residual wavering at the private meetings that followed. In these meetings he removed all doubt that he would be victorious in his clash with the rebels. This was the *coup de grâce*. The formal meeting of parliament over the following two days was simply a public display and endorsement of the parliamentarians' support: a rubber-stamping.

Ironically, it had been Chiume and Chipembere who had originally exploited Hansard and developed it into a mouthpiece for Congress. Their efforts now redounded to their disadvantage. Being public and reported in Hansard and in the media, the formal meeting made the support for Banda speedily known all over Malawi and helped to increase it in most parts of the country. Internally, too, it warned those relatively few expatriates who had openly supported the rebels, that their continued presence in Malawi was likely to be in jeopardy. Publicizing the outcome of the debate also made it known internationally: it brought forth the British government's pre-drafted and almost sycophantically worded congratulations; it helped show waverers, such as the US government, who was the winner and who were the losers; it impressed on other African countries that Banda's, rather than Chiume's, views on Malawi's external relations and pan-Africanism would prevail; and it persuaded the Chinese to lay off wooing the Malawi government, at least for a while.

Only one uncertainty persisted beyond the turning point, point of no return and *coup de grâce* sequence and into the rubber-stamping phase: Chipembere. Chiume had summoned him to return urgently from Canada and looked upon him as an ally – probably his only real ally in the marriage of convenience. Before the debate started Banda sent Kumtumanji with a letter – written before the first day's debate – asking him to stay in the government. Only to him, throughout the whole of the crisis, did Banda make such a request. Chipembere did not immediately decide. He refused to discuss the matter with Kumtumanji. He tried to meet with Banda, but unsuccessfully. He did meet with the rebels and secured their support in attempting to arrange a reconciliation meeting. His request that the meeting should be held before the start of the second day's debate infuriated Banda, who was now, after the first day's debate, absolutely confident of victory. No longer needing him to help secure that victory, he refused to see Chipembere until after the debate was concluded. This rejection induced Chipembere's immediate resignation.

Although Banda kept only two members of his cabinet – Msonthi, recently reinstated, and Tembo, recently promoted – he did not view all the others in an equal light. In only one case was he consistently adamant about disposing of them: that concerning Chiume. Between 31 August and 25 September Banda indicated to Jones at least six times what his intentions were about the various rebel ministers. In Chiume's case these were, successively, that, having himself momentarily resigned, he would not reappoint Chiume; he 'must go'; 'must go at once'; 'will have to go'; was 'quite unacceptable'; and he 'would never have him back'. With each of the others, Banda's intentions changed, some more than others. In the case of Chipembere, as with Chiume, he would not reappoint him. Then, successively, he 'might keep him'; he 'would keep him'; he 'probably could stay'; after his resignation Chipembere was 'quite unacceptable'; and finally, he 'would probably never have him back'. The third former minister he would not reappoint was Chisiza, but then Banda's views changed rapidly: he 'must go'; he 'would keep him'; he 'will have to go'; he hoped he 'might return one day'; and finally he agreed that Jones should see him to try to arrange a meeting with the prime minister. The doctor also changed his mind several times about Bwanausi. Having himself momentarily resigned, he would reappoint him; he 'would keep him'; he was 'quite unacceptable'; and finally he agreed that Jones should see him to try and arrange a meeting. Although, if he resigned momentarily, he was prepared to reappoint Chirwa, Banda was for some time consistent about getting rid of him: he would 'have to go at once'; he would 'have to go'; he was 'quite unacceptable'; but finally he said he 'would have him back but on his own terms'. Of Chokani he said that, having momentarily resigned, he would reappoint him, and he later agreed that Jones should see him to arrange a meeting: there was no change of mind over him. There were three ministers whom Banda would not reappoint following his proposed momentary resignation: Chiume, Chipembere and Chisiza. At that stage he was prepared to reappoint all the others. Later, after the debate in parliament, Chiume, Chipembere, Bwanausi and Chirwa were placed in the 'quite unacceptable' category, but not Chisiza, who Banda hoped might return some day, nor Chokani, whom he did not mention.

None of those involved – the ex-ministers, except Chokani and Bwanausi; Jones; and Banda – was prepared to let matters rest where parliament's unanimous vote of confidence left them.

Chiume, Chisiza, Chirwa and Chipembere returned to their constituencies, where, if anywhere, they might hope to secure or increase support for their position. What the first three of these – all from the north – planned to do, even if they secured constituency support and believed it to be sufficiently substantial to help them, is unclear. In Chipembere's case it is clearer. He commanded considerable support in the southern region and among civil servants generally, and he may have believed this support would be sufficient for him to re-challenge Banda or persuade him to open negotiations.

Jones, too, was not content to leave matters as they were. He tried to secure a reconciliation meeting between Banda and the former ministers so that at least some could return to the government. Although both the prime minister and his former colleagues acquiesced in his efforts to bring them together, it is likely that none of them was doing more than simply going along with him. Banda may have been looking beyond just the press when, at the close of the debate in parliament, he said, 'This is a family affair in which no outsider must try to meddle.'[15] Chipembere was the key. His colleagues refused to see Banda without him and he would not see Banda unless they were all present. This was their position when they discussed with Jones a possible meeting, but it is unlikely that they ever seriously sought a reconciliation, except possibly Chokani – and Chirwa, who was not party to these particular moves and whose later steps were directed to personal reconciliation. By this time they knew they stood absolutely no chance of Banda mending his ways or of their compelling his resignation. Their implausible excuses for Chipembere not attending Jones's meetings, and their joining Chipembere in continued criticism of Banda at the cocktail party immediately thereafter, support the view that they were disingenuous about a reconciliation. Had he genuinely been seeking reconciliation, Chipembere would have gone to see Jones, as did all his colleagues except Chiume. Instead, he dodged the arranged meetings and insisted on waiting a fortnight before they would meet Banda. Far from going out of his way to see the Governor-General – although subsequently they were in contact by telephone and letter – Chipembere never again saw Jones, whom he considered by this time to be ineffectual, after their brief meeting during the evening before he resigned.

Banda, also, did not let matters rest. He took early steps to appoint party stalwarts to fill the places vacated by the rebels, and to support them by appointing nine new parliamentary secretaries. Despite being the clear winner in parliament, like his former colleagues he appealed to the constituencies, or at least some of them. Unlike them, he was able to use the massive resources of the MCP to ensure support when addressing huge audiences at Palombe and Ngabu and then touring the northern and central regions. He wooed international opinion by flying the diplomatic corps to Lilongwe and entertaining them there. He refused to see any of the ex-ministers until he had completed this tour. He suspended them from the MCP. He took a number of precautionary steps to prevent them taking advantage of his absence from the south. He made Jones responsible for law and order and instructed him that the police were to shoot, if necessary to kill, in order to maintain the peace. He banned public meetings unless they had police permission. It is likely, too, that he gave instructions, either implicitly or expressly, that the LMY was to help in preventing illegal meetings and in suppressing demonstrations of support for the rebels, especially of Chipembere by the civil servants in Zomba. He told his youth leaguers that they knew what to do about Chirwa. Finally, he introduced regulations to confine the movement of persons and had a restriction order promptly served on Chipembere.

These moves taken by Banda, together with the failure of the steps taken by Jones to secure a reconciliation meeting, persuaded all the ex-ministers to flee the country – except Chipembere, who was restricted to his home village area. Their solidarity pact was at an end. Bwanausi and Chokani left unmolested for Zambia. Chiume and Chisiza were fortunate narrowly to escape relatively unharmed across the northern border into Tanzania. Chirwa, who took the early precaution of sending his wife to Britain, put up with a great deal before also realizing that his overtures were fruitless, that his life was in danger and that he too should flee the country for Tanzania: his car was burned out, he walked ten miles through the bush at night to seek refuge at Government House, he was

The Ministers' Revolt and Its Legacy · 313

severely beaten and humiliated when he visited Banda and asked to be given a judicial appointment and he had an uncomfortable escape hidden in the engine room of a boat. Banda was content to have the former ministers leave the country – and be out of his way – and indeed he approved their being allowed to leave, though he did not mind them being intimidated or beaten in the process. Cameron, fearful for the safety of his family and himself, also fled the country. Having already removed all the dissident ministers politically, Banda had succeeded by early November in removing them physically from Malawi – all except Chipembere.

It took some time for Chipembere to be removed from the country. The restriction regulations confined him to the Malindi area, and the detention legislation drove him into hiding. Although his attempted *coup d'état* was a failure, it, and the inability of the security forces to track him down quickly, convinced Banda that he was better out of the way. Consequently, while he immediately rejected an amnesty in exchange for Chipembere ending his guerrilla activities, he equally quickly agreed to his request to leave Malawi for the USA. To have agreed to an amnesty would have deprived him of the opportunity to wreak vengeance on Chipembere and his followers and fully teach them the lesson he intended they should never forget. Banda needed to be rid of him because he was the only significant threat remaining in Malawi, and furthermore the population of a large part of the southern region, and many civil servants, were in sympathy with him. He was the only continuing exception to Banda's victory against the ministers' revolt. Get rid of him and he would have got rid of *all* the rebel ministers and his victory would be, or would be made to appear, complete and the opposition utterly routed. Until Chipembere was out of the country, the cabinet crisis could not be considered to have come to an end. Banda would have preferred to have him hunted down, captured and killed, but since his security forces were not making enough progress towards achieving this, he seized the opportunity presented by Chipembere's request to leave the country.

Chipembere could fairly easily have joined the other former ministers in Tanzania or in Zambia, but he would have felt only slightly more safe from Banda there than in the forests and mountains east of Fort Johnston. His attempted coup had failed, his followers were being ruthlessly victimized and punished. Sooner or later his troops would lose faith in him and refuse to put up with the continued harassment of their relatives and with the hardship that living in, and being hunted in, the forests inevitably involved. Considerable as were his gifts as a politician, he had few of the qualities required of a guerrilla leader. His health was deteriorating and he needed medical treatment. He would have been reluctant to seek asylum in Britain because it would have been resisted – as indeed it was later – as embarrassing to the British government. The USA was a much better bet. The Americans had already supplied him with some medications, and high-quality medical treatment would be available in the States. The US government would be keen to secure the potential benefits of giving sanctuary to a possible – indeed, in many eyes a very likely, and in some eyes an inevitable – successor to Banda, especially if this could be achieved without alienating the doctor. Chipembere would feel safer – though far from completely safe – in America than anywhere else. From Banda's point of view, he would be rid of the man, the opposition that he led would collapse, martyrdom would be avoided and the matter could be presented as a coward, afraid of facing Banda, running away, not only from the doctor but also from those whom he purported to lead, abandoning them in an unprincipled fashion and leaving them to face Banda's vengeance.

With Chipembere's departure from Malawi the ministers' revolt drew to a close. None of the rebel ministers remained in Malawi and none was to return to his home country until Banda's presidency came to an end thirty years later. By that time the majority were dead: Chipembere, Chisiza, Bwanausi and Chirwa. Only Chokani and Chiume survived to return to Malawi. Msonthi also was dead. Tembo had continued as a leading – and increasingly prominent – member of the government and the party right up to the time when, in the multi-party elections of 1994, the MCP was defeated and was no longer the government of Malawi and Banda no longer the country's president.

Much had happened in the meantime, and much of it was attributable to, or influenced by, the cabinet crisis and the ministers' revolt. The legacy was serious and long-lasting. In October 1964, only a month after the vote of confidence in parliament, Cole said of the crisis: 'The result will be that the Government will become more of a one-man band than ever. Nor is the undiluted power which will thus be in Dr Banda's hands likely to improve his already at times arbitrary judgment.'[16]

The events of the second half of 1964 and the early months of 1965 did indeed have these consequences and had a number of major effects on Banda and the way he governed Malawi. All of these had their origins in at least embryo form during the period of colonial rule before independence, but they were greatly accentuated thereafter. They included furthering his dominant leadership of the MCP; controlling the judiciary; controlling prosecutions; using the police, especially the Special Branch, and army either directly or indirectly for political purposes; employing powers of restriction and detention without trial; and relying on informal sources of intelligence against dissidents.

The crisis confirmed for Banda the immense value of his dominant position as life president of the MCP and the power it gave him to use the party's organizational and communications resources quickly to mobilize the masses behind him and against all who might challenge him. Although the youth league and young pioneers had acted in paramilitary support of his position over the past several years, their more open and extensive activities during the crisis reinforced their great value: they 'acted as a nation-wide intelligence network, as well as intimidating potential opponents'.[17]

> [They were turned] into an armed force inder the direct control of the president, who is their Commander-in-Chief, [and they have become] a private army under his exclusive control. [Before 1966 they] were guilty of large scale intimidation, violence, robbery and rape [and] new powers give them immunity from arrest and freedom from any form of control save that of the President.[18]

Starting in 1958 with no significant power base, he developed the greatest power base of all – the MCP, its members and its organs, the youth and women's movements. Added to this was the strong and unqualified support and fostering by Macleod and Jones – given from the outset with their eyes open to the dangers involved – that greatly facilitated his rapid and inexorable rise to supreme power, from which the consequent despotism and tyranny flowed. The effectiveness of this power base was to be even greater after Malawi became a *de jure* one-party state in 1967.

There were early signs that Banda was dissatisfied with the judiciary and intended to tame or control its members. In December 1960, he made violent speeches against the high court and the magistrates' courts, accusing them of being biased against the MCP and favouring opposition parties. As a consequence, Armitage – who contemplated prosecuting him – delivered a personal reprimand which, surprisingly, Banda apologetically accepted. In 1962 he abolished the chiefs' courts and replaced them by 'local courts', subsequently 'traditional courts'. In the middle of the following year the chief justice formally expressed to the Governor his deep concerns about the local courts and their staff whose 'appointments [were] political and the members [were] inexperienced and incompetent'.[19] He did not believe that an independent judiciary could survive, nor that the constitutional provisions relating to the judiciary would be effective after independence. He was right. He asked that an inquiry be held into the running of the local courts but this was rejected by Butler and Jones – both of whom knew he was right. He was as patient and helpful as he felt able to be but, mindful of the vital role of the courts in a civilized state and unwilling to prostitute his position as head of the judiciary, he resigned before independence. To these pre-independence indications were added a number of others soon after independence.

Banda took steps to appoint a West African chief justice in his place, but when these steps failed he promoted one of the puisne judges, a European. The new chief justice was appointed on the clear understanding that 'if at any time the Prime Minister desires to fill the post of Chief Justice with another candidate of his choice [he] would be prepared immediately to resign [his] appointment as Chief Justice'.[20] This undertaking was a condition of his appointment, put to him by Jones, designed to avoid the provisions of the constitution that a judge of the high court was removable *only* 'for inability to perform the functions of his office ... or for misbehaviour' – [21]and not simply because the head of government preferred a different person. Again, when Banda contemplated appointing Chirwa to the high court bench, he was adamant that it should not be done through the judicial service commission, as the constitution required,[22] because he would want to get rid of him if he was unsatisfactory. Again, Jones went along with this proposal.[23] But it was to the traditional courts – staffed with political appointees – rather than the high court and magistrates' courts, that Banda turned more completely to secure his hold over the judicial process after the ministers' revolt.

When, in 1970, an expatriate judge, at the close of the prosecution case dismissed the case, against defendants accused of a horrific and baffling series of axe murders with dangerous political undercurrents, Banda was incensed and vowed publicly: 'No matter what anyone says or does [the accused] are not going to be let loose ... I am in charge.'[24] He immediately extended the jurisdiction of the traditional court system by setting up three regional traditional courts whose jurisdiction included murder, rape and, later, treason. Their sentencing powers were extended to include the death penalty.[25] The decision on whether a case should be heard in the high court or in the regional traditional court was at the discretion of the prosecution, and in practice all political offences were directed to the latter.

> The [regional] 'traditional court' consists of four chiefs ... appointed by the President ... and removable by him, as well as a qualified lawyer, who writes the judgment. The accused has no right of legal representation and ... receives no advance summary of the prosecution evidence in order to prepare a defence ... Procedural matters and rules of evidence are entirely at the discretion of the court [and there is no presumption of innocence]. Discretion as to whether those convicted may appeal ... lies with the Minister of Justice [Banda]. The right of appeal is only within the 'traditional court' system [and not] to the Supreme Court.[26]

These extensions of traditional court jurisdiction brought about the resignation of the whole of the high court bench.

Furthermore, in important cases, Banda regularly made his views known publicly before the trial, and 'the judges are left in little doubt as to what verdict they are to deliver'.[27] This was in spite of Chirwa's and Banda's public assurance, given at the end of 1963, that the courts would not be subject to political interference.[28] In Silombela's case, as an example, the doctor publicly announced, in advance of his trial: 'I know he is going to be found guilty. What kind of judge can acquit Silombela? ... He will be found guilty. And after that you can come and watch him swing.'[29] Banda could have pointed with justification to the 1915 public execution precedent when the colonial administration in Nyasaland had publicly both executed many of Chilembwe's followers and then displayed their bodies, and more recently to the public execution of Mau Mau terrorists in Kenya.

Not only was Banda determined that the courts should convict those whom he thought should be put away, but he was also determined that those he wished to remain free should not be convicted. He tackled this latter aspect through controls over prosecutions. He had long been opposed to an independent office of director of public prosecutions with sole power to decide whether a case should be prosecuted, though being required in cases involving questions of public policy to consult the elected minister of justice. He much preferred the minister of justice to be responsible for deciding on prosecutions. Even before the self-government constitution, which introduced the office, was brought into effect, he made it clear to Jones that: 'unless the [director] learned to accept the will of the Government, the Doctor would ensure that the system was broken up. He would be prepared to over-rule any authority on this and if necessary declare Nyasaland a Republic.'[30] The independence constitution retained the provision that the director should 'not be subject to the direction or control of any person or authority', but where he believed general considerations of public policy might be involved, he was to bring the case to the notice of the attorney-general and have regard to any views he expressed.[31] In the republican constitution the office of director of public prosecutions was retained but it provided that he should 'at all times be subject to the general or special directions of the Attorney-General', provided that where the attorney-general was not a minister, the minister of justice could at any time require that a case be submitted to him 'for the purpose of giving a direction as to whether or not criminal proceedings [should] be instituted or discontinued'.[32] Changing the words 'have regard to any views [expressed by the attorney-general]', to 'be subject to the ... directions [of the minister of justice]' contributed massively to Banda's powers over prosecutions since, at that time and continuously thereafter, the attorney-general was not a minister, and Banda, as minister of justice, henceforth personally – and constitutionally – was in complete control of prosecutions.

During the colonial period, prior to the introduction of the office of director of public prosecutions, the attorney-general was entrusted with the duty of prosecuting crimes. Constitutionally, his 'right and power of prosecuting [was] absolutely under his management and control'.[33] In practice, however, the attorney-general was subject to the views and wishes of the Governor. In 1948 a young illiterate post office messenger was convicted of stealing a postage stamp. The case was unremarkable, save that it was heard by the senior resident magistrate; that the prosecution was led personally by the attorney-general, who pressed for 'a substantial and deterrent sentence'; that the accused was sentenced to four years' imprisonment with hard labour; and that the stolen stamp was taken from a private letter written by the Governor, Colby.[34] In 1960 Armitage told the secretary of state quite clearly that he, the Governor, would decide whether or not Chipembere and Chiume were to be prosecuted. Then, when the attorney-general wished to prosecute Chiume and possibly Banda himself, Armitage overruled him, though he agreed to Chipembere's prosecution.[35] In 1960, too, as acting Governor, Jones had secret instructions issued to district commissioners that they were to turn a blind eye to all but the most serious of offences by members of the MCP, rather than rock the political boat. With the introduction of self-government in February 1963, Chirwa was appointed minister of justice, with the right to be consulted in cases involving questions of public policy. The newly appointed, and extremely experienced, expatriate director of public prosecutions encountered great difficulty in being able to consult the minister. This led to the accumulation of a large number of cases. Since he felt that the constitution was being interpreted so as to prevent the prosecution of politically motivated serious offences, the director resigned and the Governor did nothing to dissuade him. In 1963, also, instructions were issued to police officers – presumably directly or indirectly by Jones or with his knowledge and acquiescence – that they were not to proceed with politically motivated cases against members of the MCP, even when these were serious offences. These instructions prevented numerous cases being submitted to the director of public prosecutions, since they involved stopping investigations at even the preliminary stage of identifying suspects. Critics could readily have pointed to these and other cases during the colonial era when the Governor had, directly or indirectly, exercised control over prosecutions.

In dealing with the revolt and the rebels' subsequent activities, Banda recognized, more clearly than previously, the value of the police, especially the Special Branch, and the army as powerful tools of government at his disposition. He needed no additional formal powers. The colonial government and the former ministers had given him virtually all the powers he needed to rule autocratically within the law, though he continued to add to them as occasion, as he saw it, demanded. The wide powers of restriction and of detention proved their worth to him during the crisis when applied against suspects and their families, particularly when hunting down Chipembere. They were used even more extensively and ruthlessly thereafter, whether instigated by himself or by others on his behalf: 'Of the formal state institutions, the most important in maintaining political control has been the police and in particular its security wing, the Special Branch.'[36]

Although the military forces had been the federal army, which was not under Nyasaland's control, during the last decade of colonial rule, save the final few months, Banda would have remembered the way in which, as he saw it, the army was used in 1959. While it was deployed exclusively to back up the civil authorities in arresting those to be detained and to restore law and order during the first week of the emergency, thereafter the army's main task, at the Governor's direction, was different.

> It was decided that there should next be a vigorous policy of harassing and breaking up Congress organisers, supporters and hoodlums ... The objectives of the new operation were to arrest leaders still at large, to make propaganda, and to give firm but friendly displays of force in quiescent areas and to take tough, punitive action in areas where lawlessness and violence were being perpetrated or planned ... swift and offensive retribution [were] meted out to convince that lawlessness did not pay.[37]

Banda may well have seen this as a political use of the army. Without saying so, it was a precedent he followed in directing the army to harry the people of the Fort Johnston district in pursuing Chipembere and his cohorts and in wreaking vengeance thereafter. The Malawi army used precisely the same methods of cordon and search that the federal troops had used six years earlier.[38] Two years later, the army was used to pursue, capture and kill Yatuta Chisiza.[39]

The restriction and detention legislation that Banda introduced in October 1964 was copied from earlier Nyasaland legislation, though with fewer effective safeguards. The colonial legislation – 'an elaborate code giving [the Governor] extensive control over persons and property' – [40] had been used extensively during the emergency, and even when the emergency was lifted, new legislation was enacted to enable the Governor to keep the Congress hard core locked up. A few weeks after Chipembere's attempted *coup d'etat* Banda publicly proclaimed that if in order to maintain political stability he had to detain a hundred thousand people, he would do it: 'I will detain anyone who is interfering with the political stability of this country.'[41] Official figures of the number detained were never issued. Short in 1970 believed that periodic amnesties kept the number at any one time down to about four hundred, but it is widely claimed that actual numbers far exceeded this: within a year of independence over a thousand supporters of the rebel ministers were detained without trial; 'in 1968 alone, 1427 prisoners were officially released from detention'; in 1976 there were a thousand political detainees and over 5,000 Jehovah's Witnesses in detention; and in November the following year, between 2,000 and 3,500 men and women were released from detention. It has been estimated that during the three decades of his reign he detained over a quarter of a million people, and even this calculation is seen by some as a 'gross underestimate'.[42]

One of the factors that brought about the turning point at the end of August 1964 was Banda's receipt of anonymous letters and personal callers convincingly reporting allegations of disloyalty and conspiracy by the rebels. He had always paid attention to informal sources of intelligence – or simply rumour – sometimes preferring them to formal and better substantiated sources. After 1964 he paid even more heed to these sources than in the past, whether they came to him directly, or through the Special Branch or the secretary-general of the party. This reliance on informal sources of information, especially accusations against individuals, became more marked after certain key expatriate officers, in whom he placed great trust and who were able to sift and evaluate some of the rumours and allegations for him, left the country: Dewar, Secretary for Agriculture, in May 1969; Long and Lomax in July 1971; Lewis in August 1971; Freeman, secretary for education and registrar of the university, in September 1971; and Roberts in May 1973. A few days before he left Malawi in July 1966, Jones wrote privately to Banda saying that he had found these men 'to be faithful and discreet' and that if the doctor 'wished to disclose matters of a secret nature' to any of them he could rest assured that they would not divulge them to others.[43] Other senior expatriate officers in influential positions also left at about the same time, including the chief justice and all the puisne judges in the middle of 1970, the secretary for finance in December 1970, the deputy commissioner of police in January 1973 and the commander of the State House Guard – after firearms and ammunition had been reported missing from the State House armoury - [44] in March 1973. Roberts, head of the civil service, cast a revealing light on the matter of allegations against individuals and the restraining influence he and other expatriates were able to bring to bear while they were in office:

> After 1964, Dr Banda's reservations about Africanisation ... were not restricted to anxieties about a dilution of the efficiency of the service ... There was the question of political reliability as well ... The political

element, of course, and also the playing off of old vendettas ... against individual civil servants and army officers and policemen for either political or personal family reasons, did lead to a great deal of 'snakes and ladders' in the Africanisation game ... as a result of the fact that [defects] had been wrongly imputed to them by some hostile critic who sought the ear of Dr Banda in order to get rid of them ... Within a very short period of my departure, the majority of the Malawian Permanent Secretaries were out of a job. I attributed this largely to the fact that after I had gone and was no longer available as an independent investigator of the validity of complaints made against either the loyalty or the efficiency of Malawian senior officers – when I was no longer there to protect their interests – the possibility of victimising senior officers, by making false charges, either against their efficiency or their honesty, or their political loyalty, became very much easier ... I dread to think, looking back, what injustices must have occurred in many cases when one considers that Mr Muwalo [secretary-general of the MCP] was the minister responsible for these enquiries and investigations [as well as for the State House guard].[45]

The cabinet crisis also had a number of important effects on those who replaced the rebel ministers. They saw that the dissidents – well educated, experienced, skilled, and in some cases cunning, politicians – had failed to alter Banda's autocratic methods of governing. They learned that even a united, determined and courageous front at the highest level in opposition to Banda would be ruthlessly swept aside. They learned, too, that on major – and indeed any other – points of policy he would not be shifted. So there was no point in attempting to get him to alter either his methods or his policies. A major lesson was the imprudence of crossing Banda – or indeed those to whom he might listen – in any way, even if this turned them into, or confirmed them as, sycophantic yes-men. None of these attributes of Banda and his methods of governing was new, but they became much more apparent, entrenched and accepted after the cabinet crisis, and they became characteristics of his regime for the next three decades. On the very points with which the rebels had challenged him, they had not simply failed to induce him to reform: they had made him worse.

Few of the new guard who replaced the rebel ministers at the time of the cabinet crisis – the party stalwarts – or who were appointed subsequently were immune from Banda's suspicions and ruthlessness. Whereas in the past the ruthlessness had been directed en masse against opposition parties, such as Mbadwa, or against uncooperative sects, such as the Jehovah's Witnesses, or against the followers of rebel ministers, such as Chipembere, they became directed more against individuals. Kumtumanji was arrested in 1970 on the far-fetched allegation that as minister of health he had access to chloroform with which to drug the victims in a series of murders that were believed to be politically motivated to undermine Banda. He died in detention in April 1990.[46] In 1974, Msonthi was suspended from the MCP for breaching party discipline.[47] Muwalo, who had become secretary-general of the party and minister of state in the president's office, was arrested in September 1976, with Focus Gwede, head of Special Branch. Both had been 'closely associated with the highly repressive policies of the early 1970s, in particular the widespread detention of political critics and Jehovah's Witnesses'.[48] They had just 'carried out a massive purge of northerners which saw 300 highly educated people detained'.[49] It was alleged that they were in illegal possession of firearms and plotted to have Banda assassinated and effect a *coup d'état*. Early the following year, they were tried for treason, in a regional traditional court, convicted and sentenced to death. Muwalo was executed, but Gwede was reprieved at the last moment.[50] It was said of Muwalo that 'It was he who ... drew up lists of people to be detained, arrested, removed, sacked from their jobs or deported for Dr. Banda's approval [and] who ran the Land Rover squad that visited people to be deported or arrested.'[51]

On 14 January 1980 Aleke Banda – who had become minister of development and planning in 1966 and minister of finance in 1968 – was expelled from the party for gross breach of party discipline.[52] He was detained without charge and imprisoned for the next decade. Chakuamba was arrested in 1980, charged with sedition, tried by a traditional court, convicted and sentenced to twenty-two years' imprisonment.[53] It was widely believed at the time that he was arrested because at a public meeting he, rather than Banda, had been praised for the developments that had taken place in the southern region. Later, he was kept for long periods in leg irons and handcuffs because, it was claimed, he was planning to escape from prison.[54]

In May 1983, Dick Matenje, the new secretary-general of the MCP and minister without portfolio, and Aaron Gadama, minister for the central region and Leader of the House, introduced a motion in parliament, asking the president to make changes to the election procedure so that he should nominate three candidates, instead of one, to stand in each constituency. With the minister of health and the MP for Chikwawa, they were murdered. They were 'killed because, for the first time since the 1960s they were members of the ruling inner circle who wished to discuss and formulate policy rather than just carry out the President's wishes'.[55] Political murder was not new in Malawi. Pondeponde and a significant number of Jehovah's Witnesses had been murdered for political reasons before independence, during the period of British rule, and their murderers escaped punishment. Even two decades after the cabinet crisis, not everyone had learned, as had the rebels and those who replaced them in 1964, the imprudence of challenging the way Banda did things. One by one, almost without exception, Banda's closest associates in the party and the government were disposed of by being convicted, or, more usually, detained without trial, or simply murdered.

Three of those who were detained or put to death had been secretary-general of the MCP – as had Dunduzu Chisiza. This was perhaps the most hazardous job in the country,[56] because it was the secretary-general who, under the constitution, with two cabinet ministers, would form a presidential council to perform the functions of the president in the event of his death, resignation or incapacity.[57] That it was important to neutralize those who occupied that dangerous post is possibly the only indication that the doctor ever contemplated his resignation or incapacity – or mortality.

The ministers' revolt did not give birth to Banda's dictatorial attitudes or his tyrannical behaviour. They had long existed, been recognized and indeed in many respects had been fostered within both the government and the party. Rather, the crisis proved to him and others that none of his colleagues was indispensable; that none could successfully challenge him – not even the most powerful and able; that slapping them down and teaching them a lesson they would never forget was effective; and that he was right not to trust any of them. The result was that he became even more acutely and constantly vigilant for the slightest sign of dissent, indeed of even unvoiced disagreement, and was quick in acting ruthlessly whenever he detected or thought there might be any dissent or disagreement. Never again would he risk having at large anyone, particularly anyone in his cabinet, who might hamper his task of ensuring the well-being of the Malawian people. Only he could ensure this. Only he was indispensable.

Having placed Banda in a position of great power and encouraged him to use it, Britain and the MCP lieutenants could hardly have been surprised when, after independence, he capitalized on that power to preserve and strengthen his own dominant position, albeit so that he could continue to pursue the best interests of the country, as he saw them. Macleod from the very beginning strongly supported the doctor and treated him exclusively as expressing the collective will of the Nyasaland people. Jones did all he could to foster and maintain Banda's hegemony. He quickly became, and then continued to be, the doctor's devoted supporter, advocate, defender and apologist. The lieutenants built up Banda as a messiah, furthered his cause throughout the country and conferred sweeping autocratic powers on him. They all – the British government, the secretary of state, the Governor and the lieutenants – did this deliberately and with their eyes wide open, though they could not have anticipated how long Banda would live and remain in power,[58] or the degree to which he would exploit the position in which they had placed him. Nor could they have foreseen the full extent of the legacy that he – and to some extent they – would leave Malawi.

Notes

1. Introduction

1. P. Short, *Banda* (London: Routledge and Kegan Paul, 1974), p. 81.
2. H. B. M. Chipembere, Evidence to Devlin Commission, 16 May 1959, Devlin Papers, Rhodes House Library, Oxford, Box 12A.
3. Short, op. cit., pp. 82–3.
4. *Report of the Nyasaland Commission of Inquiry*, Cmnd. 814 (London: HMSO, 1959), pp. 12–13.
5. Viscount Boyd, in A. H. M. Kirk-Greene, *The Transfer of Power: The Colonial Administrator in the Age of Decolonisation* (Oxford: Inter-faculty Committee for African Studies, 1979), p. 3.
6. E. E. Bailey to author, 23 February 1995; P. E. S. Finney, Evidence to Devlin Commission, 12 May 1959, Devlin Papers, Rhodes House Library, Oxford (hereafter Devlin Papers), Box 14; R. Mushet to author, February 1995.

2. Banda and His Lieutenants

1. H. B. M. Chipembere, 'Malawi in Crisis', *Ufahamu*, 1970, vol. 1, pt 2, p. 14.
2. M. Harris, interview with author, 28 September 1995.
3. M. W. K. Chiume, *Kwacha, an Autobiography* (Nairobi: East African Publishing House, 1975), p. 90.
4. Loft Papers, Letter SP-30, 28 May 1958.
5. *Report of the Nyasaland Commission of Inquiry*, Cmnd. 814 (London: HMSO, 1959), p. 26; H. B. M. Chipembere, Evidence to Devlin Commission, 16 May 1959, Devlin Papers, Box 12A; P. Youens, interview with author, 8 December 1997; Chipembere, tape casette recording of a seminar led by Chipembere for the political geography class of Emeritus Professor Edwin Munger, Caltec, Pasadena, 1 February 1971, provided by Donal Brody and David Stuart-Mogg. Hereafter referred to as Chipembere Seminar.
6. J. H. E. Watson to author, 25 May 1995.
7. M. Harris, Evidence to Devlin Commission, Kasungu, 1 May 1959, Devlin Papers, Box 13, Transcript File 3.
8. Jones Papers (hereafter JP), Record of a discussion between Dr H. K. Banda and the acting chief secretary on Monday, 5 September 1960.
9. Loft Papers, Letter SP-30, 28 May 1958, p. 7.
10. Extracts from Banda's personal papers, enclosed with T. Walker to author 20 April 1998.

11. H. B. M. Chipembere, Evidence to Devlin Commission, 16 May 1959, Devlin Papers, Box 12A.
12. Chipembere Seminar.
13. Ibid.
14. Brody Collection: Banda, Speech at Nkota Kota, 29 September 1960.
15. Ibid. Chipembere was in Gwelo with Banda for thirteen, not fourteen, months.
16. H. B. M. Chipembere, Evidence to Devlin Commission, 16 May 1959, Devlin Papers, Box 12A.
17. Loft Papers, Letter SP-21, 13 April 1959; Letter SP-78, 3 December 1959; Visit to Gwelo prison, 29 September 1959; Chipembere to Loft 14 October 1959.
18. M. Harris, Evidence to Devlin Commission, 1 May 1959, Devlin Papers, Box 13 Transcript File 3. The question of raising hats had long been a sensitive one: see G. Shepperson and T. Price, *Independent African: John Chilembwe and the Origins, Setting and Significance of the Nyasaland African Rising of 1915* (Edinburgh: University Press, 1958), p. 369.
19. R. Purdy, Evidence to Devlin Commission, 2 May 1959, Devlin Papers, Box 13, Transcript File 3; Youens, interview with author, 8 December 1997; M. J. Bennion, conversations with author 1963–64; Chiume to author, 19 August 1994; Chiume, op. cit., p. 83.
20. CO. 1015/1518, Armitage to secretary of state (hereafter SS) 2 May 1959; *Manchester Guardian*, 6 March 1959; Loft Papers, Letter SP-21, 13 April 1959.
21. Chiume, interview with author, 13–14 December 1998.
22. H. B. M. Chipembere, Evidence to Devlin Commission, 16 May 1959, Devlin Papers, Box 12A.
23. Y. K. Chisiza, Evidence to Devlin Commission, 19 May 1959, Devlin Papers, Box 14, Transcript File No. 18,
24. Short, op. cit., p. 68, citing Chipembere interview with David Martin, Dar es Salaam, 1969; CO. 1015/1516, Armitage to SS, 9 March 1959; Loft Papers, Letter SP-50, 31 August 1959; J. D. Msonthi, conversation with author, 6 March 1959; CO 1015/1516, SS to Armitage, 9 March 1959.
25. Loft Papers, Letter SP-24, 8 May 1959; Chiume to author, 20 October 1998; JP, Jones to chief secretary, 19 April 1961. The allegation was made by T. D. T. Banda, and Jones said, 'There was no truth whatsoever in the allegation.' There is no evidence in Armitage's papers that the allegation was true; Loft Papers, Visit to Gwelo prison, 29 September 1959.
26. CO 1015/2119, Memorandum to the secretary of state, the Rt Hon. Iain Macleod, by Mr Orton Chirwa, 18 November 1959; Record of a meeting between the secretary of state for the colonies and Mr Orton Chirwa at the Colonial Office on 18 November 1959; Monson to Armitage, 3 December 1959.
27. Armitage Papers, Private Diary, 3 March 1959.
28. York Papers, Banda to Nkrumah, 24 May 1962; M. Y. Q. Chibambo to author, 8 March 1999. The other camp finalists were Kapombe Nyasulu, N. Mwafulirwa, W. Chikafa, Mtekateka, Elias Sonjo, Kachowa, Wangiba Nkhoma and Matupi Mkandawire.
29. JP, Note by Jones.
30. Hansard, Second Meeting, First Session, 8–9 September 1964, p. 91.
31. Loft Papers, Visit to Gwelo prison, 29 September 1959.
32. Short, op. cit., p. 120.

3. Banda Consolidates His Power

1. CO 1015 1977, Macmillan to Perth, 10 February 1959.
2. JP, Monson to Jones, 19 August 1960.
3. JP, Record of a discussion between Dr Banda and the acting chief secretary, Friday, 12 August 1960.
4. JP, Note for the record, 16 August 1960.
5. The Brody Collection (hereafter Brody), Banda, speech 'On the Release of the Last of the Detainees' delivered at Kota Kota, 29 September 1960, from Banda's private papers.
6. Armitage Papers, Draft memoirs, 1960 vol. 2, p. 36.
7. Chiume to author, 20 October 1998.
8. JP, Record of a discussion between Dr H. K. Banda and the acting chief secretary on Monday, 5 September 1960.
9. JP, Note for the record, 6 September 1960.
10. Banda, interview with Hans Germani, cited in Attati Mpakati, 'Malawi: the Birth of a Neo-Colonial State', *Africa Review*, 1973, vol. 3, pt 1, p. 51.
11. JP, Record of a discussion between Dr H. K. Banda and the acting chief secretary on Wednesday, 7 September 1960.
12. JP, Jones to SS, 8 September 1960.
13. JP, Macleod to Jones, 12 September 1960.
14. JP, Jones to Macleod, 15 September 1960.
15. JP, Note for the record, 15 September 1960.
16. JP, Jones to SS, 23 September 1960, and draft by Jones, n.d. but 22 September 1960.
17. Short, op. cit., p. 139.
18. Brody, Banda's speech 'On the Release of the Last of the Detainees' delivered at Kota Kota on 29 September 1960. The Nyasulu referred to here is Francis Kapombe Nyasulu, who acted as secretary and general factotum to Banda while in Gwelo.
19. Short, op. cit., p. 139, says they were flown to Kota Kota.
20. JP, Finney to private secretary to the Governor, 28 September 1960; Bailey to author, 12 July 1994.
21. Chiume to author, 20 October 1998.
22. Brody, Banda's speech 'On the Release of the Last of the Detainees', delivered at Kota Kota, 29 September 1960.
23. Chiume to author, 20 October 1998.
24. Short, op. cit., p. 145.
25. Armitage Papers, Armitage to Mrs Armitage, 19 December 1960, and private diary 18–22 December 1960.
26. Armitage Papers, Private diary, 1–3 December 1960.
27. Brody, Chipembere to Banda, 18 August 1961.
28. Armitage Papers, Private diary, 6 December 1960.
29. Armitage Papers, Draft memoirs, 1960, vol. 2, pp. 129–30.
30. *Nyasaland Times*, 3 February 1961.
31. Armitage Papers, Private diary, 16–17 December 1960.
32. H. M. Costello to author, 2 September 1996.
33. Brody, Chipembere to Banda, 18 August 1961.
34. Armitage Papers, Private diary, 24 December 1960.
35. *Nyasaland Times*, 24 January 1961.

36. Armitage Papers, Armitage to Mrs Armitage, 18 February 1961.
37. Ibid.
38. Chiume to author, 20 October 1998.
39. Brody, Chipembere to Banda, 25 January 1961.
40. Brian Lapping draws a parallel with an agreement between Lee Kwan Yew and Lennox-Boyd under which the SS had some of Lee's supporters arrested, Lee then released them and shortly had them reimprisoned and out of his way: B. Lapping, *End of Empire* (London: Paladin Grafton, 1989), p. 36.
41. Lapping incorrectly attributes Chipembere's prosecution to Jones, who he thought was Acting Governor at the time: B. Lapping, op. cit., p. 36.
42. L. Mair, *The Nyasaland Elections of 1961* (London: Athlone Press, 1962), p. 38.
43. Chiume, interview with author, 13–14 December 1998.
44. Short, op. cit., pp. 146–7.
45. DO 158 60, Minutes of a meeting between the British High Commissioner, Salisbury, and the two northern governors, 31 May 1961.
46. *Malawi News*, 3 August 1961.
47. JP, Jones to SS, 31 July 1961.
48. The term 'Malawi' referred to the Malawi Congress Party, and not to the country. For example, at this stage, before independence, when the Governor was referred to as 'Malawi Jones' it meant 'Congress Jones' and was intended to be offensive rather than complimentary.
49. JP, Jones to Macleod, 27 and 29 July 1961.
50. Roberts, interviews with author, 26 and 27 July and 6 August 1982; Short, op. cit., pp. 150–51.
51. Brody, Chiume to Banda, 17 January 1962.
52. Brody, Chipembere to Banda, 18 August 1961.
53. Hansard, Second Meeting, Seventy-sixth Session, 28–29 November 1961. The others in prison, named by Chisiza, included Msopole, Chapinga and Kaponda.
54. JP, Jones to Macleod, 19 August 1961.
55. JP, Draft note by Jones, probably to chief secretary, on meeting with Banda, 22 August 1961; Jones to Macleod, 25 August 1961.
56. *Report of the Nyasaland Constitutional Conference Held in London in July and August 1960*, Cmnd. 1132 (London: HMSO, 1960), para. 8 A (iii).
57. Ibid.
58. JP, Draft note by Jones, probably to chief secretary, on meeting with Banda, 22 August 1961; and Jones to Macleod, 23 August 1961.
59. *Nyasaland Government Gazette*, 1961, p. 303.
60. Chiume to author, 20 October 1998; Chiume interview with author, 13–14 December 1998.
61. *Proceedings in the Parliament of Malawi* (hereafter Hansard), Second Meeting, First Session, 8–9 September 1964, p. 70.
62. Cameron, interview with author, 21 March 1998.
63. Brody to author, 8 May 1997, citing 'HKB verbatim comments' in Banda's private papers. This comment is dated 2.9.1961.
64. CO 1015 2491, Jones to Macleod, 4 October 1961.
65. Ibid.
66. Extracts from Banda's personal papers, enclosed with T. Walker to author, 20 April 1998.

Notes to Chapter 4 · 329

4. In Government

1. JP, Note of a meeting between His Excellency the Governor and certain members of executive council and parliamentary secretaries, 11 September 1961.
2. JP, Note of a meeting held at Government House, Zomba, 30 November 1961, with non-official ministers and parliamentary secretaries.
3. JP, Note for the record, 18 December 1961, about meeting of 16 December 1961.
4. Cameron, interview with author, 21 March 1998.
5. Chiume, interview with author, 13–14 December 1998.
6. JP, Note of a meeting held at Government House, 30 November 1961, with non-official ministers and parliamentary secretaries.
7. JP, Note of a meeting held at Government House, Zomba, 1 December, 1961, with the official ministers.
8. Cmnd. 1132, para. 8A.
9. JP, Jones to SS, 30 December 1961.
10. JP, Draft record of meeting between Jones and Banda, 22 August 1961, probably by Jones to chief secretary.
11. *Nyasaland Government Gazette*, 1962, pp. 67, 81.
12. JP Jones to SS, 29 January 1962.
13. The former schoolmasters were Bwanausi, Msonthi, Chiume, Chirwa and Chokani. Banda himself had been a pupil teacher before he left Nyasaland in 1915.
14. M. W. K. Chiume, *Kwacha, an Autobiography* (Nairobi: East African Publishing House, 1975), pp. 150–52.
15. Brody, Chiume to Banda, 17 January 1962.
16. DO 183 136–7, Nyasaland Intelligence Committee Report (hearafter NICR) for April 1962.
17. Armitage Papers, Private diary, 24 December 1960.
18. NICR for May 1962.
19. Loft Papers, Report of a visit to the Federation of Rhodesia and Nyasaland, 9–27 April 1961.
20. DO 183 467, Visit of Dr Banda to the United Kingdom.
21. NICR for July 1962.
22. Loft Papers, Report of a visit to the Federation of Rhodesia and Nyasaland, 9–27 April 1961.
23. D. K. Chisiza, 'The Temper, Aspirations and Problems of Contemporary Africa', p. 8, in *Relating Principles of Economic Development to African Economic Development*, the Nyasaland economic symposium, 18–28 July 1962.
24. JP, Theunissen to Scott, 20 September 1962.
25. Andrew Ross to author 14 August 1997, enclosing copy of a seminar paper, *Reflections on the Malawi 'Cabinet Crisis' 1964–65* (hereafter *Reflections*).
26. JP, Stevens to Commonwealth Relations Office, 3 August 1962.
27. DO 183 168, Governor to SS, 7 August 1960.
28. Cameron, interview with author, 21 March 1998.
29. Ibid.
30. DO 183 168, Governor to SS, 7 August 1962.
31. Cameron, interview with author, 21 March 1998.
32. Chipembere, op. cit., pp. 8–9.
33. Sir Michael Caine, interview with author, 15 October 1997.

34. Chipembere, op. cit., pp. 8–9.
35. Chiume, interview with author, 13–14 December 1998. Since the 'Gwelo Cabinet' which excluded Yatuta Chisiza had been planned in Gwelo gaol in Chiume's absence, Yatuta could not rationally blame him for his exclusion. One would have expected him to blame those who were there: Banda, Chipembere and Dunduzu Chisiza.
36. Brody, Chiume to Banda, 2 August 1962.
37. Brody, Bwanausi to Chiume, 2 July 1962.
38. JP and DO 183 168, Jones to SS, 7 August 1962.
39. JP, D. K. Chisiza to Jones, 4 August 1962. Chipembere also referred to the more active of MCP members as Banda's 'soldiers'.
40. Ross, *Reflections*; Ross, interview with author, 26 May 1999.
41. Chipembere, op. cit., pp. 7–9.
42. Short, op. cit., p. 109; C. A. Crosby, *Historical Dictionary of Malawi* (London and New Jersey: Scarecrow Press, 1980), p. 35.
43. F. Chevallier, interview with author, 31 December 1997; W. L. Aucutt to author 29 December 1997; Khazir Khan Lodhi, telephone conversation with author, 20 March 1998.
44. JP, Governor to SS, 15 August 1862 and SS to Governor, 31 August 1962.
45. JP, Jones to SS, 24 August 1962.
46. Chiume, interview with author, 13–14 December 1998.
47. DO 183 296, Informal conference between the High Commissioner in Salisbury and the two northern governors, 1 October 1962.
48. JP, Jones to SS, 29 August 1962.
49. JP, Jones to SS, 7 August 1962.
50. N. Sherrin, *Oxford Dictionary of Humorous Quotations* (Oxford: Oxford University Press, 1995), p. 259.
51. JP, Jones to SS, 31 July 1961.
52. M. Llewelyn to author, 23 December 1994. The rumours persisted for many years: see Joey Power, 'Remembering Du: an Episode in the Development of Malawian Political Culture', *African Affairs* (1998), 97, 369–96.
53. M. Bowery to author, 24 January 1995.
54. M. Tadman to author, 3 December 1998.
55. NICR for September 1962.
56. P. Howard, interview with author, 30 July 1994.
57. Chiume, interview with author, 13–14 December 1998.
58. Short, op. cit., p. 168.
59. Joey Power, 'Remembering Du: an Episode in the Development of Malawian Political Culture', *African Affairs* (1998), 97, 369–96.
60. Unattributable.
61. *Nyasaland Times*, 29 May 1962.
62. D. K. Chisiza, *Realities of African Independence* (London: Africa Publications Trust, 1961), p. 5.
63. *Report of the Nyasaland Constitutional Conference Held in London in November 1962*, Cmnd. 1887 (London: HMSO, 1962).
64. JP, Press conference held by Dr Banda at his Zomba residence at 10 a.m. on 26 November 1961.
65. Brody, Chipembere to Banda, 19 December 1962.
66. Brody, K. C. Musopole to Banda, 24 February 1962.
67. JP, SS to Jones, 11 November 1962.

68. JP, Jones to SS, 11 January 1963.
69. JP, Jones to Alport, 15 January 1963. The following information on Chipembere's release, except where otherwise stated, is from NICR for the period 1–25 January 1963.
70. Short, op. cit., p. 168.
71. NICR for period 1–25 January 1963.
72. Short, op. cit., pp. 167–8.
73. Brody, Chipembere to Banda, 19 January 1963.

5. Self-government

1. Chipembere Seminar; Short, op. cit., p. 168; *Malawi News*, 20 November 1964.
2. The Malawi Congress Party Constitution, cited in Short, op. cit., pp. 169–70.
3. NICR for June 1963.
4. DO 183 136, Neale to Snelling, 10 April 1964.
5. JP, Record of a meeting with Dr Banda, 16 August 1993.
6. DO 183 468, Cole to Whitley, 30 August 1963; Cole to Shaw, 4 September 1963.
7. DO 183 468, British Ambassador Monrovia to Earl of Home, 4 September 1963.
8. DO 183 468, British Embassy Bonn to Foreign Office, 4 and 19 September 1963.
9. DO 183 468, Note of two meetings held on 23 September 1963.
10. DO 183 468, British Embassy Washington to Central Africa Office, 18 Ostober 1963.
11. JP, Jones to SS, 10 October 1963.
12. JP, Jones to SS, 30 November 1963.
13. Chiume, to author, 7 November 1999.
14. Armitage Papers, Annotated extracts from letter written by Robin Rowland to Richard Kettlewell. The extracts indicate that the letter was written on 30 October 1963.
15. *Malawi News*, 6 October 1964; Chiume, interview with author, 13–14 December 1998.
16. *Malawi Government Gazette* 1963, p. 311, General Notice No. 765, dated 9 November 1963.
17. Chiume, op. cit., p. 187.
18. Hansard, Third Meeting, First Session, 27–30 October 1964, p. 208.
19. DO 183 136, Unsigned and undated minute on October 1963 intelligence report.
20. Phillips, interview with author, 3 December 1997.
21. Chipembere, op. cit., p. 5.
22. Chipembere, op. cit., pp. 5–6, 8, 11–22.
23. Robins, to author, 10 October 1995.
24. Hansard, Second Session, Fifth Meeting, 6–13 April 1965.
25. Chiume, interview with author, 13–14 December 1998.
26. JP, Record of a meeting with Dr Banda at Government House, 29 January 1964.

27. Chipembere, op. cit., pp. 7, 9.
28. JP, Jones to SS, 10 December 1963.
29. JP, Jones to SS, 9 January 1964.
30. Sir Edgar Unsworth to author, 5 March 1995; Unsworth, interview with author, 22 September 1995.
31. JP, Jones to SS, 30 December 1963 and 9 January 1964; NICR for December 1963.
32. NICR for December 1963.
33. JP, Jones to SS, 9 January 1964.
34. NICR for January 1964.
35. JP, Jones to Sandys, 21 April 1964.
36. NICR for February 1964.
37. Ibid.
38. NICR for March 1964.
39. JP, Jones to SS, 10 March 1964.
40. JP, Jones to Chirwa, 28 February 1964.
41. Several years later, Chipembere said Banda 'extensively' used the powers to prevent prosecutions: JP, Chipembere to Jones, 26 October 1965.
42. JP, Chirwa to Jones, 13 March 1964.
43. JP, Jones to SS, 10 March 1964; JP, Note for the record by Jones, n.d. but 18 March 1964.
44. JP, Jones to Chirwa, 6 April 1964.
45. JP, Chirwa to Jones, 17 April 1964.
46. JP, Jones to Chirwa, 18 April 1964.
47. Unsworth to author, 5 March 1995.
48. JP, Jones to SS, 26 May 1964.
49. Short, op. cit., p. 171.
50. JP, Jones to Banda, 27 April 1964.
51. JP, Jones to Secretary of State, 30 April 1964; Jones to Banda, 27 April 1964.
52. JP, Jones to Banda, 27 April 1964.
53. Cynthia Magee to author, 7 February and 9 July 1999.
54. Cameron to author, 27 November 1998.
55. Foster, interview with author, 14 August 1997.
56. Nyasaland Information Department transcript of Banda's speech to the Zomba Debating Society, 29 April 1964, cited in Short, op. cit., p. 174.
57. Hansard, Fifth Session, Second Meeting, 12–14 December 1967, p. 124. It was alleged by the Chinese embassy in Dar es Salaam that Banda had himself asked for £18m. but the Chinese had turned him down because the sum was greater than that which they were giving to other East African countries: DO 183 168, British High Commission, Dar es Salaam, to Commonwealth Relations Office, 9 September 1964.
58. DO 183 137, Nyasaland Intelligence Committee Paper, 5 June 1964, drafted by Lomax.
59. Chiume, interview with author, 13–14 December 1998.
60. Chiume to author, 20 October 1998.
61. Chipembere, op. cit., p. 13.
62. Roberts, interviews with author, 26 and 27 July and 6 August 1982.

6. The Revolt

1. DO 183 457, Cole to Bottomley, Despatch No. 4, 27 October 1964.
2. DO 183 457, Cole to Sandys, Despatch No. 3, 14 October 1964.
3. Roberts, interviews with author, 26 and 27 July and 6 August 1982.
4. Clyde Sanger, 'Nyasaland Becomes Malawi: An Assesssment', *Africa Report*, August 1964, pp. 8–11.
5. Cameron, 'Malawi Reborn', *Venture*, 1964, vol. 16, pts 7 and 8, pp. 18–21.
6. H E I Phillips, 'Nyasaland – Poised for Independence', *Commonwealth Journal*, vol. VII, no. 3, June 1964, p. 95; Chipembere, op.cit, p. 4.
7. JP, Untitled and undated notes by Jones.
8. Chiume to author, 20 October 1998.
9. DO 183 457, Cole to Sandys, Despatch No. 3, 14 October 1964.
10. Cameron, interview with author, 21 March 1998.
11. Ross, *Reflections* and interview with author, 9 September 1999.
12. DO 183 457, Cole to Sandys, Despatch No. 1, 13 July 1964.
13. York Papers, Report of the Ghana delegation to the Malawi independence celebrations.
14. DO 183 61, Note by Neale, 20 July 1964.
15. *Malawi Government Gazette*, 10 July 1964, p. 3.
16. Sanger saw Chisiza as 'perhaps the most impressive of all' the ministers: Sanger, op. cit.
17. DO 183 457, Cole to Sandys, Despatch No. 3, 14 October 1964.
18. DO 183 457, High Commissioner's top-secret and personal document of 11 August 1964, addressee unknown.
19. Short, op. cit., pp. 195–6.
20. JP, Jones to SS; 12 March 1964.
21. Chipembere Seminar.
22. Short, op. cit., p. 203.
23. Chiume, op. cit., p. 200.
24. Short, op. cit., pp. 203–4.
25. Salisbury *Sunday Mail*, 18 October 1964.
26. Chipembere, op. cit., pp. 10–11.
27. Youens, interview with author, 8 December 1997.
28. Chiume, op. cit., p. 200.
29. Chiume, op. cit., p. 201.
30. Chiume, interview with author, 13–14 December 1998.
31. Cameron to author, 27 November 1998.
32. JP, Record of a meeting with Dr Banda, 6.15 p.m., 28 July 1964.
33. Chipembere, op. cit., p. 16. Chipembere later said Msonthi was alleged to have been implicated in a scandal over trading licences for Asians.
34. Chipembere, op. cit., p. 16.
35. JP, Record of a meeting with Dr Banda, 28 July 1964.
36. Chiume says the meeting was on 5 August: Chiume, op. cit., p. 212. Chipembere also says 5 August: Chipembere, op. cit., p. 17.
37. DO 183 457, Cole to Sandys, Despatch No. 3, 14 October 1964.
38. The proposal was delayed when Jones agreed to ask the Commissioner of Police to deal with the particular case, of Khofi Phiri, in a different way: JP, Record of a meeting with Dr Banda at Government Lodge, Blantyre, 31 July 1963.

39. Oxford University Colonial Records Project (hereafter OUCRP), Youens interview with Sir Kenneth Bradley, 26 November 1970. Cameron says he resigned but did not walk out: Cameron, interview with author, 21 March 1998.
40. Cameron, interview with author, 21 March 1998.
41. Chiume, op. cit., p. 212.
42. Phillips, interview with author, 3 December 1997.
43. Chipembere, op. cit., p. 17.
44. Cameron, interview with author, 21 March 1998.
45. Chipembere, op. cit., pp. 17–18.
46. Walker, to the author, 12 April 2000, reporting Catherine Chipembere, interview with Walker, 24 February 2000.
47. Ross, *Reflections*.
48. Chiume wrote that this was on 5 August, but the correct date was 29 July: Chiume, op. cit., p. 212.
49. Chiume, op. cit., pp. 212–13. The first Act passed by the Malawi parliament was the Constitution of Malawi (Amendment) Act, No. 1 of 1964, which removed the obstruction to introducing restriction and detention legislation.
50. DO 183 445, Record of a meeting on 29 July 1964, by Jones dated 30 July.
51. Moxon reported that the meeting took place the following day and that 'Banda was in a stormy mood and raved about his need for security': York Papers, paper by Moxon. Jones's account is likely to be the more accurate.
52. Banda visited the United States in December 1964 to address the United Nations General Assembly: *Malawi News*, 15 December 1964. The introduction only of an enabling clause at this stage was agreed after Cameron had left the cabinet meeting.
53. DO 183 445, Record of a meeting on 29 July 1964, by Jones dated 30 July.
54. DO 183 61, Duke of Devonshire to Governor-General 17 August 1964.
55. JP, Record of a meeting between Jones and Banda held on 11 August 1964.
56. DO 183 61, Cole to CRO, 24 August 1964.
57. When the *Gazette* notice was published it was dated 31 July and transferred Cameron's ministerial responsibilities to Bwanausi with effect from 29 July: *Malawi Government Gazette*, 7 August 1964, p. 31.
58. JP, Diary, 1 August 1964.
59. JP, Note for the record, 6 August 1964.
60. JP, Record of a meeting between Jones and Banda, held on 11 August 1964.
61. JP, Diary, 12–13 August 1964.
62. Cameron, interview with author, 21 March 1998.
63. York Papers, paper by Moxon.
64. JP, Record of a meeting with Dr Banda at Government House, 22 April 1964.
65. Chipembere Seminar.
66. Chiume, op. cit., p. 213.
67. JP, Diary, 12 August 1964.
68. JP, Notes made by Sir Glyn Jones, Governor-General, between 24 August and 26 October 1964 (hereafter Jones Notes), 24 and 25 August 1964. Although the notes in the Jones Papers purport to have been written at the time, there is evidence in them that they were later compiled or copied from notes made at the time.

Notes to Chapter 6 · 335

69. Jones, Notes, 24 and 25 August 1964.
70. Short, op. cit., p. 204n. A Government Notice dated 10 August 1964 says that 'during the temporary absence from Malawi of the Minister of External Affairs the responsibilities of the Minister of External Affairs shall be assigned to the Prime Minister': *Malawi Government Gazette*, 1964, p. 37.
71. Ross, *Reflections*.
72. Short is uncertain of the dates of various cabinet meetings, saying a crucial one was on 16 August – a Sunday – rather than 26th – a Wednesday, the usual day for cabinet meetings – and this may have thrown his other dates out of gear. Others have copied Short's dates. Chiume and Chipembere are mistaken as to the date of the cabinet meeting when Cameron resigned, believing it to have been 5 August rather than 29 July.
73. Jones, Notes, 24 and 25 August 1964.
74. Chipembere, op. cit., pp. 11–12.
75. JP, secret and personal record of Meeting with Dr Banda on 11 August 1964.
76. Chipembere, op. cit., p. 12.
77. JP, Record of a meeting between Jones and Banda on 11 August 1964.
78. JP, Secret and personal record of a meeting between the Governor-General and the Prime Minister, 11 August 1964.
79. JP, Diary, 15–19 August 1964; Chiume, op. cit., p. 213.
80. DO 183 168, Secret and personal note by Cole, 20 August 1964, no addressee.
81. Jones, Notes, 24 and 25 August 1964.
82. Chipembere, op. cit., p. 6.
83. Ibid., p. 18.
84. Chiume to author, 20 October 1998.
85. Ross, *Reflections*.
86. Jones, Notes, 24 and 25 August 1964.
87. DO 183 168, Cole to Snelling, 24 August 1964.
88. DO 183 457, Cole to Sandys, 14 October 1964.
89. Chipembere, op. cit., p. 6.
90. Chiume, op. cit., p. 213.
91. Details in the following paragraphs dealing with the cabinet meeting of 26 August 1964, unless otherwise stated, are from JP, Minutes of a meeting of the cabinet held on Wednesday, 26 August 1964, at 9.30 a.m. in the No. 1 Committee Room, National Assembly Building, Zomba.
92. Short thought it probable that Tembo was not present: Short, op. cit., p. 207n.
93. Cole says, 'Ignoring the agenda the Ministers raised, one after another, all the policy matters which had caused them concern': DO 183 457, Cole to Sandys, Despatch No. 3, 14 October 1964. Based on information from Jones gathered from Banda and other ministers, Cole said, 'Ministers from the outset, clearly by pre-arrangement, went off at various tangents all hostile to Banda': DO 183 168, Cole to CRO, 28 August 1964. It was not the case that the agenda was ignored, nor that the ministers went off at tangents, although they undoubtedly used the agenda to raise and pursue their complaints.
94. Short says the proceedings opened with a discussion on establishing the university: Short, op. cit., p. 207. This was not so.

336 · Notes to Chapter 6

95. *Malawi Government Gazette*, 28 August 1964, p. 49.
96. The Constitution of Malawi, sections 59.3 and 61.1.
97. When, shortly, the need to keep regional ministers out of the cabinet disappeared – but rather to have them in the cabinet – this need to alter the constitution also disappeared.
98. Chipembere made much the same point about Youens's successor a few years later, claiming that Roberts was 'almost the Vice-President of the country. Very powerful indeed': Chipembere Seminar.
99. Youens's account says the ministers accused Banda of using the expatriate officials as 'spies to report on their activities'.
100. Phillips, interview with author, 3 December 1997; Youens, interview with author, 8 December 1997.
101. Youens, interview with author, 8 December 1997.
102. Jones, Notes, 26 August 1964. Short, op. cit., p. 207, says the discussion turned to the total Chinese aid offer. This must have been after Youens and Ellams left, because it is not in the minutes of the cabinet meeting.
103. DO 183 457, Cole to Sandys, Despatch No. 3, 14 October 1964.
104. Jones, Notes, 27 September (*sic*, must be August) 1964.
105. Attati Mpakati, 'Malawi: The Birth of a Neo-Colonial State', *Africa Review*, 1973, vol. 3, pt 1, p. 63.
106. OUCRP, Youens, interview with Sir Kenneth Bradley, 26 November 1970 and interview with author, 8 December 1997.
107. Roberts, interviews with author, 26 and 27 July and 6 August 1982. Cole also says Banda was 'seriously contemplating resignation': DO 183 457, Cole to Sandys, Despatch No. 3, 14 October 1964.
108. It is clear from Jones's papers that Banda did not see him that evening but did so the following evening.
109. Chiume, op. cit., p. 214.
110. Hansard, Second Meeting, First Session, 8–9 September 1964, pp. 10–11.
111. Hansard, Second Meeting, First Session, 8–9 September 1964, pp. 10–12. Some of what Banda told parliament, especially about the possibility of resigning, must have taken place after Youens and Ellams left, because it does not appear in the minutes of the meeting.
112. OUCRP, Youens, interview with Sir Kenneth Bradley, 26 November 1970. The British prime minister had been briefed as early as January 1960 that 'even if standards were lowered, nothing which approached a nucleus of a locally staffed senior service would be available in Nyasaland for several decades': CO 1015 2629, Matters Arising from Prime Minister's Tour of Nyasaland, January 1960.
113. DO 183 168, Cole to Commonwealth Relations Office, 28 August 1964.
114. Jones, Notes, 26 September (*sic*, must be August) 1964.
115. Ibid. Short, op. cit., p. 207, says Banda discussed the situation with Jones 'in the interim', i.e. between the two meetings with the ministers on 26 August and at 11 a.m. the following day. Jones's account, his diary and Cole's account make it clear that Jones and Banda did not see each other or discuss the situation on 26 August, nor the following day until the evening.
116. See Short, p. 208: it became clear that the difficulties were not insuperable; the meeting ended amicably; and the ministers were to list the subjects on which they wished to have further talks and Banda would consider them point by point.
117. Jones, Notes, 27 September (*sic*, must be August) 1964.

118. Jones, Notes, 27 September (*sic*, must be August) 1964.
119. DO 183 457, Cole to Sandys, Despatch No. 3, 14 October 1964, p. 8.
120. Quoted in Trelford, 'An Editor in Malawi', *The Listener*, 6 January 1977, p. 16.
121. Short, however, claimed that it was agreed that 'On foreign policy there could be further discussions': Short, op. cit., p. 208.
122. DO 183 168, Cole to CRO, 28 August 1964.
123. P. Howard, interview with author, 30 July 1994.
124. OUCRP, Youens interview with Kettlewell, 19 February 1985.
125. Chiume, op. cit., p. 214.
126. JP, document headed 'Matters on Which Ministers Want Immediate Action Taken'.
127. John Spicer, Salisbury *Sunday Mail*, 18 October 1964.
128. Chipembere, op. cit., pp. 13–16.
129. Jones, Notes, 28 September (*sic*, must be August) 1964.
130. Hansard, Second Meeting, First Session, 8–9 September 1964, p. 12.
131. Jones, Notes, 28 September (*sic*, must be August) 1964.
132. Ibid.
133. In speaking of Chiume leading the attack against him, Banda said he thought Chirwa and Chisiza might follow him, but Jones's note of the meeting does not make it clear whether 'him' meant Banda or Chiume: Jones Notes, 28 September (*sic*, must be August) 1964.
134. Jones, Notes, 29 August 1964.
135. Hansard, Second Meeting, First Session, 8–9 September 1964, pp. 137–8.
136. DO 183 168, Cole to Commonwealth Relations Office, 30 August 1964. A good deal of Cole's information came directly from the head of Special Branch: Cole to author, November 1994.
137. Chiume, op. cit., p. 214. The date for the next session of parliament had already been altered from 3 to 2 September: *Malawi Government Gazette*, 21 August 1964, p. 49.
138. DO 183 168, Cole to Snelling, 3 September 1964.
139. DO 183 168, Watson to Cole, 3 September 1964.
140. DO 183 168, British High Commissioner to Commonwealth Relations Office, 4 September 1964.
141. DO 183 168, 10 Downing Street (signature unclear) to P. J. S. Moon, Commonwealth Relations Office, n.d. but early September 1964.
142. DO 183 168, Broadley, British embassy in Washington, to Jamieson, Commonwealth Relations Office, 2 September 1964.
143. Cameron, interview with author, 21 March 1998 and telephone conversation 11 October 1999.
144. Jones, Notes, 29 September (*sic*, must be August) 1964.
145. Chipembere, op. cit., p. 19. On the other hand, Tembo was at the cabinet meeting on 26 August and took part in the criticisms of Banda, and Chirwa told parliament that Tembo had 'been present at all the critical and tragic discussions': Hansard, Second Meeting, First Session, 8–9 September 1964, p. 99.

7. Banda's Retaliation

1. Hansard, Second Meeting, First Session, 8–9 September 1964, pp. 12–13.
2. Chipembere, op. cit., p. 19.

338 · Notes to Chapter 7

3. DO 183 168, Cole to Snelling, 3 September 1964.
4. Hansard, Second Meeting, First Session, 8–9 September 1964, pp. 12–13.
5. Ibid., p. 101.
6. Ibid., p. 52.
7. Ibid., pp. 73–4.
8. Jones, Notes, 29 August 1964.
9. Jones, Notes, 31 August 1964.
10. Chipembere, op. cit., pp. 7–9. Chiume also wrote of the consultations Banda had with the stalwarts: Chiume, op. cit., p. 215. Banda had access to Special Branch reports of his ministers' speeches and could assess them independently of any other reports he received.
11. Ibid. In this note Jones records the Saturday meeting between Banda and his ministers as being on 28 September, but this is clearly a mistake for 28 August.
12. Lusaka *Mail Magazine*, 2 October 1964.
13. Jones, Notes, 31 August 1964; JP, Meeting held at Government House on Monday 31 August 1964. The reference to not being 'Nyererized' relates to Banda's view that President Nyerere of Tanzania – who gave up the premiership of his country after a short time in that office, to concentrate on party affairs and who disappeared during the January 1964 mutiny of the Tanganyika Rifles – was a weak person unable to control people like Kambona his foreign affairs minister, a friend of Chiume: JP, Note for the Record, 22 August 1964.
14. York Papers. Visit to Dar es Salaam and Blantyre by Krobo Edusei, November 1964.
15. Jones, Notes, 31 August 1964.
16. This was in fact Banda's suggestion, though he proposed to achieve it by his momentary resignation and instantaneous reappointment.
17. Jones, Notes, 1 September 1964.
18. JP, timetable note on meetings of 2 September 1964; Jones, Notes, 2 September 1964.
19. Jones, Notes, 2 September 1964.
20. DO 183 457, Cole to Sandys, Despatch No.3, 14 October 1964.
21. OUCRP, Youens, interview with Sir Kenneth Bradley, 26 November 1970.
22. Jones, Notes, 2 September 1964.
23. Short, op. cit., p. 209.
24. Jones, Notes, 2 September 1964.
25. Ibid.
26. This may have meant that the prime minister was ultimately solely responsible for the government of the country rather than that the ministers were irresponsible in the way they acted.
27. JP, Meeting held in Government House at 6.30 p.m. on Wednesday, 2 September 1964.
28. M. Tadman to author, 3 December 1998.
29. Chipembere, op. cit., p. 18.
30. Jones Notes, 3 September 1964.
31. Ibid.
32. Chiume, interview with author, 13–14 December 1998.
33. Jones, Notes, 3 September 1964.
34. Jones, Notes, 4 September 1964.
35. B. Jones-Walters, conversations, 1992–96.
36. Cole to Snelling, 3 September 1964. Cole later said that Chiume was 'a

Notes to Chapter 7 · 339

rabid nationalist, ready to burn his fingers with Communist aid, and nobody would regret his going': DO 183 457, Cole to Sandys, Despatch No. 3, 14 October 1964.

37. Jones, Notes, 4 September 1964.
38. DO 183 168, Cole to Watson, 4 September 1964.
39. Jones, Notes, 4 September 1964.
40. DO 183 168, Cole to Watson, 4 September 1964.
41. Jones, Notes, 4 September 1964.
42. Ibid.
43. 'Attorney-General' may have been a slip in Jones's account for 'minister of justice'.
44. Short, op. cit., p. 210n. Short says Chipembere was 'apprised of events at home' when he received the telegram the day before parliament met. This would put the date of receiving the telegram as 7 September, but it would not give sufficient time for him to arrive back in Malawi the following day.
45. DO 183 168, Cole to Watson, and Cole to Snelling, both 5 September 1964. See also Neale to Cole, 5 September 1964.
46. By 5 September, the Commonwealth Relations Office already knew that Chipembere was on his way back to Malawi: DO 183 168, Neale to Cole, 5 September 1964.
47. Hansard, Second Meeting, First Session, 8–9 September 1964, p. 89.
48. Jones, Notes, 6 September 1964.
49. DO 183 168, Cole to Snelling, 6 September 1964..
50. DO 183 168, Banda to Chibambo, n.d. but probably September 1964.
51. Jones, Notes, 7 September 1964. Banda's advice on the offices to be vacated was formalized in JP, Banda to Jones, 7 September 1964.
52. Jones, Notes, 7 September 1964.
53. DO 183 168, Cole to Snelling, 7 September 1964.
54. Chiume, op. cit., p. 204.
55. Jones, Notes, 7 September 1964.
56. Ibid.
57. Chiume, op. cit., pp. 203–4.
58. Chiume, interview with author, 13–14 December 1998.
59. Chiume, op. cit., p. 204.
60. JP, Chisiza to Governor-General, 7 September 1964; Chokani to Governor-General, 7 September 1964; and Msonthi to Governor-General, 7 September 1964.
61. Chokani to author, 28 January 1999.
62. P. Howard, interview with author, 30 July 1994.
63. OUCRP, Youens, interview with Kettlewell, 19 February 1985.
64. Chiume, interview with author, 13–14 December 1998.
65. Hansard, Third Session, Fourth Meeting, 11–19 January 1966, pp. 449–50.
66. Jones, Notes, 7 September 1964.
67. Jones, Notes, 8 September 1964.
68. Youens, interview with author, 8 December 1997.
69. Hansard, Second Meeting, First Session, 8 and 9 September 1964, pp. 10–141. The wording of the motion is contained in JP, Prime Minister to Clerk of the National Asembly, 7 September 1964.
70. Loft Papers, Menzies to Loft, 11 September 1964.
71. DO 183 457, Cole to Sandys, Despatch No. 3, 14 October 1964.
72. Chiume, op. cit., pp. 204–5.

73. *Parade*, October 1964, p. 10.
74. Short, op. cit., p. 212.
75. Short, op. cit., p. 213.
76. Hansard, Second Meeting, First Session, 8 and 9 September 1964, p. 89.
77. *Parade*, October 1964, p. 10.
78. Lusaka *Mail Magazine*, 2 October 1964.
79. Hansard, Second Meeting, First Session, 8 and 9 September 1964, p. 126.
80. Hansard, Second Meeting, First Session, 8 and 9 September 1964, p. 89. See also DO 183 457, Cole to Sandys, Despatch No. 3, 14 October 1964,
81. Jones, Notes, 8 September 1964.
82. I. C. H. Freemen, conversations with author, late 1960s.
83. Jones, Notes, 8 September 1964.
84. Hansard, Second Meeting, First Session, 8 and 9 September 1964, pp. 89–90.
85. Jones, Notes, 9 September 1964.
86. Hansard, Second Meeting, First Session, 8 and 9 September 1964, p. 138.
87. Jones, Notes, 9 September 1964. See also Hansard, Second Meeting, First Session, 8 and 9 September 1964, p. 90.
88. JP, Chipembere to Jones, 9 September 1964.
89. P. Moxon, *Malawi – The 1964 Cabinet Crisis* enclosed with Tovey to author, 1 July 1999; the paper is from York Papers.
90. Mpakati, op. cit., p. 62.
91. Chiume, op. cit., p. 216.
92. Jones, Notes, 10 September 1964.
93. Hansard, Second Meeting, First Session, 8 and 9 September 1964, p. 92; *Parade*, October 1964, p. 12.
94. Chiume, op. cit., pp. 216–17.
95. Cynthia Magee to author, 7 February and 9 July 1999. Curiously, her husband had been the first police officer to examine Dunduzu Chisiza's car after the fatal crash in 1962.
96. Chiume, op. cit., pp. 217–18.
97. DO 183 168, Cole to Snelling, 6 September 1964.
98. DO 183 168, Approved draft, Commonwealth Relations Office to British High Commissioner, Zomba, 9 September 1964, and minute – 'Message issued' – Snelling to Neale, 10 September 1964. Mpakati mistakenly saw 'the fact that Britain did not use the Cabinet crisis to her own advantage by siding with one of the parties' as evidence that neither Banda nor the rebels were a threat to the British economic interest in Malawi.
99. Jones, Notes, 10 September 1964; *Malawi Government Gazette*, 1964, p. 83.
100. York Papers, n.d. but 10 September 1964.
101. DO 183 457, Cole to Sandys, Despatch No. 3, 14 October 1964.
102. DO 183 168, Cole to Snelling, 10 September 1964. For the appeal to the country, see DO 183 457, Cole to Sandys, Despatch No. 3, 14 October 1964.
103. JP, Diary, 12 September 1964.
104. DO 183 168, Cole to Commonwealth Relations Office, 12 September 1964.
105. Chiume, op. cit., pp. 218–19.
106. *Rhodesia Herald*, 10 October 1964.
107. DO 183 168, Cole to Snelling, 10 September 1964. See also Short, op. cit., pp. 216–17, and Malawi *Times*, 14 September 1964.
108. Jones Notes, 14 September 1964.

109. Jones Notes, 15 September 1964.
110. DO 183 457, Cole to Sandys, Despatch No. 3, 14 October 1964, p. 15.
111. Jones, Notes, 16 September 1964.
112. JP, Commissioner of Police to Officers in Charge of Police, Karonga and Fort Johnston, 16 September 1964.
113. Jones, Notes, 16 September 1964.
114. DO 1883 457, Cole to Sandys, Despatch No. 3, 14 October 1964.
115. *Sunday Mail*, Salisbury, 18 October 1964.
116. JP, Diary, 17 September 1964; Jones, Notes, 17 September 1964.
117. JP, Secretary to Governor-General to Governor-General, 16 September 1964.
118. *Malawi Government Gazette*, 1964, p. 89.
119. *Sunday Mail*, Salisbury, 20 September 1964. This newspaper also reported that the central executive 'split 6–5 in [Banda's] favour over the cabinet dismissals and resignations'.
120. Jones, Notes, 18 September 1964.
121. Jones, Notes, 19 September 1964.
122. Ibid.
123. Cameron, interview with author, 21 March 1998.
124. Unattributable.
125. Southern Rhodesia Radio, 20 September 1964, cited in Jones Notes, 20 September 1964.
126. Participant observation by author.
127. Malawi Information Department, press release, 20 September 1964, cited in Short, op. cit., p. 219.
128. Short, op. cit., p. 219.
129. Jones, Notes, 20 September 1964.
130. Jones, Notes, 21 September 1964.
131. DO 183 457, Cole to Sandys, Despatch No. 3, 14 October 1964.
132. Jones, Notes, 21 September 1964.
133. *Malawi Government Gazette*, 1964, pp. 91, 123.
134. DO 183 457, Cole to Sandys, Despatch No. 3, 14 October 1964.
135. JP, Diary, 21 and 23 September 1964.
136. *The Central African Examiner*, October 1964.
137. Jones, Notes, 25 September 1964.
138. Jones ,Notes, 26 September 1964.
139. *Malawi Times*, 24 September 1964.
140. *Rhodesia Herald*, 23 September 1964.
141. JP, Secret note for the record, 26 September 1964.
142. JP, Secret and personal record, 6 August 1964.
143. Unattributable.
144. Chiume, op. cit., p. 220.
145. Hansard, October 1967, p. 113; *Rhodesia Herald*, 1 October 1964.
146. OUCRP, Youens interview with Sir Kenneth Bradley, 26 November 1970.
147. *Rhodesia Herald*, 27 September 1964.
148. DO 183 457, Cole to Sandys, Despatch No. 3, 14 October 1964. See also *Rhodesia Herald*, 27 September 1964.
149. DO 183 457, Cole to Sandys, Despatch No. 3, 14 October 1964. There are photographs of the burned-out car, BA 6933, in *Rhodesia Herald*, 30 September 1964 and in Malawi *Times*, 10 October 1964.

150. Chiume to author, 7 November 1999.
151. Lewis, interview with author, 31 January 1996.
152. *Rhodesia Herald*, 30 September 1964.
153. Chiume, interview with author, 13–14 December 1998.
154. Chiume to author, 7 November 1999; *Rhodesia Herald*, 8 October 1964.
155. DO 183 457, Cole to Sandys, Despatch No. 3, 14 October 1964, pp. 19–22. For attack on Chakuamba and Chirwa, see DO 183 168, Commonwealth Relations Office to all British High Commissioners, n.d. but early October 1964. A photograph of the burned MCP headquarters building in Zomba is in *Rhodesia Herald*, 30 September 1964 and in *Malawi Times*, 10 October 1964. The words in square brackets in the Cole quotation are from *Rhodesia Herald*, 29 and 30 September 1964.
156. T. Young to author, 8 December 1999.
157. DO 183 457, Cole to Sandys, Despatch No. 3, 14 October 1964; *Rhodesia Herald*, 30 September 1964; *Malawi Times*, 2 October 1964.
158. JP, Chipembere to Jones, transcript of a telephone call from Chipembere to the Governor-General, drafted jointly by Jones and Youens, n.d. but probably 30 September 1964.
159. Chipembere Seminar.
160. *Sunday Mail*, 20 September 1964, citing Robert Conley writing in the *New York Times*.
161. JP, Chipembere to Jones, transcript of a telephone call from Chipembere to the Governor-General, drafted jointly by Jones and Youens, n.d. but probably 30 September 1964.
162. *Rhodesia Herald*, 30 September 1964.
163. *Rhodesia Herald*, 1 October 1964.
164. DO 183 457, Cole to Sandys, Despatch No. 3, 14 October 1964. See also *Malawi Times*, 2 October 1964.
165. OUCRP, Youens, interview with Sir Kenneth Bradley, 26 November 1970.
166. *Rhodesia Herald*, 1 October 1964.
167. DO 183 457, Cole to Sandys, Despatch No. 3, 14 October 1964.
168. Ibid.
169. *Rhodesia Herald*, 7 October 1964.
170. DO 183 457, Cole to Sandys, Despatch No. 3, 14 October 1964.
171. Chipembere, op. cit., p. 20.
172. Sanger to author 11 March 2000.
173. DO 183 457, Cole to Sandys, Despatch No. 3, 14 October 1964.
174. Sanger to author 11 March 2000.
175. *Rhodesia Herald*, 7 October 1964.
176. Hansard, Third Meeting, First Session, 27–30 October 1964, pp. 251–2.
177. Ibid., p. 225.
178. *Rhodesia Herald*, 10 October 1964. See also Malawi Information Department transcript of speech by Dr Banda at Kasungu, 5 October 1964, cited in Short, op. cit., p. 222.
179. OUCRP, Youens, interview with Sir Kenneth Bradley, 26 November 1970.
180. Photographs of the crowd and the police mobile force are printed in *Malawi Times*, 10 October 1964.
181. JP, Jones to Banda, 10 October 1964.
182. Ibid.

183. For an MCP account of the success of Banda's tour, see leading article in *Malawi News*, 13 October 1964.
184. JP, Secret note for the record, by Jones, 17 October 1964.
185. Jones, Notes, 19 October 1964.
186. *Malawi News*, 13 October 1964.
187. OUCRP, Youens, interview with Sir Kenneth Bradley, 26 November 1970. Jones's account says that on Youens's return he told them that Banda had said he would be pleased to see Chirwa 'for the purpose stated' and they both immediately, at about 6.45 p.m., left for Banda's house.
188. Chiume to author, 7 November 1999.
189. OUCRP, Youens, interview with Sir Kenneth Bradley, 26 November 1970.
190. Jones, Notes, 19 October 1964.
191. Chiume, to author, 7 November 1999.
192. Jones, Notes, 19 October 1964.
193. The following details of the Banda–Chirwa meeting, except where otherwise stated, are from Jones, Notes, 20 October 1964.
194. OUCRP, Youens, interview with Sir Kenneth Bradley, 26 November 1970.
195. Ibid.
196. Ibid.
197. W. Chipanda to author, 18 January and 23 June 1998.
198. Roberts, interviews with author, 26 and 27 July and 6 August 1982.
199. Jones, Notes, 20 October 1964.
200. Short, op. cit., p. 223.
201. Jones, Notes, 21 October 1964.
202. JP, Jones, no addressee, but to Chirwa, 22 October 1964.
203. OUCRP, Youens, interview with Sir Kenneth Bradley, 26 November 1970.
204. Roberts, interviews with author, 26 and 27 July and 6 August 1982.
205. *Malawi News*, 13 October 1964.
206. Chevallier to author, 11 January 1999.
207. *Malawi News*, 13 October 1964.
208. Chevallier to author, 11 January 1999.
209. *The Nationalist*, Dar es Salaam, 17 October 1964, cited in *Rhodesia Herald*, 18 October 1964. The allegations that Banda was dabbling in witchcraft were designed to lower his reputation as a well-educated Western medical doctor.
210. *Malawi News*, 20 October 1964.
211. York Papers. Visit to Dar es Salaam and Blantyre by Krobo Edusei, November 1964.
212. JP, Note by Roberts: address to civil servants, 22 October 1964.
213. Short, op. cit., p. 223.
214. Chiume, to author, 7 November 1999.
215. *The Times*, 15 December 1965.
216. Jones, Notes, 26 October 1964.
217. Chokani, to author, 28 January 1999.
218. JP, Diary, 26 October 1964.
219. Chiume, to author, 23 January 2000.
220. L. Bean, telephone conversation with author, 4 November 1997.
221. JP, Note of meeting with Dr Banda, 29 October 1964.
222. Cameron, interview with author, 21 March 1998.
223. JP, Note for the record, meeting of 3 November 1964.
224. JP, Diary, 28 September 1964.

8. Chipembere's Attempted *Coup d'État*

1. T. Stoneman to author, 1 October 1998.
2. JP, Chipembere to Jones, 7 March 1965.
3. Stoneman to author, 1 October 1998.
4. Hansard, Second Meeting, First Session, 8-9 September 1964, p. 95.
5. JP, Chipembere to Jones, 7 March 1965.
6. *Malawi Government Gazette*, 13 and 20 November 1964.
7. Hansard, Third Meeting, First Session, 27-30 October 1964, p. 164.
8. The folowing account is based on J. and D. Arden to author, 19 February 1999; Mrs Arden, conversation with author, 19 September 1997.
9. David Baptie to his parents, 3 November 1964, privately held.
10. Young to author, 8 December 1999.
11. JP, Chipembere to Jones, 7 March 1965.
12. Two hundred is the figure given by the government. Chipembere said there were only about a hundred and they were joined by about fifty others, who took advantage of the situation to loot and destroy property: JP, Chipembere to Jones, 7 March 1965.
13. Denton to author, 23 July 1996.
14. Stoneman to author, 21 October 1998.
15. R. Frasier to author, 15 August 1999.
16. W. Cleveland to author, 28 August and 10 October 1999.
17. Cleveland to author, 28 August 1999.
18. Stoneman to author, 21 October 1998.
19. R. Tovey to author, 11 March 1999.
20. W. Hayward to author, 3 August 1999.
21. Tragically, a year later, Mrs Harding returned to Fort Johnston with the specific intention of committing suicide. She died of a drug overdose taken while staying at the Palm Beach Hotel: Young to author, 8 December 1999.
22. Martha Jarrett James [Kevin Denny], *Zagwa Zatha*, a draft novel, 1999.
23. Stoneman to author, 21 October 1998; Young to author, 8 December 1999.
24. Hansard, Third Session, Fourth Meeting, 11-19 January 1966, p. 449.
25. T.J.P. Lewis, interview with author, 13 October 1998; Denton to author, 1 December 1998.
26. Ross, 'A Return to Malawi', *Edinburgh University History Graduates Association Newslatter*, No. 30, October 1998, p. 16.
27. Lewis, interview with author, 13 October 1998. Special Branch also heard nothing of canoes being used: Denton to author, 1 December 1998.
28. Stoneman to author, 21 October 1998.
29. Hayward to author, 3 August 1999.
30. Lewis, interview with author, 13 October 1998. The duty company was sent because, not having attended the mess night function, they were more immediately alert than their fellows.
31. Hansard, Second Session, Fifth Meeting, 6-13 April 1965, p. 505; Lewis, interview with author, 13 October 1998.
32. Denton to author, 23 July 1996.
33. Tovey to author, 11 March 1999.
34. Hayward to author, 3 and 12 August 1999.
35. Hansard, Second Session, Fifth Meeting, 6-13 April 1965, pp. 507-8; Young to author, 8 December 1999. See also Short, op. cit., pp. 227-8.

36. Tovey to author, 11 March 1999.
37. Short, op. cit., p. 228.
38. Young to author, 8 December 1999.
39. Cleveland to author, 28 August 1999.
40. Chipembere Seminar.
41. Bill Jackson, *Send Us Friends* (Blantyre: Claim, n.d., c. 1997), pp. 284–5.
42. Young to author, 8 December 1999.
43. Tovey to author, 11 March 1999.
44. Hayward to author, 3 August 1999.
45. B. S. Ward to author, 7 February 1995.
46. JP, Diary, 29 March 1965. During Jones's absence on leave the Chief Justice, Sir Frederick Southworth, was Acting Governor-General, a person far less likely to be confided in than Jones.
47. Denton to author, 1 December 1998.
48. JP, Banda to Jones, 1 February 1965
49. Arden to author, 5 February 1999.
50. Hansard, First Session, Fourth Meeting, 19–26 January 1965, pp. 498–9.
51. Mpakati, op. cit., pp. 66–7.
52. JP, Chipembere to Jones, 7 March 1965. Changwa was a forty-three-year old Malawian police officer who had been in the force since 1951: Staff List.
53. Stoneman to author, 21 October 1998.
54. Ross, conversation with author, 30 October 1997.
55. A. Ross, 'A Return to Malawi', *Edinbugh University History Graduates Association Newsletter*, no. 30, October 1998, pp. 12–20.
56. DO 208 2, Cole to CRO, Despatch No. 3, 7 April 1966.
57. Lucas to author, 22 April 1999.
58. Lewis interview with author, 13 October 1998.
59. Unattributable.
60. Lewis, telephone conversation with author, 12 November 1998; Staff List 1965.
61. DO 183 457, Cole to Sandys, Despatch No. 3, 14 October 1964.
62. Chiume, interview with author, 13–14 December 1998.
63. Ward to author, 7 February 1995.
64. Denton to author, 1 December 1998.
65. Chipembere, op. cit., p. 20.
66. Hansard, Second Session, Fifth Meeting, 6–13 April 1965, p. 506.
67. Ibid.; JP, Notes for a talk to university staff, 8 February 1966.
68. Hansard, Fifth Session, First Meeting, 3–6 October 1967, p. 114.
69. Chevallier to author, 11 January 1999.
70. JP, Chipembere to Bolt, 7 March 1965.
71. JP, Chipembere to Jones, 7 March 1965.
72. Chiume, interview with author, 13–14 December 1998; Chiume to author, 7 November 1999.
73. Ross also made the point that there were many followers with Chipembere from other southern districts: Ross, interview with author, 26 May 1999.
74. JP, Secret note for file, by Jones, n.d. but 10 March 1965.
75. Short, op. cit., p. 228, says £500.
76. JP, enclosed with Chipembere to Jones, 7 March 1965.
77. JP, Jones to Chipembere, 17 March 1965.
78. Chiume, interview with author, 13–14 December 1998.

346 · Notes to Chapters 8 and 9

79. JP, Chipembere to Lady Jones, 16 March 1965.
80. Hansard, Second Session, Fifth Meeting, 12 April 1965, pp. 641–2.
81. Ibid. p. 648.
82. Hansard, Third Session, Third Meeting, 9–10 November 1965, p. 250.
83. JP, Diary, 27–9 March 1965.
84. Lewis, interview with author, 31 January 1996.
85. JP, Chipembere to Jones, 25 March 1965.
86. Hansard, Second Session, Fifth Meeting, 6–13 April 1965, p. 505.
87. York Papers, Cole to CRO, 24 March 1965.
88. JP, Record of meeting with Dr Banda, 18 March 1965.
89. Hansard, Second Session, Fifth Meeting, 6–13 April 1965, p. 509.
90. JP, Secret note for the record, by Jones, 6 April 1965.
91. JP, Record of meetings on 5 and 6 April 1965, dated 6 April 1965. This suggests that Lomax had not instigated the letter from Chipembere to Gilstrap, as might have been suspected, though it does not positively dispose of the suspicion.
92. JP, Record of Meetings on 5 and 6 April 1965, dated 6 April 1965.
93. These facts are deducible from the letter Chipembere to Gideon Banda, 17 April 1965, in JP.
94. JP, Chipembere to Jones, 26 October 1965.
95. Hansard, Second Session, Fifth Meeting, 6–13 April 1965, p. 509.
96. Ibid. pp. 712–3.
97. The known wanted men, in addition to Chipembere, included Silombela, Masharubo, Lipande, Julias Motoli, Kapinda, Sinoya, Akim Harry Stambuli, Tenga Maloya and Ndomondo. JP, Reward notice.
98. Chiume to author, 7 November 1999.
99. JP, Chipembere to Gideon Banda, 17 April 1965.
100. Ibid.
101. Ibid.

9. Chipembere's Evacuation

1. Denton to author, 23 July 1996.
2. Denton to author, 19 November 1996.
3. It is known that the letter went over Gideon Banda's name because it was to him that Chipembere later replied.
4. Lewis, interview with author, 13 October 1998.
5. Lucas, interviews with author, 18 February 1997 and 12 March 1999.
6. The following details of the evacuation of Chipembere, unless otherwise stated, are from Denton to author, 2 April 1996, 9 July 1996, 23 July 1996, 19 November 1996, 24 May 1997, 12 August 1997, 17 December 1997, 1 December 1998 and 1 February 2000.
7. T. Young to author, 8 December 1999.
8. Lewis, interview with author, 13 October 1998, and telephone conversation with author, 12 November 1998.
9. Ross, interview with author, 26 May 1999.
10. Lewis, interview with author, 31 January 1996.
11. JP, Chipembere to Jones, 26 October 1965.
12. JP, Gondwe to Banda, n.d. but shortly after 8 November 1965.

13. DO 208 28, Briefing for minister of state's visit to Nairobi, n d., but early 1966.
14. Denton to author, 1 December 1998.
15. Youens to author, 5 May 1998.
16. JP, Reuters, press statement given by Chipembere to Bates on 27 May 1965, enclosed in W. B. Hussey to Jones, 4 June 1965.
17. Hansard, Third Session, First Meeting, 7–15 July 1965, p. 142.
18. Material in this and the following three paragraphs, unless otherwise stated, is from Ross to author, 14 August 1997, 30 June 1998, 30 October 1998 and 14 December 1998; Ross, conversation with author, 30 October 1997; Ross, seminar paper, 'Reflections on the Malawi "Cabinet Crisis" 1964–5'; Ross, interview with author, 26 May 1999; and Ross, 'A Return to Malawi', *Edinburgh University History Graduates Association Newsletter*, No. 30, October 1998, pp. 12–20.
19. H. B. M. Chipembere, *My Malawian Ancestors*, August 1999; Robert Rotberg to author, 2 December 1998.
20. Cameron to author, 27 November 1998.
21. JP, Notes, 6 September 1964.
22. Ross, interview with author, 9 September 1999.
23. JP, Malcolm to Lomax, 14 May 1965.
24. Ross to author, 14 December 1998.
25. JP, Malcolm to Watson, 18 May 1965.
26. A. Ross, 'A Return to Malawi', *Edinburgh University History Graduates Association Newsletter*, No. 30, October 1998, p. 16.
27. Young to author, 8 December 1999.
28. Ibid.
29. Ross, interview with author, 9 September 1999.
30. JP, Malcolm to Lomax, 14 May 1965.
31. Ibid.
32. DO 208 17 and 28; British high commission and Commonwealth Office papers refer only to the operation being arranged by Malawi Special Branch with US knowledge.
33. DO 208 28, Briefing for Minister of State's visit to Nairobi, n.d., but early 1966.
34. Youens, interview with author, 8 December 1997.
35. Ross later said that he was 'shaking and went to pieces' when he learned that Banda might not have known what was going on, though his wife 'reacted rather better': Ross, interview with author, 26 May 1999.
36. JP, Malcolm to Watson, 14 May 1965.
37. Ibid.; Ross, interview with author, 26 May 1999.
38. JP, Malcolm to Watson, 14 May 1965.
39. Ross substantially confirmed this account in 'A Return to Malawi', *Edinburgh University History Graduates Association Newsletter*, No. 30, October 1998, p. 17.
40. Material in this and the following six paragraphs, unless otherwise stated, is from JP, Malcolm to Watson, 18 May 1965.
41. A. Ross, 'A Return to Malawi', *Edinburgh University History Graduates Association Newsletter*, no. 30, October 1998, p. 17.
42. Ibid., p. 17.
43. Ross to author, 14 December 1998.
44. A. Ross, 'A Return to Malawi', *Edinburgh University History Graduates Association Newsletter*, no. 30, October 1998, pp. 12–20.

45. Ross interview with author 26 May 1999.
46. JP, Malcolm to Watson, 18 May 1965.
47. Ross's poor opinion of Chiume was matched by Chiume's poor opinion of Ross, even thirty-five years later: Chiume to author, 7 November 1999.
48. The list of sixty-four 'Daily Major Incident Reports from the Police Files, January–February 1965' contains none from the Balaka area: Chiume, *Kwacha*, pp. 233–9.
49. G.J. Bender, 'A Tribute to Henry Chipembere', *African Studies Newsletter*, vol. viii no. 6, December 1975, pp. 12–13.
50. Ibid.
51. Lucas, interviews with author, 18 February 1997 and 12 March 1999.
52. Cleveland to author, 28 August 1999.
53. Mpakati, op. cit., p. 59.
54. DO 208 18, Cole to CRO, 4 November 1966
55. Young to author, 8 December 1999.
56. Ross, *Reflections*.
57. *Malawi: Amnesty International's Concerns* (London: Amnesty International, 1989), p. 13. See also *Where Silence Rules: The Supression of Dissent in Malawi* (New York: Africa Watch, 1990), p. 27.
58. Young to author, 8 December 1999.
59. Ibid.
60. Hansard, Third Session, First Meeting, 7–15 July 1965, p. 12.
61. W. T. Zingani, interview with author, 15 December 1999.
62. Hansard, Third Session, First Meeting, 7–15 July 1965, p. 12.
63. JP, Jones to Banda, 1 June 1965.
64. JP, Chipembere to Jones, 26 October 1965.
65. Hansard, Third Session, Second Meeting, 5–7 October 1965, pp. 162–3 and see also p. 157.
66. Ibid., pp. 144–8.
67. JP, Meeting with Dr Banda at Government Lodge, 12 September 1965.
68. Ibid.
69. Hansard, Third Session, Third Meeting, 9–10 November 1965, pp. 272–3.
70. Hansard, Third Session, Second Meeting, 5–7 October 1965, p. 163; Roberts, interviews with author, 26 and 27 July and 6 August 1982; Lewis, interview with author, 13 October 1998; Young to author, 8 December 1999.
71. Young to author, 8 December 1999.
72. JP, meeting with Dr Banda at Government Lodge, 12 September 1965.
73. Hansard, Third Session, Third Meeting, 9–10 November 1965, p. 276.
74. Lucas to author, 9 December 1996.
75. Lewis, interviews with author, 31 January 1996 and 13 October 1998; Lucas to author, 9 December 1996.
76. D. McCarry to author, 2 April 2000.
77. Hansard, Third Session, Third Meeting, 9–10 November 1965, p. 251.
78. DO 208 21, Beswick to Kerby, 30 December 1965; Commonwealth Secretary to Byrne, 15 January 1966.
79. DO 208 21, Undated document, but November 1965.
80. DO 208 21. There are many letters on this file expressing fears that Silombela would not receive a fair trial and hoping that he would not be hanged, at least not in public.

Notes to Chapter 9 · 349

81. Jackson, op. cit., p. 316; Cameron, interview with author, 21 March 1998.
82. See DO 208 21 for references to the petition.
83. DO 208 21, Bottomly to Grimond, 6 January 1966.
84. DO 208 21, Cole to CRO, 21 January 1966.
85. York Papers, Nkrumah to Banda, 10 January 1966.
86. York Papers, Owusu to Nkrumah, 19 January 1966.
87. York Papers, Banda to Nkrumah, 31 January 1966.
88. York Papers, Banda to Nkrumah, 16 February 1966.
89. DO 208 21, Banda to Grimond, 31 December 1965.
90. JP, handwritten notes, dated 11 June 1969.
91. JP, note by Jones of a meeting with Banda, 5 November 1965.
92. H. S. Peters, conversations with author, 1966. In reporting Banda's acceptance of this suggestion to the Queen, Jones said it was his suggestion, but it is clear from various sources that it was in fact Roberts's: DO 208 21, Cole to CRO, 21 January 1966.
93. DO 208 21, Cole to CRO, 24 January 1966.
94. DO 208 21, Defence Adviser to High Commissioner Zomba, 2 February 1966, and Cole to CRO 3, February 1966. For other reports of the execution, see Bill Jackson, *Send Us Friends* (Malawi: Claim, n.d.), Chapter 30; *Guardian, Sun* and *The Times*, 2 February 1966. *The Times* seems to attribute the leadership of the February 1965 attempted coup to Silombela. Jackson says the padre, Rev. Fred Chintali, left Silombela at 6.40 a.m. and was not with him at the actual execution.
95. JP, Chipembere to Jones, 26 October 1965.
96. Ibid.
97. It is unclear whether any, or many, of those arrested were released. In his press statement to Reuters in May 1965, Chipembere said that Banda had 'recently released many detainees', but in his letter to Jones in October 1965 he said they had not been released.
98. P. Theroux to author, 13 July 1999.
99. JP, Arden to Jones, 16 April 1965.
100. JP, Meeting with Dr Banda, 5 November 1965.
101. JP, Archdeacon Chipembere to Jones, 21 November 1965.
102. JP, Note by Jones of meeting with Banda, 24 November 1965.
103. Rev. John Parslow to author, 31 May 1999. It is possible that Catherine's escape was in November 1964 rather than 1965.
104. Young to author, 8 December 1999.
105. DP 208 23, Nicholas to CRO, 6 and 7 January 1966.
106. JP, Arden to Jones, 21 November 1965.
107. Chiume to author, 7 November 1999.
108. DO 208 28, Briefing for minister of state's visit to Nairobi, n. d. but early 1966.
109. JP, Gondwe to Banda, n.d. but shortly after 8 November 1965.
110. Short, op. cit., p. 239.
111. *Where Silence Rules: The Supression of Dissent in Malawi* (New York: Africa Watch, 1990), Africa Watch Report, October 1990, p. 100.
112. JP, Note by Jones of meeting with Banda, 24 November 1965.
113. JP, Meeting with Dr Banda, June 1966.
114. G. J. Bender, op. cit., pp. 12–13.

10. The Fate of the Ministers

1. DO 208 21, Cole to CRO, 30 June 1966; DO 208 2 Cole to CRO, 16 July 1966.
2. DO 208 35, Cole to CRO, 16 November 1966.
3. DO 208 17, CRO to Cole, 16 November 1966.
4. DO 208 2, Cole to CRO, 16 July 1966.
5. DO 208 2, Cole to CRO, 29 June 1966.
6. Ibid.
7. For example, as late as 1978, Chokani was visited in Zambia by Sangaya, who was attending a church meeting there. When he returned to Malawi, he was interrogated by the police. He admitted meeting Chokani and was detained by the police for three days: Silas S. Ncozama, *Sangaya* (Blantyre: Claim, 1996), p. 21.
8. York Papers, Document vol. 1, no. 4, n.d. but probably mid-1967, published by the PDP of Malawi, Lilongwe.
9. Mpakati, op. cit., p. 67n.
10. John Lwanda, *Kamuzu Banda of Malawi: A Study in Promise, Power and Paralysis* (Glasgow: Dudu Nsomba Publications, 1993), p. 164.
11. York Papers, Document vol. 1, no. 4, n.d. but probably mid-1967, published by the PDP of Malawi, Lilongwe.
12. Chiume to author, 23 January 2000.
13. Chiume, interview with author, 13–14 December 1998.
14. Reuters, Blantyre, 7 February 1966: copy in DO 208 23.
15. JP, Jones to his bank manager, 15 June 1967; Lomax to Jones, 12 August 1967.
16. Chiume, interview with author, 13–14 December 1998.
17. JP, Jones to Banda, 27 June 1967.
18. Lewis, interview with author, 31 January 1996.
19. JP, Secret note by Jones, 22 March 1968.
20. Chiume, interview with author, 13–14 December 1998. The additions in parentheses are from Chiume to author, 7 November 1999.
21. John Lwanda, *Kamuzu Banda of Malawi: A Study in Promise, Power and Paralysis* (Glasgow: Dudu Nsomba Publications, 1993), pp. 237–8; *Where Silence Rules: The Suppression of Dissent in Malawi* (New York: Africa Watch, 1990), pp. 37–40.
22. H. Brind, *Lying Abroad* (London: Radcliffe Press, 1999), p. 231.
23. Amnesty International, *Malawi: Preserving the One-Party State – Human Rights Violations and the Referendum*, 18 May 1993, pp. 15–17.
24. Hansard, Fifth Session, Second Meeting, 12–14 December 1967, pp. 121–36.
25. Attati Mpakati, *African Review*, 1973, vol. 3, pt 1, p. 67.
26. D K Chisiza, Evidence to Devlin Commission, 18 May 1959, Devlin Papers, box 12A.
27. Chiume, interview with author, 13–14 December 1998. Banda alleged that Chisiza was 'being kept by an American girl who was a Peace Corps worker' in Malawi: Hansard, Fifth Session, First Meeting, 3–6 October 1965, p. 115.
28. *Malawi Government Gazette*, 1967, p. 391.
29. Hansard, Fifth Session, First Meeting, 3–6 October 1965, p. 14.
30. Hansard, Fifth Session, First Meeting, 3–6 October 1965, pp.14–15 and 114–17.

Notes to Chapter 10 · 351

31. *Malawi Government Gazette*, 1967, p. 391.
32. Lewis, interview with author, 13 October 1998.
33. Hansard, Fifth Session, First Meeting, 3–6 October 1965, p. 122.
34. Ibid. F. Mwalyambwile was also killed.
35. *Malawi Government Gazette*, 1967, p. 367.
36. Lewis, interview with author, 13 October 1998.
37. Chevallier, interview with author, 31 December 1997; Chevallier to author, 11 January 1999.
38. C. Munro, conversation with author, late 1965. There is a great deal more detail on the invasion and its outcome in Hansard, Fifth Session, Second Meeting, December 1967, pp. 14–15, 121–36.
39. Roberts, interviews with author, 26 and 27 July and 6 August 1982; Mpakati, op. cit., p.67. The condemned men were G. Bonongwe, Timango Chipwati, Suwedi Masamba, Harris Phombeya, James Kamanga, M. Moyo, G. M. Mwakawanga and M. L. Mphwante.
40. York Papers, *Malawi Freedom News*, published by the Panafrican Democratic Party of Malawi, vol. 1.
41. Brody, Banda to Kaunda, 28 November 1967.
42. Hansard, Fifth Session, Second Meeting, 12–14 December 1967, p. .
43. JP, Meeting with Dr Banda, June 1966.
44. DO 208 17, Cole to CRO, 14 June 1966.
45. Hansard, Fifth Session, Second Meeting, 12–14 December 1967, p. 123.
46. DO 208 21, Application for United Kingdom Entry Certificate.
47. DO 208 21, Cole to CRO, 14 June 1966.
48. Ibid.
49. DO 208 17, Minute, CRO, to SS, 16 June 1966.
50. DO 208 17, Norris to SS, 16 June 1966.
51. DO 208 17, Saville-Garner minute, 17 June 1966.
52. DO 208 17, Scott to Cole, 5 August 1966; Norris to Scott, 26 August 1966.
53. DO 208 17, Undated and unsigned note.
54. DO 208 17, note on file, n.d., probably June 1966.
55. DO 208 17, Chipembere to Bottomley, 23 June 1966.
56. DO 208 17, MacGilligin to Chipembere, 8 July 1966.
57. DO 208 17, Minute, Cole to Deputy High Commissioner Zomba, 24 June 1966; Cole to CRO 26 June 1966.
58. DO 208 17, Cole to CRO, 30 June 1966.
59. DO 208 17, Cole to CRO, 9 July 1966.
60. G. J. Bender, op. cit., pp. 12–13.
61. DO 208 17, Cole to CRO, 15 June 1966.
62. JP, D. D. Chavundula, *Pan-African Democratic Party of Malawi: Formation of Branches*, circular letter, n.d.
63. *Daily Telegraph*, 31 October 1966.
64. York Papers, Document vol. 1, no.4, n.d. but probably late July, early August 1967, published by the PDP of Malawi, Lilongwe.
65. Hansard, Fourth Session, Third Meeting, 16–21 December 1966, pp. 286–7.
66. JP, Record of press conference, March 1967.
67. York Papers, Document vol. 1, no.4, n.d. but probably late July, early August 1967, published by the PDP of Malawi, Lilongwe.
68. DO 208 17, Cole to CRO, 28 May 1966.

352 · Notes to Chapters 10 and 11

69. DO 208 17, High Commissioner Dar es Salaam to CRO, 2 December 1966.
70. DO 208 17, CRO to Cole, 8 and 22 December 1966.
71. The following account is from JP, Secret note by Jones, 22 March 1968.
72. G. J. Bender, op. cit., pp. 12–13.
73. Ibid.; Chiume interview with author, 13–14 December 1998.
74. Lwanda, *Kamuzu Banda of Malawi: A Study in Promise, Power and Paralysis* (Glasgow: Dudu Nsomba Publications, 1993), p. 275.
75. JP, Jones to Banda, 3 November 1969.
76. Bender, op. cit., pp. 12–13.
77. Phillips, interview with author, July 1998.
78. Bender, op. cit., pp. 12–13.
79. Details of the event and quotations from it are from Brody, tape recording of seminar addressed by Chipembere at California Institute of Technology, 1 February 1971.
80. Hansard, 20 December 1968, cited in Mpakati, op. cit., p. 63.
81. See also Mpakati, op. cit., pp. 53–4.
82. This had been an argument made by Banda and Chokani when considering the WNLA agreement just after independence.
83. Chiume to author, 7 November 1999.
84. Mpakati, op. cit., p. 59.
85. DO 208 2, Cole to Bowden, 22 December 1966.
86. JP, Chipembere to Jones, 21 December 1973.
87. See also D. Trelford, '"Chip" Dies in Exile', *Rand Daily Mail*, 15 October 1975.
88. Chiume only once saw Chipembere take alcohol and that was a bottle of beer on the eve of his departure from Tanzania for the USA: Chiume, interview with author, 13–14 December 1998.
89. Bender, op. cit., pp. 12–13.
90. Ibid.
91. Chiume, interview with author, 13–14 December 1998.

11. The Ministers' Revolt and Its Legacy

1. JP, Roberts to J, 'Malawi: the next phase', 15 March 1965.
2. JP, Roberts to Jones, 8 January 1963.
3. Chiume, interview with author, 13–14 December 1998.
4. JP, Jones, to SS 14 April 1962.
5. Chibambo to author, April 1999.
6. JP, D. K. Chisiza to Jones, 4 August 1962.
7. Chiume to author, 7 November 1999.
8. JP, SS to Jones, 3 January 1964.
9. JP, Jones to SS, 13, 17 and 25 February 1964.
10. Cmnd. 814, para. 26.
11. DO 183 136, Intelligence Report for June 1962.
12. The resignation issue was raised towards the end of the meeting because Chirwa suggested an adjournment shortly thereafter.
13. Cameron, interview with author, 21 March 1998; Chiume, interview with author, 13–14 December 1998.

14. Photograph in Armitage Papers and in Chiume, op. cit.; Jackson, op.cit., p. 276.
15. Hansard, Second Meeting, First Session, 8–9 September 1964, p. 141.
16. DO 183 457, Cole to Bottomley, despatch no.4, 27 October 1964.
17. *Where Silence Rules: The Suppression of Dissent in Malawi* (New York and London: Africa Watch, 1990), p. 2.
18. Mpakati, op. cit., p. 65.
19. JP, Unsworth to Jones, 28 May 1963.
20. JP, Roberts to Jones, n.d. but July 1964.
21. The Malawi Independence Order 1964, Statutory Instrument, 1964, no. 916, Schedule 2, s. 77(2).
22. Ibid., s. 76(2).
23. JP, Note of meeting, 21 October 1964.
24. Short, op. cit., p. 271.
25. Laws of Malawi, Traditional Courts (Amendment) Act, no. 38 of 1970.
26. *Where Silence Rules: The Suppression of Dissent in Malawi* (New York and London: Africa Watch, 1990), pp. 16–17.
27. *Where Silence Rules: The Suppression of Dissent in Malawi* (New York and London: Africa Watch, 1990), pp. 31–2.
28. *Proceedings of the Tenth Meeting of the Sixty-sixth Session of the Legislative Assembly*, 10–16 December 1963, pp. 988–93.
29. Speech at Chileka, 3 November 1965, cited in Short, op. cit., p. 269.
30. JP, Roberts to Jones, 8 January 1963.
31. The Malawi Independence Order, 1964, Schedule Two, section 70(6).
32. The Republic of Malawi (Constitution) Act, 1966, section 58(6).
33. The Laws of Nyasaland, Chapter 21, The Criminal Procedure Code, section 81.
34. Colin Baker, 'The Governor and the Post Office Messenger: Nyasaland, 1948', *South African Philatelist*, vol. 73, no. 3, June 1997.
35. Armitage Papers, draft memoirs 1960, vol. 2; Diary 28, and 30 December 1960.
36. *Where Silence Rules: The Suppression of Dissent in Malawi* (New York and London: Africa Watch, 1990), p. 15.
37. Cmnd. 814, para. 258.
38. Cmnd. 814, section 4, pp. 132ff.; Lucas, interview with author, 22 April 1999.
39. *Where Silence Rules: The Suppression of Dissent in Malawi* (New York and London: Africa Watch, 1990), p. 15, however, claims that 'The army has largely remained out of politics and has played no significant role in internal repression.' At the very least this ignores the part played by the army in harrying the Fort Johnston district in 1965.
40. Cmnd. 814, para. 182.
41. Banda, speech to commemorate his release from Gwelo, cited in Short, p. 256.
42. Lwanda, op. cit., pp. 24, 273, 247–8, 273 and 279–81.
43. JP, Draft by Jones to Banda, n.d. but early July 1966.
44. JP, Report by commander of events between 10 and 29 March 1973.
45. Roberts, interviews with author, 26 and 27 July and 6 August 1982.
46. *Where Silence Rules: The Suppression of Dissent in Malawi* (New York and London: Africa Watch, 1990), p. 31n.

47. Lwanda, op. cit., p. 278.
48. *Where Silence Rules: The Suppression of Dissent in Malawi* (New York and London: Africa Watch, 1990), p. 33.
49. Lwanda, op. cit., p. 279.
50. *Where Silence Rules: The Suppression of Dissent in Malawi* (New York and London: Africa Watch, 1990), pp. 33–6.
51. Lwanda, op. cit., p. 279. It will be recalled that the Land Rover squad had threatened Cameron and McAdam in 1964 and that it was Muwalo who called them off. Ross had also associated Chakuamba with a Land Rover squad.
52. Lwanda, op. cit., p. 283.
53. Ibid.
54. *Preserving the One Party State*, Amnesty International, p. 14.
55. *Where Silence Rules: The Suppression of Dissent in Malawi* (New York and London: Africa Watch, 1990), p. 53.
56. Ibid. p.16.
57. Republic of Malawi (Constitution) Act, Schedule Two, sections 12 and 13.
58. Dr Banda was removed from office, constitutionally, in 1994 and died at the age of ninety-nine in 1997.

Biographical Notes

ARMITAGE, Robert Perceval, b. 1906; educated Winchester and Oxford; Colonial Administrative Service, Kenya, 1929; Administrative Secretary, 1947; Financial Secretary, Gold Coast, 1948; Minister of Finance, 1951; Governor of Cyprus, 1954–55; Governor of Nyasaland, 1956–61; d. 1990.

BANDA, Aleke, b. 1939; educated Southern Rhodesia; Secretary of Que Que branch of Nyasaland African Congress; arrested 1959 and briefly detained; deported to Nyasaland; co-founder, with Orton Chirwa, of Malawi Congress Party, 1959; founder of *Malawi News*; Secretary-General Malawi Congress Party, 1966; held various ministerial posts, 1966–72; dismissed 1973 and subsequently twice detained; re-entered political life with multi-party elections in 1994.

BANDA, Dr Hastings Kamuzu, b. 1898; medical practitioner and politician; worked in Southern Rhodesia and South Africa as a young man; educated USA and Scotland; practised medicine Liverpool, Tyneside and London, 1939–52 and Ghana 1953–58; returned to Nyasaland 1958 and took over leadership of Nyasaland African Congress; detained March 1959 to April 1960; Leader of Majority Party and Minister of Natural Resources and Local Government, 1961–63; Prime Minister of Nyasaland and then Malawi, 1963–66; President of Republic of Malawi, 1966–94; d. 1997.

BLACKWOOD, Michael Hill, b. 1917; lawyer and politician; member of legislature of Nyasaland and Malawi, 1954–74; member of Executive Council, 1956–61; CBE, 1963.

BWANAUSI, Augustine, b. 1930; schoolmaster and politician; educated at Makerere College, Uganda; worked in Tanganyika and became a senior member of the Tanganyika African National Union; returned to Nyasaland 1959; held various ministerial posts, 1961–64; dismissed 1964; exile in Zambia and Tanzania; died in car crash in Zambia.

CAMERON, Colin; lawyer; elected to legislature, 1961; Minister of Works and Transport, 1961; Transport and Communications, 1963; resigned ministerial post, July 1964; fled country and returned to Scotland, November 1964.

CHAKUAMBA, Gwanda, born 1935; elected to legislature, 1961; held various ministerial posts from 1964; convicted of sedition, 1981 and sentenced to twenty-two years' imprisonment; re-entered political life with multi-party elections in 1994.

CHIBAMBO, Rose; organizer and leader of Women's League, 1958–64; dismissed from Parliamentary Secretary post and suspended from Malawi Congress Party, September 1964; exile in Zambia 1964; returned to Malawi with multi-party elections in 1994.

CHIDZANJA, Richard, born 1921; detained March 1959 to September 1960; Regional Minister, 1964; various cabinet and diplomatic posts from 1964; d. 1978.

CHIPEMBERE, Henry Blasius Masauko, b. 1930; politician; graduated Fort Hare, South Africa; District Assistant, Nyasaland Civil Service; member of legislature, 1956–64; Treasurer of Nyasaland African Congress, 1958; detained March 1959 to September 1960; imprisoned for sedition, January 1961–January 1963; Minister of Local Government, 1963–64; Minister of Education, 1964; resigned from office, September 1964; led unsuccessful *coup d'état*, February 1965; evacuated to live in USA, 1965 to 1975, with temporary return to Tanzania, 1966–69; d. 1975.

CHIRWA, Orton Edgar Ching'oli, b. 1919; teacher, lawyer and politician; educated Zambia and Fort Hare, South Africa, 1947–51, graduating BA and BEd with Diploma in Education; returned to Nyasaland 1951 and taught at teacher training college; London, studying law, 1955–58; called to Bar, 1958; returned again to Nyasaland and became legal adviser to Nyasaland African Congress, 1958; briefly detained 1959; co-founder, with Aleke Banda, Malawi Congress Party and was its first President, 1959; various ministerial posts, 1961–64: Parliamentary Secretary to the Ministry of Justice, Minister of Justice, Attorney-General; dismissed September 1964; exile in Tanzania; abducted and returned to Malawi in 1981, convicted of treason in 1984; sentence of death commuted; d. 1992.

CHISIZA, Dunduzu, b. 1930; younger brother of Yatuta Chisiza; worked in Southern Rhodesia; Secretary-General of Nyasaland African Congress, 1958–59; detained March 1959 to September 1960; reinstated as Secretary-General; Parliamentary Secretary to Ministry of Finance, 1961–62; killed in car crash, September 1962.

CHISIZA, Yatuta, b. 1926, elder brother of Dunduzu Chisiza; police officer, Tanganyika; returned to Nyasaland 1958; detained March 1959 to September 1960; personal bodyguard to Dr Banda, 1959–64; Parliamentary Secretary, Ministry of Labour, 1963–64; Minister of Home Affairs, 1964;

Biographical Notes · 357

dismissed September 1964; exile in Tanzania and Zambia, 1964–67; killed in armed invasion of Malawi, 1967.

CHIUME, Murray William Kanyama, b. 1929; teacher and politician; educated Tanganyika and Uganda; taught in Tanganyika; returned to Nyasaland; member of legislature, 1956–64; Publicity Secretary of Nyasaland African Congress and later Malawi Congress Party; overseas during state of emergency, 1959–60; Minister of Education, 1961–64; Minister of External Affairs, 1964; dismissed September 1964; lived in exile in East Africa, 1964–94; returned to Malawi 1994.

CHOKANI, Willie, b. 1930; schoolmaster and politician; educated in Blantyre; graduated Delhi, India; detained, 1959; Minister of Labour, 1962; dismissed 1964; exile in Zambia, 1964; Malawi ambassador to the USA, 1994.

COLE, David, b. 1920; diplomat; British High Commissioner to Malawi, 1964–67; MC, 1944; CMG, 1965; KCMG, 1975.

FOSTER, Robert, b. 1913; graduated Cambridge; Colonial Administrative Service, Northern Rhodesia, 1936; Provincial commissioner, 1957; Secretary, Ministry of Native Affairs, 1960; Chief Secretary, Nyasaland, 1961–63; Deputy Governor, 1963–64; High Commissioner, Western Pacific, 1964–68; CMG, 1961; KCMG, 1964; KCVO, 1970; GCMG, 1970.

GILSTRAP, Sam, US ambassador to Malawi 1964–65.

JONES, Glyn Smallwood, b. 1908, graduated Oxford, Colonial Administrative Service, Northern Rhodesia, 1931; Commissioner for Native Development, 1951; Provincial Commissioner, 1955; Secretary, later Minister, for Native Affairs, 1958; Chief Secretary, Nyasaland, 1960; Governor, Nyasaland, 1961; Governor-General, Malawi, 1964–66; MBE, 1944; CMG, 1957; KCMG, 1960; GCMG, 1964; d. 1992.

KUMTUMANJI, Gomile; member of legislature; regional chairman MCP; various ministerial posts, 1964–70; detained 1970 until death in 1990.

LEWIS, Paul, Commander of the Malawi Army, 1964–65 and 1967–71 as Colonel and then Brigadier; CBE.

LOMAX, Douglas George, b. 1915; Hampshire Constabulary, 1936–42; Special Police Corps, Germany, 1946–50; Nyasaland Police, 1950–71; Senior Assistant Commissioner, 1966; Head of Special Branch, 1964–71; CPM; QPM, 1966; OBE, 1969; d. 1998.

LONG, Peter, b. 1915; Metropolitan Police, 1936–38; Jamaica Police, 1938–51; Nyasaland-Malawi Police, 1951–71; Commissioner, 1964; CBE, QPM, CPM.

MKANDAWIRE, Mikeka; b. early 1920s; storekeeper and politician; detained 1959; Minister without portfolio, 1961–64; exile in Scotland, 1965; returned to Malawi; d. 1995

MSONTHI, John, b. 1928; schoolmaster and politician; educated Zomba Secondary School and graduated at Bombay, India; detained 1959; Minister of Transport, 1962; suspended from Cabinet and then reinstated, 1964; temporarily resigned as minister, 1964; various ministerial posts from 1964.

MUWALO, Albert; Secretary-General of MCP; Minister of State in President's Office; arrested, tried and convicted of illegal possession of arms and sentenced to death 1976; executed 1978.

PHILLIPS, Henry Ellis Isadore, b. 1914; Institute of Historical Research, University of London, 1936–39; served in war, 1939–45; prisoner of war, 1942; Colonial Administrative Service, Nyasaland, 1946; Development Secretary, 1952; seconded to Federal Treasury of Rhodesia and Nyasaland, 1953–57; Financial Secretary, Nyasaland, 1957–64 and Minister of Finance, 1961–64; MBE, 1946; CMG, 1960; Kt, 1964.

ROBERTS, Bryan Clieve, b. 1923; lawyer and administrator; called to Bar, 1950; Colonial Legal Service, Northern Rhodesia, 1953–61; transferred to Nyasaland, 1961; Solicitor-General, Attorney-General, Minister of Justice; Secretary to the President and Cabinet, 1965–73; QC; JP; CMG, 1964; KCMG, 1973; d. 1996.

ROSS, Rev. Dr Andrew, b. 1931; ordained minister, 1958; Church of Central Africa Presbyterian, Malawi, 1958–65; fled country and returned to Scotland, May 1965.

TEMBO, John, b. 1932; schoolmaster and politician; educated Malawi, Botswana and Zimbabwe; Parliamentary Secretary to Ministry of Finance, 1962; Minister of Finance, 1964; Minister of Trade and Industry, 1969; Governor of reserve bank, 1971.

YOUENS, Peter William, b. 1916; Colonial Administrative Service, 1939; naval service, 1939–40; Sierra Leone, Assistant District Commissioner, 1942; District Commissioner, 1948; Colony Commissioner, 1950; Assistant Secretary, Nyasaland, 1951; Deputy Chief Secretary, 1953–63; Secretary to the Prime Minister and Cabinet, Malawi, 1964–66; company director, London, 1966–94; OBE, 1960; CMG, 1962; Kt, 1965; d. 2000.

Sources

Primary sources

1. The Glyn Jones Papers, deposited in Rhodes House Library, Oxford.
2. The Robert Armitage Papers, deposited in Rhodes House Library, Oxford.
3. The Oxford University Colonial Records Project papers, including transcripts of interviews with Sir Peter Youens, Sir Bryan Roberts and Sir Roy Welensky, deposited in Rhodes House Library, Oxford.
4. The Devlin Papers, covering the 1959 commission of inquiry into the Nyasaland disturbances, deposited in Rhodes House Library, Oxford.
5. The Brody Collection. This is an extensive collection of Dr Banda's papers, either originals or copies, by Dr Donal Brody of Lynnwood, Washington, USA. The use in this book of material from the Brody Collection is with Dr Banda's and Dr Brody's permission.
6. The Loft Papers, copies of letters, reports and other documents in the possession of George Loft of Sharon, Connecticut, USA. Loft was the representative in the Federation of Rhodesia and Nyasaland of the American Friends Service Committee from 1957 to 1960. The use in this book of material from these papers is with Mr Loft's permission.
7. The 1993 York University Conference Papers on the Cabinet Crisis, copies supplied by Professor George Shepperson.
8. Files in the Public Record Office, Kew:

CO 1015 2491, Governor's Reports on Current Situation, Nyasaland.
DO 158 60 and 296, Informal Conference Between British High Commissioner, Salisbury, and the Two Northern Governors.
DO 183 61, Republican Status of Malawi.
DO 183 136 and 137, Intelligence Reports, Nyasaland.
DO 183 168, Executive Council (now Cabinet), Nyasaland (now Malawi).
DO 183 176, British Embassy Washington to Foreign Office.
DO 183 444, Appointment of Governor-General.
DO 183 445, Despatches from the Governor-General of Malawi.
DO 183 457, Despatches from the British High Commissioner in Malawi.
DO 183 467, Visit of Dr H. Banda to the UK, 1962.
DO 183 468, Visit of Dr Banda to Europe, USA and UK.
DO 208 2, Despatches from British High Commissioner, Malawi.
DO 208 17, Movements of Chipembere and Position if Living in UK.
DO 208 18, Malawi: Internal Security – LMY.

DO 208 21, Malawi: Capital Punishment.
DO 208 23, Malawi: Political Crisis of 1965.
DO 208 28, Malawi: Various Briefs and Memoranda from CRO.
DO 208 34, Malawi: Presidency and Succession.
DO 208 35, Detention of Citizens in Malawi.
DO 208 38, Malawi: Leading Personalities.
DO 208 40, Malawi: Detainees and Banishment of Fr Tovey to Likoma.

9. Correspondence: Correspondence with former Nyasaland and Malawi cabinet ministers and other politicians, civil servants, police officers, army officers, diplomats, Peace Corps and VSO volunteers, all of whom are acknowledged in endnotes.

10. Interviews: Sir Douglas Hall, Sir Henry Phillips, Sir Peter Youens, Sir Robin Foster, Sir Bryan Roberts, Sir Edgar Unsworth, Sir Edgar Williams, Sir Michael Caine, Lady Emma Nicholson, Lady Jones, Lord Perth, Dr Kenneth Kaunda, Kanyama Chiume, Richard Kettlewell, Frank Chevallier, Syd Peters, Peter Smith, Paul Lewis, Charles Lucas, Robert Dewar, Elisabeth Perchard, Colin Perchard, Ruth Conybeare, John Sheriff, Dr. W.M. Chirwa, Bishop Donald Arden, Jeremy Armitage, Rev. Eric Pocklington, Kenneth Neale; Kevin Denny.

12. Miscellaneous:

Extracts from the private papers of Dr H. K. Banda, provided by Dr D. Brody and T. Walker.

Tape recording of H. B. M. Chipembere's political geography seminar at California Institute of Technology, 1 February 1971.

Andrew Ross, Reflections on the Malawi *'Cabinet Crisis'*, *1964–65*, a seminar paper sent by Ross to author on 14 August 1997.

Secondary sources

1. *Government publications*

Cmnd. 814 (1959) *Report of the Nyasaland Commission of Inquiry.*

Cmnd. 1132 (1960) *Report of the Nyasaland Constitutional Conference.*

Cmnds. 1148–1151 (1960) *Report of the Advisory Commission on the Review of the Constitution of the Federation of Rhodesia and Nyasaland.*

Cmnd. 1887 (1962) *Report of the Nyasaland Constitutional Conference.*

Statutory Instrument, 1964 No. 916, The Malawi Independence Order in Council 1964.

The Erosion of the Rule of Law in Nyasaland (Salisbury, July 1963).

The Erosion of the Rule of Law in Nyasaland: The Local Courts (Salisbury, September 1963).

The Rule of Law in Nyasaland [Nyasaland Rejoinder], 1963.

Proposals for the Republican Constitution of Malawi (Zomba, November 1965).

Republic of Malawi (Constitution) Act 1966 (Zomba, June 1966).

Nyasaland Government Gazette (Zomba: Government Press, to July 1964).
Malawi Government Gazette (Zomba: Government Press, from July 1964).
Proceedings of the Nyasaland Legislative Council (to May 1964).
Proceedings of the Nyasaland National Assembly (May–July 1964).
Proceedings of the Malawi Parliament (from July 1964).

2. Journals

Intimidation in Central Africa: Vote for Me or Else (London: East Africa and Rhodesia, 1962).

Gerry Bender, 'A Tribute to Henry Chipembere', *African Studies Newsletter*, vol. viii, no. 6, December 1975, pp. 12–13.

Colin Cameron, 'Malawi Reborn', *Venture*, 1964, vol. 16, pts 7 and 8, pp. 18–21.

H. B. M. Chipembere, 'Malawi in Crisis: 1964', *UFAHAMU*, vol. 1, 1970, pp. 1–22.

H. B. M. Chipembere, *My Malawian Ancestors* (mimeo.).

H. B. M. Chipembere, 'Dr Banda's Opposition in Exile', *Manchester Guardian*, 7 July 1966.

Attati Mpakati, 'Malawi: The Birth of a Neo-Colonial State', *Africa Review*, 1973, vol. 3, pt 1, pp. 33–68.

Joey Palmer, 'Remembering Du: An Episode in the Development of Malawian Political Culture', *African Affairs* (1998), 97, 369–396.

Henry Phillips, 'Nyasaland – Poised for Independence', *Commonwealth Journal*, vol. VII, no. 3, June 1964, p. 95.

Andrew Ross, 'A Return to Malawi', *Edinburgh History Graduates Association Newsletter*, no. 30, October 1998.

Clyde Sanger, 'Nyasaland Becomes Malawi, An Assessment', *Africa Report*, 1964, pp. 8–11.

3. Books

Africa Watch, *Where Silence Rules: The Suppression of Dissent in Malawi* (New York and London: Africa Watch, 1990).

Amnesty International, *Malawi: Preserving the One-Party State – Human Rights Violations and the Referendum* (London: Amnesty International, 1993).

Colin Baker, *State of Emergency: Crisis in Central Africa, The Nyasaland State of Emergency, 1959–1960* (London: Tauris Academic Press, 1997).

— *Retreat from Empire: Sir Robert Armitage in Africa and Cyprus* (London: Tauris Academic Press, 1998).

— *A Proconsul in Africa: The Life of Sir Glyn Jones* (London: Tauris Academic Press, 2000).

Harry Brind, *Lying Abroad, Diplomatic Memoirs* (London: Radcliffe Press, 1999).

D. K. Chisiza, *Realities of African Independence* (London: Africa Publication Trust, 1961).

Kanyama Chiume, *Kwacha, an Autobiography* (Nairobi: East African Publishing House, 1975).

Cynthia Crosby, *Historical Dictionary of Malawi* (London and New Jersey, Scarecrow Press, 1980).

Andrew Doig, *It's People That Count* (Edinburgh: Pentland Press, 1997).

Bill Jackson, *Send Us Friends* (Malawi: Claim, n.d., c. 1997).

A. H. M. Kirk-Greene, *The Transfer of Power: the Colonial Administrator in the Age of Decolonisation* (Oxford: Inter-faculty Committee for African Studies, 1979).

Brian Lapping, *End of Empire* (London: Paladin Grafton, 1989, first published by Granada Publishing, 1985).

John Lwanda, *Kamuzu Banda of Malawi: A Study in Promise, Power and Paralysis* (Glasgow: Dudu Nsomba, 1993).

Lucy Mair, *The Nyasaland Elections of 1961* (London: Athlone Press, 1962).

Edwin Munger, *President Kamuzu of Malawi* (Hanover, N.H.: American Universities Field Staff Reports, 1969).

S. S. Ncozama, *Sangaya* (Blantyre: Claim, 1996).

Henry Phillips, *From Obscurity to Bright Dawn* (London: Radcliffe Press, 1998).

Nick Priggis, *From Dictatorship to Democracy: Malawi in Transition* (Milton Keynes: World Vision, 1998).

George Shepperson and Thomas Price, *Independent Africa: John Chilembwe and the Origins, Setting and Significance of the Nyasaland African Rising of 1915* (Edinburgh: University Press, 1958).

Philip Short, *Banda* (London: Routledge and Kegan Paul, 1974).

J. R. T. Wood, *The Welensky Papers: A History of the Federation of Rhodesia and Nyasaland* (Durban: Graham, 1983).

Index

African National Congress (ANC), 279
African unity, 90
Africanization, 66, 92, 124, 129, 131, 132, 133, 150, 178, 219, 301, 320-1
Algeria, 275
All Africa People's Conference, 7; Banda's speech at, 297
amnesty, 32, 224, 225, 231, 235, 241, 247, 248, 266, 267, 268, 313, 320; Banda's proposal of, 18, 20; rejected by Banda, 226, 227
Amnesty International, 278
Anderson, Loren, 210
Anglican Church, 269
anonymous letters received by Banda, 140-1, 156, 307, 320
Arden, Bishop Donald, 206-8, 269, 270
Arden, Jane, 206-8
Armitage, Sir Robert, 5, 6, 10, 13, 14, 17-19, 21, 25, 26, 27, 29, 82, 84, 315; succeeded by Jones as governor, 30
army of Malawi, 102, 186, 187, 188, 203, 213, 216, 226, 228, 239, 247, 262, 276, 314, 318; Africanization of, 219; political use of, 319; relations with Chipembere, 219, 221; violence of, 229; white officers in, 219
attorney-general, position of, 34, 317-18

Banda, Aleke, 12, 13, 14, 27, 47, 59, 83, 84, 85, 107, 115, 128, 129, 130, 132, 141, 154, 190, 251, 296, 322; appointed commander of Young Pioneers, 72; appointed head of community development, 105, 116
Banda, Gideon, pseudonym, 233, 234, 235, 238, 241, 244, 248, 249, 250, 252, 266
Banda, Dr Hastings Kamuzu, 32, 33, 89, 153, 249, 251; appointment of ministers, 34, 35, 37, 38, 45, 80-2, 91; appointment of MCP candidates, 158, 312; arrival in Nyasaland, 3; as Prison Graduate Number One, 24, 29; assassination threat to, 218, 260; attitude to African nationalism, 47; attitude to Europeans, 4, 6-7, 10, 14, 66, 81, 110; attitude to judiciary, 315-18; attitude to public executions, 265; character of, 86, 88, 90, 105, 167-8, 177-8, 192, 214-15, 275, 294-5, 296, 297, 303, 323; choice of own portfolios, 35-6, 39; chosen as leader, 3, 6; consolidation of power, 17-41, 67, 84-5, 86; criticism of, 111, 117, 120, 199, 306, 312; detention in Gwelo prison, 13, 16; granted freedom of Blantyre, 73; introduction of public executions, 262-3; introduction of treason law, 227-8; longevity of, 324; meeting at Ngabu, 178; opposition to, 88, 99, 100, 103, 105, 107, 111, 119, 276, 299, 323; persuaded to return to Nyasaland, 2, 8, 15, 17, 81, 300, 301, 305; possibility of resignation, 106, 107, 117, 118-19, 121, 123, 127, 128, 138, 141, 144, 145, 146, 148, 149, 150, 306, 308; possible title as chief minister, 42, 43, 44, 67, 82; press conference with Chiume, 63; qualifications of, 2, 4; question of membership of Executive Council, 18; relations with FRELIMO, 247; relations with lieutenants, 4-16; relations with Lonrho, 91, 96; relations with Macmillan, 25; relations with ministers, 39-40, 41, 51, 54, 59-60, 68, 70, 72-4, 93, 95-6, 97, 98, 100, 104, 106, 107, 109, 111, 117, 119-20, 123, 136, 137, 146-7, 162, 171-2, 175, 180, 307 (with Chipembere, 9-10, 232, 237, 244, 250, 287, 314; with Chisiza, 36; with Chiume, 5, 62, 82, 83, 125, 143); relations with UK, 285; released from detention, 13, 18, 81, 84; retaliation of, 140-203; songs in praise of, 29; sources of intelligence, 305; speeches of (address to Zomba Debating Society, 83; at All Africa People's Conference, 297; at Chileka, 93-4, 95, 102, 103, 257, 305-6; at Kasungu, 189; at OAU summit, 92-3, 94, 111; during motion of confidence, 164); supplied with intelligence supports, 85; sworn in as prime minister, 69; takes control of

youth pioneers, 74; threats of violence against opponents, 181; travel by, 72 (to Europe, 259; to Ghana, 70; to London, 13–14, 24–5, 90, 92; to Portugal, 6, 83; to US, 13–14; tour of Malawi, 182 (for electoral registration, 29–30)) *see also immediately below*

Banda, Dr Hastings Kamuzu, meetings and correspondence of: with Butler, R.A., 71; with Chipembere, 27–8, 31–2, 33, 51–2, 64, 66–7; with Chisiza, 128; with Chiume, 46–7, 51–2; with Jones, 20–1, 22, 28, 33, 34–5, 38, 42, 45, 55–6, 56–7, 71, 81, 95, 101, 104, 121–7, 134–7, 138–9, 143, 145, 149–50, 151, 152, 154, 155, 156, 158, 166, 167, 168, 170, 171–2, 177, 179–80, 181, 187, 190, 193, 196–7, 201–2, 203, 216, 226, 232, 244, 269, 270, 272, 273, 277, 284, 291, 307, 310, 311, 317, 320; with Mkandawire, Cameron and Chisiza, 50; with Youens, 21

Banda, Thomas, 14
Bandawe, Mrs, murder of, 205
Bango, Page, 260
Baptie, David, 207
Bean, Leonard, 201
Bell, Francis, 209, 215
Bender, Gerry, 292
Blackwood, Michael, 26, 31, 33, 37, 100, 104, 125
Bolt, John, 205, 206, 209, 211, 212, 222, 228
Bottomley, A.G., 285; letters from Chipembere, 286–7
British Central Africa, name changed to Nyasaland, 1
British South Africa Police (BSAP), 241, 243
Burdon, John, 211, 212, 215
Butler, 55, 56, 63, 64, 65, 315
Bwanausi, Augustine, 24, 27, 28, 29, 37, 38, 45, 47, 50, 51, 52, 55, 56, 59, 60, 61, 66, 72, 73, 81, 82, 91, 112, 114, 115, 120, 141, 145, 156, 157, 171, 172, 173, 174, 175, 176, 177, 178, 179, 180, 181, 191, 196, 283, 300, 303, 304, 306, 314; accusations against, 83; appointed minister (of development and housing, 80; of labour and social development, 36); at August cabinet meeting, 108; considered for minister of finance, 80; criticism of, 71; dies in car crash, 275; in exile in Zambia, 274, 312; relations with Banda, 37; sacking of, 158–9, 309, 310; tour of Tanzania, 104
Bwanausi, Dr Harry, 12

cabinet meeting of 26 August, 108–21

cabinet system, introduction of, 63
Cameron, Colin, 33, 35, 37–8, 43, 51, 52, 54, 55, 63, 81, 85, 89, 90, 91, 99, 101, 138, 152, 156, 202, 203, 251, 302, 303; appointed minister (of public works, 80; of works and transport, 36); disagreement with Banda, 304; 'feud' with Chiume, 50, 51, 55, 61, 68; leaves Malawi, 203, 256, 313; meeting with Jones, 99–100, 101, 105, 154–5; meets with Banda, 50; on detention without trial, 97; resignation of, 98, 99, 103, 108, 306; view of Banda, 177–8
Canada: approached by Chipembere, 289–90; visited by Chipembere, 303
Carnegie, Dale, 11
Catchpole, Mr, executioner, 266
Central Africa Office, 72
Central African Federation, 24, 127; withdrawal from, 48, 49
Central Intelligence Agency (CIA), 237, 242, 255, 268
Chakuamba, Gwanda, 14, 45, 75, 143, 146, 153, 154, 189, 190, 257, 322; appointed minister for community and social development, 170; attack on, 169, 183, 184
Changwa, Inspector, wife and child killed, 209, 218, 223, 297–8
Chevallier, Frank, 198–9, 282
Chibambo, McKinley, 14, 108, 146, 153, 154, 164–5, 171, 303, 304, 308, 309; appointed regional minister, 167
Chibambo, Rose, 71–2, 153, 155, 157, 174; sacking of, 158–9
Chidzanja, Richard, 72, 76, 85, 141, 143, 146, 154, 167, 257, 265, 266; appointed minister of works and transport, 170
Chijozi, D., 2, 14
Chikarema, James, 279
Chikowi, Chief, 75, 184, 221
Chimondo, George, 259
China, 110, 275, 310; aid from, 83–4; ambassador in Dar es Salaam, 83; fears of plotting by, 163; relations with, 131, 134, 138, 153; visit by Y. Chisiza, 274, 276
Chinyama, J.R.N., 2, 14
Chipanda, Wilfred, 194, 195
Chipembere, Arthur, 244, 259, 268
Chipembere, Catherine, 206–8, 231, 233, 244, 246, 269; leaves Malawi, 270
Chipembere, Archdeacon Habil, 30, 66, 156, 167, 206–7, 245, 269; leaves Malawi, 270
Chipembere, Henry, 2, 3, 5, 6, 8, 12, 13, 14, 15, 17, 22, 24, 25, 26, 27, 30, 32, 40, 45, 47, 50, 72, 73, 74, 82, 83, 86, 91, 93, 98,

99, 100, 104, 106, 109, 118, 122, 123, 133, 134, 139, 142, 143, 145, 148, 151, 155, 156, 164, 167, 169, 172, 173, 174, 176, 177, 178, 179, 180, 181, 185, 186, 187–8, 190, 191, 194, 195, 196, 275, 279, 280, 283, 303, 304, 305, 308–9, 310, 312, 318, 321; accusations against, 83; applies to enter UK, 284–8, 313; appointed minister (of education, 80; of local government, 69); attempted *coup d'état*, 204–36, 313, 319; attitude of Banda towards, 234; attitude to Europeans, 10; changes strategy, 230; criticism of, 71–2; death of, in US, 298; evacuation to US, 237–73, 274, 287, 293, 314; goes into hiding, 205–8, 216; goes to Tanzania, 273, 288, 292; hope for amnesty, 224; hunting of, 230, 319; imprisonment of, 27, 28, 29, 40, 47, 62, 84, 95, 300; in view of Ross, 257; letters (to Banda, 27–8, 31–2, 33, 64, 66–7; to Bottomley, 286–7; to Jones, 222–6, 287–8, 297; to Lady Jones, 227; to Ross, 245–6, 248–9, 252–7); levels of support for, 28; Marxist view of failure of, 218; meetings of (at Fort Johnston, 171; in Limbe banned, 182–3; with Banda, 65; with Jones, 165–6, 184–5); mention of name banned by Banda, 288; orders end to violence, 260; organizes 'tea parties', 204; plans to leave for US, 232–6; press statement to Reuters, 244; pressure to leave US, 273, 284; prosecution considered by Armitage, 26; refusal to drive car, 294; refusal to leave Malawi, 224; release from prison, 11, 16, 22, 23, 52, 56, 63–7, 304; resignation of, 167, 168; restriction order imposed on, 188–9, 202, 204–5, 312, 313; reward offered for, 226; rumoured invasion attempt by, 283; sacking of, 168, 311; speeches of (at California Institute of Technology, 294; in Blantyre, 25; in Lower River, 85; in Port Herald and Chikwawa, 70; in US, 270, 272; in Zomba, 9); study at university in US, 231, 237, 248, 250, 256, 257; suffers from diabetes, 208, 231, 234, 246, 293, 298; suitcase captured, 214; summons issued, 26; taken on at California State University, 293–4; threat of military takeover, 289–92; travels of (to Canada, 105, 108, 121; to US, 69, 70); view of Banda, 4, 54, 93, 230; warned of assassination threats, 205
Chirwa, Fumbani, 278
Chirwa, Mackenzie, 278, 280

Chirwa, Orton, 12–3, 14, 16, 23–4, 27, 29, 37, 38, 39, 43, 45, 47, 51, 67, 69, 77–81, 83, 84, 85, 91, 95, 99, 109, 112, 113, 116, 117, 118, 120, 121, 122, 125, 134, 135, 136, 137, 139, 140–1, 148, 149, 151, 152, 153, 155, 157, 168, 171, 172, 173, 175, 180, 190, 191, 192, 197, 200, 201, 220, 233, 275, 276–8, 283, 284, 289, 290, 292, 302, 307, 308, 311, 312, 314, 317; appointed minister (for natural resources, 70; of justice, 80, 318); appointed parliamentary secretary, 36; as principal representative of Congress party, 13; at August cabinet meeting, 108; attack on, 183 (during visit to Banda's house, 192–3, 196); escapes to Jones, 183; in exile in Tanzania, 274, 312–13; leaves Malawi, 197–8; meetings (with Banda, 78; with Jones, 103, 114, 115, 120–1, 142–3, 136–7, 196 (secret, 105–8)); relations with Banda, 12; sacking of, 158–9, 162, 168, 309; sentenced to death, 278
Chirwa, Vera, 276–8; sentenced to death, 278
Chisiza, Dunduzu, 3, 6, 8, 9, 11, 13, 14, 17, 22, 24, 27, 30, 32, 35, 37, 38, 39, 40, 42, 45, 47, 48–9, 50, 51, 52–6, 61, 62, 63, 67, 68, 83, 84, 85, 89, 98, 99, 114, 115, 139, 143, 172, 174, 179, 180, 221, 222, 304, 308, 323; appointed minister for home affairs, 80; as parliamentary secretary, 36, 55, 70; chosen as secretary-general of Congress party, 15; death in car crash, 57–60, 65, 169, 182, 275, 300 (rumours about, 59); dispute with Chiume, 307, 309; freed from detention, 16, 23; letter to Jones, 303–4; meets with Banda, 50; offer to oust Chiume, 54; view of Chiume, 53–4
Chisiza, Yatuta, 8, 9, 11–12, 13, 14, 15, 22, 24, 27, 37, 39, 40, 49, 51, 52, 59, 71–2, 81, 83, 85, 91–2, 96, 100, 102, 105, 109, 113, 120, 124, 145, 148, 154, 156, 157, 171, 173, 175, 177, 178, 181, 190, 191, 196, 275, 277, 283, 289, 290, 302, 306, 314; as Banda's secretary and bodyguard, 12, 15–16, 62; at August cabinet meeting, 108; death of, 319 (mourning made illegal, 282); groomed as police commissioner, 55, 56, 59, 62, 83; in exile in Tanzania, 274, 312; leaves Malawi, 198; meets with Jones, 175, 176; organizes incursion into Malawi, 279, 279; release from detention, 23; resignation of, 160, 162, 168, 309, 310,

366 · *Revolt of the Ministers*

311; tour of Tanzania, 104; visit to China, 274, 276
Chisuze, Moir, 12
Chiume, Murray, 2, 3, 5, 6, 9, 10–11, 13, 14, 16, 18, 19, 20, 21, 24, 25, 26, 27, 31, 35, 38, 39, 42, 43, 45, 47, 48, 50, 52, 56, 60, 61, 62, 65, 72, 73, 74, 81, 82, 84, 86, 89, 90, 91, 93, 94, 95, 103, 109, 110, 112, 113, 115, 121, 124, 128, 133, 135, 136, 137, 138, 141, 143, 145, 146, 148, 150, 152, 153, 154, 155, 156, 157, 158, 169, 171, 172, 173, 175, 180, 181, 200, 201, 203, 223, 227, 234, 259, 260, 261, 271, 272, 275, 277–8, 283, 290, 292, 298, 300, 303, 304, 305, 306, 307, 308, 310, 312, 314, 318; account of confrontation with Banda, 99; accusations against, 83, 85; appointed minister (of education, 36; of health, 70; of information and independence, 72, 80); at August cabinet meeting, 108; attends Commonwealth education conference, 46; Banda's view of, 7–8; calls Jones an imperialist, 160; car attacked in Fort Hill, 198; complaints against, 51, 53–4, 61, 67, 71; description of motion of confidence, 163–4; dispute with Chisiza, 307, 309; exile in Tanzania, 274, 276, 312; 'feud' with Cameron, 50, 51, 55, 61, 68; in view of Ross, 256–7; letter to Banda, 46–7, 51–2; prosecution considered by Armitage, 27, 29; relations with Banda, 14–15; sacking of, 158–9, 162, 168, 309, 311; travels of (study tour of US, 69, 70; to London, 59, 62; to Northern Rhodesia, 115; to Tanzania, 104); unpopularity of, 83; view of Banda, 7–8 *see also* Banda, relations with ministers (Chiume)
Chiume, Mrs, 5
Chiwanda, Alfred, appointed minister of labour, 179
Chiweta, Isaac, 280, 282
Chokani, Willie, 12, 45, 50, 51, 55, 56, 61, 71, 83, 94, 111, 112, 114–5, 116, 138, 139, 145, 154, 171, 172, 173, 175, 176, 177, 178, 179, 180, 181, 191, 196, 275, 283, 309, 311, 314; appointed minister of labour, 80; at August cabinet meeting, 108; exile in Zambia, 274, 276; leaves for Zambia, 312; resignation of, 160, 161, 162, 168, 309; risk of returning to Malawi, 201
Christian Democrat Party, 25
Church of Central Africa Presbyterian (CCAP), 240, 245, 251
Church of Scotland, 1

Cicewa language, 3
civil servants, 47, 135, 189, 212, 312; African (criticized by Banda, 216; loyalty to Banda, 190; strike by, 185–6); criticized for undue familiarity, 108; economies introduced, 299; expatriate, 109, 115, 124, 131, 295, 299 (power of, 105–6; retention of, 133; salaries raised, 133); threat of attacks on, 184, 190, 199
Cleveland, Bill, 209–10
coffee, growing of, 5
Colby, Sir Geoffrey, 255, 318
Cole, David, 88, 89, 105, 107, 114, 120, 121, 137, 150, 153, 154, 155, 157–8, 163, 169–70, 172, 187, 220, 243, 244, 246, 248, 250, 263, 265, 275, 285, 287, 297; meets Banda, 90; report to Commonwealth Relations Office, 125–6
Colonial Office, 13, 26
Colvin, Rev. Tom, 251
Commonwealth Relations Office, 90, 125–6, 138, 155, 169, 170, 285
Commonwealth Scholarship and Fellowship Plan, 46
communism, 83, 93, 221, 246; literature of, 85
Congress party, 5, 8, 15, 81
Congress for the Second Republic (CSR), 276, 292
Conner, Wayne, 253–4, 255, 256
constitution of Malawi, 33
corruption and nepotism, 96, 130, 132, 136, 164, 199
Cram, Judge, 263
crime levels, 77

death penalty, 297, 316; proposed by Banda, 228; public executions, 262–3
Denny, Kevin, 211–12
Denton, Keith, pseudonym, 237–44, 249, 255; leaves Malawi, 243
detention without trial, 96, 97, 98, 99, 101, 103, 104, 136, 151–2, 155, 205, 216, 302, 305, 307, 319
Development Plan, funding of, 110
Devlin, Sir Patrick, 10, 12, 305
Devlin Commission, 6, 12, 17
Dewar, Robert, leaves Malawi, 320
Dillon, Thamar, 14
Director of Public Prosecutions, role of, 78, 80

Economic Commission for Africa, 112, 113
elections, 31, 32, 33, 34, 63
Elizabeth II, Queen, 100
Ellams, 108; criticism of, 117

Executive Council, proceedings of, 39–40
expatriate Europeans, leave Malawi, 202

Federation of Rhodesia and Nyasaland, 3; imposition of, 1
Finney, Philip, 25, 27
Fort Johnston, 171, 181, 186, 205, 209, 210, 212, 214, 215, 216, 2!7, 218, 238, 258, 259, 260, 262, 263, 266, 298, 319; attack on, 223, 229, 248; Jones tours district, 228; major damage at, 213; tensions at, 185–6
Foster, Sir Robert, 37, 44
Frasier, Roy, 209
Freeman, Ifan, leaves Malawi, 320
FRELIMO, 190, 247, 258, 259, 280, 296
French, Margaret, 70

Gadama, Aaron, 322
Ghana, 2, 7, 46, 70, 90, 100, 106, 117, 120, 142; Banda's experience of, 4; Banda's visit to, 41
Gilstrap, Sam, 138, 233, 243, 244, 246, 248, 249, 250, 253, 254, 255, 256, 267, 268, 272; letter from Chipembere, 231
Gondwe, Vincent, 12, 271–2
Grimond, Jo, 263, 265
guerrilla war, 224, 225, 227, 230, 235, 242, 248, 261, 266, 267, 313
Gulliver, Colonel R.F.L., 77
Gwede, Focus, 322
Gwelo prison, detention in, 8, 9–10, 11, 12, 15, 16, 28, 39, 40, 48, 55, 64, 81, 83, 84, 301

Hansard: reporting in, 309; revision of, 185
Harding, George, 210
Harvard, Chipembere's application to, 286
Hayward, Bill, 211, 214, 215
Home, Alec Douglas, 138
Hoover, J. Edgar, 57
hospital charges: imposition of, 116, 129, 132, 133, 137, 140, 150, 299, 301; modification of, 178
hot pursuit, threat by Banda, 283
housing, distribution of, 130
Howard, Philip, 161, 162

independence of Malawi *see* Malawi, independence of
Ingham, John, 45; appointed minister of urban development, 37
Itimu, I.B., 205

Jackson, Bill, 215
Jacobson, Jay, 271, 286

Jardim, Jorge, 113; appointed as consul in Beira, 105, 136
Jehovah's Witnesses, 321; detention of, 320, 322; violence against, 76, 77, 78, 80, 322
Jennings, Pamela, 212
Johnson, Lyndon B., 57
Johnstons, a European couple, 215
Jones, Sir Glyn, 19, 20, 21, 22, 31, 32, 34, 40, 41, 43, 44, 52, 53, 54, 61, 62, 64, 65, 67, 76, 78, 79, 82, 92, 96, 98, 102, 103, 104, 118, 119, 120, 141, 144, 145, 146, 154, 171, 172, 173, 179, 183, 188, 195, 196, 225, 233, 234, 237, 240, 242, 248, 249, 250, 253, 279, 294, 303, 307–8, 312, 315, 316, 318; account of dismissals of ministers, 161–2; appointed Acting Governor, 18; appointed Governor-General, 30, 89; assents to public executions bill, 263, 265; functions of, 151; holds vespers, 179, 183, 185, 190, 194; negotiates Chipembere's return to Malawi, 290; on leave in Britain, 216, 217; private diary of, 216; support for Banda, 86, 151, 300–1, 308, 315, 323; threat of resignation, 173–4; tour of Fort Johnston district, 228; treatment by Banda, 174; trip to Mozambique, 113; view of sackings of ministers, 165–6 *see also immediately below*
Jones, Sir Glyn, meetings and correspondence of: with Banda *see* Banda, meetings and correspondence of; with Cameron, 99–100, 101, 105, 154–5; with Chipembere, 165–6, 184–5, 222–6, 227, 228, 231, 232, 238, 247, 266–9, 287–8, 297; with Chirwa, 78–9, 103, 105, 114, 115, 120–1, 136–7, 142–3, 148–9, 191, 196, 199; with D. Chisiza, 303–4; with Y. Chisiza, 175, 176; with Chiume, 159–60; with Chokani, 179, 200–1; with Gilstrap, 232, 233; with Kaunda, 201; with Macleod, 39–40; with Msonthi, 121–2; with Roberts, 147–8, 174–5, 178; with Youens, 174–5, 178, 185, 187, 192; judiciary, Banda's attitude to, 315–18

Kadzamira, Cecilia, 9, 71, 129, 132, 146, 147, 151, 152, 161, 194, 195, 227
Kadzamira, Mary, 70
Kanduma, Corporal Frederick, 281, 282
Kanjedza, 23, 24; detainees in, 19, 20
Kasungu, visit by Banda, 6
Katsonga, Chester, 25
Kaunda, Kenneth, 49, 50, 201, 283, 284
Kenya, 46, 100, 110
Kenyatta, Jomo, 93, 201

Kettlewell, Richard, 36, 45; appointed minister of land and mines, 37
King's African Rifles, 212
Kota Kota conference, 81, 84
Kota Kota district, violence in, 30
Kuchawe manifesto, 128–34, 140, 307, 308
Kumtumanji, Gomile, 108, 141, 153, 154, 164, 167, 181, 183, 187, 189, 190, 257, 265, 266, 310; appointed to MCP central executive, 170; arrest of, 321–2
Kuntaja, Chief, 5, 15
Kwenje, N.D., 2, 14

labour unrest, 113, 114
Lancaster House agreements, 19, 20, 29, 31, 40, 44, 45, 67, 84
Lancaster House conference, 44, 81; Banda attends, 14, 16, 19
Lea, General, 102
League of Malawi Youth (LMY), 25, 26, 30, 75, 85, 155, 182, 187, 190, 196, 202, 203, 222, 234, 240, 245, 260, 312, 315; rioting by, 183; special action squads, 75, 76
Lennox-Boyd, Alan, 3
Lewis, Paul, 220, 226, 233, 234, 237, 240, 261, 262, 277, 282; leaves Malawi, 320
Liberia, 70
Lilongwe, 312; idea of moving capital to, 90, 128, 132, 142; prison camp at, 216
Listowel, Judith, Lady, 290–1
Lomax, Douglas, 91–2, 155, 175, 226, 233, 234, 237, 238, 240, 255, 276, 291, 292
Lomax, Norah, 242
Long, Peter, 213, 226, 233, 234, 237; leaves Malawi, 320
Lonrho *see* Banda, relations with Lonrho
Lubani, Lali, 181, 189
Lucas, Charles, 262
Lumba Church, 181

Macleod, Iain, 13, 17, 18, 20–1, 22, 25, 26, 32, 44, 263, 300, 323; support for Banda, 315
Macmillan, Sir Harold, 17, 138
Malawi: African states have no embassies in, 134; foreign policy of, 115, 116, 124, 131–2, 134, 140, 154; image of, in the world, 114, 115, 173, 180, 202; independence of, 92, 96, 116 (celebrations of, 89, 90); landlocked situation of, 295, 296, 299
Malawi army *see* army of Malawi
Malawi Congress Party (MCP), 8, 11, 13, 15, 19, 27, 30, 33, 39, 40, 41, 44, 60, 63, 64, 67, 69, 76, 77, 78, 82, 88, 163, 169, 170, 172, 174, 183, 203, 221, 260, 312, 322; Banda made life president of, 314–15; candidates appointed by Banda, 30, 75, 85, 158; conferences, 19, 22; detainees presented to conference, 24; disciplinary regulations of, 69; dissidents within, 72; founding of, 12, 16, 308; growing power of, 47; members not to be prosecuted, 318; party songs of, 29; prisoners victimized, 28; seats won in elections, 31; secretary-generalship of, dangerous post, 323
Malawi Freedom Movement (MAFREMO), 278, 292
Malawi Rifles, 199–200, 213, 214, 240, 281
Malcolm, C.B., issue of Chipembere's letters, 250–7
Malindi, rioting in, 229
Mambique, part offered to Malawi, 296
Mao Zedong, 282
Marlborough House conference, 63, 64
Martin, David, 293
Matenje, Dick, 322
Matthews, Major, 226
Maudling, Reginald, 43, 44
Mbadwa party, 74–5, 321; attacks on members of, 75; members flee Nyasaland, 75
Mbawa, John Ali, 264
McAdam, Albert, 251, 203; leaves Malawi, 203, 256
Menzies, Gordon, 163
St Michael's teacher training college, 204–5, 208, 209
migration of labour, 300; to South Africa, 111, 113, 295
Mkandawire, Mikeka, 35, 38, 50, 51, 52, 54, 55, 61, 63, 82, 89, 304; appointed minister without portfolio, 36; meets with Banda, 50
Mlomba, Chief, killing of, 261
Momela resolution, 104
Monckton Report, 18
Mondlane, Eduardo, assassination of, 292–3
Morgan, R.G., 101
motion of confidence in Banda, 157, 158, 159, 163, 311
Moxon, Major Peter, 101, 102, 201, 203, 220–1; career of, 101–2; leaves Malawi, 203; view of Banda, 167–8
Mozambique, 112, 223, 245, 247, 258, 280; relations with, 113, 134, 142, 296, 304
Mponda, Chief, 171
Msonthi, John, 12, 31, 45, 50, 55, 61, 108, 123, 161, 163, 314; appointed minister (of education, 179; of transport and communications, 80); dismissal of, 91, 92, 95, 96, 105, 115, 122, 302, 305

Index · 369

(resigns, 160, 162, 168); meeting with Jones, 121–2; reinstatement of, 128, 145, 309, 310; suspended from MCP, 322
Msopole, Flax, 26
Mtembo, store-owner, 228, 238
Mtiesa, Matola, 259, 268
multi-racialism, 46, 47
Munro, C., 253
Munthali, Machipisa, 262; imprisonment of, 259
Muwalo, Albert, 70, 128, 140, 141, 143, 145, 154, 183, 259, 321; appointed minister of information, 170; arrest of, 322; attack on, 183, 184
Mvahiwa, G., 262
Mwahimba, C.J.L., 282

Nacala rail link, 136, 142
Nasser, Gamal Abdel, 8, 93
Ndache, Sergeant-Major Manfred, 281–2
Ndangwe, Banarba, 260
Ndomondo, George, 268
Neale, Kenneth, 90, 91, 96
nepotism *see* corruption and nepotism
Nigeria, 46
Nkrumah, Kwame, 61, 93, 219, 263; message to Banda, 263–4
Nkula Falls hydro-electricity scheme, 60
non-alignment policy of Malawi, 134
Ntaja police station, attack on, 221
Nyandoro, George, 279
Nyasaland: independence of, 74; level of development in, 5; new constitution for, 17
Nyasaland African Congress, 1, 13; banning of, 14
Nyasaland Railways Board, 304
Nyasulu, Kapombe, 23, 141, 143, 153, 154, 156, 157; appointed minister for natural resources, 170; release from prison, 23
Nyerere, Julius, 49, 50, 115, 143, 147, 150, 156, 177, 199, 201, 274; attempts rapprochement with Banda, 289

'Operation Stunt', 23
Organization of African Unity (OAU), 96, 112–13, 134, 294, 295; Committee of Nine, 139

Panafrican Democratic Party of Malawi (PDP), 288, 292
Peace Corps, 279, 285
petrol bombs, use of, 75
Phillips, Earl, 293
Phillips, Henry, 73, 89, 98, 116, 135–6, 304; as minister of finance, 80, 97

Phiri, Gloria, 288–9
Pine, John, 37
police, 77, 239, 240, 262, 276, 312, 318; Africanization of, 219; control of, 38; non-intervention in political crimes, 76, 85, 318; relations with Chipembere, 220; white officers in, 219
political cases, prosecution of, 76, 78, 85, 318
political killings, 322
Pondeponde: house destroyed by arson, 75; murder of, 75, 169, 322
Port Herald, riot in, 25
Portugal, 247; relations with, 6, 93, 105, 112, 113, 114, 115, 120, 134, 135, 138, 294, 296, 299; troop incursion into Malawi, 258–9
postage stamp, theft of, 318
Privy Council, appeal to, 228

registration for elections, 29, 30, 75–6, 80; failure to register, 76
release of detainees, 21, 22, 24, 32 *see also* amnesty
republican status for Malawi, 96, 100, 104, 106, 125, 126, 142, 174, 274, 302, 317
resignation of Banda *see* Banda, possible resignation of
restriction orders, imposition of, 188, 224, 319
Rhodesia, Northern, 115, 180, 243, 250
Rhodesia, Southern, 18, 115, 116, 230; relations with, 134, 135, 138, 300
Roberts, Bryan, 31, 86, 88, 118–19, 143, 144, 147–8, 149, 150, 152, 163, 226, 232, 233, 234, 237, 238, 261, 265, 288, 291, 295, 300; appointed attorney-general, 170; leaves Malawi, 320; meets with Jones, 174–5, 178; present in Zomba for troubles, 199; visit to Banda, 148 *see also* Banda, Gideon
Ross, Andrew, 49, 90, 99, 103, 240, 241, 245–6, 250, 268, 294; attitude to Chiume, 256–7; departure from Malawi, 250–7; letters (from Chipembere, 245–6, 248–9, 250, 252–7; to Ross, 250); view of Chipembere, 257
Ross, Mrs I.J., 245, 252
Rowland, H.R.H, 72
Rubadiri, David, 12

Sacranie, Sattar, 38, 152, 155
Salazar, Antonio, 6; visited by Banda, 83
Sangala, James Frederick, 14
Sangaya, Rev. Jonathan, 251, 255
Sanger, Clyde, 88–9, 304
Scullion, M., 253

Selassie, Haile, 93
Shire Highlands protectorate, 1
Short P., 25, 92, 103, 164, 320
Silombela, Medson, 221, 260; capture of, 262; hanging of, 317; hunt for, 230; reward offered for, 226; trial of, 263–6
Singo, John, 280, 282
Skinner report, 86, 116, 129, 130, 132, 133, 135, 136–7, 140, 150, 301; Banda's acceptance of, 105
South Africa, 111, 112, 230; migration of labour to, 295; proposed boycott of, 112; relations with, 93, 113, 114, 119, 134, 294, 295, 300, 301
Special Branch, 25, 47, 51, 56, 58, 62, 65, 66, 70, 72, 75, 82, 91, 92, 95, 100, 138, 158, 171, 179, 190, 209, 214, 216, 220, 237, 238, 243, 245, 248, 250, 251–2, 253, 254, 255, 256, 262, 270, 283, 314, 318, 320, 322; European officers of, 131
state of emergency (1959), 6, 8, 15, 18, 20
Stoneman, Gill, 209
Stoneman, Terry, 209, 219
Surtee, I.K., 35, 38, 63, 289, 292

Taliwa village, destruction of, 258
Tanganyika, 46, 73, 115
Tanganyika African National Union (TANU), 11
Tanzania, 198, 199, 202, 222, 225, 227, 260, 261, 269, 275, 284, 288, 293, 312
taxation, 31, 116
Tembo, John, 59, 70, 80, 81, 85, 105, 109, 110, 112, 114, 115, 116, 122, 123, 129, 132, 139, 161, 162, 163, 310, 314; appointed minister of finance, 95; at August cabinet meeting, 108
Timbiri, Sub-Chief, murder of, 200
Tovey, Rev. Ron, 210–11, 214, 215
traditional courts, 315, 316, 322
treason 316; law introduced by Banda, 227–8
Tubman, William, 70

Uganda, 46
Union of Soviet Socialist Republics (USSR), 110, 275
United Federal Party (UFP), 25, 26, 28, 30, 31, 33, 34, 63
United Kingdom (UK), 31, 42, 46, 49, 96, 120, 323; and evacuation of Chipembere, 246–7; assistance with budget of Malawi, 137; attitude to independence, 299, 300; declares protectorate over Shire Highlands, 1; entry application by Chipembere, 284–8, 290; recognition of MCP, 27; relations with Banda, 17, 275, 303, 310; relations with Malawi, 287; views on public hangings, 266
United National Independence Party (UNIP) (Rhodesia), 49
United Nations (UN), 90, 96, 201, 294
United States of America (USA), 120, 138, 140, 232, 233, 243, 248, 253, 256, 270, 310; involvement in evacuation of Chipembere, 246–7, 254, 269, 271, 272, 285
University of Malawi: possible location in Zomba, 128, 128; proposed, 109–10, 119
Unsworth, Sir Edgar, 75, 79

violence, 27, 66, 85, 259; against opposition, 29, 169; Banda's attitude to, 20; choice of non-violence, 208; political, 76, 183, 187, 202, 204, 236, 257, 300; pre-election, 74

Welensky, Sir Roy, 3, 27, 28, 71
Wilfred, chauffeur *see* Chipanda, Wilfred
witchcraft, Banda's adherence to, 199
Witwatersrand Native Labour Association (WNLA), 111–15; agreement, 114, 115

Youens, Peter, 10, 18, 19, 20, 93–4, 98, 103, 105, 108, 109, 116, 118, 120, 121, 127, 143, 145, 146, 147–8, 150, 157, 161, 182, 186, 189, 194, 195, 196, 197, 226, 232, 233, 234, 237, 244, 250, 305–6; criticism of, 117; meets Jones, 174–5, 178, 185, 187, 192; present in Zomba for troubles, 199–200; visit to Kanjedza, 23, 24
Young Pioneers, 182, 185, 186, 200, 205, 214, 223, 224, 234, 260, 261, 262, 269, 270, 276, 298, 304, 315
Young, Canon, 270, 271
Youth League *see* League of Malawi Youth

Zambia, 223, 275, 284; relations with South Africa, 295; role in facilitating Chisiza's incursion, 283–4
Zimbabwe African People's Union (ZAPU), 279
Zomba: established as capital, 189–90; idea of moving capital from, 90, 128–9; rioting in, 222–3; tension at, 186; 'virus', 20, 21

www.ingramcontent.com/pod-product-compliance
Lightning Source LLC
Chambersburg PA
CBHW070008010526
44117CB00011B/1470